WORLD HISTORY
A Brief Introduction

JOSEPH REITHER, Professor of History, teaches European history at New York University and directs the history honors program at its University Heights campus. He has also lectured at Hunter College, as well as on radio and television and in appearances before cultural organizations in New York and elsewhere.

Professor Reither received his B.S. and M.A. degrees from the University of Virginia, and pursued further graduate studies as a fellow at the University of Rome and at the University of Pennsylvania. During World War II he directed two branches of headquarters intelligence in the United States Air Force.

Also knowledgeable in music, he is on the Board of Advisors of the Rachmaninoff Society, and has written on that composer. For a number of years he lectured at the Manhattan School of Music.

Joseph Reither has written numerous articles on modern European history and is also the editor of *Masterworks of History*. Now in its sixth updated English version, *World History: A Brief Introduction* has so far been translated into Danish, Swedish, Hebrew, Chinese, Portuguese, and Spanish.

WORLD HISTORY
A Brief Introduction

JOSEPH REITHER
Professor of History
New York University

McGraw-Hill, Inc.

New York • St. Louis • San Francisco • Auckland • Bogotá
Caracas • Hamburg • Lisbon • London • Madrid • Mexico
Milan • Montreal • New Delhi • Paris • San Juan
São Paulo • Singapore • Sydney • Tokyo • Toronto

World History: A Brief Introduction
(formerly published under the title *World History at a Glance*)

Copyright © 1942, 1949, 1952, 1957, 1965, 1973 by Copeland & Lamm, Inc. All rights reserved. Printed in the United States of America. No part of this publication may be reproduced, stored in a retrieval system, or transmitted, in any form or by any means, electronic, mechanical, photocopying, recording, or otherwise, without the prior written permission of the publisher.

Maps by Stephen Kraft

First McGraw-Hill Paperback Edition, 1973

9 10 11 12 13 14 15 BKPBKP 9 8 7 6 5 4 3 2 1

Library of Congress Cataloging in Publication Data

Reither, Joseph.
      World history.

      Previous editions published under title: World history at a glance.
      1. World history.   I.   Title.
D21.R38   1973   909   73-6500
ISBN 0-07-051875-0

INTRODUCTORY NOTE

Fundamentally, history is the story of men's efforts to get along with one another. It is as simple as that. But men have not found the problem of getting along together a simple one. At times they have tried to solve it with clubs and knives and arrows, with guns and tanks and poison gas. They have also sought through peaceful intercourse to overcome fear and suspicion of one another to the end that each might enjoy the fruits of his daily labor with some degree of security and safety.

Through patience and perseverance, through toil and intelligence, men have at various times succeeded in creating great civilized societies in which order and decency prevailed over the disintegrating forces of violence and greed; in which the impatience of unwise or evil men was curbed by laws and customs which long experience had tried and proven sound.

But at other times, human frailty—weakness of judgment, shortsighted selfishness, failure of spirit—has caused men to surrender many of the gains so hardly won. Great civilizations have disintegrated and passed away, and the slow work of establishing a new civilized order has had to be begun all over again. In broad outline, there is nothing new in history. And yet, in particulars, things are never the same. Each civilization has its own infinite variety, its own special emphasis, its own unique interest for the reader of history.

Since the struggles and perplexities of each era are in some sense also the problems of earlier ages, history is of interest and concern to everyone. Students of history and all those who seek to enhance their understanding of the main trends of past events will find in this book a broad survey of the whole field of human history.

World History: A Brief Introduction is different from other surveys of the subject in several respects. The account is divided into fifteen parts, each part preceded by a chronological table which will help the reader to fix events in time without suffering the inconvenience of having to remember dates scattered through the text. In the same way, the fourteen specially-drawn maps, introduced at various points in the book, show important changes in the political complexion of the world at different periods in history.

The student and general reader will readily understand that in presenting so large a subject within a limited space it has often been necessary to mention only briefly many persons and events which are each often the subject of whole volumes. In a review of history such as this, that fact is not to be regretted. The book is not offered as a substitute for more detailed study of particular periods of history. But it should help a reader who is fascinated by the Reformation or by the Revolutionary Era, or by any other period, to view that period as one among many by seeing history whole and in perspective.

In its several revisions and again in this new edition, the book has been strengthened by the addition of new and important material concerning recent developments in all parts of the world, offered under clear and convenient headings. And at the same time, where recent research called for changes in certain pages in the earlier sections of the book, these also are incorporated in the present edition. In this way the book is of increased usefulness to students, and it continues its compact, authoritative coverage in keeping with the pattern indicated in its title, *World History: A Brief Introduction*.

J. R.

CONTENTS

INTRODUCTORY NOTE   *v*

PART ONE
The Earliest Civilizations

1 PREHISTORIC MAN   *3*

2 EGYPT   *6*
   The Earliest Nile Dwellers   *6*
   The Pyramid Age and the Disunity of Egypt   *7*
   The Egyptian Empire   *12*

3 MESOPOTAMIA   *16*
   Early Man in Western Asia   *16*
   The Triumph of Babylon   *18*
   The Assyrians and the Chaldeans   *20*

4 EAST MEDITERRANEAN PEOPLES   *23*
   The Aegeans   *23*
   The Hebrews   *25*
   The Phoenicians   *27*

5 INDO-EUROPEANS IN WESTERN ASIA   *28*
   The Persians   *29*
   The Persian Empire   *30*
   Conflict with the Greeks   *32*

6 EARLY CIVILIZATION IN EASTERN ASIA   *33*
   India   *34*
   China   *36*

PART TWO
Greek and Roman Civilization

7 THE GREEKS   *43*
  Advance of the Indo-Europeans and Flight of the
    Aegeans   *43*
  The Greeks Develop a Settled Life   *44*
  The Greeks Become Traders and Colonizers   *46*
  The Struggle with Persia   *47*
  Final Defeat of the Persians   *49*

8 HELLENIC GREECE   *51*
  Political Development   *51*
  Greek Civilization   *55*
  Rivalry of Athens and Sparta   *57*
  The Peloponnesian War   *59*
  Aftermath   *61*

9 THE AGE OF ALEXANDER THE GREAT   *61*
  The Rise of Macedonia   *61*
  Alexander and the Greek States   *63*
  World Conquest   *66*

10 THE HELLENISTIC WORLD   *68*
  Struggles of the Hellenistic Kingdoms   *68*
  Hellenistic Civilization   *69*
  Alexandria   *71*

11 THE WESTERN MEDITERRANEAN   *72*
  Rome   *74*
  Roman Expansion in Italy   *76*
  War with the Greeks   *77*

12 THE STRUGGLE FOR THE DOMINATION
    OF THE WESTERN MEDITERRANEAN   *79*
  The First Punic War   *80*
  The Second Punic War   *82*
  The Third Punic War   *85*

13 ROME AND THE EAST   86
    The Illyrian and Gallic Wars   86
    New Wars in the East   87
    Trouble with Antiochus   88

14 WORLD DOMINION
    AND THE END OF THE REPUBLIC   89
    *The Province of Asia and the Political Crisis at
    Rome*   90
    The Gracchi   94
    Marius   95
    Sulla   96
    Pompey   98
    Caesar   98
    Dictatorship   100

15 TWO CENTURIES OF WORLD PEACE
    UNDER THE EMPIRE   101
    The Age of Augustus   103
    The Era of Roman Peace   104

16 DECLINE   105
    Constantine   108
    The Rise of Christianity   109
    The Council of Nicaea   113
    Constantinople   114
    Julian and the Pagan Reaction   114
    The Authority of Christianity   115

PART THREE

*The Collapse of the Roman West
and the Revival in the East*

17 THE BARBARIANS   119
    Peaceful Infiltration into the Empire   119
    The Breaching of the Barriers   120
    The Barbarians Overrun the Empire   121
    Collapse of the Empire in the West   125

18 THE AGE OF JUSTINIAN   127
    Military Exploits   127
    The Legal Reforms of Justinian   129
    Byzantine Art   130
    Theodora and the Nika Riot   131

19 MOHAMMED AND THE
    EXPANSION OF ISLAM   132
    The Arabs   132
    Mohammed   133
    Mohammed's Religion   134
    The Hegira and After   135
    The Expansion of Islam   137
    Moslem Culture   139

PART FOUR
Feudal Europe

20 THE FRANKS   143
    The Conquests of Clovis   143
    Charlemagne   146
    The Carolingian Empire   147

21 BREAKUP OF THE CAROLINGIAN EMPIRE   150
    Louis the Pious and the Grandsons of Charle-
        magne   150
    Feudalism   152
    Lord and Vassal   153
    The Serf   155

22 THE CHURCH IN FEUDAL EUROPE   155
    Monasticism   156
    The Papacy   158

23 THE NORSEMEN   159
    Early Norse Attacks upon Europe   159
    Permanent Settlement of the Norsemen   160

PART FIVE
Medieval Europe

24 THE HOLY ROMAN EMPIRE   165
   Otto the Great   166
   *Feudalization of the Church and the Plight of
      Rome*   166
   Otto in Italy   167
   The Successors of Otto   168

25 THE RIVALRY OF EMPIRE AND PAPACY   169
   The Cluniac Movement   171
   The Normans in Italy   172
   Henry IV and Germany   173
   Canossa   174

26 THE CRUSADES   175
   The Seljuk Turks   176
   The Council of Clermont   177
   The First Crusade   177
   The Siege of Antioch   179
   The Crusading States   180
   The Crusades Continue   181
   The Papacy and the Fourth Crusade   182
   The Children's Crusade   185

27 EFFECTS OF THE CRUSADES
      UPON EUROPE   186
   Commercial Expansion   186
   The Rise of the Towns   187
   The Guilds   188
   Money   189
   Reaction to the New Authority of the Church 191

28 THE FLOWERING OF
      MEDIEVAL CIVILIZATION   193
   Medieval Education   193
   Medieval Literature   195

Gothic Art   196
Other Aspects   198

PART SIX
The Formation of European States

29 CAPETIAN FRANCE   203
    The National State   203
    The Early French Monarchy   203
    Policies of the French Monarchy   204
    Philip Augustus   205
    Expansion of Government   207
    Louis IX   207

30 SAXON AND NORMAN ENGLAND   208
    Earliest Inhabitants   208
    Anglo-Saxon England   209
    The Norman Conquest   212
    Norman England   212

31 GERMANY AND ITALY   217
    Hohenstaufen Successes   218
    Innocent III and Frederick II   220

32 RUSSIA AND THE EAST   222
    Eastern Europe in Early Times   222
    Expansion of the Slavs and the Coming of the Rus   222
    Kiev and Novgorod   223
    The Mongols   224
    Tamerlane   225
    The Rise of Moscow   225
    The Two Ivans   225

33 RIVALRY OF ENGLAND AND FRANCE   226
    Crécy   229
    The Black Death   230
    Poitiers   231
    Civil Strife in France and England   231
    Renewal of the War   233
    Joan of Arc   234

34 THE AVIGNON PAPACY AND
   THE GREAT SCHISM 235
   The Babylonian Captivity of the Papacy 237
   European Reaction to the Avignon Papacy 237
   The Great Schism 238
   The Council of Constance 238

PART SEVEN
The Renaissance and the Reformation

35 EUROPE DISCOVERS THE FAR EAST 243
   Venice and the Eastern Trade 243
   Henry the Navigator 243
   Columbus 246
   Further Portuguese Explorations 247
   The Spanish in America 247

36 THE AGE OF THE DESPOTS AND THE
   RENAISSANCE IN ITALY 249
   The States of Italy 250
   The Renaissance 251
   The Collapse of the Eastern Empire 251
   Humanism 252

37 THE REFORMATION 253
   John Wyclif 254
   John Hus 255
   The Abuse of Indulgences 256
   Martin Luther 257
   Spread of the Lutheran Revolt 258
   Zwingli 258
   John Calvin 259
   Geneva under Calvinism 259

38 TUDOR ENGLAND 260
   Henry VIII 262
   Henry VIII and the Church 263
   The Renaissance in England 265

PART EIGHT

The Age of Monarchy

39 THE PREDOMINANCE OF SPAIN 269
The Empire of Charles V 269
The Many Problems of Charles V 272
The Situation in France 272
The Turks 273
Germany in Relation to Charles V 274
Philip II and England 275
The Problems of Philip II 276
Philip and the Turks 277
The Revolt of the Netherlands 278
Philip and England 278
The Invincible Armada 280

40 THE ABSOLUTE MONARCHY IN FRANCE 281
The Wars of Religion 282
The Reign of Henry IV 283
The Regency of Marie de' Medici 284
Richelieu 285
Mazarin 286

41 GERMANY AND THE
THIRTY YEARS' WAR 287
The Bohemian Revolt 288
The Danish War 288
Sweden Intervenes 289
The French Phase of the War 290
The Peace of Westphalia 290

42 DEVELOPMENT OF CONSTITUTIONAL
MONARCHY IN ENGLAND 291
Charles I 295
The Commonwealth and Protectorate 297
The Later Stuarts 297
The Glorious Revolution 298

43 RUSSIA AND SWEDEN   299
      Peter the Great   *299*
      Peter's Reforms   *300*
      War with Sweden   *301*

44 THE AGE OF LOUIS XIV   302
      The Government of Louis XIV   *303*
      Versailles   *304*
      Louis and the Huguenots   *304*
      The Wars of Louis XIV   *305*
      The War of the Spanish Succession   *306*

PART NINE

Industrial Progress and the Beginnings
of European World Dominance

45 EUROPEAN COLONIZATION   311
      The Search for a Sea Passage to the East   *311*
      Dutch Enterprise   *312*
      French Settlement   *313*
      English Colonization   *313*
      The French and English in America   *314*

46 THE AGRICULTURAL AND
        INDUSTRIAL REVOLUTIONS   316
      The Agricultural Revolution   *317*
      The Industrial Revolution   *319*

PART TEN

Despotism and Revolution

47 THE ENLIGHTENED DESPOTS   323
      Russia and Catherine the Great   *323*
      The Partitions of Poland   *325*
      Prussia and Frederick the Great   *325*
      Austria and Joseph II   *328*

48 THE ERA OF REVOLUTION   329
      The American Revolution   *329*
      The French Revolution   *329*

49   NAPOLEON   *333*
     The Egyptian Campaign   *334*
     The Consulate   *334*
     The Empire   *335*
     The Wars of Liberation   *337*
     The Hundred Days and After   *338*

50   REACTION AND REVOLUTION   *339*
     Liberal and Conservative   *340*
     Revolutionary Outbreaks of 1820–1821   *340*
     Revolutionary Outbreaks of 1830   *341*

51   THE REVOLUTIONS OF 1848   *343*
     The Industrial Revolution and Liberal Reform   *343*
     The French Revolution of 1848   *345*
     The Revolutions of 1848 in Italy and Germany   *346*
     Reform in England   *347*

PART ELEVEN

Nationalism and Imperialism

52   THE UNIFICATION OF ITALY AND OF
         GERMANY   *351*
     The National Movement in Italy   *351*
     The Risorgimento   *351*
     The Prussian Leadership in Germany   *352*
     The North German Confederation   *353*

53   THE SECOND FRENCH EMPIRE   *354*
     The Crimean War   *354*
     The Mexican Venture   *355*
     The Franco-Prussian War   *355*
     Collapse of the Second Empire   *356*

54   IMPERIALISM AND THE EUROPEANIZA-
         TION OF THE GLOBE   *357*
     Africa   *358*
     The Struggle for Africa   *359*
     Expansion in Asia   *361*
     Changing Attitudes toward Colonies   *363*

PART TWELVE

The United States

55 THE THIRTEEN COLONIES AND
   THE WAR OF INDEPENDENCE 367
   Colonial America 367
   Background of the Revolution 368
   The Outbreak of the War 368
   Peace 369

56 GROWTH AND DEFENSE OF THE UNION 370
   The War of 1812 371
   The Mexican War 371
   Anti-Slavery Agitation 373
   The Civil War 375

57 THE UNITED STATES BECOMES
   A WORLD POWER 376
   The South after the Civil War 376
   The Industrial Revolution in the East 376
   The Spanish-American War 378
   New Problems and Reforms 379

58 THE UNITED STATES AND
   LATIN AMERICA 380
   Spanish Rule in America 380
   Struggles for Independence 381
   Latin America in the Nineteenth Century 382
   Latin America and the United States 383
   The United States and World History 385

PART THIRTEEN

The First World War

59 BACKGROUND OF THE
   FIRST WORLD WAR 389
   Economic Background 389
   Diplomatic Background 390
   The Growing International Tension 390

60 THE FIRST WORLD WAR   391
    Outbreak of the War   *391*
    The Eastern Front   *394*
    The War on the Sea   *395*
    Italian Entry into the War   *395*
    The United States and Warring Europe   *396*
    Further Course of the Conflict   *396*
    German Successes   *397*
    The Turn of the Tide   *397*
    Allied Victory   *398*

61 THE YEARS AFTER THE
    FIRST WORLD WAR   398
    The Fourteen Points and the Peace Treaties   *398*
    Reparations and the League   *399*
    A Decade of Adjustment   *401*
    New Alliances and the Kellogg Pact   *402*

PART FOURTEEN
The Second World War

62 THE ERA OF REPUDIATION   407
    The International Scene in the 1920's   *407*
    The Problem of Reparations and War Debts   *409*
    A Decade of Growing Disillusionment   *410*
    Fascism in Italy   *412*
    The Rise of Hitler in Germany   *413*
    The Socialist Experiment in Russia   *416*

63 A PERIOD OF DEPRESSION AND
    AGGRESSION   421
    The War of Ideas   *421*
    Appeasement   *423*

64 THE BEGINNING OF THE SECOND
    WORLD WAR   424
    The Collapse of France   *425*
    The Battle of Britain   *426*
    The Battle of the Atlantic   *426*

The Balkans and Libya   427
Japanese Activities on the Asiatic Mainland   427
The Nazi Attack upon Russia   428

65 THE UNITED STATES AND THE SECOND
    WORLD WAR   429
    Prelude to Pearl Harbor   431
    Pearl Harbor and After   431
    Military Events in Europe and Africa   433
    The Turn of the Tide   434
    The Russian Front   434
    The Collapse of Italy   434
    The Assault on Nazi Europe   435
    The Invasion of France   435
    Russian Advances in 1944   436
    The Fall of Germany   437
    The Japanese War   437
    The Fall of Japan   438

PART FIFTEEN

Recent History

66 AFTERMATH OF THE SECOND
    WORLD WAR   441
    Formation and Early Years of the United Nations   441
    Postwar Demobilization and Disarmament   442
    Problems of the Peace Treaties   443
    The Iron Curtain   444
    Postwar Europe   445
    Postwar Asia, Africa, and the Pacific   446

67 THE FIFTIES AND EARLY SIXTIES   448
    Formation of NATO   448
    The Korean War   449
    Southeast Asia   450
    Other Far Eastern Matters   452
    Developments in Europe   453
    The Middle East and North Africa   457
    Central Africa   459

South Africa 460
Latin American Developments 461
Developments in the United States 463
The United Nations in the 1960's 465

68 THE SIXTIES AND EARLY SEVENTIES 465
The Changing International Climate 465
The War in Vietnam 466
The Middle East 468
Africa 469
Pakistan and India 470
China 471
Latin America 472
Western Europe 473
Northern Ireland 475
The Soviet Union and Eastern Europe 476
International Cooperation 477
Retrospect and a Forward Look 479

INDEX 483

MAPS

Ancient Egypt and Mesopotamia   *13*
The Empire of Alexander the Great, 323 B.C.   *64–65*
The Roman Empire at Its Greatest Extent, 117 A.D.   *92–93*
The Byzantine Empire at the Death of Justinian,
    565 A.D.   *128*
The Mohammedan Domination, 750 A.D.   *136*
The Empire of Charlemagne, 814 A.D.   *148*
The Holy Roman Empire, about 1100 A.D.   *170*
Exploration and Colonization, 1418–1660   *244–45*
The Empire of Charles V   *270–71*
Europe after the Peace of Westphalia, 1648   *292–93*
Napoleon's Domination of Europe, 1812   *336*
The Expansion of the United States   *374*
Europe before World War I, 1914   *392–93*
Europe before World War II   *414–15*

PART ONE
The Earliest Civilizations

B.C.

4241	Beginning of Egyptian calendar: "earliest dated event in history"
4000–2900	Era of Sumerian city-kingdoms
3400	Accession of Menes begins first Egyptian dynasty
3400–2700	"Old Kingdom" in Egypt
3000	Commercial contact established between Egypt and Crete
3000–2500	Pyramid Age
2900	Predominance of Lagash over Sumerian cities
2800	Akkadian conquest of Sumer under leadership of Sargon I
2600	Cultural flowering during reign of Gudea
2500	Highly developed Indian civilization flourishing in the valley of Indus River
2160–1800	Egyptian Middle Kingdom
2100	First predominance of Babylon. Age of Hammurabi
2000	Hittite invasion of Babylonia
	Indo-Europeans settled in Iran
1900	Greeks began to settle in Greek Peninsula
1800	Kassite conquest of Babylonia
1800 (?) –1560	Hyksos rulers of Egypt
1600–1500	"Grand Age" of Crete, highest development of Cretan civilization
1580–1150	The New Kingdom, the Egyptian Empire
1500–1200	Mycenaean Age of Greece
1500	Achaean and Dorian Greeks settle in Peloponnesus
1375–1358	Amenhotep IV (Ikhnaton)
1360–1350	Tutankhamen
1292–1225	Rameses II, "The Great"
1000	Zoroaster
	Indian *Rig-Veda*
	Kingdom of Israel established by Hebrews
814	Phoenicians found city of Carthage
722–705	Sargon II
674–665	Egypt made subject to Assyrian Empire by Esarhaddon and Assurbanipal
612	Destruction of Nineveh. Fall of Assyria
612–539	Chaldean or second Babylonian Empire

586   Nebuchadnezzar destroyed Jerusalem and took He-
                brews into captivity in Babylon
563–483   Gautama the Buddha lived in India
551–479   Confucius lived in China
550–529   Cyrus established and ruled the Persian Empire
525   Cambyses conquered Egypt
521–485   Darius the Great
492–479   Wars between Persia and the Greeks
323   Revolt of India against the Macedonian rule. Chand-
                dragupta became ruler in Punjab and Magadha
274–236   Asoka's Empire in India
214   Completion of the Great Wall of China

1 PREHISTORIC MAN

Men have probably ranged over the face of the earth for more than a million years. Yet it is possible to trace the course of human history back over less than one percent of that vast expanse of time, for it was not until "relatively recent" times that men formed the habit of passing on some kind of record of their achievements and, in so doing, established the beginnings of what we know as history. Despite this fact we are not altogether without knowledge of prehistoric man. It is evident from scattered remains found in different parts of the world that in remote ages representatives of the human race were to be found in Europe, Asia, and Africa. These earliest known men probably moved about the earth following the animal herds which constituted their main supply of food. As the climate changed and the great ice fields moved down over the continental land masses, the animals retreated southward where they could still find vegetation to feed upon. And primitive men seem to have followed the animals during the first three advances of the northern ice fields. In the earth thus covered by masses of ice lay the bones of men who had died, bones which we have found covered over by as much as eighty feet of earth.

When, for the third time, the ice melted and large parts of the northern continents once again became covered with vegetation, men re-established themselves in the lands most familiar to us today. During this warm period, which lasted some thousands of years, primitive men learned to fashion for themselves rude weapons of stone. One of the first of these was the fist hatchet which was used as both a weapon and a tool. For many thousands of years men continued to depend upon stone implements in their struggles for existence, but a marked improvement was made in these implements during the period when, for the fourth time, the ice mass descended upon the northern continents. This time, instead of retreating southward, men took refuge in caves, where their descendants continued to live. Perhaps the greater difficulties they confronted sharpened their wits, for the men of the Fourth Ice Age made many improvements upon the earlier crude tools. From this era there survive arrowheads, hammers, chisels, drills, polishers, and scrapers, which were formed of stone chipped by pressure. The life of this man of the Middle Stone Age was similar in many respects to that of the modern Eskimo. The tusks of the mammoth and the horns of the reindeer provided him with useful materials which he was able to carve with his improved stone tools. He learned the use of the bow and arrow and invented a throwing stick which gave him greater range and speed in the use of his bone-tipped spear. Fine bone needles are evidence that he had learned to clothe himself with the skins of animals as a protection against the intense cold.

The developed imagination which enabled this Stone Age ancestor of ours to invent new tools and to devise comfortable garments for his body early expressed itself artistically. With hands and mind skilled in the use of his stone instruments he often fashioned objects which were beautiful as well as useful, and which, in their sculptured embellishments, give us a very accurate notion of the kinds of animals he was familiar with. Not only could he carve, he could draw and paint as well. Upon the walls of a cave near Altamira in northern Spain, preserved for ten thousand years, there are painted pictures of a group of bison which provide an astonishing example of the artistic skill of these early men. It is evident, too, that the man of the Middle Stone Age developed some conception of his relationship to God and of an existence after death, for bodies have been found surrounded by evidences of careful burial, equipped with ornaments and weapons.

Eight or ten thousand years before the beginning of the Christian Era, the ice pack which covered a good part of Europe receded once more. As the climate of Europe became less rigorous, men left their caves and established themselves along the shores of seas and lakes where they formed small villages. The tools now sharpened by grinding on a whetstone were further improved by the addition of wooden handles.

Thus we find many implements which strongly resemble tools of the present day, forerunners of our ax, chisel, knife, drill, and saw. And experiment has proven that these tools were much more efficient than one is at first likely to assume, for a modern mechanic, unused to such implements, was able to shape the necessary timber and build a house in eighty-one days with stone tools.

In the Late Stone Age the evidences indicate important advances. During this era men discovered the use of pottery. They learned to plant seeds and thus to raise part of their food supply. And they began to domesticate animals. In Switzerland plentiful remains of Late Stone Age lake villages have been found. At Wangen over fifty thousand piles supported the wooden dwellings of Stone Age men. Twenty-foot logs, sharpened at one end, were driven into the bottom of the lake at a place where the water was eight or ten feet deep. The dwellings were constructed upon platforms which were connected with the shore by a bridge. A section of the bridge could be removed to protect the village by night. Through a trap door in the floor the lake dweller could fish with a bone hook, or he might suspend nets between the piles. He constructed boats from hollowed-out logs. He still hunted on the shore, and, in addition to his diet of fish and meat, contrived dishes of barley, wheat, and some millet which he had learned to plant in the soft earth along the shore of the lake. In addition, he had learned how to make yarn and cloth out of flax.

We do not know whether this early European ever encountered his contemporaries in Asia or Africa; whether, for example, he learned to domesticate sheep and goats as was being done by his distant Asiatic neighbors. It seems likely that men learned these things for themselves in different parts of the world during the long period of the Late Stone Age.

As time went on, men in one region or another discovered newer and better ways to insure to themselves the necessities of everyday existence, and devoted themselves more and more to activities which increased their comfort and gave variety and interest to life. With advances in housing, in language, in group organization, in the arts and crafts, men began to emerge from primitive life and to enter upon the threshold of civilization.

2   EGYPT

The Earliest Nile Dwellers. The earliest known civilizations developed contemporaneously in two great river valleys of the Near East: one in the rich lands between the Tigris and Euphrates rivers in western Asia, the other in the fertile valley of the Nile in North Africa. The Nile River, flowing northward to the Mediterranean Sea, during the course of many long ages had worn a deep channel in the eastern part of the Sahara Desert. Through the centuries the river waters have deposited in this valley, hardly thirty miles wide, a rich covering of soil that has been carried down from the mountains to the south. Throughout most of the year the river flows through the center of the valley, leaving a strip of land on either side. There is little rainfall in Egypt, but once a year, as it has throughout history, the great river overflows its banks and during the period of its flood leaves a deposit of rich soil along the valley floor, thus assuring the continued productivity of the land. Enclosing the valley along much of its length are steep cliffs which shut off the barren deserts on either side.

It is fairly easy to understand how this land, watered and enriched by the river and protected on east and west by expanses of burning desert, nurtured one of the earliest civilizations. The dry air has marvelously preserved those abundant remains of ancient Egyptian civilization which stand outside the area annually covered by the river flood. Thousands of mounds along the desert edge preserve the bodies of Stone Age men where, surrounded by weapons and utensils and pottery jars containing food, they were buried by their fellows over six thousand years ago.

The ancient Egyptians were a Hamitic people. The Hamites, one of the three branches of the Caucasian or white race, have through the ages lived principally in northern Africa along the Mediterranean and have characteristically dark complexions and black hair. In ancient Egypt there were also considerable numbers of Negroes who had migrated there from the neighboring central parts of Africa.

In very early times the Egyptians had devised a kind of picture writing that was not essentially different from that which was in use among the North American natives. And long before 3000 B.C.—three thousand years before the birth of Christ—the Egyptians had improved their system of writing and had developed an alphabet of twenty-four letters. That is, the pictures with which they wrote did not represent ideas, as before, but instead represented sounds. The Egyptians could thus combine these sounds on paper to form words, as we do. And they had also learned to make paper and to write with pen and ink. In addition they had solved the problem of time measurement. At first, like the American Indian, they measured time by the change of the moon. But they then observed (the Indian failed to take account of this) that the moon-month varied from twenty-nine to thirty days. They also noted that the moon-month does not divide the year evenly. So after careful calculation they worked out a year of three hundred sixty-five days. Thus the ancient Egyptians developed the essentials for recording history: an accurate time measurement and a system of writing. The earliest recorded event is accordingly the date of the beginning of the Egyptian calendar, 4241 B.C. And in addition to all this, probably some time before 4000 B.C. the Egyptians discovered copper and thus entered the Age of Metals.

The Pyramid Age and the Disunity of Egypt. When the Nile returned to its channel after the period of flood, the soft, moist soil left behind was ready to receive the seeds which men had saved over from the last harvest for planting. But the burning tropical sun would soon bake the earth dry if men did not haul water up from the river and irrigate the fields in which they had planted their crops. Very early the Egyptians learned to build canals and ditches running from the riverbanks out through the cultivated fields. The control of this water supply was of vital importance to all, for if the farmer near the river used all the water from the canal, those fields lying further away would dry up and their owners would be without food. It was important therefore that each citizen receive his fair share of the water. Another problem confronted them. The overflowing river destroyed the familiar landmarks which showed where one man's field left off and his neighbor's began. Each year then the Egyptians had to arrange an allotment of land to each farmer and the regulation of the water supply. The supervision of these arrangements naturally fell to the chieftains of each of the groups of people living along the river. And since it was impossible for any one man to fence off a piece of land and say "This is mine" for longer than the period of months between the annual floods, the Egyptian never thought of himself as an *owner* of land. The land belonged to the god, and part of it was allotted to him each year for his use by the chieftain who thus represented the god. Government and religion were in this fashion very closely associated in the mind of the Egyptians from the earliest times.

In all ages men have recognized that behind the familiar cycle of birth and life-struggle and death is a regulating force which lies beyond the sphere of human understanding. The ancient Egyptians could no more explain what life is or what brought the universe into being than can the modern scientist. They observed that the living creatures about them and the vegetation on which they depended would burn and die under the blazing sun were it not for the great river—that the river was their source of life. The river was a life-giver. And so the river and all it brought him became the symbol of a god, Osiris. The sun too, with its power to give and to destroy life, became the symbol of another god, Ra. As we have seen, in their writing, the Egyptians used pictures, known as hieroglyphics, to represent sounds and ideas. It is not surprising therefore that they employed images or pictures of animals to represent the gods which were the invisible forces regulating the life of the universe around them. Thus they developed the idea of many gods or spirits, the most important of which were Ra and Osiris.

The very early Egyptians, like the Stone Age Europeans, believed that a man's spirit did not die with his body. They did not know whether, when a man had died, his spirit might wish to return to his body, perhaps to dwell in it from time to time like a house. They therefore carefully dressed the dead in his familiar clothing and ornaments and surrounded him with jars of food, tools, and weapons, and placed him in a prepared grave. The dead chieftain or king, accustomed in life to be attended by servants, to being dressed in official robes, to ride upon the river in boats, was accompanied in death by models of the things which surrounded him in life. The tomb of the king was naturally larger than that of other men and women and, for its protection, was covered by a mound of sun-dried bricks, sand, and gravel.

About 3000 B.C. the Egyptians began to use stone in their buildings. Then the grand vizier, or chief official, of King Zoser, slightly later than 3000 B.C., designed the oldest all-stone building that has survived from those remote times, a tomb for his king. From that event the development of construction in stone was amazingly rapid. No longer were the kings' tombs built of brick, but great pyramids of solid stone masonry were constructed over the carefully concealed burial chambers in which the kings' bodies were placed. By the end of the thirtieth century B.C. the Great Pyramid of Gizeh was being prepared for King Khufu. Some notion of the astonishing progress that had been made may be had from the fact that this pyramid, which is seen in the background of most photographs of the Sphinx, is a solid mass of masonry containing 2,300,000 blocks of stone, each stone weighing about two and a half tons. The base of the pyramid covers an area of thirteen acres and the structure rises to a height of nearly five hundred feet. Not only is the mass of this monument impressive, the fineness of workmanship is even more so. Great blocks of stone weighing tons are fitted together with seams showing a joint of less than ten thousandths of an inch. Herodotus, a Greek historian of a later date, tells us that it took a hundred thousand workmen twenty years to complete the great structure.

Obviously this massive pyramid is not the tomb of a minor chieftain but that of a great emperor who ruled all Egypt, an emperor who was looked upon by his people as a god as well as a ruler. It is not very clear by what steps Egypt had thus come to be united under a single king. The local kingdoms which we mentioned earlier had long since been united to form the two kingdoms of Upper and Lower Egypt. About 3400 B.C. they were brought together under the rule of Menes, whose capital was the city of Memphis. There then followed an era of remarkable progress under the Old Kingdom which endured for nearly a thousand years. The extraordinary development of pyramid building is no more than a single evidence of a progress which was manifested in many ways, for not only do these pyramids testify to the efficiency and wealth of the Pharaoh's government, they indicate the means by which a benevolent ruler cared for his people. The once popular notion that these hordes of workmen were driven to their tasks with whips is not supported by evidence. "What presided over the erection of the Great Pyramid was not brute force, but organized ability, magnificently trained to use to the best advantage the strength of a race of fine workers." It now seems likely that the greater number of these workers were employed during the months when the river was in flood. At such times the fields would be covered with water and many men would be without work. Those who had been unable to put aside sufficient stores of food to carry them through the season would have found themselves in difficulties were it not for the employment provided by these great public undertakings, the pyramids.

Let us note that the Egyptians never developed a system of coinage of their own. Barter, or the exchange of commodities, was practiced down to the fourth century B.C. when coinage was first introduced in imitation of the Greeks. Taxes were collected in kind, and the grain and other produce thus paid into the public treasury were stored in warehouses supervised by the priests and by the king's officials. This great store of reserve taxes was used to put large numbers of men to work during the flood season when, incidentally, it was also easier to float the massive blocks of limestone across the river from the quarries to the site of the pyramid. The last great king of the Old Kingdom was Pepi I who ruled around 2700 B.C. His popularity and energy are attested by the large number of inscriptions from all parts of Egypt which bear his name. Under Pepi Egypt's commerce continued to flourish—for it must not be supposed that the great state we are now dealing with remained isolated from the rest of the world. Egyptian traders ventured southward into Nubia and brought back precious woods, ivory, gold, and scented gums. Her commerce reached out along the coast of the Red Sea to the land of Punt (modern Somaliland) and northward and eastward to the peninsula of Sinai and beyond. Goods were exchanged with Palestine and Syria and the islands of Crete and Cyprus. But after Pepi I the power of the rulers of the Old Kingdom declined.

Egypt was divided into districts called nomes; the rulers of the nomes were thus known as Nomarchs. The Nomarchs acquired such power in their own provinces that the kings could no longer control them, with the result that the next period of Egyptian history is characterized chiefly by wars among the small states which had broken away from the great kingdom. The prosperity of the country declined as a result of frequent wars and the records of the period are very confused. This state of affairs lasted until near the end of the third millennium B.C., when the rulers of Thebes in the southern portion of Egypt succeeded to some extent in unifying the country once again. Thebes now replaced Memphis as the capital of Egypt.

The Theban kings, all of whom were called either Amenemhet or Senusret, were energetic men. They created the new fertile province of Fayum where the waters of Lake Moeris were used in irrigation works and in the reclamation of large tracts of land. The Theban god Amon was identified with Ra and thus religious unity was restored. Commerce was revived and trading fleets set out for Palestine, Syria, Cyprus, and Crete. A canal was dug connecting the Red Sea with one of the branches of the Nile Delta so that Egyptian ships might travel from the Nile directly into the Red Sea and down the African coast. This first Suez Canal was constructed four thousand years ago. Not content with restoring Egypt, the Theban rulers undertook conquests in Nubia and Asia. But this period of Egyptian successes was relatively brief. About 1800 B.C. the peoples of Mesopotamia were overwhelmed by conquering tribes from the north. Many moved southward toward Egypt in search of new lands. The Egyptian records show a period when their country was under the domination of foreigners from the north whom they called Hyksos. The Hyksos rule, which began about 1800 B.C., did not fundamentally affect the civilization of Egypt although later records indicated that much material damage was done. The military success of the conquerors was apparently due to the fact that they possessed horse-drawn chariots and were more experienced in warfare than the Egyptians. They naturally retained their interest in the lands they had left and sought through commercial penetration and conquest to extend their influence along the coast of the eastern Mediterranean and the western edge of the Arabian Desert. As a result the peoples of these areas developed close contacts with Egypt and the development of their own civilizations was hastened. The exact duration of the Hyksos rule is uncertain for, in accordance with custom, when the foreigners were driven out all the records and monuments of their rule were destroyed. But in two ways the Hyksos domination prepared Egypt for the great conquests of her later rulers. The Hyksos introduced the horse and chariot into Egypt and they taught the Egyptians how to organize warfare on a large scale.

The Egyptian Empire. The Egyptians, under the leadership of Ahmose, finally overthrew the foreigners about 1580 B.C. After liberating the country Ahmose established himself first ruler of the Eighteenth Dynasty, that is, first of the eighteenth line of hereditary rulers of Egypt. The Hyksos domination had taught the Egyptians much besides the use of the horse and large-scale warfare. It made them realize that their country was open to attack on the north. The great kings of the

Eighteenth Dynasty determined that Egypt would dominate the lands and waterways of the eastern Mediterranean. It seemed to be a question of whether Egypt or her enemies would control those approaches; her able kings provided their own answer.

The first great conqueror of the line was Thutmose I. After the brief reign of his son Thutmose II, the succession passed to Egypt's first queen, Hatshepsut, who was probably the daughter of Thutmose I. She married Thutmose III. During the lifetime of the queen her husband remained in the background. Hatshepsut devoted herself to peaceful pursuits and the development of commerce. The prosperity of her reign is attested by the magnificent palace she constructed at the base

ANCIENT EGYPT and MESOPOTAMIA

of the cliffs at Thebes, by her restoration of the old buildings, and the completion of those begun before the Hyksos conquered Egypt. She boasts of her achievements in many inscriptions and in commemoration of the fifteenth year of her reign erected one of the most impressive monuments of ancient Egypt. The great engraved obelisk erected in the courtyard of the temple of Karnak is a single shaft of granite standing ninety-seven and a half feet high and weighing nearly three hundred fifty tons. It was quarried far up the river at the first cataract. When we consider that the Egyptians were completely without our modern steel girders and power-driven machines, we may properly marvel at the ingenuity and skill they exhibit in quarrying, transporting, and erecting this huge shaft.

Upon the death of the great queen her husband, Thutmose III, revealed himself to be possibly the ablest and most energetic ruler Egypt ever had. He launched an era of conquest which has earned him the name of the Napoleon of Egypt—which is a compliment to Napoleon rather than to Thutmose. His exploits are recorded on the walls of the great temple of Karnak. He conquered Syria, Phoenicia, and Palestine, and made them subject kingdoms paying tribute to Egypt. In the interests of imperial solidarity, he educated the ruling families of conquered territories in Egypt. Strong Egyptian garrisons were stationed at important centers in the subject states under the command of Egyptian generals. The control of Egypt was extended into Nubia to the south, and powerful Egyptian fleets sailed the Mediterranean while Cyprus and the confederation of Cretan cities were forced into an alliance with the great conqueror. Thutmose's military prowess was matched by his abilities as an organizer and administrator—there is an interesting account of his ruthless treatment of an extortionate taxgatherer. And when he found moments of leisure, this versatile and tireless man gave himself to the designing of exquisite vases.

The successors of Thutmose III devoted themselves to the defense and extension of the empire. Their relationships with other countries are revealed in a collection of state papers found in the ruins of the palace of Amenhotep IV at Tell el-Amarna. The diplomatic language of the time was the language of the Mesopotamian city-states of Sumer and Akkad. The letters which cover the reigns of Amenhotep III and IV reveal an international intercourse strikingly similar to that of our own day. But although at peace with the Egyptian Empire, the rival Hittite and Assyrian states fomented unrest among the peoples subject to Egypt. It required the greatest vigilance and energy to control and rule the great state.

Upon the death of Amenhotep III there ascended the throne one of the strangest and most tragic figures of history, the young Amenhotep IV. The empire was being threatened by unrest in the provinces, by a large immigration of desert nomads called the Khabiri, and by a Hittite advance from the north. Instead of placing himself at the head of his army and marching into the northern provinces, Amenhotep IV sought to bring about a sweeping religious reform by instituting the worship of one god, Aton. The tragedy of Amenhotep IV, or Ikhnaton as he called himself, is that he ruled at a moment when Egypt needed a military leader more than she needed a philosopher, poet, and reformer. Ikhnaton was a man of great abilities, but his overthrow of the ancient religion rent the state asunder at the moment when all of its forces should have been concentrated against the enemy. The old priesthood held out against him until his death.

During the forty years of political anarchy which followed the death of Ikhnaton, one brief reign was that of young Tutankhamen (whose perfectly preserved tomb was uncovered in 1923). In the fourteenth century B.C. Seti I and his son Rameses II, known for the great buildings of their period, partially restored the empire. But the era was one of constant conflict with rival neighboring empires, especially the Hittites. The Egyptians were no longer willing to fight ceaselessly for the existence of the Egyptian state. The great story of ancient Egypt as an independent country came to an end.

3   MESOPOTAMIA

Early Man in Western Asia. The early history of Mesopotamia in many ways resembles that of Egypt. For here, too, is a fertile valley. This valley is watered by two great rivers, the Tigris and the Euphrates—Mesopotamia means between the rivers—and it was particularly well adapted to serve the needs of an emerging civilization. Both rivers originate in the mountains of Armenia to the north, and in the course of making their ways southward to the Persian Gulf the rivers annually overflow their banks, depositing a covering of rich mud upon the valley floor. We do not know when men first began to sow seeds in this soft, freshly deposited mud and then settled down to await the ripening of their crops. But, like the Egyptians, they discovered that the hot sun would soon bake the earth dry and kill their crops unless they devised some method of carrying the river water to their fields.

The Tigris-Euphrates Valley is much broader than the Valley of the Nile, and the rivers were often some distance from the places where seed had been sown. But in natural hollows pools of water remained when the flood subsided and men used the water from these pools to irrigate their crops. Thus natural accident probably became the basis for the irrigation system developed in Mesopotamia. For men learned to build catch basins and to surround them with dikes and dams so that each year, after the flood subsided, there would remain in these artificially constructed reservoirs sufficient water for irrigation. As in Egypt, canals and ditches carried the water to the fields.

Again it becomes apparent that these irrigation systems were the product of co-operative effort, that the members of each community developed rules governing the fair distribution of water and agreed upon some kind of leadership and authority in the application and enforcement of those rules. In Mesopotamia there were other factors which tended to strengthen men's sense of community and to emphasize the need for capable leadership. For the land of the Tigris-Euphrates Valley is not surrounded by protecting desert barriers. Fierce nomadic peoples dwelling in the neighboring hills and mountains looked down with covetous eyes upon the ripening harvests and upon the well-fed flocks of the valley folk. Warfare was part of their life for they were in the habit of seizing what they could. If the men of the valley were to enjoy the fruits of their labors they had to be prepared to fight for their possessions and their land. And among them those individuals whose superior ingenuity had devised the catch basins and irrigation ditches, whose judgment foresaw dangers and counseled preparation against inevitable attacks, became chieftains. His superior talents were an indication to the citizen that the chieftain enjoyed the special favor of the gods. As a result the chieftain became the priest. By 3000 B.C. each of the little communities of agricultural folk located near the mouths of the two rivers was governed by a priest-king called a patesi.

We do not know the racial origins of these people. They called themselves Sumerians and their country Sumer—*Shinar* it was called in the Bible by the Hebrews. Probably through trade with their neighbors to the north they became possessed of metals and developed the manufacture of copper. Like the Egyptians they devised a kind of picture writing to keep records of trade and government. But the materials they employed were those at hand; with a triangular wedge or stylus they made impressions upon soft clay tablets, in a form of writing known as cuneiform. They then baked the tablets in an oven and in the hardened clay possessed a permanent record of each transaction. They measured the year roughly by moon-months, and thus their time records are not as dependable as the Egyptian.

The chief cities of Sumer—Kish, Ur, Eridu, Lagash, Nippur—fell to quarreling with each other for predominance. Around 3000 B.C. Lagash united a large part of the district. Somewhat after 2900 B.C. a Sumerian king called Lugalzaggizi conquered the territory around the Persian Gulf and extended his sway along the northern part of the Arabian

Desert to the shores of the Mediterranean Sea. But the struggles of the Sumerian city-kingdoms probably weakened them, for about 2800 B.C., as we shall now see, their land was conquered by their northern neighbors.

The Triumph of Babylon. To the north of the Sumerians in the Tigris-Euphrates Valley there dwelt a Semitic people whom we know as the Akkadians from the name of their chief city Akkad. (The Semites are a branch of the Caucasian or white race; we have mentioned the Hamites—in Egypt—as another branch of the white race; the third branch, the Indo-Europeans, will appear first in our account in Chapter 5.)

About 2800 B.C. the Akkadians, under the leadership of Sargon I, conquered Sumer. The Akkadians seem to have been culturally inferior to the people they conquered. Little change was made in the district. Each city kept its own patesi and the conquerors seem to have adopted the ways of the superior Sumerian civilization.

As a result there followed a new cultural flowering under the rule of Gudea, priest-king of Lagash around 2600 B.C., during which Sumerian civilization reached its highest development. Although the Sumerian believed in a life after death, he conceived it to be a drab existence under the rule of a stern goddess. So instead of building tombs, like the Egyptians, he bent his energies to the construction of great palaces and temples to the gods. As there is no stone in the land, his buildings were constructed of sun-dried brick and adorned with carpets and tiles and the walls of these buildings were covered with fantastic animal designs. Among the most striking of these structures were the towers, or *ziggurats,* dedicated to the sun god. But at the peak of its flowering, Sumerian civilization received a severe shock. Savage mountain tribes from Gutium invaded the country and during the course of about a century destroyed cities and temples and palaces.

The next people to conquer Sumer and set up a new kingdom came from the city of Babylon, located on the Euphrates River north of Sumer. These people, the Babylonians—like the Akkadians—were Semites. Their great ruler, Hammurabi, defeated the Elamites, who were the chief rivals of the Sumerian cities, and then conquered Sumer. Mesopotamia became a united state under the rule of Babylon. The land was now known as Babylonia and the non-Semitic Sumerians disappear from the record. Local governments were crushed, the independence of the cities destroyed, and a strong centralized government was established. When Hammurabi ruled, his governors throughout the country collected tribute, enforced the laws that had long been in existence and, with the aid of a standing army, protected the country from attack. But some confusion resulted from the fact that the laws were not the same in all parts of the country. Accordingly Hammurabi collected all the laws and organized them into a general Code. This famous Code of laws was engraved upon a stone shaft and set up in the temple of the god Marduk in Babylon. It has survived to our day, the oldest preserved code of ancient law. And it gives us a very complete idea of the life of ancient Babylonia.

Trade was a much more important factor in the lives of the Babylonians than it was among the early Egyptians. This is undoubtedly due in part to the fact that they were surrounded by neighbors with whom they could profitably exchange what they produced. The rapid development of commerce may also have been aided by the fact that the Sumerian and his successors owned land as individuals and were able to increase their wealth by purchase and exchange. Women owned property and engaged in business. Although coined money had not yet come into use, silver and some gold in small lumps were used as a medium of exchange. The Babylonian system of justice was based upon the old conception "an eye for an eye and a tooth for a tooth." For example, if a badly built house fell and injured the householder's son, under the law the householder might inflict a similar injury upon the son of the builder who was responsible for the bad workmanship. The business character of this civilization is evident from the fact that the temples loaned money like banks, exchanged goods, and were often large landowners. The religious functions of the priests were to keep the gods well disposed toward the people by making sacrifices and, through the study of the stars and the internal organs of animals, to attempt to foretell the future.

The Assyrians and the Chaldeans. The wealth and civilization of the Tigris-Euphrates Valley continued to provoke the greed and ambition of warlike neighbors. The Babylonian Kingdom of Hammurabi was short-lived. Under his successor a period of internal disorder and foreign invasion began. The Hittites from Asia Minor seized Babylonia around 2000 B.C. and ruled it for a time. They were followed by the Kassites, the eastern neighbors of the Babylonians, who had never ceased to raid her borders and who now, around 1800 B.C., conquered Babylonia which they continued to rule for a period of 576 years. It is about this time that the peoples whom the Egyptians called Hyksos sought to escape the invaders by establishing themselves in Egypt.

The era was most violent and confused. The Hittites, although withdrawn from Babylon, continued to be a formidable power. To the north of the Arabian Desert, and along the coasts of the Mediterranean, many groups of peoples whose progress had been accelerated by their commercial contacts with Egypt and Mesopotamia fought with each other for land and commercial advantage. For a while, under her great conqueror Thutmose III, Egypt gained an empire which extended all the way to the Euphrates. Then in the latter part of the second millennium there occurred a new movement of peoples which further disrupted the Near East, for expansion of Indo-European peoples through central Asia and Europe pressed upon those who had long dwelt in the Balkan Peninsula, the islands of the Mediterranean, and Asia Minor, and drove them in large numbers into Syria and Egypt. The story of Mesopotamia as such continues at the moment of a later conquest.

About two hundred miles north of Babylon on the Tigris was the ancient city of Ashur, which dominated a mountain plateau inhabited by herdsmen and farmers. These were the Assyrians, another Semitic people. For many centuries they were too busy defending themselves against their local neighbors to figure largely in the history of Mesopotamia. Their civilization was borrowed to a considerable extent from the peoples to the south whose history we have traced. As early as the fourteenth century B.C. they appear as dangerous rivals to the Hittites and Babylonians. With the fall of the Hittite Empire, the Assyrian king, Tiglath-pileser I, decided to extend the dominion of his country and succeeded in conquering territory as far as eastern Asia Minor to the Black Sea. However, the Assyrians failed to hold these territories. Again in the ninth century the Assyrians sought to enlarge their holdings by conquest but with indifferent success. Finally, during the second half of the eighth century B.C., they made a third and more successful attempt. An able Assyrian general seized the throne and as an indication of his ambition took the name Sargon II. Under his leadership the foundation of the Assyrian Empire was laid.

Assyria established the first purely military empire in history. Its strength was based upon a well-organized permanent army rather than a militia called together for a particular war. From the Hittites the Assyrians had obtained iron which gave them superiority over their enemies in weapons. Their infantry, well armed with pikes and bows and swords and protected by breastplates, fought in close formation. There were companies of swift-moving cavalry whose charges broke up the enemy ranks as well as the heavy armed chariots which may perhaps be regarded as the tanks of ancient warfare. The Assyrians also developed a siege technique for reducing fortified cities. They employed the battering-ram against walls and gates. Where the walls were too thick to be breached in this fashion they undermined them by digging. They also employed the technique of terror, often slaughtering the populations of whole towns. As if this were not enough, they sometimes flayed their enemies, i.e., skinned them alive, or impaled them on sharp stakes. Various forms of mutilation were also practiced.

With these "gentle" methods the Assyrians succeeded in conquering Babylonia, the Syrio-Phoenician coast, and Palestine. Their attacks to the west, beginning as plundering raids, ended with the subjugation of large territories. Esarhaddon, the grandson of Sargon, attacked Egypt and made it an Assyrian province. But while they were victorious in their westward expansion, the Assyrians possessed an eastern frontier that required protection against their Chaldean neighbors. From their various new capital cities, Kalhu, Dur Sharrukin, and Nineveh, successive Assyrian emperors sought to break the power of the Chaldeans. But the latter proved hardy enough to withstand their attacks. And the strength of the Assyrians, their militarism, proved in the long run to be their weakness too. For the empire was soon beset by so many revolts that the distracted rulers forced their unhappy subjects into the larger armies which they now needed to suppress rebellion. It was the beginning of the end, and the Chaldeans were quick to take advantage of the weakened state of the empire.

Finally, in 612 B.C. the Chaldeans took Nineveh and destroyed the city. They established a new empire with Babylon once again the capital city. While many had hailed the victory of the Chaldeans over the Assyrians because it meant release from those brutal conquerors, they did not willingly submit to the new empire. Egypt, again independent and fearful of the power of the Chaldeans, stirred up revolts among the peoples of the Mediterranean coast. In punishment for one such revolt the Hebrew people of Judah were transported in large numbers from their homeland. In spite of his long wars, the greatest of the Chaldean rulers, Nebuchadnezzar, enlarged and beautified the city of Babylon. The beautiful gardens which he created on the terraced roof of his palace were known to the ancient world as the Hanging Gardens of Babylon, one of the seven wonders of the world. Over the city towered the great ziggurat temple to the Babylonian god Marduk, very possibly the Tower of Babel of the Bible. Under Chaldean rule Babylonian civilization flourished once more.

4   EAST MEDITERRANEAN PEOPLES

The Aegeans. There is evidence that as early as 3000 B.C. the Egyptians had begun to exchange goods with people from over the seas to the north. Just which people these were is not clear. But the eastern Mediterranean area was settled very early. Along its eastern coast, the coast of later Syria and Phoenicia, were Semites who had come from the east. The islands, including Crete and Cyprus, and the coasts of Asia Minor and what was later the Greek peninsula, were inhabited by people who were probably not Semitic and who very likely arrived there from the north.

These East Mediterranean peoples soon came in contact with their more civilized neighbors to the east and south, the Sumerians and the Egyptians. Remains which have been uncovered by excavation indicate that they borrowed heavily from both. For example, the Cretans, who achieved an advanced state of culture during the sixteenth century B.C., seem to have learned cuneiform writing from Mesopotamia while it is possible they also adopted the Babylonian system of weights and measures. Most of their crafts, however, were learned from the Egyptians. And this seems to have been the case also with the Semites on the Asiatic mainland.

The Cretans, whose island was protected by the sea, did not find it necessary to fortify their cities. With that exception, the Cretan towns resemble in plan the earliest cities of the Greek mainland, best known of which are Mycenae and Tirens. These latter were surrounded by strong walls. The development of Aegean civilization—it is convenient to refer to it as Aegean since the islands and coasts bordered the Aegean Sea—was hastened as a result of intercourse with Mesopotamia and Egypt. The land was not particularly fertile but it did produce olives and grapes in abundance. Consequently the Cretans and Aegeans sought to obtain many of the things they desired from other people in exchange for their excellent wine and olive oil. Their history and their prosperity

were accordingly commercial, their might largely sea power.
The seizure of Babylonia by the Hittites at the beginning
of the second millennium, and the invasion of Egypt by the
Hyksos, made the eastern Mediterranean the center of rivalry
between the two great states. Commerce was much increased
and the cultural flowering of Crete from 1600 to 1500 B.C.
is based upon the era of prosperity which resulted. The Cretan
and Aegean cities of this period reflect a more democratic
type of life than that which was to be found in Mesopotamia
and Egypt. There was not the same contrast between the palace of the king and the dwelling of the private citizen. True,
the palace of Cnossus, in Crete, was large, but that was because of the many small apartments necessary to house the
large number of people who shared the palace with the king.
These cities, too, possess some improvements which were not
found elsewhere; they had drainage systems and paved streets.
Incidentally, plumbing is not a modern invention. In Egyptian
homes of 4500 years ago were to be found kitchen sinks of
limestone finished with metal trim. The faucets turned on
and off as ours do and the sinks were equipped with stoppers
attached to metal chains. They were not greatly different from
those that may still be found in older American homes.
    About 1500 B.C. three great powers dominated the eastern
Mediterranean. They were the Hittites who, although driven
out of Babylonia by the Kassites some two centuries earlier,
still formed a strong kingdom in Asia Minor; Egypt, under
the Eighteenth Dynasty; and the Aegean kingdoms united in
an alliance under the headship of Crete. But the balance of
power did not last for long. The great pharaoh Thutmose III
conquered Syria and dominated the Mediterranean league.
However, in her turn Egypt had to surrender the leading role,
for she was seriously weakened by the religious revolution
under Ikhnaton and the period of chaos which followed. The
Hittites were prompt to take advantage of her weakness; eventually Syria and Phoenicia fell into their hands.
    In the fourteenth century Crete, at the height of her de-
velopment, received a crushing blow from which she never
recovered. This was the revolt of the Aegean city-states of

the mainland which were under Crete's rule. The revolt became possible because an enormous eruption on the nearby island of Thera devastated Crete, thus permitting Mycenae to gain cultural and political leadership. The kings of Mycenae waged many wars early in the next century, the most famous being that against Troy and the league of cities on the western coast of Asia Minor.

During the thirteenth century (B.C.) great changes took place. New people began to invade the region from the north, coming principally from eastern Europe, and moving down the Greek peninsula and across into the Peloponnesus, attacking the Aegean peoples already settled there. Many Aegeans and Cretans fled before these persistent foes, some finding refuge in Egypt and Syria. (Egyptian chroniclers refer to "sea peoples.") The newcomers who subjugated and later largely displaced the Aegean peoples absorbed what remained of the Aegean culture and made it part of a new tradition. We will soon come to know these newcomers as the Greeks.

The Hebrews. The history of the Semitic peoples who came from the east and settled in Syria and Palestine and Phoenicia parallels that of the Cretans and Aegeans. They, even more than their non-Semitic neighbors of the sea, were forced to submit to the successive domination of Sumerians, Babylonians, Egyptians, Hittites, and Assyrians. Among these peoples two are of particular interest to us because of the influence of their contributions to history. They are the Hebrews and the Phoenicians.

The Hebrews, a nomadic folk from the Arabian Desert, migrated slowly westward in small groups constantly in search of fresh pastures for the flocks upon which they depended. The Hebrews settled with their flocks upon the hillsides of Palestine and by degrees adopted the civilization of the Canaanites who had long been dwellers in the land. Later members of a wandering Hebrew tribe coming from the east found their way into Egypt where they were enslaved and cruelly treated by the pharaoh—possibly Rameses II who died about 1225 B.C. Finally they were led out of Egypt by Moses and then found their way into Palestine. In the north of Palestine particularly the Hebrews intermarried with the Canaanites and adopted their settled life and civilization. In so doing they acquired a civilization that had in its turn been derived from Babylonia and Egypt. But they never entirely gave up their pastoral life, and in the south of Palestine they continued to live among their flocks, following the wandering life of the nomad. They had become dwellers in the land but at that time were in no sense a nation.

During the twelfth and eleventh centuries Palestine and Syria were attacked by peoples fleeing before the conquerors of the Aegean region, who ravaged the coasts of the Mediterranean. Some of them, the Philistines, became firmly entrenched upon the shores of Palestine. The Hebrews were forced to defend themselves against the newcomers, and the effort seems to have brought them together as a people. Around 1000 B.C., under their first king, Saul, they were defeated by the Philistines, but under Saul's successor, David, they successfully met the Philistine threat and became united in an extensive kingdom.

We have already seen how, from earliest times, the intermediary position of the region, lying between the centers of the two great ancient civilizations, determined that its people would develop skill in commerce. And throughout the whole of history the region has remained a center through which has passed the commerce between east and west, between north and south.

Solomon, David's son and successor, became one of the leaders of the Near East. He joined in partnership with the Phoenician king of Tyre to launch a trading fleet. He was known far and wide as a trader in horses. From Phoenicia he borrowed workmen. He developed the city of Jerusalem and planned the magnificent temple of stone which became the chief Hebrew place of worship. But the splendor of Solomon's reign was costly and the burden of taxation became so irksome that after Solomon's death the northern tribes withdrew from the union. The united Hebrew kingdom had lasted less than a century.

Contact with the Phoenicians was important to the Hebrews in many ways but particularly so in the development of writing. They abandoned clay tablets and learned to write in the Egyptian fashion with pen and ink on papyrus—the paper made from river reeds. They also borrowed the Phoenician alphabet, which was superior to that of the Egyptians, and which, through its adoption by the Greeks, became the alphabet of the Europeans of later history and ultimately our own.

Palestine, as we know, lay in the path of the great eastern conquerors. The land of Israel fell before the Assyrians. When, toward the end of the seventh century, the Chaldeans conquered Nineveh, the Hebrews, like the other victims of Assyrian power, hoped for a release from foreign dominion. But Chaldea in turn gained control of Palestine, and the Hebrews were taken into exile in distant Babylon. The Hebrews from about this time on were to be known as the Jews—the name being derived from Judaea, the region around Jerusalem. It was not until the conquest of Babylonia by the Persians that they were released and permitted to return to their homeland.

The Phoenicians. The Phoenicians were a Semitic people who, as early as 3000 B.C., found their way westward from the Arabian Desert and settled on the shores of the Mediterranean. By 2000 B.C. they had borrowed heavily from Egypt and Mesopotamia and developed a considerable civilization. Their most important cities—Sidon and Tyre—lay along the coast and from earliest times they gave themselves to the cultivation of sea-borne commerce. From time to time they fell under the domination of the great states, but whether independent or subject to the dominion of a distant pharaoh or king, they remained an important factor in East Mediterranean commerce and prospered accordingly. With the final collapse of Egyptian power toward the close of the thirteenth century, the Phoenicians enlarged their commerce and traveled farther and farther along the coasts of the Mediterranean in search of markets, new sources of raw material, and strategically located harbors where they might set up colonies in the interests of extended commercial activity. Phoenician captains explored the entire Mediterranean coast. Some found their way through the passage which the Greeks called the Pillars of Hercules—the Straits of Gibraltar—and sailed along the west European coast. It is likely that they found their way to the island of Britain, for they brought back quantities of tin, a metal that is still found abundantly in England. Phoenician trading ships stopped along the coasts of Greece and tempted these primitive people with fine cloths, ivory combs, perfume bottles of Egyptian manufacture fashioned of glass and alabaster, richly engraved bronze, and robes dyed the famous Phoenician purple. For three centuries after the year 1000 B.C. the Phoenicians were the most important traders of the Mediterranean. They established a trading post at Gades—modern Cadiz—in Spain; and on the north African coast opposite the island of Sicily they founded the city of Carthage which, after Phoenicia fell to the Persians, became a great independent power.

5   INDO-EUROPEANS IN WESTERN ASIA

We have dealt with the great civilization of the Hamitic people in Africa. We have described the series of Semitic empires in Mesopotamia and have traced the history of smaller Semitic groups, the Hebrews and the Phoenicians. We now turn to another Caucasian or white-skinned people known as the Indo-Europeans, who were in time to spread out from the middle East into most of Europe.

The Indo-European peoples originated in the northern grasslands of central Asia. A branch of these people, around 2000 B.C., migrated eastward and eventually settled in northern India. Another group pushed in a southwesterly direction and settled in the mountains north and east of Mesopotamia. These were the Aryans from which come the names Iran and Iranian. Other Indo-European tribes advanced farther westward and settled about the Caspian and Black seas while still others pushed on into Europe all the way to the Atlantic Ocean. From these are descended the Greeks, the Romans, and the Celts of France. All these latter folk are not properly Aryans although they are often spoken of as such. They do, however, have the same original ancestry as the Aryans of central and western Asia.

Among the Indo-Europeans who settled in the mountains east of Mesopotamia were two powerful tribes, the Medes and the Persians. At the time of the collapse of the Assyrian Empire in 612 B.C., before the onslaughts of the Chaldeans, the Medes had established an extensive empire east of the Tigris River. The Persians, associated with them, were located to the south at the Persian Gulf. The empire continued in a northwesterly direction through the mountains to the Black Sea region.

The Aryans were united by a single religion which had been preached by the prophet Zoroaster around 1000 B.C. The religion was based upon a recognition of the struggle evident throughout history between good and evil. This conflict in the lives of men was, to the Zoroastrian, part of a larger struggle between the forces of the god of light and goodness, Mazda, or Ahuramazda, and the forces of the god of evil and darkness, Ahriman. Zoroaster called upon men to place themselves upon the side of Mazda and the forces of good. In their temples the priests kept sacred fires burning as symbols of their god of light. At a much later date, when the Medes and Persians had learned to write, they gathered together the old hymns and fragments of Zoroaster's teaching; a thousand years after the prophet's death they were copied down in a book known as the *Avesta*.

The Persians. About the middle of the sixth century there came to the throne of Anshan, a small kingdom subject to the Medes, a ruler named Cyrus who was a Persian. He succeeded in uniting the Persian tribes and, as leader of a new Persian nation, attacked the Medes, their overlords. In three years he had broken the Median power and made himself master of their territory.

The great states to the west took alarm at the rapid rise of

Cyrus and formed a powerful coalition against him. Chaldea, Egypt, Lydia in Asia Minor, and even Sparta in Greece, joined forces against the new conqueror. Without an instant's hesitation Cyrus attacked Lydia, a rich Greek kingdom on the western coast of Asia Minor whose king Croesus had brought about the hostile alliance. Sardis, the Lydian capital, fell, and in 546 B.C. Croesus was a prisoner in the hands of the Persian king. The Persian army was patterned to some extent upon the efficient armies of Assyria. Most of the army was made up of bowmen. Great flights of arrows at long range broke up the enemy ranks. Then the infantry advanced to engage the confused enemy in hand-to-hand combat while swift-moving cavalry on either wing circled about to take the enemy in the flank and complete the destruction.

Having defeated Lydia, Cyrus turned eastward and overwhelmed the army of the young Chaldean prince Belshazzar. Nebuchadnezzar had surrounded Babylon with huge walls, but after the defeat of Belshazzar's army the city surrendered with slight resistance in 539 B.C. Ten years later Cyrus fell in battle while subjugating some nomadic tribes in the eastern part of his empire. He was buried in his capital of Pasargadae, which is near the later and more famous capital at Persepolis.

The Persian Empire. Cyrus' son, Cambyses, inherited the energy and ambition of his father. Three years after his accession to the throne Cambyses conquered Egypt. Within the period of twenty-five years since the overthrow of the Medes by the Persians, Cyrus and Cambyses had conquered and united the whole civilized East. The Persian Empire now extended from the Aegean Sea and the Nile Valley in the west almost to India in the east.

Great as was the achievement of the Persians in conquering this vast empire, their brilliant organization and government of the many peoples of superior civilization who were now their subjects rank as an even greater feat. The growth of commerce and the growing interdependence of the different parts of the region had prepared the way for political unification. Businessmen had discarded the clay tablets and cuneiform writing of the Babylonians and now employed the more convenient Egyptian system of writing on papyrus with pen and ink. Aramaic had become the language of traders and was now in general use throughout most of the East. The new empire accordingly employed two languages: Aramaic, the language of commerce, and Persian, the language of the conquerors, for which an alphabet was now devised.

One of the most interesting facts revealed by the period of history we have covered thus far is the enduring quality of the institutions of civilization. The Sumerians gave way to their Semitic conquerors who, in turn, were subjugated by the Kassites. Then came the new Babylonian domination followed by that of the Assyrians, the Chaldeans, and finally the Indo-European Persians. And each conqueror was in turn conquered by the civilization of the subject peoples. Let us note here the great importance of religion and the autocratic power of the king through all the long course of early history. The king's power was absolute; he was responsible only to the gods. And in the great empires the king himself was looked upon as a god and a high priest as well as a political ruler. There was as yet no hint of democracy.

The ability of the Persians to absorb and master the complicated civilization of their subjects is astounding. Their genius is evident in the organization and administration of their empire, a work begun by Cambyses and brought to completion by his successor, Darius the Great (521–485 B.C.). The one-man rule of Darius "was just, humane, and intelligent," says an authority on the period. He planned no new conquests but gave his attention to the maintenance of his empire. He made himself king in Babylonia and Egypt. The rest of the empire he divided into twenty provinces under the rule of governors called "satraps." The government did not interfere much with the local life of the people so long as they behaved themselves.

The first coined money in history was invented by the Lydians. Darius perceived the advantage of this new money and introduced coinage throughout the empire. The convenience of a medium of exchange issued by the state stimulated commerce. Darius instituted a kind of secret service called the Eyes and Ears of the King which kept watch on the governors and reported signs of rebelliousness or misgovernment. Good roads were maintained with post horses at stations along the main roads so that communication was rapid.

During the decline of Egypt the canal which connected the Red Sea with the Nile had been allowed to fill with sand. Darius commanded that it be restored, and once again ships were able to sail from the Red Sea into the Mediterranean. An efficient postal system was instituted for the dispatch of official communications. Herodotus, the Greek historian, has recorded the motto of the Persian postal service: "Neither snow nor rain nor heat nor gloom of night stays these couriers from the swift completion of their appointed rounds." Today the motto of the Persian postal service appears inscribed upon the façade of the main post-office building in New York City.

Conflict with the Greeks. As we have already noted, the western coast of Asia Minor bordering the Aegean Sea had been taken possession of by the same people who had destroyed the Mycenean Empire that flourished on the mainland of what was later to become Greece. These people, who became the Greeks of history, were now settled about the coasts and islands of the Aegean Sea. The Ionian Greeks of Lydia were now subjects of the Great King, as the ruler of Persia was called. Yet in race, in culture, in religion, in political and economic interest, they formed part of Greece. They were not content to remain obedient subjects of a distant oriental despot.

In 499 B.C. some of the Greek cities of Asia Minor revolted against their Persian governors. An army was dispatched to put down the rebellion, but the struggle was a long one. During its course Athens, the leading maritime city of the Greek peninsula, dispatched a fleet of twenty ships to help her kinsmen. But in the end the Persian armies prevailed and cruel punishment was meted out to the rebel cities. Miletus was burned to the ground and her prosperity destroyed.

The Greek ships were the only important rivals of the Persians and Phoenicians in the Mediterranean. Darius determined to punish Athens for the encouragement and aid she had given his rebellious subjects and to destroy Greek sea power. A Persian army crossed over from Asia Minor into Europe and a great Persian fleet followed them along the coast. The arduous march cost the army many men and the fleet, in attempting to round the high promontory of Mount Athos in 492 B.C., was wrecked. The expedition was abandoned and a new one organized.

Two years later a second expedition set forth. It met with a catastrophe which had certainly not been envisaged by the Persians. But this event makes one of the glorious pages of Greek history and we shall leave the telling of it to its proper place.

6 EARLY CIVILIZATION IN EASTERN ASIA

Thus far we have been dealing with people who belong to the white race. In Asia we encounter the Mongolians, who evidently originated in central and eastern Asia and during the course of many migrations spread eastward into China and Japan, southward into Malaysia and the islands of the Pacific, westward to the Near East and Russia. The American Indians, who do not comprise a single race, are a mixture of many types most of which are Mongoloid. The Negroid peoples extended in a belt across Africa and southern Asia. The tall and the pygmy types of Negro are found in both places. In Asia and in the Pacific islands sub-races are found which were produced by the mixture of Negro, Mongolian, and white peoples. We have already spoken of the white Indo-Europeans who migrated into northern India, western Asia, and Europe.

Little is known of the earliest civilizations of eastern Asia. The two principal reasons for this are a lack of early written records and a scarcity of archeological investigation in these regions.

India. Excavations in the valley of the Indus River in northwestern India, at Mohenjo-daro and Harappa, have revealed that around 2500 B.C. there flourished in this region a remarkable culture rivaling that of Mesopotamia and Egypt. The fate of this culture can only be guessed. And there is as yet no evidence of similar areas of early civilization elsewhere in India.

As we have already seen, around 2000 B.C. or shortly thereafter, there took place an invasion of northern India by Indo-Europeans from the grasslands of central Asia. During an indefinitely extended period which may have lasted until 800 B.C. the Indo-Europeans of India worshiped nature gods, engaged in agriculture and cattle raising, practiced monogamy, and were frequently at war with each other and with the surrounding tribes native to the region. The *Rig-Veda,* which dates from around 1000 B.C., contains a collection of their sacrificial hymns, many of them dating from a much earlier time. During the course of the next two centuries there were added to this literature other collections of hymns, magical formulae, and religious prose.

Still later the origins of the Indian caste system began to appear. The slaves were the first to be set apart from other classes because of their black color—they were evidently the natives who had been subjugated by the Indo-Europeans. Among the freemen were three classes or castes: the priests, the nobles or warriors, and the common folk including farmers and craftsmen.

In the sixth century B.C. there lived among these people Gautama, or Siddartha, the Great Buddha, teacher and prophet. His teaching constituted a revolt against the teachings and practices of the priestly class called Brahmans. He accepted the older belief that the soul passed through a series of rebirths in different bodily forms. He taught that the soul would receive rewards and punishments in a heaven or hell. And he preached that the soul might escape from the normal series of rebirths through a discipline of strict morality and self-sacrifice and by withdrawal from the world in meditation and personal religious experience.

During the reign of Darius, the great Persian general Skylax, sent to explore the Indus, seized the district of Gandhara, western Punjab, from the disunited Indo-Europeans and added it to the Persian Empire. It remained a Persian satrapy for a century and a half. One of the effects of this Persian conquest is that the Indians devised an alphabet for themselves based upon Persian which was used by them until the fourth century A.D. Unlike the Chinese, the Indians were not interested in chronology. The result is that the first precise date in Indian history is fixed by the Greeks. It is the date of the invasion by Alexander the Great in the spring of 326 B.C. Alexander found resistance weak as a result of the fact that the peoples of northwestern India were divided into many rival states. Those states which resisted him he conquered. The rulers who submitted to him immediately had all their powers restored to them on condition that they acknowledge Alexander as their suzerain.

From the inhabitants of the Punjab region Alexander learned of a rich Indian state, Magadha, lying to the southeast. He determined to conquer it, but at this point his soldiers refused to go further away from home. It had been four years since they had started eastward from the conquered Persian capital of Ecbatana and eight years since they had crossed the Hellespont into Asia. Alexander therefore left behind him governors and garrisons to rule the new province and returned home. But upon his death in 323 B.C. the Indians revolted and re-established their freedom.

Among the princes who had submitted to Alexander was Chandragupta Maurya of Magadha whose family had been overthrown and who was living in exile in Punjab. Chandragupta led the revolt of the Indians against the Greeks and became ruler of Punjab. At about the same time the Nandas regime was overthrown in Magadha and Chandragupta was able to re-establish himself as ruler in his native land. He thus controlled an empire stretching across northern India from the Ganges Delta on the east to the western limits of Punjab. He set up his capital at Pataliputra (modern Patra), and under the Maurya dynasty northern India flourished for a hundred thirty-seven years to 185 B.C.

Before this empire was secure, however, Chandragupta had to defend it against the Greek general who became the ruler of the eastern part of Alexander's empire after the great conqueror's death. Seleucus Nicator was so badly beaten by Chandragupta that he surrendered the vast territory that is now modern Afghanistan and Baluchistan.

The most famous ruler of the Maurya dynasty after Chandragupta was Asoka. His fame does not rest upon conquest. It was he who made Buddhism a great Indian religion. Until Asoka's conversion to Buddhism it was but one of a number of minor religious sects. But Asoka sent out missionaries and spread the teachings of Buddha throughout India, Malaysia, and China. His missionaries traveled throughout western Asia to the Mediterranean, disseminating the teachings of Buddha and spreading the fame of their prince.

China. The Chinese seem to have been dwellers in their own land from earliest times. While they were still a primitive people there occurred a division which resulted in the southward migration of large numbers of Chinese. Many settled finally in south China, in Tibet, in Indo-China, and in Siam. Little is known of early Chinese history. There have come down to us chronological records of ancient dynasties along with many legends which describe a golden age in the remote past. But some of those records have been proven to be forgeries, and it is therefore impossible to accept this legendary history until it is supported by other evidence.

Around 1000 B.C. the Chou rulers established a western capital at Hao in the Wei Valley. Under the Chou dynasty land and offices were held by an aristocracy with hereditary rights. The peasantry lived a communal life in villages during the winter and in the fields during the summer. They tilled the common land which was held by their noble overlords. But the Chou emperors were feudal suzerains who had little control over their nobles. The western Chou dynasty came to an end in 771 B.C., and while an eastern Chou dynasty continued to exist until the third century B.C. its power was more nominal than real. Chinese influence and political domination was spread eastward to the sea and southward to the Yangtze River, but this was the work of ambitious feudal nobles and not of the reigning house.

The foundations of Chinese civilization were laid during this feudal era. They learned to irrigate the land and private ownership was established. A system of picture writing was devised which became the basis of the present Chinese system and a literature was developed. The Chinese religion based upon ancestor worship was elaborated. A supreme being was recognized although nature spirits were also worshiped, and a ceremony and ritual were built up.

Chinese history to the middle of the third century B.C. is a story of the continuous struggles of various states to extend their dominion at the expense of their neighbors. As the more powerful succeeded and consolidated their realms the contest passed from a condition of small-scale feudal warfare to a pattern more nearly resembling the modern rivalry of national states in Europe. In the middle of the sixth century Hsiang Hsu, minister of the Duchy of Sung, proposed that the rival states of the two existing alliances enter into a treaty for the renunciation of war as an instrument of policy. In 546 B.C. fourteen states signed this solemn convenant which was renewed five years later in 541 B.C. But the king of Ch'u, observing the growing weakness of the neighboring state of Ch'in, attacked his neighbor and inaugurated thereby a period of Chinese history that is known as the Age of the Warring Kingdoms.

The period is marked by revolutionary upheavals and alignments which continued until the Ch'in domination toward the end of the third century. Interestingly enough it is an era of great intellectual activity. Philosophers, usually holding official positions, devoted their attention to questions of social welfare and sought to devise a new social order. Their ideas often seem very modern. In the sixth century Lao-tze, the founder of Taoism, declared that the social and political systems devised by men were mischievous and the cause of most of the ills which afflicted humankind. He preached a surrender to the forces of the universe and the removal of all man-made restrictions.

A contemporary, Confucius (551–479 B.C.), sought to save society by a return to ancient principles. He believed that men should be disciplined in right conduct by moral education and an emphasis upon ethics. He insisted upon the importance of the leadership and example of the educated and believed that society should be regulated by ceremonies or conventions and tradition. In the fourth century Mencius insisted upon the right of subjects to revolt against unjust rulers.

The Chinese states were finally united toward the end of the third century by the rulers of Ch'in. Ch'in was located on the northwestern frontier and as a result of its position experienced a strong infiltration of non-Chinese blood. It was a buffer state grown strong through the necessity of defending itself. In the fourth century Ch'in abandoned the cumbersome war chariot employed by the other Chinese states and adopted the Tartar method of fighting on horseback. The state was strengthened internally by the abandonment of the peasant system in a reform which set up in its place a system of small landholdings. Under a series of able leaders during the course of a century Ch'in overpowered the other Chinese states in a series of wars. In 246 B.C. the Ch'in ruler assumed the title Shih Huang Ti, meaning First Emperor.

The First Emperor divided his empire into thirty-six provinces ruled by salaried officials responsible to the emperor. To protect his empire against the Hsiangnu Tartars to the north the emperor undertook the construction of the great Chinese Wall which extended from the sea along fourteen hundred miles of the northern border to the desert sands. Many reforms were undertaken, including the simplification of the Chinese written character. There was inevitably much opposition to the changes so rapidly being brought about; and to criticize these actions of the emperor, many continually recalled the great and happy eras of the past. In response to this reaction, the emperor decreed the destruction of all books except the *Annals of the State of Ch'in* and a selected list of scientific books in addition to the libraries of certain scholars who were approved by the state.

But the reign of Ch'in was brief. In 202 the throne was seized by Liu Pang, founder of the Han dynasty. The ancient period of Chinese history ends with the fall of the Ch'in dynasty.

PART TWO
Greek and Roman Civilization

B.C.

776	First Olympiad in Greece: beginning of Grecian calendar
735	Greeks settled at Syracuse in Sicily
700	Homeric poems written down
509–264	First period of Roman supremacy in Italy
490	Battle of Marathon
480	Battle of Thermopylae and Battle of Salamis
478	Herodotus' history ends
461–431	Age of Pericles in Greece
431–404	Peloponnesian War between Athens and Sparta
399	Death of Socrates
387	Sack of Rome by the Gauls
359–336	Philip, King of Macedonia
336–323	Age of Alexander the Great
325–304	The Samnite War
309–307	War with the Etruscans
281–272	War with Tarentum and Pyrrhus
264–241	First Punic War
220	Shi Hwang-ti became King of Ts'in
218–201	Second Punic War
149–146	Third Punic War
146	Carthage and Corinth destroyed
60	First Triumvirate—Caesar, Crassus, and Pompey
55	Caesar invaded Britain
	Caesar completed invasion of Gaul
48	Julius Caesar defeated Pompey at Pharsalus
44	Julius Caesar assassinated
31 B.C.–14 A.D.	Reign of Augustus (Rome)

A.D.

30	Jesus of Nazareth crucified
54	Nero succeeded Claudius
64	Martyrdom of St. Peter and St. Paul in Rome
68	Suicide of Nero
69–79	Vespasian
70	Destruction of Jerusalem. End of Jewish rebellion against Rome
79–81	Titus, Emperor

81–96	Domitian, Emperor
117	Hadrian succeeded Trajan, Roman Empire at its greatest extent
161–180	Marcus Aurelius
250	Serious persecution of Christians by Decius
284–305	Diocletian, Emperor
301	Edict of Prices
302–304	Edicts against Christians
306–337	Constantine, Emperor
311–313	Edicts of Toleration
325	Council of Nicaea
330	Constantinople, new capital of Roman Empire
361–363	Julian the Apostate attempted to substitute Neo-Platonism for Christianity
426	St. Augustine's *City of God*

7 THE GREEKS

Advance of the Indo-Europeans and Flight of the Aegeans.
The Greeks were the descendants of a number of Indo-European tribes which turned southward, after reaching the pasture lands along the Danube River, and found their way into Greece. It is probable that they first looked down from the highlands of northern Greece upon the waters of the Aegean and Mediterranean seas not later than 2000 B.C. For a long time the newcomers remained in the upland valleys, pasturing their flocks and gazing with wonder and bewilderment at the busy life of the Aegean cities below. Across the blue waters they could follow the flash of sails as Cretan, Phoenician, and Egyptian ships carried their cargoes back and forth from one thriving city to another. Gradually they pressed southward into Greece and settled in the countryside around the Aegean towns in very much the way the Hebrews distributed themselves among the Canaanites of Palestine.

The southern part of the Greek peninsula, called the Peloponnesus, is almost an island, for it is separated from the rest of Greece by the Gulf of Corinth except where, on the east, a tiny neck of land called the Isthmus of Corinth ties it to the mainland. Before 1500 B.C. at least one Greek tribe, the Achaeans, had penetrated the Peloponnesus. Around 1500 B.C. a more aggressive group of Greeks called Dorians reached this region.

The Dorians attacked the Aegean towns and their Greek kinsmen as well and subdued both. Like barbarian conquerors through the ages, they destroyed much of the civilization they were unable to understand. Despite that fact they must have learned a good deal from their Aegean subjects. When they had been settled in the Peloponnesus long enough to become familiar with the sea and the handling of ships, they launched an attack on the island of Crete. This was around 1400 B.C.

Between 1300 and 1000 B.C. the Greeks spread over the

entire Aegean area. Roughly the Aeolian Greeks established themselves in the north, the Ionians in the center, and the Dorians in the Peloponnesus, in the southern islands, and upon the southern part of the coast of Asia Minor. While the Greeks were gradually taking possession of the Aegean Islands and the coast line of Asia Minor, other Indo-European peoples, the Phrygians and the Armenians, invaded Asia Minor from the north and attacked the Hittite empire. The power of the Hittites was broken. Meanwhile the defeated Aegeans and Cretans left the smoking ruins of their towns and palaces and fled across the seas to Egypt and Syria where they fought desperately for the right to settle in these already occupied lands.

The Greeks Develop a Settled Life. "The political organization of Greece was dictated by the geographical and economic conditions" of their land, observes a great historian. The land is mountainous. Many small valleys are open to the sea but are closed in on the land side by those mountains. The effects of this conformation of the land upon the inhabitants is interesting.

Each valley became the home of a small group or tribe of settlers. These nomads pastured their flocks in the grasslands and upon the hillsides and tilled the most fertile stretches of soil. For safety and convenience they built their dwellings close together, often about an outcropping platform of rock to which they might withdraw if attacked. This was the "acropolis," which means in Greek, "highest part of the city." Upon it, when their villages grew larger, the Greeks erected their temples and public buildings and accordingly here they often met to discuss the affairs of the community. They also met daily in the market place which might be located below the acropolis where it would be more accessible to the citizens.

It was easier for the Greeks to travel upon the sea than to make their way inland across the mountains. And the Aegean is dotted with more than five hundred islands, which was a very important factor in the early expansion of the Greeks. For it was relatively easy for the Greeks to venture forth in their small boats when nearly always there was some bit of land in sight upon which they might seek refuge in case of storm.

Each valley developed a self-centered existence revolving about the village that in time developed into a city. The "country" to which a Greek belonged was not Hellas, the land of all the Greeks, but his own little city-state, the town and the surrounding countryside that belonged to it. Almost any Greek could stand upon the mountainside and overlook his entire fatherland.

The poems of Homer give a picture of the simple life of the early Greeks. These first city-states had kings who, like the heads of other important families, were believed to be descendants of the gods. Government was by an oligarchy, or an aristocracy, made up of the heads of the chief families. The wealth of these city-states was mostly in the form of land, cattle, and slaves—the slaves were conquered enemies who became the property of the citizens. Among the freemen were serfs or tenants who rented farmland, men who worked for wages, craftsmen, and property owners.

However, the modern meaning of all these words is likely to convey a false impression of ancient Greek life. Let us recall that when Homer's shipwrecked hero, Odysseus—whom the Romans called Ulysses—landed on a strange shore, he found the king's daughter on the beach doing the family washing. Nausicaä brought Odysseus home and introduced him to her father, and while the hero talked with the old king, swine wandered in and out of the house through the open door.

Life in all households was very much the same. Everyone worked including the queen. The womenfolk did the cooking and washing, cared for the children, spun yarns, wove cloth, and made the family clothing. The men cared for the fields and flocks, built and repaired the house, made the furniture, and fought in wars. The slaves did pretty much the same work as everyone else, although no doubt the less pleasant tasks more often fell to their lot. But no one regarded labor as a burden. A landless freeman might move to the outskirts of the community, clear the land by draining a swamp or felling the forest, and become a landowning farmer.

The Greeks Become Traders and Colonizers. It will be remembered that after the final collapse of the Egyptian Empire around 1200 B.c. Phoenicia was left in control of commerce in the Mediterranean. Her enterprising businessmen beached their ships along the Greek coasts and offered tempting merchandise for whatever the Greeks could give in exchange. They had little enough to offer, but they soon discovered what articles were most acceptable to the Phoenicians. The grape and the olive were two products that flourished in Greece. The wine of Syria was inferior and the Greek article much in demand. The demand for wine and olive oil soon had an effect on Greek agriculture.

Before long the Greeks learned that from the clay of their country could be fashioned pottery of superior quality. In due course, when they acquired skill in making pottery and taste and originality in shaping and decorating their product, the Greeks became important producers of one of the chief articles of ancient commerce. For in the ancient world pottery had many uses. Jars for storing grain and wine, nearly all household utensils, vessels used in the crafts like dyeing and the tanning of leather, burial urns, unguent jars, statuettes, and often images of household gods—all were fashioned of clay.

Of course it took time for the Greeks to learn to produce marketable commodities. At first they had little to offer in exchange for the things they wanted and their ships more often engaged in piracy than in trade. But with the growth of legitimate commerce, it became necessary for the Greeks to seek markets. As the Greek towns grew into cities, with numbers engaged in the production of articles for trade, as the fields were replaced by olive groves and vineyards, it was necessary to import grain, as well as iron, from Asia Minor, cloth and luxury articles from Syria and Egypt. The Greek cities founded colonies wherever suitable lands could be found.

Extensive areas of the Black Sea coast, a rich grain-producing region, were colonized by Greeks. In the west the Greeks established themselves in the eastern part of the island of Sicily and in the southern part of Italy; these lands, too, became part of Greater Greece. The Phoenicians already had settled Carthage and Utica in north Africa and the western part of Sicily as well. Central Italy was held by the Etruscans. And the Adriatic was controlled by the piratical Illyrians. A Greek colony was, however, established in southern Gaul, at Massilia—modern Marseilles—and settlements were made along the coast of Spain.

The Struggle with Persia. The Greeks were politically divided. Each city was the rival of all the others for trade and colonies. Even the colonies were not ruled by the home city from which the settlers originally came; they became self-governing city-states in their turn, although they remained associated with the mother city in trade, in religious belief, and often in war. The rivalries of the Greek cities led to many wars among them. And they were so busy with their own affairs that the Greeks remained ignorant of the great political changes that were taking place in Asia.

After the collapse of the Hittite Empire several kingdoms were formed in western Asia Minor, the most important of which was Lydia. The culture of the Anatolian Greeks, as those in Asia Minor were called, was much influenced by the civilization of Lydia. Lydia, in turn, adopted much from the Greeks, so that in time the Greeks came to think of Lydia as part of the Greek world. A series of astute Lydian kings took advantage of the political disunity of the Greeks and gradually absorbed the cities of the coast into their kingdom.

Such was the situation in the Greek world when the rise of Cyrus the Persian caused Croesus, the Lydian ruler, to propose an alliance of the great powers against Persia. It will be remembered that Croesus consulted the Greek oracle at Delphi as to the consequences of a war with Persia. The oracle replied that did Croesus undertake such a war a great kingdom would be destroyed. It apparently never occurred to the optimistic Croesus that Lydia might be the kingdom referred to and not Persia.

Lydia was conquered by the Persians in 546 B.C. and the Greeks of Asia Minor became subjects of the Great King. As we know, the Greek cities were dissatisfied with Persian rule and revolted in 499 B.C. In 494 B.C., after a long struggle in which they had the assistance of an Athenian fleet, the rebellious cities were put down and severely punished.

Darius probably had many reasons for deciding to revenge himself upon Athens for the assistance she had given her Anatolian kinsmen. The prestige of the great Persian Empire could be maintained only if it were certain that every injury to it would be avenged. Then, too, the destruction of Greek maritime power would enable the Great King's Phoenician subjects to monopolize the lucrative commerce of the Mediterranean. And the disunity of the Greeks, intensified by jealousy and bitter rivalry, made them seem an easy prey.

The disastrous fate of the expedition of 492 B.C., which we have already described, did not cause the Great King to abandon the project. Two years later another fleet of warships and transports set out from the island of Samos. The army was set ashore in Attica, in which Athens was located, with the purpose of marching from the Bay of Marathon along the coast to Athens.

The Greek states were in confusion. Darius might have waited to bring together a larger army, but he calculated that his twenty thousand men would suffice if he attacked before the Greeks had had time to prepare. Callimachus, the Athenian commander-in-chief, wisely yielded to the judgment of his subordinate Miltiades, who was familiar with Persian tactics. The Greeks decided not to wait for the arrival of the Persians but to march across the peninsula and block the Persian approach along the coastal road.

The Athenians, reinforced by a thousand men from Plataea, could not possibly have numbered half the Persian host. They took up a strong position commanding the coastal road. The Persians tried to draw the Greeks from their position, but failed. They then attempted to cover their line of march with a force spread out in battle formation.

Miltiades knew that the Persians massed their main strength in the center of the battle line. He therefore weakened the Greek center and massed his troops in the wings. As the armies met, the weak Greek center gave way while the heavy wings pressed forward and surrounded the bulk of the Persian army. At close quarters the Persian bowmen were helpless and the Greek spearmen wrought a frightful havoc. The Persians fled to their ships, leaving over six thousand dead on the field. The Athenians lost less than two hundred men. A runner was dispatched to carry the news to Athens. The youth who bore the great news refused to spare himself over the twenty-five miles which separated Marathon from the city. When he reached Athens he had barely strength enough to proclaim the glorious tidings before he fell dead.

When the Persian fleet sailed around Attica and appeared before Athens the victorious Greek army, which had returned by the short overland route, was waiting to meet them. It would have been foolhardy to attempt a landing, so the Persians headed for home.

Final Defeat of the Persians. At Marathon, Athens, almost alone, had saved Greece from the immediate danger of Persian domination. For the first time the Greek world understood that a war with Persia might end in the enslavement of the Greeks. During the next ten years, in spite of political division and mutual jealousy, Greek public opinion was prepared for united resistance against the inevitable renewal of the attack. But Darius was old. And in 486 Egypt revolted. The following year Darius died. His successor, Xerxes, needed time to establish his position at home, and it was not until 480 that the new ruler was able to give his attention to the conquest of Greece.

Meanwhile Themistocles insisted that Athens could not hope to resist the invasion successfully unless she possessed a great fleet. Athens built a fleet, but most of the Greek states took no important steps to prepare for the coming attack.

Xerxes' preparations were carefully made. He determined to follow the plan of 492 B.C. and send an army overland accompanied by a fleet sailing along the coast. The Greeks, warned of Persian preparations, considered two plans of defense. The Spartans of the Peloponnesus, who possessed the strongest army, proposed that all Greece north of the Peloponnesus be abandoned and that the Persians be met on the narrow Isthmus of Corinth where the advantage of their great numbers would not count so heavily. The other Greek states wished to save central Greece from destruction by meeting the enemy at the pass of Thermopylae which led into central Greece.

The second plan was practicable if an army of sufficient strength defended the pass. But Sparta and some of the other allies dispatched only small forces for the defense of Thermopylae. The fleet, according to plan, prevented any attempt to reach the Greek flank from the sea. But the insufficiency of the Greek land forces prevented them from protecting all the mountain paths, and the Persians were able to march around to the Greek rear and attack from two directions at once. The Greek defense was heroic; Leonidas and his small force of Spartans fought to the last man, but victory fell to the Persians. At once Boeotia and most of central Greece capitulated and the Persian army advanced into Attica to enjoy their long-deferred revenge.

It was now impossible to defend Athens, and her people were removed to the island of Salamis off the Attic coast. The Persians arrived and set fire to the city. Even at this moment of crisis the Greeks were still divided. Sparta stubbornly insisted that her strategy be followed and threatened to withdraw her fleet if the wishes of her commanders were not followed. Themistocles barely succeeded in holding the Greek fleet together and in forcing the enemy to meet him in the narrow gulf between Salamis and the mainland where the Persians would be unable to deploy their ships and enjoy the advantage of great numbers.

The Greeks were completely victorious. And with the Greeks in command of the sea, Xerxes had to reorganize his whole plan. A strong Persian army was left in northern Greece and the remainder marched back to Asia.

The Persians returned to the attack in the spring of 479 B.C. Sparta still refused to send her armies into central Greece, with the result that the Persians again entered Athens and completed their destruction of the city. At last, when the Spartans realized that the discouraged Athenians might give up the war and make peace with the enemy, her generals sent a strong army into Attica. It was promptly joined by the militia of other Greek states.

The Persian forces were united under the command of their general Mardonius. The Greek generals quarreled even on the field of battle. Plataea might easily have been a Persian victory. But Mardonius mistook a shift in the Greek position for flight and attacked at a moment when his cavalry could not be brought into play. Again, as at Marathon, the heavy-armored Greek infantry, equipped with spears, proved superior in close combat to the lighter-armored Persians. Mardonius was himself killed and the Persian army fled.

At once the Greek fleet sailed eastward and attacked the Persian fleet and army stationed at Mycale. The Persian force was cut to pieces, and by this victory the Greek cities of Asia Minor were freed. In the meantime Carthage, the Phoenician colony in north Africa, had attacked the Greeks of Sicily in an attempt to win possession of the eastern half of that island for herself. Her cavalry was wrecked in the crossing from Africa and her army was defeated in a great battle near Himera. In all quarters the Greeks triumphed.

8 HELLENIC GREECE

The Greek world, saved from oriental domination by a combination of valor, tactics, and good fortune, has had a profound effect on all succeeding ages. It is important therefore that we know something of the civilization of these people whose culture and institutions have so greatly affected the whole course of future history.

Political Development. The life of the primitive city-state described by Homer was much changed during that period of Greek expansion through commerce and colonization which we have discussed. The men who fought in the wars between city-states, who engaged in piratical raids upon the seas, were those possessed of sufficient lands and wealth to provide themselves with expensive weapons, armor, war chariots, and ships. These were the nobles who, by their enterprise and shrewdness, greatly increased their land holdings and, through their power as a group, came to dominate the affairs of the community.

In Athens the king was gradually deprived of his power. During peacetime the nobles chose one of their number as archon, to "assist" the king in his government. In time of war a noble was chosen to lead the state during the crisis. The Spartans, jealous of the power that would be wielded by a single ruler, chose two kings, each of whom would provide a check upon the powers of the other. Twenty-eight elders assisted the kings and, jointly with the kings, possessed the power to initiate legislation. The tendency was the same throughout Greece so that by the end of the seventh century B.C. kings had disappeared in most places.

Probably the era of active colonization which occurred during the rule of the nobles was partly the result of the increasing monopoly of the land by this class. But, as we have seen, Greek colonization increased the market for Greek products. As a result there grew up in the Greek cities a considerable group of prosperous merchants and manufacturers who had no voice in the government. And taxes fell so heavily upon the independent small farmer that many were heavily in debt to the state.

The laws of the early Greeks were simply the customs which had grown up among them. These unwritten laws were so freely administered in their own interest by the nobles that in 621 B.C. they were written down and published by Draco in response to popular demand. This publication of the old law helped the Greeks to realize how severe and unreasonable many of their customs were. They soon began to demand changes. The introduction of coined money made it possible for many to borrow at high rates of interest and these soon found themselves more hopelessly in debt than ever. Under the old law, if a man could not pay his debts and the sale of his property was not sufficient to satisfy his creditors—in many cases the chief creditor was the state and the debt back taxes—the debtor might be sold into slavery in order to satisfy the debt. Thus many farmers lost not only land, but freedom as well. The freemen who retained their small holdings had to compete with the products of the large estates operated by slave labor, and this became increasingly impossible. The situation became so bad that in 594 B.C. popular demand forced the appointment of Solon, a member of the middle class, as archon. Solon introduced a series of sweeping reforms. All debts were canceled. All debt slaves in Attica were freed. Draco's laws were revised. A council of four hundred was given the right to initiate legislation and the Assembly of the People had the right to accept or reject these proposed laws, just as in our day we vote on the acceptance or rejection of constitutional amendments.

But Solon's reforms failed to restore prosperity and tranquillity to the citizens. The freed debt slaves were still without lands and consequently without a means of livelihood. And no measures had been taken to help the sharecroppers who received only a sixth of the produce of their land and labors. The reforms also failed to establish political rights for the growing class of merchants and artisans who were not landowners.

Taking advantage of this situation, Pisistratus, an exiled noble, returned home with an army of followers and established himself Tyrant. His government was a wise one and under it Athens once again enjoyed an era of prosperity. When Pisistratus died in 528 B.C. he was succeeded by his two sons who ruled together as tyrants. Although they were able men, the Athenians hated them because their power was exercised without the consent of their subjects. In 514 B.C. two young men, Harmodius and Aristogiton, attempted to free the state from the tyrants. Hipparchus was killed and his brother Hippias, escaping assassination, fled.

The Athenians now accepted as their leader a nobleman who was devoted to the interests of all classes of citizens. The reforms of Clisthenes reserved to the nobles, who were experienced leaders, the right to hold the most important offices. But once a year the citizens had the right by vote to declare any prominent citizen a danger to the state and might banish him for a period of ten years. Thus around 500 B.C. the Athenian citizens had secured a means of protecting themselves against excessive ambition in a ruler and were thereby assured that government would seek to serve the interests of all the citizens.

In the meantime Sparta had conquered a large part of the Peloponnesus. The revolt of the new subjects forced the Spartans to revise the political organization of the state. Sparta was a state without industries. Whatever prosperity and influence she enjoyed was chiefly the result of her military strength. Long before 600 B.C. Sparta had forced the neighboring states of the Peloponnesus into an alliance under her domination, the Spartan League, and her control of this combination made her the most powerful military state in Greece. Around 610 B.C. the state was reorganized into a military camp. The military training of the Spartan boy began at the age of seven. Men of military age lived in barracks and ate at a common table.

At this point in our narrative let us note a very important difference between the Greeks and the other peoples whose history we have traced. Whenever the civilized peoples of Asia or Africa found intolerable the rule of a wicked or incompetent king, they revolted, overthrew their king, and promptly submitted to another monarch. It was the Greeks who, for the first time, sought to protect themselves against a repetition of the bad situation by devising new types of government. We have observed the change from monarchy, the rule of one man; to oligarchy or aristocracy, government by a few or a limited class; to tyranny, government seized and exercised by force; to a form of government which approached democracy. The Greeks devised and defined these types of government for all time; the words we still use to describe them are Greek—monarchy, oligarchy, aristocracy, tyranny, democracy.

We have dealt with the development of two Greek states,

Athens and Sparta. There were many other Greek city-states, of course. But Athens and Sparta were perhaps the two most important. And they do represent in their particular histories two types of development, one or the other of which characterized the history of all the other city-states.

Greek Civilization. Although Greece evolved forms of government which have been resorted to by men ever since, this is but one of her many contributions to future civilizations. These people were active at the same time in politics, in war, in colonization, in commerce, and in industry. More lasting and of greater influence were their achievements in science, in philosophy, in mathematics, in art, in literature, in the drama.

Herodotus, who wrote the history of the Persian Wars has become known through the ages as the father of history. Here for the first time is a full account of a great event which discloses its background, causes, development, and immediate consequences. This is no mere table of dynasties or calendar of years. The tradition was carried on by Xenophon, Thucydides, and Polybius who produced great histories which were also great works of literature.

The oath taken by our students today upon graduation from medical school is the oath of Hippocrates, great physician of Cos, and it reveals to us how modern was the role of the physician in Greece five centuries before the birth of Jesus. Thales, philosopher and scientist of Miletus, was able to predict the eclipse of 585 B.C. The great advancements made in Greek science are the result of the fact that for the first time men conceived that the earth, nature, and man, were all phenomena which could be understood. The Greeks' persistent search for a *reasonable* explanation of the natural universe resulted in the development of habits of analysis and classification which are the fundamentals of modern scientific and philosophical thinking.

Perhaps the very nature of Greek religious belief provides an explanation of why the Greeks were so ready to rely upon their own intelligence in such matters. Like other ancient peoples, the Greeks believed in many gods. At the head of the family of gods was Zeus. At the time of the Homeric poems, the gods were thought to dwell upon the top of a high mountain in northern Greece, Mount Olympus. They controlled the forces of nature and the destinies of men. But to the Greeks the gods were very human. They looked and acted like men. Hera, the wife of Zeus, was a nagging spouse, jealous, and particularly troublesome when Zeus's attention was attracted by the beauty of some young goddess or by a beautiful mortal. The gods quarreled among themselves, carried on feuds, and often played pranks upon men. A too successful mortal might provoke the jealousy of the gods and through their interference in his affairs would be likely to suffer unforeseen misfortune. But the Greek was not barred from inquiry by a paralyzing awe of the gods. He dealt with them tactfully, showed them respect, and won their good will by sacrifices. He then proceeded to live his life in his own way, depending upon his own efforts rather than the assistance of the gods for his success. Although at all times he hoped that the gods would be well disposed toward him, he was likely to act upon the principle that the gods assist those who help themselves.

Nevertheless, as beings greater than men, superior in wisdom and knowledge as well as in power, the gods were worshiped and their patronage and friendship sought. Each city was dedicated to a particular god or goddess. Athena, daughter of Zeus, for whom Athens was named, was loved for her beauty and wisdom. Apollo, the sun god, also beautiful and wise, was favored by all the Greeks. Temples of unsurpassed beauty were erected to the gods and goddesses in all the Greek cities and were adorned by statues of the particular deity to which the temple was dedicated; these statues were large and sometimes fashioned of ivory and gold.

The temples to the gods were usually erected upon the acropolis which, as we have seen, was the highest part of the city. Other public buildings surrounded the temples, and in the intervening spaces were erected statues of the heroes and athletes who had brought fame and honor to the city. No sculpture before or since has equaled the perfection of that of the Greeks in the presentation of the human body. Poetry and drama also played an important part in the lives of the ancient Greeks. Comedy and tragedy were defined by them. The great dramatists of the fifth century B.C. established the forms and rules which still govern this art. Aeschylus, Sophocles, and Euripides wrote plays which have the power to stir men of our day as profoundly as they moved the Greeks of the fifth century. And only a short time ago a play by Aristophanes, *Lysistrata,* enjoyed a record run on Broadway.

Rivalry of Athens and Sparta. When, in 479 B.C., the defeated Persians at last withdrew from Greece, the Athenians returned to the smoke-blackened ruins of their city, to fields of scorched earth, to ash heaps that were once farmhouses. As they set about the slow labor of reconstruction they must have remembered with bitterness that the Persians could have been held at Thermopylae had Sparta sent sufficient help. In recalling the victory of their fleet at Salamis they must have remembered also how nearly it had been made impossible by Spartan selfishness.

Under the leadership of Themistocles, the Athenians set about making themselves safe against further attack. The new city was surrounded by fortified walls. Although the city of Athens had become a maritime power, it was located some distance back from the coast. So in order to protect her commerce and her access to the sea, Themistocles fortified the little town of Piraeus, the port of Athens—this despite protests from the Spartans. The Athenian fleet was enlarged to give it undisputed supremacy on the sea.

But Athens did not stop here. She formed a defensive league of Greek city-states against any future Persian attack. Member cities contributed either ships or treasure to the league. The treasure, in charge of the Athenian Aristides, was placed in the temple of Apollo on the Island of Delos—the league accordingly came to be known as the Delian League.

There ensued in Athens a bitter dispute over future policy.

Cimon favored a continuance of close friendship with Sparta; Themistocles, believing Sparta untrustworthy, advocated a more independent policy. The supporters of Cimon prevailed and, embittered, Themistocles fled and found employment among the Persians. But when the Athenians sent troops to help Sparta put down a revolt, the Spartans curtly demanded the withdrawal of this aid.

Incensed at such treatment, the Athenians ostracized Cimon in 461 B.C., and instituted a new constitutional reform which restricted the functions of the conservative Council of Elders and placed the real government in the control of a popular Council of Five Hundred. This council was divided into ten groups of fifty; each group controlled the affairs of the state for a little over a month and then was replaced by the next group. All citizens except propertyless laborers were made eligible to hold the office of archon.

Through the Assembly of the People, through the enlarged council and the enlarged juries, through new eligibility to the highest offices, the Athenian citizen now developed political experience and intelligence under a democratic order. Only in military direction was it necessary to restrict the highest offices to those of experience and proven skill. Nevertheless, from among the available strategoi, or generals, the people selected the one who was to be given charge of military and state policy. In 460 B.C. they elected to this important office Pericles, scion of an old and distinguished family. So able and popular was the rule of Pericles that he continued to be re-elected strategos until his death more than thirty years later.

The magnificent cultural and intellectual flowering which marks this era, based as it was upon an unprecedented commercial and industrial prosperity, has made the Periclean Age one of the most famous in history. The prosperity of Athens may be judged by some figures provided by Prof. Breasted. Money could be borrowed at rates from ten to twelve percent. An expedition to the Black Sea area might bring a return of one hundred percent after all expenses were paid. Manufacture frequently brought a return of thirty percent.

The wealth of Athens was lavished upon the improvement

of the city. A new temple to Athena was built—the Parthenon —a building as nearly perfect as any ever conceived. Its architects were Ictinus and Callicrates. It was adorned with sculptures and a frieze by Phidias, one of the greatest sculptors of all time. The Piraeus was connected with Athens by a series of long walls so that in wartime the city might not be cut off from the sea. Literature, philosophy, drama, all the arts flourished. Sophists trained the young Athenians in clear thinking and skillful debate, to fit them to exercise intelligently and responsibly the privileges of free citizenship.

But the era was not one of peace. During Pericles' first term as strategos, Athens became involved in a war with the states of the Peloponnesus, and when he died Athens was already engaged in her last struggle as a great power. Nearly all the Greek states had been drawn into one or the other of the two leagues, the Delian or the Spartan. The fear of each alliance that the other might become predominant in the Greek world—fear of the destruction of the balance of power—was the underlying basis of the war.

Hostilities began with a quarrel between Corinth and Corcyra. Athens, having made an alliance with Corcyra, came to her aid when she was about to lose the war (433 B.C.). This was the prelude to the Peloponnesian War which lasted from 431 to 404 B.C. with a suspension of hostilities between the main powers during an interim of seven years from 421 to 414 B.C.

The Peloponnesian War. The war opened with an attack on Athens' ally, Plataea, by the Thebans. The struggle promptly resolved itself into a contest between the two city-states heading the two great coalitions, Athens and Sparta, between the greatest sea power and the greatest land power.

Pericles' strategy was to withdraw behind the defensive walls of Athens and her port, to permit Sparta to ravage the countryside while Athens supplied herself from the sea, and to wear down the Peloponnesian power by destroying her commerce and raiding her coasts. The Spartan strategy was to destroy Attica by annual campaigns, to split the Delian alliance by causing division among the allies—an ancient Fifth Column—and ultimately to force Athens into risking a land battle.

It is impossible to trace here the long course of the war. In general each side adhered to its original strategy. Often it was necessary for Athens to send out armies to punish allies that had deserted the alliance and come to terms with Sparta. By 422 B.C. both powers were shaken by the long struggle. Sparta was threatened by revolt and the reserves of Athens were exhausted. The following year a peace was negotiated by Nicias which was to last for fifty years.

Despite the peace, hostilities continued, chiefly among the smaller allied cities. Then there came to the fore in Athens a brilliant but overambitious and reckless young man, Alcibiades. First he persuaded Athens to resume the war. Sparta did not immediately respond with hostilities. He then conceived a great expedition against Syracuse, the chief Greek city of Sicily and a colony of Corinth.

Had Alcibiades been left in command of the Sicilian expedition it is possible he might have brought it to a victorious conclusion. But he was withdrawn from the command after the expedition had started in order to stand trial for misconduct at home. Alcibiades at once deserted and proffered his services to Sparta. The Sicilian campaign went badly from the start. Nicias was cautious when he should have been bold, and blundering in execution. Instead of abandoning the ill-fated project, Athens exhausted her strength in sending reinforcements. The costly venture met disastrous defeat in 413 B.C.

Sparta had resumed the war in 414 by sending aid to Syracuse upon the advice of Alcibiades. The following year, again on the advice of Alcibiades, Sparta invaded Attica. The bad conduct of the war had caused great discontent among the people of Athens. In response to popular clamor many political changes were made and this further weakened the war effort.

Meanwhile the ambitious Alcibiades, who had gone over to the Persians, was engaged in stirring up revolt among the Greek cities of Asia Minor. The Athenian fleet, much reduced in size, was more than ever in need of an able leader. Without obtaining the consent of Athens, the fleet appealed to Alcibiades to lead them against the Peloponnesians. He seized this opportunity to restore himself to favor in his own land. Under Alcibiades' skillful leadership the Athenian fleet completely destroyed the Peloponnesians. Alcibiades then returned to Athens and was elected strategos.

However, by this time political faction, sharpened by military reverses, had destroyed the morale and unity of the Athenians. They were unable to follow any leader long enough to permit his strategy to bear fruit. When a portion of the fleet not under Alcibiades' personal command met with a small reverse, the Athenians failed to re-elect Alcibiades strategos. He retired to his castle on the Hellespont where he ultimately was assassinated by a Persian.

A series of defeats brought Athens to her knees in 404 B.C. She escaped complete destruction by giving up her fleet and all her foreign possessions, and becoming a member of the Spartan League.

Aftermath. As we have seen, the Spartan state was above all else a military organization. The Spartans were not fitted by experience to rule the states now subject to them. Many Greeks, left without a country to which they felt loyalty, hired themselves out as professional soldiers and many found employment in Persia. Before long the Spartans were forced to surrender the Greek states of Asia Minor to Persia.

Revolts broke out among the Greek cities. Athens participated but never regained her old ascendancy. For a time Thebes rose to a position of leadership. But while, by degrees, prosperity was restored to most of Greece, the Greeks remained a weak and divided people.

9   THE AGE OF ALEXANDER THE GREAT

The Rise of Macedonia. North of the eastern half of the Greek Peninsula lay Macedonia, a country, largely mountainous, inhabited by a hardy and warlike people. The civilization of Macedonia was derived from Greece with the result that the Macedonians regarded themselves as part of the Greek world. Here Greek culture and Greek genius was highly respected.

In 360 B.C. there came to the throne of Macedonia a man who had received a Greek education. While living as a hostage at Thebes, Philip had taken full advantage of the opportunity to study Greek politics and Greek military tactics. The new king set about recruiting a permanent or standing army among the peasants of his kingdom which he armed as heavy infantry. He then introduced the Greek formation known as the phalanx. The phalanx was a solid body of infantry protected by the interlocked or overlapping shields of the outside ranks. The soldiers within the phalanx lowered their spears over the shields of the outer ranks so that the phalanx presented on all sides a solid row of protective shields topped by bristling rows of spears. The famous Macedonian phalanx was larger than the Greek and the spears carried by the soldiers longer.

In addition Philip trained a heavy cavalry force to operate in massed formation on either side of the infantry phalanx. When he had perfected this military organization, Philip possessed an irresistible fighting machine.

Philip's next step was to toughen his disciplined army in actual warfare. He wisely turned away from Greece and proceeded to conquer all that territory which lay north of the Aegean Sea to the Hellespont (the modern Dardanelles).

These startling developments to the north were noted by the Greeks with mixed feelings. In Athens one group, headed by Isocrates, was ready to accept Philip as the leader and uniter of the Greek world. They were opposed by the orator Demosthenes who looked on Philip as a tyrant who aimed to enslave the Greek world. In a series of speeches against Philip, his "philippics," Demosthenes aroused the Athenians against Macedonia. A series of hostilities followed in spite of many indications of friendliness on the part of Philip. The struggles were brought to a close by an overwhelming Macedonian victory at Chaeronea in 338 B.C. as a result of which Philip placed himself at the head of a league of all the Greek states except Sparta.

Philip next turned his attention to Asia Minor which he invaded with the intention of freeing the Greek cities there from Persia. But in 336 B.C. he was stabbed by a conspirator while celebrating the marriage of his daughter.

Alexander and the Greek States. Philip was succeeded on the throne by his young son Alexander, then only twenty years of age. Alexander had received an excellent education. When he was only thirteen Philip had placed him under the tutelage of the great philosopher Aristotle, pupil of Plato, whom he had summoned to his court. Thus Alexander, like his father, developed a deep understanding of and affection for Greek culture. In addition to providing him with a splendid education, Philip left his son a group of able and loyal advisers.

Upon the accession of Alexander the Greek city of Thebes revolted in the belief that so young a king would be unable to hold the conquests of his father. Alexander had inherited a war with Persia. But he realized that it would not be safe to take his army into Persia until he had given the Greeks evidence of his determination and ability. He conquered Thebes and completely destroyed the city. However, as an indication of his reverence for Greek genius, he left standing the house of the great poet Pindar.

Having made sure of Greece, Alexander marched eastward with an army made up of Macedonians and Greek allies. The Persians had been given time to make preparations and they had strengthened their forces with large bodies of hired Greek mercenaries. The two armies met at the River Granicus in Asia Minor. The young king threw himself into the fray at the head of his troops and barely escaped with his life. The Persian army was scattered and Alexander was able to march southward and free one Greek city after another.

In the course of their long wars the Greeks had destroyed their own maritime supremacy in the Mediterranean. Taking advantage of this situation, the Phoenician subjects of the Great King had built up a large fleet, superior to anything the Greeks were now able to assemble. In view of the Persian domination of the sea it was clear that if Alexander crossed the mountains of Asia Minor and entered Asia he would be cut off from the Greek world. However, he had left at home an army sufficiently large to ward off Persian attack and he believed that the Greeks had come to accept him as their leader. Accordingly he pushed boldly forward.

At the head of the Gulf of Issus in northern Syria, the main Persian army, under the personal command of Darius III, awaited the approach of Alexander. The Persians had taken a strong defensive position behind a stream. But, following the

policy of his father always to be the attacker, Alexander took the initiative. Massed cavalry, led by the young king, plunged into the stream and attacked the Persian left. The Persian center and right wing held firm against the Macedonian and Greek infantry which had to wade across the stream. But the weight and fury of the cavalry attack broke their left wing. Alexander was able to check the advance of his disciplined horsemen as soon as the forces opposing them were put to flight. His cavalry then took the Persian center in the rear and the battle was won (333 B.C.).

Darius, who had escaped from the field of battle, now

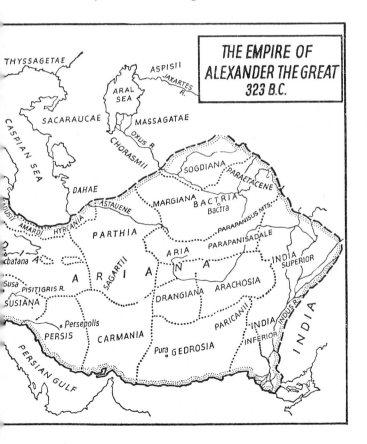

THE EMPIRE OF ALEXANDER THE GREAT 323 B.C.

proposed terms of peace. He offered to surrender all Asia west of the Euphrates River and to pay an indemnity of 10,000 talents. Alexander's generals advised him to accept, pointing out that the Persians still controlled the seas which lay between him and Greece. But the twenty-three-year-old king demanded unconditional surrender and this was refused.

World Conquest. Alexander's next move reveals his mastery of broad strategy. There was no time to build a fleet and secure the seas which would lie behind him as he marched into Asia. He therefore proceeded southward along the coast of Syria and Phoenicia and reduced the great coastal cities which provided bases for the Persian navy. He then crossed the Isthmus of Suez into Egypt and that rich land quickly submitted to him. The Persian fleet, now deprived of all its bases, soon scattered and the Greeks once more regained control of the Mediterranean.

There is more to the establishment of an empire than the subjugation of people by force. If such dominion is to endure, the conquered peoples must find it possible to accept the new rule. They must be able to recognize that under it they will receive substantial justice and security and respect for their rights as human beings. Here once again Alexander revealed the breadth of his genius.

He saw that throughout the East people looked upon the king as both a man and a god. In Egypt, therefore, he visited the oracle at the temple of Amon at Siwa where he was greeted as the son of Zeus-Amon. In this manner the Egyptian priest proclaimed that the chief Greek god, Zeus, was the same as Amon, the principal god of the Egyptians, while at the same time he declared to the Egyptians that Alexander was destined by the god to rule over them. Before returning to Asia Alexander founded the city of Alexandria which became a center for the dissemination of Greek culture among the Egyptians.

Having obtained Egypt as a source of supply for his forces, in the spring of 331 B.C. Alexander led his men into Persia. Darius had gathered an army together for a last stand at

Arbela. But the new Persian war chariots, with sharp blades projecting from the axles on either side, were of no avail against the seasoned Macedonian and Greek soldiery. The Persian army was crushed and in his flight Darius was assassinated by one of his own attendants.

At Persepolis, the Persian capital, Alexander once again displayed wisdom and tact in dealing with a defeated people. In revenge for the Persian destruction of Miletus and for the burning of the temples of the Athenian Acropolis, Alexander, with his own hand, set fire to the Persian palace. But it was a symbolical act merely, and before the flames could do serious damage he ordered the fire extinguished.

Alexander now controlled an empire vaster than that of any ruler in history. Such an achievement might satisfy the ambition of any man. But the restless young ruler, after setting up a government for his new conquest, pressed on in search of new worlds to conquer. During the course of the next five years he crossed the Iranian plateau, marched northward across the Oxus and Jaxartes rivers, and then turned southward into India. After forcing the submission of the princes of the Indus valley he pushed eastward into the valley of the Ganges where, as we have seen in another chapter, his troops refused to go further.

In India Alexander constructed a fleet which he sent out to explore the Indian Ocean and the coasts of southern Asia. At last, seven years after leaving Babylon, the returned conqueror re-entered the ancient Mesopotamian capital. During the course of his long marches this extraordinary genius had established some twenty-five cities, named for himself and garrisoned with Greek troops, which remained centers of Greek influence and culture in Asia.

In Babylon Alexander planned new conquests. The Arabian peninsula and the western Mediterranean remained to be subjugated. But in 323 B.C. he fell ill and a few days later died. He was thirty-three years of age.

10   THE HELLENISTIC WORLD

Struggles of the Hellenistic Kingdoms. After Alexander's death, Roxana, the Persian princess whom he had married, gave birth to a son, Alexander II. But Alexander's generals soon fell to quarreling among themselves for possession of his empire. After a generation of warfare the empire split into three parts, Europe, Asia, and Africa. Antigonus, grandson of the general of the same name, gained possession of Macedonia. He sought to control Greece. The territories of the Persian Empire fell to Seleucus, one of Alexander's generals, and another general, Ptolemy, became ruler of Egypt.

The smallest division of the empire was, of course, Macedonia. But before Antigonus could establish himself upon the throne, the Greek world confronted a new and unexpected danger. This was the invasion of the Celts, or Gauls, descendants of the Indo-European peoples who had settled in France and central Europe. They now descended into the Balkan Peninsula and entered Macedonia, Thrace, and Greece. By 277 B.C. Antigonus had driven the invaders out of Macedonia and, having put down a revolt of the Greek cities, had himself crowned king.

Meanwhile, Alexander's general, Ptolemy, had made himself king in Egypt. He realized that the Egyptians, who submitted passively to his rule, could not provide him with a good army and that he would have to depend upon Greek mercenaries. While Antigonus was busy with the Greek revolt and the Gaulish invasion, Ptolemy constructed a great fleet which gave him domination of the Mediterranean and permitted him to bring mercenary troops from Greece whenever necessary.

Ptolemy wisely adjusted his policy to the conditions which confronted him in Egypt. Over his Egyptian subjects he ruled as Pharaoh, both absolute monarch and god. His administration was filled with Greeks. And under the wise rule of a line of Ptolemies, northern Egypt, especially the city of Alexandria, became the most important center of Greek civilization and culture in the Hellenistic world.

Seleucus, the general who had obtained the Asiatic portion of Alexander's empire, sought to carry on the work of spreading Greek culture which had been begun by Alexander. He founded a new city, which he named Antioch in honor of his father, and made it his capital. Antioch became the greatest commercial center of the north Mediterranean and the rival of Alexandria.

The history of the eastern Mediterranean during the next two centuries is chiefly a history of the rivalry of these three Alexandrian kingdoms. The Greek city-states remained politically weak. They tried to overcome this condition by forming alliances or leagues among themselves. But Greece never regained the political and military ascendancy she had once enjoyed.

However, it is to be remembered that the civilization of the post-Alexandrian world was Greek. Greece remained its source and one of its principal centers although in time Alexandria became a great center of Greek civilization. For centuries to come the greatest philosophers, artists, scientists, and writers were Greeks.

Hellenistic Civilization. The Age of Alexander divides two great cultural epochs. It separates the earlier Hellenic culture from the later Hellenistic civilization. Hellenic means simply Greek, and Hellenic culture was confined in general to the area we have defined as Greater Greece, including Sicily, southern Italy, the western coast of Asia Minor, and the islands of the Aegean, as well as Greece itself. Hellenistic civilization is the civilization brought about through the agency or influence of Greece. It was strongest in the eastern Mediterranean area where Greek influence was felt most, but extended throughout the territories of the Greek-ruled Alexandrian kingdoms.

The conquest and unification of most of the civilized world by Alexander had brought about conditions that made possible the era of prosperity and civilization which followed.

. Macedonian domination brought peace to the eastern Mediterranean. No longer were pirates and the fleets of warring states a serious hazard to peaceful commerce.

Political and military careers were opened up to Greeks all over the world, for the Egyptians had too long been ruled by conquerors to rely upon themselves, and the Persian satraps, who were at first permitted to retain their offices, soon proved unreliable or disloyal. The Greeks developed a taste for eastern products and the plunder of conquest furnished a means for gratifying such tastes. As people and goods moved more freely about the world, the Greeks found new markets for their pottery, oil, and wine.

For generations the Persian rulers had stored up a great treasure of gold and silver which Alexander seized. Thus at a moment when trade and commerce were being stimulated there was made available a store of precious metals which, converted into coined money, greatly facilitated the exchange of goods. While it is true that the rivalry of the Hellenistic kingdoms produced wars, the better organized conduct of military affairs proved less disruptive to commerce than had the petty plundering of the small states before the time of Alexander.

While Greek influence predominated throughout a large part of the Hellenistic world, the Greeks were in their turn affected by other people and new conditions. In the small city-states of the Hellenic period the Greek citizen was personally known to nearly all his fellow citizens. His life was public. He was a member of the Assembly of the People and participated directly in his government. He spent much of his leisure time in the market place, in attendance at religious festivals and athletic contests, at the theatre, in the company of large numbers of his fellow citizens. The greatest honor he could have was the esteem of his fellows, his own people. Rich men lavished their fortunes upon religious fêtes, the adornment of public buildings, and the beautification of the acropolis. Alcibiades caused a scandal by employing an artist to decorate the walls of his own house.

It was impossible to live this kind of a life in the larger

Hellenistic world and men's ambitions took new directions. Many sought wealth for the power and prestige and physical security it would bring them. Others sought the prestige and power of political office or military commands. These were now something different from what they had been in Hellenic times. In the Hellenistic monarchies men did not obtain political and military office through the good opinion of their fellow citizens as they had in the little democracies of the Hellenic era. The materialistic emphasis of the new age resulted in science becoming more practical. Scientific knowledge was applied to the solution of problems of material comfort and efficiency. Invention flourished. The individual enjoyed many conveniences that were not thought of in earlier times. He was surrounded by gadgets.

Alexandria. Under the intelligent fostering and patronage of the Ptolemies, Alexandria became the brilliant center of Hellenistic civilization. Perhaps we may best appreciate the achievements of the age by noting some modern aspects of the life of this city.

Alexandria was a new city. It had not grown up by haphazard, it was planned. Its avenues were broad and its streets regularly laid out. The location and grouping of its public buildings were carefully considered. Squares and intersections were adorned by monuments and statues. It had a zoological garden, theatres, stadia, and race courses. The harbor was dominated by a lighthouse atop a skyscraper that reached a height about that of a thirty-story modern building.

Hero, who built a steam-engine 1500 years before James Watt observed the steam issuing from a kitchen kettle, invented a penny-in-the-slot machine for selling water in the temples. Sprinkler systems protected many public buildings from fire hazard. The girls of Alexandria bobbed their hair and had permanent waves, plucked their eyebrows, painted their toenails and fingernails dark red, and used rouge.

The Ptolemies supported a great museum and a library containing a half-million volumes. They endowed research and provided not only studies but living quarters for scholars who came from all over the world to carry on their researches at Alexandria. They turned condemned criminals over to surgeons for scientific vivisection while the courts debated whether vivisection was legal.

Books were produced in quantity. Many were now written primarily for entertainment rather than for the instruction or edification of the reader. Art became realistic. Portrait sculpture became accurate and lifelike although the Greeks never again produced the moving, idealized sculptures of the fifth century B.C. In mathematics, as in medicine and surgery, great advances were made. Hipparchus counted over a thousand stars and arranged them in constellations. Eratosthenes estimated the circumference of the earth with an error of less than fifty miles.

But let us not fail to note how firmly this great civilization rested upon the work of the earlier Hellenic Greeks. It is interesting to observe how completely in the course of time Hellenistic civilization passed away, while the great works of the Hellenic era lived on to contribute powerfully to the development of later civilizations.

11   THE WESTERN MEDITERRANEAN

Thus far we have had little occasion to refer to the western Mediterranean and to the various peoples who settled upon its shores. We observed briefly that both Phoenicians and Greeks established colonies at points along the African and European coasts and we noted the tragic consequences of Athens' attempt to conquer Sicily during the Peloponnesian War. But we must now go back and trace the early history of the region which became the center of one of the mightiest empires of history.

As one looks at a map of the Mediterranean one notices that toward the middle of its length two peninsulas of land thrust southward from the continental mass of Europe. Both peninsulas, the Greek and the Italian, present roughly the same features. They are both mountainous and people are therefore likely to settle along or near the coasts where the land slopes to the sea. Latitude, exposure to the sea, northern mountain barriers which shut out cold continental winds, account for similar climatic conditions. As we now trace the history of the Italian peninsula we shall come upon many other factors which link the history of that peninsula with Greece. During the Ice Age Italy was joined to Africa as well as to Europe. This fact will help us to understand the remains of primitive cave-dwellers which indicate that there were two types of men living in Italy in the Old Stone Age, one of which was Negroid. Roughly from 2500 to 2000 B.C. the Italians of the New Stone Age developed agriculture, kept herds, learned to make pottery and to use copper.

Then, around 2000 B.C., about the time the Greeks first appeared in the Balkan mountains north of Greece, a group of closely related Indo-Europeans began invading Italy from the north. Some of them may have come from Switzerland for they built villages on piles in the waters of the north Italian lakes like the Stone-Age men of Wangen, in Switzerland. As they moved southward away from the lakes they continued to live in compact villages which they surrounded by ditches, or moats, filled with water. These were the *Terramare* or Black Earth villages. The invaders were soon followed by their kinsmen from the Danube region and in time they spread themselves over the entire peninsula.

As these early Italians settled throughout Italy—in Samnium toward the south, in Umbria along the upper Adriatic, in Latium south of the Tiber—their kinsmen, the Greeks, also pushed toward the centers of Aegean civilization in southern Greece. The Italians adopted a primitive agricultural life, but the Greeks soon found themselves at war with the Cretans and Aegeans as we have seen.

During the era of violence which marks the spread of the Greek peoples over the Aegean area, many of the older civilized populations fled and sought safety in other lands. One such group, probably from Asia Minor, settled upon the west coast of Italy north of the Tiber. These were the Etruscans and the land upon which they settled still bears their name in the modern form, Tuscany. The Etruscans soon extended their dominion to the Lombard plain in the north and eastward along the Po valley. They founded colonies upon the eastern shores of Corsica and along the Italian coast south of their Latin neighbors, in the vicinity of Naples.

The Phoenicians, located on the extreme eastern coast of the Mediterranean Sea were active traders and colonizers from earliest times. Toward the close of the ninth century B.C., the date usually given is 814, the Phoenician city of Tyre founded the colony of Carthage on the north African coast opposite Italy and Sicily, near modern Tunis. Carthage in turn established colonies in western Sicily and Sardinia and soon became the greatest center of Phoenician commerce in the western Mediterranean. When the mother country was conquered first by the Babylonians and then by the Persians in 538 B.C., Carthage became an independent state.

During the Age of the Nobles many Greek city-states established colonies in the western as well as in the eastern Mediterranean. Corinth founded the city of Syracuse on the eastern coast of Sicily. Spartans settled at Tarentum (modern Taranto) in southern Italy. And Phocaea set up a colony at Massilia in southern Gaul around 600 B.C. (modern Marseilles).

Thus we see that by the sixth century B.C. Italy and the Italian islands were settled by many peoples differing in language and origin. Chief of these were the Etruscans, the Carthaginian-Phoenicians, the Greeks, and the primitive Italic people.

Rome. "The location of Rome, on the Tiber at a point where navigation for seagoing vessels terminated and where an island made easy the passage from bank to bank, marked it as a place of commercial importance. It was at the same time the gateway between Latium and Etruria and the natural outlet for the trade of the Tiber valley." Thus concisely does Boak establish the strategic advantages of Rome's position.

The early history of the city-state of Rome is shrouded in

legend. But it seems clear that a primitive form of kingship existed in early times, similar to that found in the Homeric Greek cities. The agricultural Romans were the victims of plundering raids, for the neighboring tribes, many of them pastoral hill folk, were often tempted to seize the harvests, flocks, and other possessions of the industrious Roman farmers. In self-defense the Romans subdued their troublesome neighbors and established a loose dominion over them.

The early Romans were inevitably influenced by the civilization of their more advanced neighbors to the north, the Etruscans. For a time, it appears, Rome was ruled by Etruscan kings. But around 508 B.C. the Etruscan rulers were overthrown and the control of the Roman state passed into the hands of a Latin nobility.

The free Roman citizens fell into two classes, patrician and plebeian. The patricians were the nobles, the great landholders who, because of their superiority in military equipment and training, and the support of their clients, held political control and enjoyed the right to sit in the Senate. The plebeians were also free citizens; less wealthy landowners, tradesmen and craftsmen, laborers, and clients or tenants of the patricians. The client was a kind of feudal dependent who held the land under a patrician overlord to whom he owed respect, obedience, and military aid; his patron in return owed him protection.

The Etruscans under Lars Porsena of Clusium made an attempt to subjugate Rome once again and may have succeeded in doing so for a brief time. At any rate the struggle with Clusium weakened Rome's control over her Latin neighbors.

When freed again from Etruria, the Romans set about strengthening their position. They made a trade treaty with Carthage and began the reconquest of their former allies. It was a difficult period and the plebeians, burdened by taxes and debt, were without influence in the government. They revolted. But the form of their revolt is evidence of the disciplined responsibility of the Roman citizen. The plebs did not resort to violence; they simply withdrew a short distance from the city and refused to return until they were assured the means of protecting their interests against the misuse of their powers by the patrician magistrates. The tribunes, the new representatives of the people, were given the right to intervene on behalf of anyone threatened by the power of a magistrate. Aedils were also appointed to collect fines and to supervise public works and poor relief.

Around 486 B.C. Rome established the Latin League which bound her in an offensive and defensive alliance with her Latin neighbors. The treaty also guaranteed the status of the citizens of each community in all the others through rights of trade (*commercium*), and of marriage and inheritance (*conubium*).

During the fifth century the Etruscans continued to threaten Rome. At last the Romans determined to destroy once and for all the power of their ancient enemy. Veii, the center of Etruscan power twelve miles north of Rome across the Tiber, was captured and destroyed in 392 B.C. and its population sold into slavery.

No sooner had the Romans disposed of one enemy than another confronted them. During the fifth century, wild Gaulish tribes from western Europe crossed over the Alps and drove the Etruscans from most of the Po valley. In 387 B.C. a horde of tribesmen crossed the Apennines and, after besieging Clusium, attacked Rome. The Roman army was defeated and the citizens, fleeing from the city, sought refuge in neighboring towns. After seven months the Gauls accepted a ransom for the city, 1,000 pounds of gold, and marched home.

The Romans rebuilt their city which they now fortified with a stone wall. Again in 368 B.C. the Gauls threatened the city. But when they returned for a third time in 348 B.C. the Romans were strong enough to force the Gauls to sign a treaty of peace.

Roman Expansion in Italy. It is impossible to describe here the many struggles by which Rome established her dominance over the peoples of central Italy. Whenever she was seriously weakened by the attacks of Etruscans or Gauls, her Latin allies showed an inclination to rebel. In the Latin War of

338–336, the rebellious states had the help of the Campanians. Within two years the Latins were subdued and, instead of regaining their status as free allies, they were incorporated into the Roman state. Campania accepted a Roman alliance by which the Campanian military resources were joined with those of Rome. By this treaty Roman influence was extended to the Bay of Naples (334 B.C.).

Between 325 and 280 B.C. Rome was engaged in wars with three different enemies. The Samnites, to the south, attacked Campania. Rome came to the aid of her ally and suffered two serious defeats. Encouraged by these reverses, the Etruscans and their allies attacked in the north. Despite reverses the Romans refused to consider defeat. They fought on and finally conquered both the Etruscans and the Samnites. Many central Italian cities now at their own request became allies of Rome.

In 298 B.C. war broke out again. This time the Samnites allied themselves with the Etruscans and Gauls. In a series of vigorous campaigns the Romans defeated each enemy in turn. The Samnites and Etruscans became allies of Rome and the Gauls were driven back into the Po valley. Roman overlordship was now acknowledged in all parts of the peninsula except among the Greek settlements in the extreme south.

War with the Greeks. Sicily and the southern part of the Italian peninsula, as we know, had been settled by Greek colonists. On the mainland Tarentum, the strongest city, had assumed the role of protector of the Greeks against their Italian neighbors. Even so, Tarentum usually had to rely upon assistance from Greece or the Syracusan Greeks of Sicily.

The Greeks had watched the growth of Roman power with uneasiness. By treaty Tarentum had obtained a promise that Roman ships of war would not enter the Gulf of Tarentum in the arch of the Italian boot. But in 282 B.C. the Greek city of Thurii was attacked by the Lucanians, allies of Rome, and appealed to Rome for help. Rome responded by sending a force to relieve and garrison Thurii although to do this she had to send troops through the Gulf of Tarentum. The Tarentines, however, were determined to prevent the extension of

Roman influence to Greek territories. They attacked the Roman fleet and occupied Thurii. Roman demands for reparations were flouted and the war began.

Tarentum obtained the aid of Pyrrhus, King of Epirus, just across the Aegean from the heel of Italy. Pyrrhus brought with him a well-equipped army of 20,000 heavy armed infantry, 3,000 cavalry, and 20 war elephants. He met the Roman armies at Heraclea in 280 B.C. Superior generalship and his elephants, the heavy tanks of ancient warfare which were a new experience to the Romans, enabled Pyrrhus to drive the Romans from the field although his losses were heavy. He advanced northward into Latium and the following year defeated the Romans at Ausculum. His losses were so great however that he remarked, "Another such victory and we are lost." A "Pyrrhic victory" has come to mean ever since one which is so costly that it is the equivalent of a defeat.

The Romans were ready to make peace, but the Carthaginians, fearing for the security of their colonies in Sicily, offered the Romans an alliance and the assistance of the great Carthaginian fleet. The war continued.

The Carthaginians had renewed their attacks on the Sicilian Greeks and these now appealed to Pyrrhus for aid. He crossed the Straits of Messina and quickly defeated the Carthaginians, leaving them with but one city, Lilybaeum. But the weakness of the Greeks in Italy, as in Greece, was their distrust of each other. Fearing that Pyrrhus would make himself their master, the Sicilians concluded a separate peace with Carthage, and Pyrrhus was forced to withdraw to Italy.

Disgusted with the attitude of the Greeks whom he had aided, discouraged by the loss of his fleet in a battle with the Carthaginians and by the Roman repulse of his forces at Beneventum, Pyrrhus withdrew to Greece. One by one the Greek cities capitulated and joined the Roman alliance. During the course of the next five years a few revolting and unsubdued communities were disciplined. By 265 B.C. Rome had completely subjugated the Italian peninsula.

12   THE STRUGGLE FOR THE DOMINATION OF THE WESTERN MEDITERRANEAN

In the middle of the third century B.C. an observer would undoubtedly have adjudged Carthage to be the greatest power in the western Mediterranean area. She had subjugated the Libyan population of the African mainland and these now paid her tribute and rendered military service. The Carthaginian Empire extended from the Gulf of Syrtis westward beyond the Straits of Gibraltar. Corsica, Sardinia, the western part of Sicily, and the smaller islands of the western Mediterranean were Carthaginian. So was a long stretch of the southern and eastern coast of the Spanish peninsula.

The wealth of Carthage depended upon her monopoly of the commerce of this area and her exploitation of the resources of her colonies, particularly the Spanish silver mines. It was for these reasons that Carthage was ever ready to check the colonial and commercial expansion of the western Greeks.

Sea power was of supreme importance to Carthage, and to render her extended empire secure she had established an undisputed naval supremacy west of the Straits of Messina. Since the activities of most Carthaginians were in one way or another connected with the sea, they never comprised a national citizen army. For her land forces Carthage depended upon the Numidians and upon mercenaries recruited in all parts of the ancient world.

Compared with this great empire Rome seemed a relatively weak state. She had no navy. She had only just completed her unification of the peninsula and it might reasonably be assumed that many subject cities were only too ready to revolt at the first opportunity. Her wealth was much inferior to that of Carthage. Her citizen army was excellent, but it might be doubted whether it was good enough to conduct a war against a first-class power and to hold the allies in line at the same time.

The First Punic War. On the Sicilian side of the narrow strip of water which separated the island from the Italian mainland lay the town of Messina. After the Tarentine war the town remained in the hands of the Mamertini, a group of Campanian mercenaries who had deserted from the armies of Syracuse and seized the city. As a result of their plundering and brigandage, the energetic king Hiero, who had come to the throne of Syracuse in 265, blockaded these raiders in their city. Its capture seemed certain.

The desperate Mamertini appealed to Carthage for help and, in line with her policy of checking the Greeks at every point, Carthage sent a force to strengthen the garrison. But on second thought, the Mamertini decided they would rather have Roman protection so they addressed an appeal to the Roman Senate. The senators realized that aid to the Mamertini was likely to involve Rome in a war with Carthage. Anxious to avoid the responsibility for so grave a decision, they referred the matter to the people represented in the Assembly of the Centuries. Elated by their recent victories over the Greeks, greedy for plunder and tribute, little realizing what fateful consequences might be in store for them, the people voted to admit the Mamertini to the Roman alliance. This decision marks the beginning of what are known to history as the Punic wars. For the Romans called the Carthaginians "Phoenicians" or *poeni,* hence these wars were wars against the *poeni* or Punic wars.

In 264 B.C. the Mamertini tricked the Carthaginian garrison into withdrawing from the city and admitted the Romans. Carthage at once allied herself with the Syracusan Greeks. The following year, however, the Romans defeated the Syracusans so badly that Hiero made peace with Rome and entered the alliance. The Romans and their Greek allies now sought to drive the *poeni* from Sicily.

Carthage held control of the sea and the long Italian coast was exposed to her attacks. Consequently the Romans determined to build themselves a fleet. With the help of Greek craftsmen, they constructed a navy of 120 vessels, one hundred of which were *quinquirems,* the first-class battleships of the time. Two victories at sea decided the Romans to attack Carthage in Africa.

In 256 B.C., after another naval victory, the Romans landed in Africa and overwhelmed the Carthaginians in a land battle. Although mercenary reinforcements were on the way from Greece, Carthage sought to make peace. But the Roman terms were so severe that the war was continued. At this point the Greek mercenaries arrived. Among them was an able leader, the Spartan Xantippus, who reorganized the Carthaginian army. Making expert use of war elephants and cavalry, Xantippus inflicted a crushing defeat upon the Romans. The remnants of the Roman army were rescued by the fleet. But off the coast of Sicily this force was almost totally destroyed in a storm (255 B.C.).

The Romans set about building another fleet. In 254 it was ready and they concentrated their attack upon Sicily. On land their campaign was successful. However, they were unable to dislodge the Carthaginians from Lilybaeum and Drepana. In 253 B.C. a number of ships were lost on the way back to Rome. In 250 a Roman fleet was destroyed in a naval battle off Drepana. The next year still another fleet set out and was smashed in a storm off the Sicilian coast.

In 247 B.C. Hamilcar Barca took command of the Carthaginian forces and infused fresh energy into their efforts. He harassed the Romans in Sicily and attacked the unprotected coasts of Italy, evidently with the intention of breaking up the Roman alliance. The Roman treasury was exhausted and the Senate was unable to undertake the construction of another fleet.

At this point the Roman people exhibited the qualities which later made them rulers of the world. Despite overwhelming disasters they did not consider capitulation. Through private subscription they built a fleet of two hundred vessels. War contractors provided materials at their own expense and gambled on being paid if Rome won. The new fleet blockaded Lilybaeum and Drepana and destroyed the relief expedition sent out by Carthage. With Sicily now completely cut off, Carthage made peace in 241 B.C.

Under the terms of the peace Carthage surrendered Sicily and agreed to pay a large indemnity, 3,200 talents, in twenty years. Rome had lost over five hundred ships and 200,000 men. But the allies had remained loyal and Rome was now mistress of the sea.

Carthage had been much weakened by the war. She now had difficulty in meeting the demands of her mercenary soldiers. These revolted and were joined by the Libyans in a struggle to destroy Carthage. Both sides were guilty of frightful atrocities. It was three years before Hamilcar Barca put down the revolt and restored order (in 238 B.C.).

While Carthage was fighting for her life against the Libyans and mercenaries, Rome again declared war upon her and occupied the islands of Sardinia and Corsica. Carthage was helpless to resist. She bought peace by surrendering the islands and promising to pay an additional indemnity of 1,200 talents.

The Second Punic War. In the interval between the first and second Punic wars, Rome was engaged in long struggles with the Illyrians and the Gauls. However, we shall pass over them for the moment in order to follow to its conclusion the struggle with Carthage.

After putting down the revolt of the mercenaries and Libyans in 238 B.C. Hamilcar Barca crossed into Spain where he found the Carthaginians hard pressed by the native Iberian peoples. By force and diplomacy he extended the Carthaginian control of southern Spain. Upon his death in 229 B.C. he was succeeded by his son-in-law, Hasdrubal, who continued his policies. These policies were popular in Carthage. For in addition to increasing the Carthaginian dominion, the Spanish wars developed a large seasoned military force. In addition, the annual revenues of 2,000 to 3,000 talents from the Iberian silver mines enabled Carthage to pay off the Roman indemnity.

The Romans and the Greek colony of Massilia, now an ally of Rome, became concerned over the northward advance of the Carthaginians in Spain. By a treaty of 226 B.C. the Romans and Carthaginians fixed the Ebro River as the boundary between Roman and Carthaginian spheres of influence in this region. Carthage also agreed to respect the independence of the Greek town of Saguntum south of the Ebro which now became allied with Rome. But upon the assassination of Hasdrubal in 221 B.C. the Spanish command was given to Hannibal, the son of Hamilcar Barca. When a boy Hannibal had listened with horror to accounts of Rome's perfidy at the time Carthage was fighting for her life against the mercenaries. He now determined to avenge that injury.

Saguntum was attacked and appealed to Rome. Rome insisted upon observance of the treaty. But Hannibal laid siege to Saguntum and took it. The Romans then sent an ambassador to Carthage who, when his demands were rejected, presented a declaration of war.

The Romans were masters of the sea and it appeared that they would be able to determine when and where hostilities would break out. An army under the command of Publius Cornelius Scipio was dispatched to Spain to deal with Hannibal while another under Tiberius Sempronius was assembled in Sicily preparatory to an invasion of Carthage. But Hannibal's plans were well advanced. Leaving his brother in Spain to recruit another army, Hannibal marched his men across the Pyrenees into Gaul. He had crossed the Rhone by the time Scipio reached Massilia. Hannibal withdrew northward to avoid a battle with Scipio for his intention was to invade Italy. Scipio returned to Italy to raise another army while his men continued on to Spain. Hannibal then led his men through the difficult passes of the Alps and entered Cisalpine Gaul in northern Italy in the autumn of 218 B.C.

Hannibal lost nearly all of his elephants and many men in crossing the Alps. Scipio determined to attack quickly before he could strengthen his forces but was defeated. Upon the arrival of Sempronius both consuls attacked again but suffered a crushing defeat through the superior generalship of Hannibal. As a result of these victories many recruits joined the Carthaginian army.

The Romans now put two large armies in the field. Advancing rapidly across the marshes of Etruria, Hannibal surprised one of the armies at Lake Trasimene and annihilated it. The second Roman army suffered a similar fate. In the spring the Romans advanced with another great army and the two forces met at Cannae for a decisive trial of strength. The Romans were numerically superior but the generalship of Hannibal triumphed. Cannae was one of the worst defeats in Roman history (216 B.C.). At once a number of allied cities deserted Rome and opened their gates to Hannibal. Philip of Macedonia offered Hannibal an alliance and Syracuse went over to the Carthaginians.

Although Hannibal was invincible in the field, he was cut off from reinforcements and supplies. In consequence he found it necessary to be continually on the march in order to seize provisions for his army. In moving from city to city he sought to break the Roman alliance by ravaging the country surrounding those cities which refused to open their gates to him. In their turn the Romans, after Cannae, returned to the tactics of Quintus Fabius Maximus—the Delayer. They avoided an open battle. But by following Hannibal about and constantly threatening him they prevented the Carthaginians from dispersing their forces. Systematically they reduced the towns which had submitted to the enemy. They too devastated the countryside in order not to leave supplies that could be used by Hannibal's army. Thus Italy was ravaged repeatedly by both armies.

While the Roman fleet prevented Macedonia from sending an army to Italy and Scipio gradually conquered Spain, Hasdrubal, the brother of Hannibal, broke away with ten thousand of his men and reached north Italy in the spring of 207 B.C. Through the capture of a messenger the Romans learned Hasdrubal's plans. Leaving a small force to make a show of strength in sight of Hannibal's camp, they withdrew their main armies and, falling upon Hasdrubal at the Metaurus, completely destroyed his army. The first news Hannibal had of the catastrophe was when his brother's head was tossed into his camp by a Roman messenger. His plight was now desperate; his last hope of reinforcement gone.

In 204 B.C. the Romans invaded Africa. The following year

Scipio, son of the general of the same name, routed two Carthaginian armies and the enemy was forced to sue for peace. Under an armistice Hannibal was permitted to return to Africa with his veterans. He had spent nearly fifteen years in the enemy's country cut off from reinforcements and supplies. He had won many victories and had never once lost a battle.

When their great general arrived in Africa the Carthaginians broke the armistice and resumed the war. At Zama in 202 b.c. the Roman and Carthaginian armies met; each was headed by its greatest general. Scipio made skillful use of his superior cavalry and when his mercenaries broke from the field Hannibal's hope of victory was gone.

By the terms of the peace Carthage surrendered all her territory except the city of Carthage and the surrounding countryside. She promised to pay an indemnity of 10,000 talents. She further engaged not to make war without Rome's consent. The Numidians were organized into a strong state allied with Rome.

The Third Punic War. Before turning to other matters, let us record the final destruction of Carthage. The Carthaginians, deprived of their empire, now directed their energies to the restoration of their commercial prosperity. Their success soon awakened the envy and fears of Roman commercial interests. Aware of this Roman attitude, Masinissa, the Numidian prince, claimed Carthaginian territories knowing that under the terms of the peace Carthage might not resort to force to protect her interests. Carthage appealed to Rome.

A member of the commission sent to investigate the claims was the elderly Marcus Porcius Cato who became alarmed when he observed the degree of Carthage's recovery and the wealth of the city. The commission decided in favor of Masinissa. And upon his return to Rome, Cato instituted a campaign of propaganda against Carthage, ending all his speeches in the Senate with the words: "Carthage must be destroyed."

In 151 b.c. Masinissa again attacked Carthage. This time the angry Carthaginians took up arms. Rome issued an ultimatum which demanded that the Carthaginians abandon their city and retire ten miles from the coast. In despair the Carthaginians prepared to defend their city.

The siege of Carthage was badly handled and lasted nearly three years. In the spring of 146 B.C. the Romans broke into the city. Although weakened by hunger during the long siege, the Carthaginians nevertheless fought furiously through the streets and even in the houses of the city. The small number of survivors of this last desperate struggle were sold into slavery. The city was leveled to the ground and the land of Carthage became the Roman province of Africa.

13   ROME AND THE EAST

The Illyrian and Gallic Wars. Under her alliance system Rome assumed responsibility for protecting the interests of her allies whose relationships with foreign states she controlled. When, therefore, in 230 B.C. the cities of south Italy appealed to Rome for protection against the raids of the piratical state of Illyria, she was obliged to respond.

In 229 B.C. Rome sent a fleet and an army across the Adriatic into Illyria. Queen Teuta was compelled to relinquish part of her territories and to pay tribute to Rome. The surrendered cities became allies of Rome. Nearly ten years later these cities were attacked by Demetrius, ruler of Corcyra. Rome acted promptly, defeated Demetrius, and took possession of his chief fortresses.

Meanwhile Rome was endangered by an attack by the Gauls in northern Italy. We saw that in the early part of the third century Greece and Macedonia were invaded by the same people but that the enemy was driven out by Antigonus. Numbers of these Gaulish people crossed over into Italy and joined their kinsmen in the Po valley. In 225 B.C. a Gaulish force of some 50,000 infantry and 20,000 cavalry advanced into Etruria. Threatened with a second Punic war, the Romans acted with energy. The Gauls were surrounded by Roman armies and annihilated. As a result of this victory, all northern Italy to the Alps was brought under Roman control.

New Wars in the East. In 202 B.C., the year of the battle of Zama which ended the Second Punic War, there occurred a crisis in the east which soon involved Rome, much against her will. Ptolemy IV, who died in 203 B.C., was succeeded by an infant son. The government of Egypt fell into the hands of corrupt and incompetent politicians.

Antiochus III, ruler of the Seleucid kingdom of Syria, determined to take advantage of the weakness of the Egyptian government and seize some of her Asiatic provinces. Philip V of Macedonia then decided to match the exploits of his rival and ally by seizing several of the independent Greek cities and islands. Two other states, Pergamum, in Asia Minor, and the island kingdom of Rhodes, appealed to Rome to help them check these aggressors. The Romans were most unwilling to involve themselves in an eastern war, but Egyptian grain had fed the Italians when Hannibal destroyed the fields in Italy, and the Romans were unwilling to permit the source of these essential supplies to fall into the hands of a potential enemy.

The Romans demanded that Philip of Macedonia refrain from attacking Egypt or the Greek cities and insisted that he submit his differences with Pergamum and Rhodes to arbitration. Philip refused and Rome declared war. Not wishing to fight two great powers at the same time, Rome sent an embassy to Antiochus assuring him of Rome's desire to remain at peace with the Seleucid kingdom. Her diplomacy was successful.

In spite of the fact that Rome had come into the war partly to protect the independence of the Greeks, she had the support of only a portion of the Greek cities. Nevertheless her armies were successful and Philip was forced to accept Roman terms. In 196 B.C. the Roman general Flamininus proclaimed the independence of the Greek states. After settling the claims of these states, the Romans withdrew from Greece and left the cities to enjoy their newly restored freedom. It is clear that the Romans had no ambition to extend their dominion to the eastern Mediterranean.

Trouble with Antiochus. The Romans soon found they could not isolate themselves from the affairs of the east Mediterranean sphere. The Aitolian League of Greek cities was dissatisfied with Rome's preservation of peace, for this coalition hoped to replace Macedonia as the dominant power in Greece. They sought now to undermine Roman influence by bringing Antiochus and the Seleucid kingdom into conflict with Rome.

The Aitolians succeeded by misrepresentation and false promises. Probably they were helped by Hannibal who was in exile at the court of Antiochus. In 191 B.C. Antiochus was driven from Greece by Roman armies. The following year the Romans crossed over into Asia and attacked him in Asia Minor. By their victory at Magnesia in 190 B.C. the Romans forced Antiochus to surrender Asia Minor and withdraw beyond the Taurus Mountains. Once more Rome declined to take any territory for herself. Friendly Rhodes and Pergamum received additions to their territory and the rest of Asia Minor was divided into small independent states. The Aitolian Confederacy was forced into an alliance with Rome.

But before Rome could devote herself wholly to the organization and administration of her western empire, it was necessary to subdue Macedonia once again. The son of Philip V, Perseus, inherited a well-trained army and a war treasury from his father. The inexperienced young ruler felt himself strong enough to challenge Rome's authority in Greece. As usual many of the Greek cities hoped to win advantages for themselves by aiding Perseus against Rome. When confronted with actual warfare Perseus hesitated and tried, too late, to conciliate Rome. He had failed to use his war treasure to provide himself with mercenaries and to win the support of his near neighbors. The Romans invaded and conquered Macedonia in 168 B.C. This time the troublesome Greek cities were severely punished and the sons of many of the leading families were carried off to Rome where they were held as hostages to guarantee the good behavior of the Greeks.

14   WORLD DOMINION
AND THE END OF THE REPUBLIC

It is worth noting at this point in our history that the extension of Roman dominion over other peoples and countries was largely the result of accident rather than design. We have seen how, from earliest times, it was necessary for Rome to protect herself against nearby enemies. We have seen how, when the Latin tribes could not be trusted to remain at peace, Rome forced them into an alliance under which Rome decided questions of peace and war. But we know that the alliance system did not, in fact, bring peace to Rome's citizens, for under it they were obliged to protect their allies against attackers.

Of course Rome was not simply an innocent victim of aggression. We saw how her citizens, blinded by greed and ignorance of their danger, voted to risk a war with Carthage. The seizure of Corsica and Sardinia, when Carthage was engaged in a struggle for her life against the mercenaries and Libyans, was a dishonorable act no matter what arguments may be put forward to justify it.

But for the most part, Rome had not *planned* her conquests —they happened. Wars became conquests often because the Romans refused to recognize defeat. Other nations encountered defeats, became fearful, and sued for peace. In both the first and second Punic wars the Romans suffered an appalling series of reverses, but apparently they never thought of giving up the fight until they were victorious.

The Romans were by no means a stupid people. They were very quick to appreciate the practical advantages which victories brought them. However, at the end of the third century B.C. they were in possession of the western Mediterranean and nearly all its coasts and islands. Unwillingly drawn into wars outside that sphere, they repeatedly refused to involve themselves permanently in the affairs of the eastern Mediterranean by accepting territorial concessions there.

In 196 B.C. the Roman general Flamininus proclaimed the independence of the Greek states and withdrew to Italy. In 189 B.C. the Romans withdrew once more after setting up independent states in Asia Minor and punishing the trouble-making Aitolian League. In 167 B.C., after defeating Perseus, the Romans carried off Greek hostages in order to secure the peace. But in 149 B.C. Roman fleets and armies were again operating in the Aegean area in a double war with both Macedonia and the Achaian Confederacy. Victory once again crowned her efforts but Rome's patience was at last at an end. In 146 B.C., the year of the final destruction of Carthage, Corinth too was razed to the ground and her citizens sold into slavery. Macedonia was made a province of Rome and the Greek cities, warned by the fate of Corinth, became vassal states of Rome under the supervision of the governor of Macedonia.

The Province of Asia and the Political Crisis at Rome. In 133 B.C. Attalus III, King of Pergamum, died without issue. He willed his rich kingdom to Rome, hoping thereby to save his people from the civil war and invasion that were likely to attend a struggle over the succession. The Romans might have refused the legacy were they determined to stay out of Asia. But they accepted. And in order to understand their action it will be necessary for us to review the changes that had been taking place in Rome itself.

The economy of old Rome was fundamentally agricultural. But in the course of prolonged wars the citizen was forced to spend much of his time in the army. During the absence of the father and grown sons, the womenfolk and boys were often unable to keep up the small farms. Large landowners however operated their estates with slave labor and thus continued to produce for the market. As a result of these conditions many a small farm was mortgaged and eventually sold, probably to be incorporated into the lands of a neighboring estate. Then also soldiers returned home from the wars were apt to find country life dull and were likely to settle in town to spend what remained of their share of war plunder. Accordingly the city population rapidly increased while the number of small farmers decreased.

Army contracts and the exploitation of the products and commerce of newly acquired territories gave rise to a new class of wealthy business organizers and enterprisers. They were the *equestrians,* so called because although not noble they were nevertheless, unlike the plebs, able to appear for military service expensively equipped and mounted on horseback. The growth of this class greatly changed old ideas of wealth and standards of living.

The patrician, or senatorial order, continued to furnish the leadership in Roman affairs and to occupy the chief offices. But in order to be elected to office the senators needed the votes of the plebs. Political campaigns were expensive. There were no "party chests"—the candidate paid his campaign expenses out of his own pocket. Now from early times the Roman state had, with each conquest, set apart a portion of the land as public domain. The senators had leased this land to themselves and for generations had cultivated it as their own. But the returns from such a senatorial estate might now amount to less than the income of an international banker of the equestrian order.

In the government of the provinces the senatorial order found an opportunity to recoup their dwindling fortunes. During a term as governor of a province, limited to two years or even one, the ambitious administrator sought to squeeze as much profit out of the district in his charge as possible. Thus while in other respects Roman provincial government was fair and efficient, the greed of its governors made it extremely costly.

But the most numerous part of the citizen population of the city of Rome was made up by the plebs. For the most part these were propertyless individuals without useful skills. Some found occasional employment while others frankly lived a parasitical existence. This urban mob however was made up of men who still possessed the privileges of Roman citizenship although they were a far different body of men from the sturdy farmers whose loyalty and courage had made Rome

THE ROMAN EMPIRE
at its GREATEST EXTENT
117 A.D.

great. It was to this crowd that the office seekers catered when in need of votes. Gifts of food and entertainment—pageants, athletic games, races—were showered upon them by aspirants to public office.

Many thoughtful men did not like the changes in Roman life that we have described. They felt that the Romans had been corrupted by their success. The few independent-spirited men remaining on their small farms were unable to come to Rome to vote whenever a question was referred to the Assembly. And the mob which dominated the Assembly was likely to support the candidate from whom it could expect the biggest hand-out.

The Gracchi. In 133 B.C. Tiberius Gracchus, an aristocrat who became tribune in that year, sought to bring about reforms which would re-establish the class of free Roman farmers. He proposed that private holdings of public lands be strictly limited in size; this would return large tracts of land to the state. This land he proposed to let out in small plots to the landless Roman citizens. The senators immediately tried to block this bill, but Tiberius had the support of the citizen Assembly. The question then arose; how were the impoverished Roman citizens to find the means of setting themselves up as farmers on their new land? Tiberius then put forth another proposal which struck further at senatorial privilege. He planned to use for this purpose the treasure recently bequeathed to the Romans by King Attalus of Pergamum. The control of the provinces, as we have already seen, had always lain with the senators.

The senators and their followers and clients formed a very powerful group. When, the following year, Tiberius Gracchus came up for re-election, there was much excitement in the city. Tiberius and a group of his supporters were set upon and slain in the streets of Rome and their bodies thrown into the Tiber.

In 124 B.C. Gaius Gracchus, brother of Tiberius, became tribune. He secured the passage of a law which provided for the monthly distribution of grain to the populace at half the market price. No doubt this act provided relief and security for the poor and freed them from dependence upon the bounty of ambitious candidates for office. It also placed a strain on the treasury and, when misapplied, put a premium upon idleness.

The land law of Tiberius Gracchus was re-enacted. A program of road building and improvement was undertaken in connection with the new distribution of land. After the death of Tiberius, the senators had been able to render the land law inoperative through their control of the courts. Now Gaius Gracchus reformed the courts by so changing the qualifications of those permitted to act as justices that he was able to replace the senatorial judges with members of the equestrian order.

In 122 B.C. Gaius Gracchus left Rome to oversee the establishment of a new commercial colony, Junonia, at Carthage. It was a tactical mistake for he was away from Rome seventy days. During that time his opponents accused Gaius of aiming to be a dictator and in other ways so successfully created mistrust in the minds of the citizens that he failed to be elected in 121 B.C. The senators soon found a pretext for declaring martial law. Gracchus and his followers were attacked by the senatorial forces and defeated. Gaius had himself killed by a loyal slave.

Marius. Despite the failures of the Gracchi, the Senate had demonstrated that it was corrupt, incompetent, and devoted to its own interests. The careers of both Gracchi also revealed how a strong leader who had the support of plebs and equestrians might override the Senate. Roman history now became a struggle among power-seeking individuals many of whom, however, were genuinely devoted to the public good. One such was Gaius Marius.

Marius was a military leader of the equestrian order. He had sufficiently distinguished himself in the war against the rebellious African prince Jugurtha to be elected consul in 107 B.C. In two more years, with the able assistance of his friend and aid Sulla, Marius brought the Jugurthine war to a close. But in this same year, 105 B.C., two Roman armies were destroyed in Gaul by forces of the barbarian Cimbri and Teutons. The way lay open for the barbarians to invade Italy. Marius was appointed to the command against the Cimbri and Teutons. Instead of attempting a fresh levy of the effete Roman citizens for military service, Marius called for volunteers. This change of plan opened up careers in the army to men who, in the course of time, came to look to their leaders to secure them lands or bonuses upon their retirement from the army. But in the emergency, Marius obtained an army of good fighting men with which he defeated the enemy and saved Italy from invasion. A slave war in Sicily, a war with the pirates, and the need for suppressing a rebellion of the Spaniards, gave Marius further opportunities to distinguish himself as a general and to win popular support in Rome.

Meanwhile, the Italian cities, which had supplied soldiers for Rome's conquests, were aggrieved that they were without voice in the settlement of conquered territories and did not share in the great wealth that victories had brought to Rome. Many of these cities revolted, some demanding Roman citizenship, others their independence. The war which resulted lasted from 90 to 88 B.C. The final result was that Roman citizenship was extended to all Italy. And one of the Roman generals who distinguished himself in these campaigns was L. Cornelius Sulla.

Sulla. While Rome was busy with the revolting Italian cities, Mithridates, King of Cappadocia in eastern Asia Minor and of Pontus on the Black Sea, organized a widespread revolt against Rome in the east. The eastern provinces had long suffered the depredations of the greedy Roman tax gatherers. To these provinces and to the vassal Greek cities Mithridates seemed a deliverer. When he had easily defeated the local Roman armies sent against him, Mithridates called for the revolt of the whole East. Some 80,000 Roman and Italian residents were slaughtered in eastern cities.

The Senate appointed L. Cornelius Sulla, who still headed the army he had led in the Italian war, as commander in the

East. But the plebs, supported by the equestrians, refused to accept the Senate's appointment and elected Marius commander in the East. Marius had no army under his command at the moment, so when Sulla marched on Rome with his troops, Marius was forced to flee to Africa. Sulla then forced the passage of a law which seriously restricted the powers of the Assembly, for it obliged that body to obtain the consent of the Senate before it could vote on a measure. Sulla then, having humbled the foes of the Senate, marched off to Asia. In Sulla's absence Marius returned and instituted a massacre of the leading men of the senatorial party. He was then elected consul. But the strain was apparently too much for the seventy-year-old leader, for shortly afterward he died.

Meanwhile, Sulla was revealing himself a great general and a ruthless one. He seized Athens, pursued Mithridates into Asia and made terms with him. He punished the rebellious Greeks by exacting an enormous indemnity and by quartering troops upon them.

The popular party knew that Sulla would seek revenge for their rebellion. Accordingly armies were raised and sent out to prevent his return to Italy. These Sulla easily defeated. Then in the spring of 83 B.C. he landed in Italy with an army of seasoned veterans numbering some 40,000, all of whom had taken an oath of allegiance to himself. Overthrowing the forces sent against him Sulla advanced on Rome and entered the city as master of the state.

Sulla then had himself appointed Dictator. As Dictator he began the systematic slaughter of the followers of Marius and the confiscation of their property. Sulla revealed shortly, however, that personal power was not his aim. After his harsh revenge, he put through a series of laws which placed the powers of government securely in the hands of the Senate. Failing to appreciate the degree to which the senatorial order had degenerated, Sulla apparently sought to restore the condition of affairs that had prevailed in ancient Rome when under the able and unselfish leadership of that class Rome had become great. Having restored the power of the Senate, Sulla retired to private life in 79 B.C.

Pompey. After Sulla's death in 78 B.C. agitation was begun for the repeal of his hated laws. But the people of the Assembly knew that they would need a military champion if their powers were to be restored to them. They chose as their favorite Gnaeus Pompey who had distinguished himself in Spain. Pompey was elected consul in 70 B.C. when he agreed to repeal the laws of Sulla.

After fulfilling his promise Pompey was assigned by the Assembly the task of freeing the seas of piracy. He was given supreme command in the Mediterranean and upon its coasts. The pirates were routed out of their strongholds with such thoroughness and speed that the Assembly then placed Pompey in charge of the war already under way against Mithridates. Mithridates' power was already broken. As a result Pompey quickly obtained his submission as well as that of Tigranes, King of Armenia. He then crushed what remained of the Seleucid kingdom and made Syria a Roman province.

Toward the close of the year 62 B.C. Pompey returned to Italy and the following year celebrated a triumph. Any fears that he might be another Sulla were allayed when Pompey disbanded his army and submitted to the Senate a report on his eastern settlement and a request for land allotments to his men. But the Senate, now having nothing to fear, proceeded to earn the ill will of Pompey and his men as well by debating these matters for the next two years. Pompey cast about for political allies.

Caesar. During Pompey's absence in the East there had risen into prominence at Rome a young nephew of Marius named Gaius Julius Caesar. Just before Pompey's return to Italy, however, young Caesar had drawn suspicion upon himself through his association with Catiline, whose attempt to seize the government by violence had been thwarted by Cicero, a lawyer and the greatest orator and man of letters of his generation. However, the Senate delayed two years over giving its approval to Pompey's settlement in Asia and during that time Caesar came forward in Pompey's support.

Pompey and Caesar took into personal alliance with them

the wealthy Crassus, thus forming what was known as the "triumvirate," which was designed to advance the interests and careers of the three members. Caesar, elected consul, forced the ratification of Pompey's settlement in the East and passed other laws settling Pompey's veterans in Campania. To relieve the conditions in Rome he settled an additional 20,000 colonists on Campanian land.

Caesar saw clearly that it was no longer possible for a man to achieve distinction by constitutional means. Essential to the exercise of power was the backing of an army. With the help of his friends he obtained passage of a law which made him governor of Illyria and Gaul for five years. The appointment was later renewed. In eight years' time, from 58 to 50 B.C., Caesar conquered all Gaul north of the Alps from the Rhine to the English Channel and the ocean. He thereby made subject to Rome all of the land of modern France and Belgium. To secure these conquests he crossed the Rhine and defeated the Germans. He also crossed the Channel and invaded Britain to the Thames River. And during all this time he made sure that his achievements were being followed and appreciated by the Romans.

But the Senate, which followed these exploits with apprehension, dreaded the moment when Caesar would return to Rome and demand a triumph. They remembered that Caesar was the nephew of Marius. Accordingly when the term of Caesar's second governorship expired, the Senate appealed to Pompey to support them. Crassus had since been killed in action in the East and the triumvirate was dissolved. Pompey, whose ambition was personal, had no hesitation in championing the Senate although he had risen to favor with the backing of the Assembly. Thus assured of the support of the great conqueror of the pirates and of Asia, the Senate ordered Caesar to disband his army.

Caesar hesitated not an instant. Swiftly he crossed the River Rubicon and entered Italy in 49 B.C. Unprepared for such prompt action, the Senate and Pompey retreated as Caesar approached Rome. They were soon forced to leave Italy and cross over into Greece. Let us recall that Pompey still controlled the fleet with which he had swept the pirates from the seas. He was regarded throughout the world as the greatest man in Rome and his prestige made it easy for him to raise an army in either the eastern or western Mediterranean. While Pompey gathered together an army, Caesar surprised everyone by the speed of his movements. Crossing over into Spain he forced the capitulation of the armies there that were still led by Pompey's officers. Secure in their control of the sea, Pompey and the Senate prepared at leisure for the invasion of Italy. Before they had begun the crossing, to their amazement they learned that Caesar had returned from Spain victorious and that, still more surprising, he had crossed the Adriatic into Epirus and was preparing to attack the senatorial armies. The two great generals and their armies met at Pharsalus in 48 B.C. Pompey's plan was skillful, but despite the fact that his forces were the smaller, Caesar proved himself much superior in generalship. The senatorial army was shattered and Pompey fled to Egypt.

Upon his arrival in Egypt Pompey was treacherously murdered. Caesar, following in pursuit, met in Egypt the beautiful and talented queen, Cleopatra, last of the Ptolemies. Here Caesar intervened on Cleopatra's behalf in a conflict over the succession between the twenty-year-old queen and her thirteen-year-old brother who was also, in accordance with Egyptian custom, her husband. Succumbing to the charms of Cleopatra, Caesar remained in Egypt until the spring of 47 B.C. when an outbreak in Asia Minor demanded his immediate attention. From Asia Minor Caesar dispatched his famous report to the Senate: *Veni, vidi, vici,* "I came, I saw, I conquered." He then hastened westward to meet the republican forces which had gathered in north Africa and in Spain. After scoring fresh triumphs over his enemies, Caesar returned to Rome to celebrate a triumph.

Dictatorship. From July 28, 46 to March 15, 44 B.C. Caesar ruled the Roman Empire as Dictator. Men wondered what use he would make of his power. Would he, like Sulla, attempt to restore the form if not the substance of the old republican government? Caesar continued to rule as an autocrat, but he made his power legal by concentrating in his own hands the chief offices of the state. He was elected Dictator, consul, and also was given the tribunician authority without the office. He was Pontifex Maximus, head of the state religious organization. He received the powers of censorship. He appointed both Roman and provincial magistrates. And he possessed the right to make peace and war without consulting the Senate.

In fairness to Caesar let us acknowledge that it was no longer possible to restore anything that was worth restoring. What was needed was to give Rome a strong, responsible, efficient government. That Caesar undertook to do. His mind was full of great plans for the improvement of the city, the reform of the administration and local city government. One reform which he did fortunately bring about was the substitution of the Egyptian calendar for the old Graeco-Roman moon calendar. With modifications this Roman form of the Egyptian calendar is the one we use today.

But there were still men devoted to the old ways who were unable to see that the Senate and Assembly had long since ceased either to represent the state or to possess the capacity for ruling it. Under the leadership of Cassius and Brutus, a group including some sixty senators determined to murder Caesar. On the Ides of March (March 15th), 44 B.C., as Caesar entered the senate chamber, he was surrounded by the conspirators who drew concealed weapons and stabbed him to death. He fell at the foot of Pompey's statue.

15 TWO CENTURIES OF WORLD PEACE UNDER THE EMPIRE

If the murderers of Caesar expected to be hailed as the saviors of the republic, they were disappointed. Marc Antony, Caesar's fellow consul, took possession of Caesar's estate and sought to be acknowledged Caesar's successor. But upon receiving news of his uncle's death, an eighteen-year-old nephew, Octavian, hastened to Rome. Octavian learned there that he had been legally adopted by Caesar and made his sole heir. Antony, however, refused to recognize his claims.

Octavian was too young to be regarded as dangerous, and to that fact he owed his life. Despite his youth he soon revealed himself a worthy successor to his illustrious uncle. He promptly rallied Caesar's veteran soldiers and won over some of Antony's legions. So skillful was he in judging and acting upon the local political situation, that he forced his own election as consul when he was only twenty years of age. He then formed an alliance with Antony and another of Caesar's followers, Lepidus. This was the second triumvirate.

The two leading murderers of Caesar, Brutus and Cassius, had fled from Rome and now headed a powerful army encamped in Macedonia. Antony and Octavian moved against the conspirators. At the great battle of Philippi the champions of the old republic were completely defeated (42 B.C.).

Octavian and Antony then divided the empire between them; Octavian returned to Italy where he set about establishing order in the west. Antony remained in the east with a view to bringing it into full subjection to Rome. Octavian pursued his aims with ruthless skill. He defeated young Pompey, son of the great general, who had taken possession of Sicily. He then overthrew Lepidus, the member of the triumvirate who had been given the province of Africa. He thus united the entire western part of the empire under his rule.

Antony meanwhile had fallen under the influence of Cleopatra's charms. This ambitious woman, who once had hoped to rule the Roman Empire with Caesar, now, as Antony's queen, hoped once more to realize her ambition. In Antioch and in Alexandria Antony maintained himself in a court of oriental splendor that recalled the days of the great Persian monarchy. Reports of the ambitions of Antony and Cleopatra reached Rome along with accounts of the absolutism of their eastern courts. It was not long before Octavian found the Senate willing to declare war on Cleopatra.

The two rivals, Octavian and Antony, met, with their armies and fleets, at Actium on the western coast of Greece. As the naval battle turned in favor of Octavian, Antony fled in the queen's galley followed by the royal Egyptian flotilla. The armies, having watched the desertion of their leader, soon surrendered to Octavian. The following year Octavian landed in Egypt. Only a feeble resistance was offered. In desperation both Antony and Cleopatra took their own lives.

The Age of Augustus. The rule of Octavian over a united Roman Empire inaugurated an era of two centuries of world peace and prosperity. This, as history goes, was a very great achievement. The stability of the empire during this period is in no small degree the result of the wise organization of the imperial government instituted by Octavian and based to a considerable extent upon the plans of Julius Caesar. For Octavian fortunately lived long enough to carry out many of those plans; he ruled from 27 B.C. to 14 A.D.

Octavian tactfully avoided provoking another revolt on the part of the republicans by regarding himself as an official of the Roman Republic appointed by the Senate. He avoided titles like that of Dictator which bore unpleasant associations for the Romans. But he accepted many titles of honor such as "Augustus," or "Princeps"—*first* among the citizens—or "Imperator," director or commander. And he retained control of the armies.

The boundaries of Augustus' empire were established along natural and defensible lines wherever possible: the Rhine and Danube rivers on the north, the Black Sea and Euphrates on the east, the Sahara Desert to the south, the Atlantic Ocean in the west. To defend this great empire and maintain order a standing army was essential. Augustus recruited his soldiers among the provinces. In addition to their pay, they received upon retirement a grant of land and Roman citizenship. The soldiers were stationed along the borders except for the Praetorian Guard maintained in Rome for the defense of the palace.

Augustus reformed the administration throughout the empire. A high degree of local self-government was permitted. Roman governors maintained order, administered the laws, and collected taxes. But they were now answerable to Augustus for their behavior. For the first time in Rome's history Augustus assessed taxable property and made some reasonable attempt to adjust taxation to the wealth of the province and the individual.

The governing bureaucracy established and trained by Augustus so efficiently carried on the functions assigned to it that during the reigns of wicked or incompetent emperors like Nero or Caligula, the government practically ran itself. During the course of the next two centuries whatever elaboration or improvement of the administration took place was based upon the original structure established by Augustus.

Augustus, with the able assistance of his wife Livia, raised the level of manners and morals in Rome. Together they revived an admiration for the virtues and character of the earlier Roman. Augustus stirred the civic pride of the citizen by beautifying the city of Rome and by making his capital a great artistic and intellectual center as well as a political one. Under the patronage of Augustus, Livy devoted forty years to writing the hisory of Rome. Horace's poems preserve for us a picture of the Rome of Augustus' day. This too was the age of Virgil and his great epic poem, *The Aeneid*.

The Era of Roman Peace. During the first two centuries of the empire, the era of the *Pax Romana* or Roman Peace, the emperors concerned themselves principally with protecting and maintaining the great *regnum*. There was no serious threat to the security of the empire. But occasionally tribes or states across the borders endangered the lives or security of people within the empire and these situations called for rectification. The three chief problems were: the maintenance and protection of the boundaries, administration, and the establishment of the imperial succession. During the reign of Claudius, southern Britain was conquered and incorporated within the empire. Later emperors, Domitian for example, strengthened portions of the existing frontiers. It was not until the reign of Trajan (98–117 A.D.) that this policy was momentarily abandoned.

Trajan, an able general, seems to have dreamed of emulating the feats of Alexander and uniting both East and West in a single empire. At any rate he sought to increase the size of the Roman Empire. He crossed the Danube into Dacia, which had for some time been a source of trouble to Rome, and after conquering the Dacians, settled colonies of Romans throughout the land. Next he moved eastward against Parthia, or Persia, which had never been subdued by Rome and which remained hostile. Crossing the Euphrates, Trajan broke the Parthian power and added Armenia, Mesopotamia, and Assyria to the Roman Empire as provinces.

But Trajan's successor, Hadrian, himself a great soldier, realized that the over-extension of the empire would create grave administrative problems. Also the more extensive the boundaries, the more difficult they would be to protect. In the interests of peace and stability, Hadrian gave up all the territory conquered by Trajan east of the Euphrates River. He then devoted himself to strengthening the established boundaries. It was Hadrian who completed the line of fortifications along the exposed border between the Rhine and the Danube rivers. And it was Hadrian who built the wall across Britain to hold back the Picts and Scots.

The work of Trajan and Hadrian secured the Roman frontiers until the end of the great era of peace. Throughout that time Roman administration remained efficient and stable although toward its close, with the expansion and elaboration of bureaus, we are able to note that administration is becoming unwieldy. The question of the imperial succession was never solved satisfactorily for very long. The consequences of that important failure we shall have occasion to deal with in detail later on.

16 DECLINE

When Julius Caesar made himself head of the Roman State, he adopted as son and heir his nephew Octavian. The wisdom of that choice was made evident by the subsequent career of Octavian.

In his turn Octavian (as the emperor Augustus) adopted as heir and successor his stepson Tiberius whom he then associated with him in the government. Tiberius had already won support among the armies by his conquest of Noricum and a term as military governor of Illyria. Upon the death of Augustus in 14 A.D., Tiberius assumed command of the army and called the Senate into session. The Senate bestowed upon him the title of Augustus along with other titles and powers that had been held by Octavian. In this manner there came to be established in the empire a system of succession which prevailed for two centuries.

However, it did not always work smoothly. Upon the assassination of Caligula in the year 41, the Praetorian or palace guard dragged Claudius, Caligula's uncle, from his hiding place in the palace and proclaimed him emperor while the Senate was still debating the question whether to restore the Republic. And again in 68 A.D., upon the revolt of the armies of Gaul and Spain, when Nero fled from Rome and became a suicide Galba, leader of the Spanish armies, bought the support of the Praetorian guard and was acclaimed emperor. The Senate again accepted the choice of the armies. In the course of a single year, 68–69 A.D., the army deposed and set up four emperors and in each instance the Senate gave its approval.

Two factors saved the empire from collapse. One was the efficient bureaucracy, set up by Caesar and Augustus and improved by Claudius, which continued to function in spite of the disturbed condition of affairs in the city of Rome and other portions of the empire. Another was the fact that fortunately many of those raised to the imperial dignity by the support of the army were men of real ability and sincere patriotism. Such men were Vespasian, who reformed and strengthened the Senate, and Trajan and Hadrian to whom we have already referred. These men in their turn sought to train as their successors the ablest among the younger generation.

In 161 A.D. Marcus Aurelius succeeded Antoninus Pius. During his long reign he revealed himself an able man wholly devoted to the public service. He is also well known to readers of our generation as the Stoic philosopher whose *Meditations* have long been a standard work in European literature. This respected emperor, sadly mistaken in his judgment of the character of his own son, abandoned the customary method of succession and tried to establish a dynasty. Commodus proved utterly unfit for the office. Sunken in debauchery he neglected state affairs and was finally assassinated in a palace plot on the last day of the year 192 A.D. Once again the army seized control of the imperial office.

By the end of the second century the Roman armies were much changed in character from what they had been in the days of Augustus. For during the long period of peace, security, and material prosperity, citizens avoided military service. The empire was really not in danger and military service entailed a long enlistment during which the citizen would probably find himself assigned to a frontier post among semibarbarous peoples, far from the lively centers of civilization. It was much less difficult to obtain recruits among the outlying provinces or among the barbarians who sought service in the Roman armies than from among the older racial stocks of the empire. The barbarian in particular was proud to become a Roman soldier because it brought him prestige among his own people and, in the long run, it also brought him Roman citizenship and a grant of land upon his retirement from service. These were the soldiers who in the third century seized control of the state. They set up and deposed emperors. They demanded gifts and land, and often, in their impatient greed, they looted the provinces. Between the years 235 and 285 there were twenty-six emperors, only one of whom died a natural death.

Heavy taxes, the growing inefficiency of the over-large bureaucracy, and the depredations of the soldiers seriously disrupted the economic organization of the empire. As a consequence many abandoned their callings and sought a livelihood in other fields. These shifts caused further dislocation in essential industries and services. Further hardship resulted from rising prices which were in part due to the uncertainties and risks involved in doing business.

In 285 Diocletian was chosen emperor by the armies. He devoted his great abilities to checking the disintegration of the empire which was now evident on every hand. He saw that one of the chief threats to the stability of the imperial government was the ambition of the governors of large provinces who were in charge of armies. Diocletian divided up the empire into over a hundred provinces so that the governor of no one province would be strong enough to challenge the authority of the imperial government. In addition he separated the civil from the military authority.

Diocletian realized that the administration of the empire and the defense of its far-flung boundaries posed a problem too complicated for a single ruler. He therefore selected as co-emperor Maximian who, like himself, held the title *Augustus*. Diocletian took up his residence in the East, which had become the center of population and economic activity in the empire, and established his capital at Nicomedia in Asia Minor. Maximian headed the administration in the West and made his headquarters in Milan in northern Italy.

Each of the two *Augusti* then chose a younger officer as an assistant and associate in the government. These men were given the title *Caesar* and were adopted as the sons and successors of the *Augusti*. In 305 Diocletian forced Maximian to resign with him and the government was turned over to the two *Caesars* who now became *Augusti*. Each of the new *Augusti* then chose a *Caesar* and the new succession was launched.

Before his retirement Diocletian had given his attention to the economic plight of the empire. It was too late for any but strong and arbitrary measures. In 301 he issued an Edict of Prices which fixed the prices not only of commodities but of wages and every form of labor and professional service in the empire. He also decreed that every man should continue in his original trade or profession and that the son should follow the trade of his father.

Constantine. Diocletian's attempt to re-establish an orderly succession failed. The successor of Maximian was Constantius who died in 306. At once Constantius' British soldiery hailed his son Constantine as *Caesar* although he had not been so designated by either *Augustus*. As soon as the succession was disrupted others entered the contest. Maxentius, son of Maximian, caused himself to be proclaimed *Caesar* likewise and Maximian emerged from retirement in support of his son. There followed a series of civil wars which finally ended with the triumph of Constantine over all rivals. For a time Constantine ruled jointly with Maxentius. Later he shared the rule of the empire with Licinius. But in 324 Licinius was eliminated and Constantine became sole emperor. He confronted substantially the same difficult questions that Diocletian had sought to solve: How re-establish the unity and stability of the Roman Empire under a government which all would accept and support? How determine the imperial succession so as to bring the ablest men to the office and avoid an illegal grab for power by army leaders?

We shall not be able to understand Constantine's resolution of these problems, however, until we give some attention to the spiritual forces at work among the people of the far-flung empire.

The Rise of Christianity. Jesus was born during the reign of Augustus, when the great Roman Empire was settling down to an era of two centuries of world peace and prosperity. Yet despite the greatness of Roman achievement there were evident, even during the first decades of the imperial era, abundant signs of spiritual unease. The Romans, like the Greeks before them during and after the age of Alexander the Great, came to know and respect the peoples of many different civilizations and religious faiths who were now subject to them. They began to see that their traditional ideas about the gods were naïve and in many ways inferior to the religious concepts of older civilized peoples.

The Romans, like nearly all the other peoples of the ancient world, believed in many gods. In very early times the Romans had worshiped nature gods and the gods of the household, the Lares and Penates. As the state assumed increased importance the Romans borrowed the Greek hierarchy and bestowed upon them Roman names. Zeus became Jove. Hera became Juno. Aphrodite was called Venus and Ares, Mars. Athena became Minerva. These gods were the patrons and protectors of the Roman state so that patriotism and religious allegiance were inextricably bound together.

We saw that when Alexander conquered the East he found it necessary to appear before his new subjects as the son of Zeus-Amon. The conquered people continued to worship their old gods. But since they had been overcome by the Greeks, it seemed obvious that the god of the Greeks was more powerful than Marduk, or Bel, or Ashur, or Ra. They simply acknowledged the new god and added the statue of Zeus or Alexander to the statues of the other gods in their temples. Very much the same formula was followed when Rome became mistress of the world. The Roman emperors were deified and their statues placed in temples throughout the Empire.

But in this respect the position of the Jews was peculiar. Their god, Yaweh or Jehovah, was, as he had declared himself, a jealous god and would have no strange gods before him. He was conceived by the Jews to be the supreme ruler over all things and over all men. The Jews, therefore, could not place in their temples the statue of the deified Augustus without disobeying the explicit command of Jehovah. With their usual practical good sense, the Romans recognized the special difficulty of the Jews and made them an exception. But the Jews promptly ran into another difficulty. How could they render military service when the soldier's oath of allegiance involved the recognition of the emperor as the deified head of the state? Here again the Roman government acted with sense and generosity. The Jews were practically exempted from military service.

Christianity, originating as a Jewish sect, claimed the same exemptions as the Jews. But after the revolt of the Jews throughout the Empire in 66 A.D., which ended with Rome's destruction of Jerusalem in the year 70, the Christians were naturally suspect. They were not an officially recognized sect and were therefore often forced to hold their meetings in secret. Although, after the conversion of Paul of Tarsus, they increasingly sought converts outside the Jewish communities, for a long time the Christians were a small and little understood minority in the Roman Empire.

Even before the Jewish rebellion the Christians became the victims of official persecution. During the reign of Nero a great fire destroyed a thickly populated quarter of Rome. The rumor spread that Nero himself had caused the fire to be set in order to clear a space for his new palace, the Golden House. In order to quash the dangerous rumor it was necessary to find a scapegoat. The Christians were blamed and many were sacrificed in punishment for the deed.

For three centuries the Christians suffered intermittent persecution. The extent of that persecution is easily exaggerated however. It is well to remember that for long periods the Christians were permitted to worship as they wished without interference, that during long periods of freedom and relative security they won many converts among all classes and nationalities in the Empire. This is easy to understand when we recall that Christianity was but one of a number of eastern religions that were being taken up by the Romans and Greeks who had long since ceased to believe in the old gods.

Outstanding among the cults widely current in the third century was that of Cybele, the Great Mother. Others who were worshiped were: Attis; the Egyptian Isis and Serapis; the Babylonian goddess Ishtar; and Bel and Atayatis. Most widely followed of all, and similar to Christianity in many of its teachings and practices, was the cult of Mithras, one of the Persian deities. Points of similarity between Mithraism and Christianity were to be found in their belief in heaven and hell, in the immortality of the soul and the last judgment, in their concept of the unceasing struggle between the forces of good and evil in the world. Both religions sanctified Sunday among the days of the week and as a special feast the twenty-fifth of December. In their ceremonies both made use of the bell, holy water, and the candle. Mithraism reached the height of its popularity around 275 A.D. after which it underwent a decline. It is very likely that because of the similarity of many of its teachings to those of Christianity it prepared the way for a wider acceptance of Christianity in the Empire. The facts that Mithraism excluded women and had no general organization to unify and direct its course were points of weakness which help explain its decline.

The last serious persecution of the Christians occurred under the Emperor Decius (250–251). When Diocletian began his reign he sought to suppress Christianity, still regarded as a hostile sect, in the interests of the unity of the Empire but he quickly realized the futility of such a policy and abandoned it. Edicts of toleration, which put Christianity on an equal footing with other recognized religions, were issued in 311 and 313 by Galerius and Constantine.

The Emperor Constantine recognized that while the Christians numbered scarcely a tenth of the population, they constituted the most potent spiritual force in the Empire. For the Christian was willing to die for his faith in an age when very few men were willing to die for Rome. In addition, the Christians were organized under their bishops many of whom were men of distinguished birth and ability. Far too much has been made of the fact that Christianity appealed to the poor. Of course it did. But too frequently we are inclined to overlook the fact that from the time of St. Peter patrician Romans of wealth and position were also among its converts. It appealed to the educated as well as the uneducated. The spiritual emptiness of a too materialistic era affected men of all classes. Turning from the materialistic ambitions and pursuits of the time the Christian sought to make himself worthy in the eyes of God. To those who were ignorant of the beliefs of the Christians, this often appeared to represent an unnatural contempt for all the things that the majority of men held to be good. Combined with the Christian's unwillingness to worship the emperor as a god, this attitude made him seem a hater of mankind and of the state and a very subversive influence indeed.

By the fourth century, in spite of popular misunderstanding, and occasional persecution, Christianity had become a legally recognized religion. Constantine now sought to strengthen the unity of the Empire and to buttress a government which had already revealed many signs of weakness by winning the allegiance of the Christians. Christian bishops were appointed to posts in the Roman administration. They proved efficient and honest. Churchmen were admitted to the counsels of the emperor. In time, ancient temples were turned over to the Christians as places of worship, their property was exempted from taxation, they were permitted to hold and inherit property, and the emperor made rich gifts to Christian churches.

The Council of Nicaea. At the very moment when Constantine succeeded in strengthening the unity and administration of the Empire with the help of the Christians, there occurred a serious division in the ranks of the Christians themselves. The Greek-speaking eastern half of the Roman Empire had always exhibited a taste for philosophical and religious controversy. The very language lent itself to the refinement of distinctions and the logical opposition of concepts.

There now arose a controversy revolving about the exact nature of the divinity of Jesus. The long accepted view of God was that he was one and indivisible but possessed of three divine persons: God the Father, God the Son who had come among men and died on the cross, and God the Holy Ghost. An Alexandrian preacher, Arius, insisted that Jesus was inferior in divinity to God the Father. His reasoning, in part, was that Jesus, unlike the Father, had been created and had therefore not existed from the beginning; that he could not have been truly man without at the same time being less god. The question had many aspects and its debate stirred up the most intense excitement. In a letter to a friend a traveler of the time complained that one could not enter a shop to buy a loaf of bread or a piece of meat without having to listen to an argument upon the manner in which the persons of God were united by having the same substance but a different essence or the other way around. Arius was opposed by many churchmen, most prominent among whom was the bishop Athanasius who, at one stage in the controversy, had to flee to Rome for safety.

In 325 A.D. there assembled in Nicaea, a city in Asia Minor

not far from Constantinople, a council called together from all Christendom by the emperor for the purpose of settling the controversy which had created a schism in the church. After long debate the bishops condemned the doctrines of Arius and affirmed the principles upheld by Athanasius. Arian books were burned and the preaching of Arian doctrines prohibited.

Constantinople. Constantine, like Diocletian, took account of the fact that the life of the western empire had seriously declined. The Greek-speaking East was again, after several centuries, the center of population, wealth, and cultural vitality. Constantine determined to establish his capital permanently in the East. On the site of ancient Byzantium he built a great new city, strategically located at the point where the Bosphorus joins the Sea of Marmora. Here he constructed for himself and his court a magnificent palace. In 330 A.D. the imperial court officially took up its residence in the new city which was appropriately called Constantinople.

Before his death in 337 Constantine was baptized a Christian. While during his life he had favored Christianity among other officially recognized religions, he had not made it the religion of the state.

Julian and the Pagan Reaction. Constantine was succeeded by his three sons, Constantine II, Constans, and Constantius, who ruled jointly. Upon the death of Constantius, who had survived his brothers, the succession passed to his cousin Julian in 360 A.D. Julian had been called from the seclusion of a scholar's life to be associated in the *imperium* with his cousin. He proved, surprisingly, an exceptionally able general and an extraordinarily upright and competent administrator.

But what particularly distinguished the reign of Julian was his attempt to make paganism once more the religion of the Empire. His early study of Hellenic literature laid the basis for his conversion to Neo-Platonism, a fact which he proclaimed publicly upon the death of Constantius. While he tolerated the Christians, he deprived them of many of their privileges. But the pagan religions had lost their hold upon the peoples of the Empire. The only converts were those servilely ambitious ones who sought Julian's favor.

The Authority of Christianity. The authoritative place which Christianity had come to hold in the Empire is revealed by the submission of the Emperor Theodosius the Great (379– 395) to Bishop Ambrose of Milan. In 390 the commander of the garrison in Thessalonica was killed by the mob during a riot. When the news reached Theodosius in Milan he angrily ordered the punishment of the citizens. Some seven thousand were reported to have been slain as a consequence of this hasty order, which the emperor promptly regretted. Bishop Ambrose excluded the emperor from his church and refused him communion until he had done public penance for his rash act. Though he waited eight months, Theodosius finally made public acknowledgment of his sin, thus recognizing that the emperor was subject to the same moral rules as other men.

Earlier, Gratian (375–383) had withdrawn the state support of the heathen temples, and when Theodosius extinguished the fires of the ancient temples, Christianity was left the only legal religion in the Empire.

PART THREE

The Collapse of the Roman West and the Revival in the East

378–395	Theodosius I, Emperor
395	Division of Empire between Arcadius and Honorius. Revolt of Visigoths
406	Barbarian invasions of Gaul. Roman garrisons withdrawn from Britain
410	The Visigoths under Alaric captured Rome. Death of Alaric
429	Vandals under Gaiseric invaded Africa
439	Vandals took Carthage
449	Anglo-Saxon conquest of Britain
451	Attila and Huns invaded Gaul. Turned back at battle of Châlons
452	Pope Leo persuaded Attila to withdraw from Italy
453	Death of Attila. Huns withdraw from Europe
462	Saint Patrick began conversion of Ireland
476	Odoacer, King of Teutonic tribes in Italy
481	Clovis, King of the Franks
493	Theodoric the Ostrogoth conquered Italy and became King of Italy
496	Clovis converted to Roman Catholic Christianity
527–565	Justinian, Emperor
529	St. Benedict founded monastery at Monte Cassino
532	"Nika" riot
568	Lombards conquer northern Italy
590–604	Pope Gregory the Great
618	T'ang dynasty began in China
622	The Hegira or flight of Mohammed. Date begins Mohammedan calendar
632	Mohammed died
732	Franks defeated Mohammedans at Tours

17 THE BARBARIANS

Peaceful Infiltration into the Empire. Outside the European boundaries of the Roman Empire were many barbarian tribes which had for generations enjoyed friendly relations with the Romans. Numbers of these, as we know, crossed the boundaries and settled peaceably in the provinces or enlisted in the Roman armies. This process of infiltration had been going on quietly for so long a time that there had come to be a very large barbarian element not only in the outer provinces and the armies along the borders, but also in the very heart of the empire itself, the city of Rome. While it is true that the barbarians were to some extent civilized and Romanized by their life in the army, their numbers became so great that in many ways Roman life became barbarized. Some of the effects of this process in the army were the tendency of the troops to give allegiance to a leader rather than to the Senate or the emperor. To their leaders the troops looked for rewards of land and plunder. In their impatient greed they did not hesitate to loot the Roman provinces themselves.

The tribes settled along the European boundaries of the empire were nearly all Germanic. Along the lower Rhine were the Franks. Further to the south the Alamanni had settled. Eastward and bordering the upper Danube were the Burgundians and Lombards. North of the Balkan peninsula in the region roughly bounded by the Carpathian Mountains and the Dniester and Danube rivers were the West Goths or Visigoths. Along the north shores of the Black Sea between the Dniester and the Don rivers were the East Goths or Ostrogoths. And beyond the Don, north of the Caucasus Mountains, were the Alans.

As a rule the barbarians were not disposed to clear the forest and bring the land under cultivation. When the population of a tribe became too large to live upon the game of the nearby forest and the slender yield in crops and flocks of the natural clearing which had been settled, the tribe was split up into groups which then drew lots to determine which would migrate and search for new homelands. At such times the stretches of uninhabited fertile land across the borders of the empire tempted the barbarians to seize what they wanted. In 250 the Alamanni broke through the border defenses and entered northern Italy. Some Franks ventured across the lower Rhine at about the same time. In the same year the Emperor Decius suffered a defeat at the hands of the Visigoths. But for more than a century thereafter Rome held the borders against barbarian attack.

In the meantime the barbarians were converted to Christianity by one of their own number, Ulfilas, a Goth of mixed blood born around 310. Ulfilas was himself converted to Christianity by a follower of the teachings of Arius whose views, as we saw, were condemned at the Council of Nicaea. But Arianism was not exterminated. Even before the death of Constantine Arian doctrines were openly supported at the imperial court. Ulfilas, who was ultimately made a bishop, spread Arian Christianity among the Germanic tribes. He found it necessary to invent an alphabet for the Goths who as yet had no written language. He then translated much of the Bible into Gothic.

The Breaching of the Barriers. Around 370 A.D. a great horde of fierce nomads poured into Europe from central Asia. These were the people known to Europe as the Huns—possibly they were the Hsiungnu Tartars, we cannot be sure. Mounted on small but swift horses they moved through the forests so quietly that their attacks nearly always came as a surprise. Since they dispersed into the woods after an attack it was almost impossible to pursue them and inflict retaliatory punishment.

The Alans and Ostrogoths found themselves helpless before the Hunnish invaders and surrendered to them. A small body of West Goths fled into Transylvania, but most of the Visigoths crowded the borders of the Roman Empire and demanded permission to enter. In 376 the emperor Valens gave them permission to cross the Danube and settle on Roman land. Until they could be permanently distributed in the unoccupied regions, Valens promised to furnish them with food. In return, and as a guarantee of good behavior, the Visigoths were to surrender their arms. But the Roman officials sought to profiteer at the expense of the needy Goths. Unfortunately they also neglected to relieve the Goths of their weapons. In 378, driven to desperation by hunger, the Visigoths mutinied against Rome. Valens hurried out to meet them at the head of an army. He failed to await the reinforcements which were on the way from the West. At Adrianople the emperor and two thirds of his army were slain.

The Barbarians Overrun the Empire. During the reign of Theodosius (379–395) the Visigoths were peacefully settled upon lands which had been granted to them or which they had seized. Their young king Alaric was dealt with tactfully by the emperor who held out to him the promise of a Roman generalship—such an office held much more glamour for Alaric than the kingship of a tribe of some 150,000 barbarian Visigoths.

When Theodosius died in 395 he was succeeded by his two young sons Arcadius and Honorius. Alaric at once demanded the military appointment which had been promised by their father. The young Arcadius who had become emperor in the East not only refused the appointment, he suspended payment of the annual subsidy which had been granted by Theodosius in return for the Visigothic pledge to defend the Roman boundary. Alaric acted promptly. He led his Goths southward into Greece and seized Athens and Corinth. Then after ravaging the Peloponnesus, he headed northward into Illyria.

Upon the death of Theodosius his second son Honorius, a child of eleven, had become emperor in the West. The real ruler of the western empire however was Stilicho, an able general who had served under Theodosius. Stilicho, who was of Vandal descent, had achieved his high position through his ability and devoted service to the empire. He marched eastward with an army and in 403 at Polentia decisively defeated Alaric and his Visigoths. So long as Stilicho lived Alaric was unsuccessful in his attempts to invade the West.

The advance of the Huns through central Europe had stirred up the German tribes which for so long had been peacefully settled outside the Roman boundaries. Stilicho was kept busy marshaling his forces wherever danger threatened. Northern Italy was invaded by a horde of mixed peoples but Stilicho was able to beat them back. In 406–407 Gaul was partly overrun until Stilicho brought his armies to the scene.

During his twenty-three years as commander of the Roman armies and adviser to the young emperor, Stilicho had made many enemies. Courtiers of Roman descent were jealous of the powers of this Vandal, one of whose daughters had married the emperor. Stilicho, like most of the Germans, was an Arian Christian; he was on that account opposed by many of the Athanasian Italians who considered him a heretic. His defense of the empire was complicated by the fact that he dared not leave court for any length of time lest his enemies turn the weak-minded emperor against him.

At last Stilicho's fears were realized. Jealous courtiers persuaded the emperor that his general was disloyal. With Honorius' consent the conspirators assassinated Stilicho in Ravenna. At once Alaric led his Goths into Italy. The courtiers were incapable of meeting the crisis and the emperor fled to Ravenna, a stronghold protected from land attack by stretches of marshland and from which it would be possible to withdraw by ship. Alaric advanced upon Rome. The citizens prepared to defend the city but traitors admitted the Visigoths and the city was put to a three-day sack.

This year 410 was long remembered throughout the Roman world. During the course of a thousand years Rome had been the conqueror. Even the great Hannibal had failed to take the city of Rome. Mistress of a vast empire, for long the center of its civilization, now residence of the Pope whose authority was greater than that of any other Christian bishop, Rome was still the symbol of all the greatness associated with its name even though the center of imperial administration had for some time been located in the East.

After the sack of Rome the Goths marched southward to the tip of the Italian peninsula where Alaric began to assemble a fleet, possibly with a view to carrying his people across the straits into Sicily or even into the rich African provinces. But the fleet was destroyed by storm and Alaric shortly thereafter fell ill and died. Lest the Romans desecrate the grave of their leader, the Visigoths diverted a small river from its course and buried their chieftain in its bed. When the river was again turned back into its natural channel, all those who had secretly buried the body of Alaric were slain so that the secret might never be disclosed.

Alaric was succeeded by his brother-in-law Athaulf who sought to come to terms with the Romans. The Visigoths now progressed northward along the western coast of Italy. They had had enough of plundering and wanted to settle down in a homeland of their own. Athaulf besought the Romans to assign to them a territory where they might establish themselves as Roman subjects.

In the meantime, other tribes poured across the boundaries north of the Alps. Stilicho had been forced to withdraw troops from Britain and Gaul in order to defend Illyria and northern Italy. Britain was abandoned finally by the Romans in 409. In Gaul many of the inhabitants moved back from the boundaries where they would be less likely to suffer from barbarian raids. And the German tribes, pressed by the Huns in their flank, hastened to seize the fertile lands left vacant within the Roman boundaries.

From eastern Germany the Vandals, accompanied by a smaller tribe, the Suevi, crossed the territories of the Burgundians, Franks, and Alamanni, and swept into Gaul, plundering its cities, burning its crops and villages, and slaughtering as they went. The word "vandalism" to this day means ruthless and senseless destruction. By 416 the Vandals had reached the sea and settled in a district bounded roughly by the Loire and Garonne rivers, the region of Aquitania.

The Romans cannily hit upon a means of solving two difficult problems at once. They granted the Visigoths permission to settle in Aquitania on condition they drive out the Vandals. In this the Visigoths were entirely successful and the Vandals and Suevi withdrew southward across the Pyrenees into the

Iberian, or Spanish, peninsula. In 418 the Romans made another treaty with the Visigoths under the terms of which the Visigoths agreed to drive the Vandals out of Spain. In 429 Gaiseric, the young leader of the Vandals, decided to take his people across the straits into the rich Roman provinces of north Africa. For a time the Berbers put up a fierce resistance, but conquest was made easy by the machinations of the ambitious Roman governor of Africa, Count Bonifacius, who had long wished to rule independent of Roman suzerainty. He allied himself with Gaiseric against Rome. Bonifacius very soon regretted his action. The Vandals proved to be no more amiable as allies than as enemies. Bonifacius was soon begging Rome to free him from the Vandals. After subduing Africa the Vandals took to the sea and became pirates.

The Huns, who had entered Europe toward the end of the fourth century and whose attacks had driven the German tribes into the Roman Empire, created a loose empire of their own extending vaguely from the Ural Mountains southward to the Black Sea, thence westward to the Roman borders. Ruling over the formidable tribesmen who had subjugated this extended domain was an able chieftain named Attila. The Romans had purchased peace with the Huns by agreeing to pay an annual subsidy.

In 459 the eastern emperor Marcian suspended payment of the Hunnish tribute. Attila sought compensation at the expense of the weakened western empire. He proposed to the western emperor Valentinian III an alliance by which Attila would marry the emperor's sister and would receive as the lady's dowry, Gaul. The offer was rejected. Attila reconciled himself to the rejection of his suit but decided to take possession of Gaul anyway.

Like Honorius, Valentinian was served by a loyal general of barbarian descent named Aetius. Proceeding into Gaul with a small Roman army, Aetius called upon the Visigoths and other barbarian tribes to join him against the Huns. Near Châlons the Roman and Hunnish armies met in 452. Attila was defeated but his armies were not destroyed. He withdrew eastward into central Europe. At this point Aetius was confronted with a difficult decision. He might keep his allies in the field, pursue and destroy the Huns. But Aetius knew that at any moment his allies might get out of hand and it might be impossible to disband their armies after he had destroyed the enemy. He also knew that one of the reasons he could count on the support of the Germans was the fact that they were united with him against a powerful common enemy. Hoping that Attila's defeat might decide the Hun against another attempt on the Empire, Aetius disbanded his army and returned to Italy.

When the news of Aetius' action reached Attila he turned southward through the Tyrol and entered northern Italy. Fugitives who sought refuge from the Hun in the marshes and islands of the northern Adriatic settled on the spot and founded the future city of Venice. Valentinian fled to Ravenna like Honorius before him. Aetius was without sufficient forces at hand to stop the invader and Italy lay at the mercy of the Hun.

At this critical moment the bishop of Rome, Pope Leo I, led a delegation from Rome to the headquarters of the chieftain Attila. The Hun was much impressed with the bearing and words of his distinguished visitor. By the use of persuasion and gifts the pope obtained Attila's withdrawal from Italy. The following year Attila died and shortly thereafter most of the Huns returned to Asia.

No sooner had the Hunnish threat been removed than Rome received another heavy blow. Through the folly of the emperor, Aetius was killed and shortly thereafter Valentinian himself was assassinated. The next emperor was stoned to death by the populace in the streets of Rome within a year of his accession. Three days after this incident Gaiseric and his Vandals descended upon Rome from the sea and subjected the city to a two weeks' sack (455).

Collapse of the Empire in the West. After the withdrawal of the Vandals the Roman soldiers in Italy, now mostly Germans, seized control of the government and set up a series of puppet emperors. Ricimer the Sueve was succeeded by a former lieutenant of Attila named Orestes. The soldiers then placed upon the imperial throne the son of Orestes who was still a child, calling him Romulus Augustulus or "Romulus the Little Augustus." Orestes, who ruled in the name of his son, earned the ill will of the soldiers perhaps because he failed to provide sufficient gifts and land grants. He was seized and killed and the Little Augustus was retired to a villa on a pension. Odoacer, who had brought about the overthrow of Orestes, now decided to end the sham of imperial rule in Italy. In 476 he sent the imperial insignia to the eastern emperor Zeno. This act, by convention, dates the fall of the Roman Empire in the west. Actually it was no more than an acknowledgment of what was already a fact.

But Zeno was not satisfied to allow Odoacer to govern Italy as his lieutenant. The Ostrogoths, who had submitted to the Huns a century before, had been recently settled inside the boundaries of the empire in Pannonia. Zeno had a high opinion of their young king Theodoric who had spent half his life in Constantinople and had developed a respect for and an understanding of Roman institutions. The emperor commissioned Theodoric to conquer Odoacer. Italy finally came under Ostrogothic control in 493 when Theodoric treacherously pretended to make peace with Odoacer and invited him to a banquet. Theodoric assassinated his enemy with his own hands, cleaving him in half with a single blow of his sword. In astonishment the Ostrogoth exclaimed, "The wretch can have no bones!"

By the end of the fifth century the Latin-speaking western half of the Roman Empire was broken up into Germanic kingdoms ruled over by barbarian minorities who had made the older and more civilized population subject to them. To the south lay the Vandal Kingdom of Africa. On the west, stretching across the Pyrenees into Spain and western France, was the Kingdom of the Visigoths. Farther to the north the Franks had begun the westward and southward expansion which was eventually to give them control of all Gaul. Along the Saone and Rhone rivers the Burgundians were making their way southward, while the Ostrogoths held the Ligurian coast east of the Rhone, all Italy and Sicily, and a considerable area stretching northward from the east coast of the Adriatic to the Danube.

18 THE AGE OF JUSTINIAN

In 527 there came to the throne of the Eastern Roman Empire a man of thirty-five who had been carefully trained by his uncle and predecessor for the important office which he was to hold for thirty-eight years. The reign of Justinian was both glorious and tragic. His achievements were great; his ambitions even greater. He sought to restore all the glory and greatness of the Roman past. His ambitious program involved the reconquest of the West, the reform of the unwieldy administration in the East, the successful union of the two halves of the Empire under a single administration, and the reinvigoration of the cultural, political, and economic life of the whole. The wonder is not that Justinian failed to realize his designs but rather that he came so near to succeeding.

Military Exploits. When Justinian ascended the throne, the Empire was at war with its powerful enemy Persia. This war continued until 533 when Justinian arranged a peace with Chosroes I in order that he might devote his entire attention to the reconquest of the West. His first move was against the Vandal Kingdom of Africa. A carefully organized expedition, carried in five hundred transports and guarded by ninety-two war galleys sailed from Constantinople in 533. The Vandals for a while maintained a vigorous resistance but Justinian's armies, under the leadership of the able general Belisarius, finally triumphed.

With Africa under his control, and while his fleets subjugated the Mediterranean islands, Justinian organized his forces for the conquest of Europe. He undertook what would in modern times be called a gigantic pincers movement. Belisarius landed in Italy with one army in 535 and began the conquest of that peninsula. Later another army landed in Spain

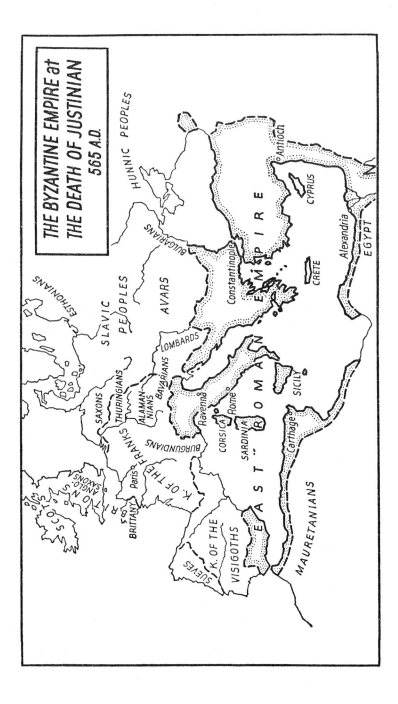

THE BYZANTINE EMPIRE at
THE DEATH OF JUSTINIAN
565 A.D.

HUNNIC PEOPLES

BULGARIANS

ESTHONIANS

SLAVIC PEOPLES

AVARS

SAXONS

THURINGIANS

ALAMANNIANS

BAVARIANS

LOMBARDS

EMPIRE

Constantinople

Antioch

CYPRUS

CRETE

Alexandria

EGYPT

SCOTS

PICTS

ANGLO-SAXONS

BRITANNY

Paris

FRANKS

BURGUNDIANS

K. OF THE

SUEVES

K. OF THE
VISIGOTHS

CORSICA

SARDINIA

Ravenna

Rome

EAST

ROMAN

SICILY

Carthage

MAURETANIANS

and succeeded in subjugating only the southern part of the peninsula. The undertaking was made difficult by resistance in Africa; the Berbers in particular continued to resist and this tied up a number of Justinian's troops that might otherwise have been used in the conquest of Europe. Had sufficient forces been placed at the disposal of Belisarius, the conquest of Italy might have been achieved quickly. As it was the struggle lasted twenty years. Of course Justinian was not unreasonable in expecting that since he had come to free the Athanasian Italians from the rule of the Arian Goths, the least the Italians could do would be to join Belisarius and fight for their freedom. This they seemed unwilling to do. And new dangers made necessary a dispersal of the forces of the Empire.

The Avars, an Asiatic people related to the Huns, invaded Europe in the sixth century and, settling in Dacia, attacked the Roman border districts. A southward expansion of the Slavic peoples of northeastern Europe forced the Lombards into Pannonia and threatened Justinian in still another quarter. In 540 Chosroes resumed his war with the Empire. From 542 to 546 Constantinople and the Empire were ravaged by a disastrous epidemic of the bubonic plague. In 559 the Avars and Slavs advanced to the very gates of Constantinople but were driven off by Belisarius.

The Legal Reforms of Justinian. Justinian's military conquests would have sufficed to make his name memorable in history. And yet, had he not conquered an inch of territory, his great legal reforms would have secured his fame. By the sixth century the laws under which the Empire was governed were in a very confused state. For centuries emperors had issued edicts called *constitutio* or constitutions, which now comprised a formidable mass of law often contradictory or repetitious. In addition there had been accumulated the opinions and decisions of recognized jurists, far too large a mass of material to be digested by the individual even were it made available in a single collection, which it was not.

Justinian appointed a committee of jurists to study the imperial constitutions and to reduce them to a single body of useful law. In 529 this volume of laws was issued as a single imperial edict which canceled and replaced all previous constitutions. The book was called the *Codex Constitutionem* and is known as *The Code*. Another committee then made a study of judicial decisions and opinions. These in turn were coordinated and issued in a book known as *The Digest*. The great lawyer Tribonian, who had served on both committees, then drew up a shortened text or summary of the laws of the Empire to be used by lawyers and students of law. This was called *The Institutes*. These three works, plus a collection of new edicts issued by Justinian, constituted a great legal reform which profoundly influenced later history. For during the Middle Ages *The Code,* as the whole collection came to be known, was made the basis of the study of civil law from the twelfth century onward.

Byzantine Art. With the help of the able but venal John of Cappadocia, Justinian reformed taxation and the administration of the government. Normally this reform would have lightened the tax load for the citizen. But although the reform resulted in a greater tax yield to the government, extraordinary expenditures actually increased the tax burden during Justinian's reign. In many ways, however, the citizen was able to recognize that the revenues were being employed for his benefit. A series of formidable border fortresses were erected in the north to keep out Huns and Slavs. And Justinian launched a program of public works which added much to the convenience and beauty of the capital and other eastern cities.

Most famous of the edifices erected by Justinian was the magnificent church of St. Sophia in Constantinople. Its great central dome, 108 feet in diameter, rose to a height of 180 feet above the floor. It was supported upon pillars between two lower half-domes which spanned an area 216 feet in length. The great church was adorned with many-colored marbles and lavishly decorated with intricate mosaics against backgrounds of dark blue and gold. These mosaics, which characterize Byzantine decoration, were of many patterns and pictured scenes formed of literally millions of bits of colored glass skillfully fitted together.

The Byzantine style was employed in Italy particularly in Ravenna, which became the headquarters of the imperial government there, and in Rome. It continued to be employed in the Eastern Empire and its influence is marked in later Moslem architecture, in Russia, and in many parts of Europe. St. Mark's cathedral in Venice is an excellent example of Byzantine architecture of a later date.

Theodora and the Nika Riot. During the early part of his reign Justinian was aided by his wife, the beautiful and talented Theodora. Theodora, the daughter of a bear-keeper in the circus in Constantinople, was a well known actress when she first met Justinian. Despite the opposition of the court the young heir to the throne insisted upon marrying the woman of his choice and when he was crowned emperor in 527 he had Theodora crowned empress with him.

Theodora's firmness and judgment often helped her husband to face difficult situations. Shortly after his accession Justinian was confronted with a revolt of factions in Constantinople which sought to change the dynasty. For several days the city was in the hands of the rioters and the weakened palace garrison appeared unable to cope with the situation. Preparations were made for flight although it seemed probable that if the emperor abandoned his capital the people might regard the act as an abandonment of his cause. At this point Theodora announced her intention to die as empress rather than flee from the revolution. She persuaded the council, advising Justinian to attack the triumphant rebels as they gathered in the Hippodrome to celebrate their victory. The factions were taken completely by surprise and the famous Nika revolt was suppressed with great slaughter. The throne was never again seriously imperiled in Justinian's lifetime.

19   MOHAMMED AND THE EXPANSION OF ISLAM

Toward the end of his life, as the emperor Justinian looked out over his vast empire, he must have sought to judge the permanence of his achievement. What forces threatened its security? Parthia, or Persia, populous and rich, had ever been hostile to Rome. Was Persia the menace of the Roman future? Or would the greatest danger reveal itself in another quarter, to the north where already the Avars—Asiatic nomads who had overridden the Bulgars and Slavs—were advancing southward into the Balkan peninsula? Further to the west the Lombards threatened Italy, now the Exarchate of Ravenna. And still further away beyond the Alps the Franks, having conquered Aquitania, Burgundy, Provence, Alamannia, Bavaria, and Thuringia, now, under the grandsons of Clovis, seemed content to rule what was already in their possession. Would they soon be stirred up to covet and seize the Roman lands of the West?

The West, North, and East—each held a threat. But to the south all seemed secure. Yet within a decade of Justinian's death there was born in Arabia the prophet of a new religion whose teaching was to kindle a fire of religious zeal that was to sweep across the world from the Atlantic Ocean to India and China.

The Arabs. Between Asia and Africa lies the Arabian peninsula. Except for the narrow neck of the Isthmus of Suez it is cut off from Africa by the Red Sea and the Gulf of Aden, which opens into the Indian Ocean to the south. To the east are the Arabian Sea and the Persian Gulf into which flow the waters of the great rivers of Mesopotamia, the Tigris and Euphrates. The Arabian peninsula is a dry tableland. In most places it receives just enough rainfall to provide sparse pasturage for the few flocks which the nomadic Arabs must ceaselessly drive along to fresh pastures as soon as the thin verdure is consumed. So rigorous are the physical conditions that prevail throughout most of the peninsula that nature has imposed upon man a mode of existence which successive waves of civilization have left unchanged. Life in the dry wastes of Arabia is the same today as it was in the remote past. In Mohammed's day, as in ours, the desert Arab, or Bedouin, was a nomad and a herdsman. The family group or tribe, led by its elder or sheik, moved from one sparse pastureland to another. Often tribes fought for possession of the grassland or water supply essential to maintain life. The only unity that existed among these tribes was a similarity of custom and belief. They all worshiped the same type of tribal nature gods. One object of reverence they held in common. That was the great black stone at Mecca—possibly meteorite in origin—which was enclosed in a rectangular structure and referred to accordingly as the Kaaba or Cube. During the sacred months pilgrims came from all over Arabia to worship before the great stone and the idols erected within the enclosure.

Mecca was situated in the western part of the peninsula in Hejaz which bordered the Red Sea. Between the low mountain ranges of Hejaz ran the caravan routes connecting the Red Sea with the Fertile Crescent to the north—a populous region bordering the north Arabian Desert which included Syria, Mesopotamia, and, linking these two, a strip of fertile land which stretched between the desert and the Taurus Mountains.

Mohammed. The city of Mecca was dominated by the Kuraish, a tribe that had established the right to levy a tax on all pilgrims. One clan of the Kuraish, the Banu Hashim, held a monopoly of the privilege of selling drinking water to the pilgrims. It was to this clan that Mohammed belonged.

Mohammed, who was born around 570 A.D., was early left an orphan. As a boy he tended sheep and camels for his relatives and as he grew older accompanied caravans into Yemen and Syria as a camel driver. In time he entered the employ of a wealthy widow, Khadijah. After conducting Khadijah's commercial ventures with marked success for some years, he married his employer.

For fifteen years Mohammed lived the life of a man of business. Little is known of this period in his life. He was subject to occasional seizures during which he lost consciousness, foamed at the mouth, and suffered fever and headaches. Impressed by Mohammed's utterances during these fits or seizures, his family and associates came to regard them as divinely inspired. The family formed the practice of noting down his words upon shards of broken pottery, palm leaves, or flat stones and these were collected in a box.

Mohammed eventually became convinced of his prophetic mission. He retired to the caves of Mt. Hira near Mecca where, during periods of fasting and meditation, he clarified his religious views. When he began to preach, his fellow Meccans, who had known him from childhood, laughed at him. But by degrees he won a following among his own clan.

Mohammed's Religion. The religious teachings of Mohammed embodied the principal ideas of the three great religions of the Near East with which he had undoubtedly become familiar during the course of his travels with caravans. God or Allah he conceived to be the creator and judge of mankind. He believed in an after life, a day of judgment, heaven and hell—beliefs which were common to both Christian and Jew. The struggle of forces of good and evil in the world, the central thought of the Persian religion of Zoroaster, had a great influence upon Mohammedan teaching as it had upon the religions of the Jews and Christians.

Mohammed's conception of heaven was one which would surely appeal to the desert dweller who so often suffered from heat and thirst. To him paradise was a place of cool glades and green meadows, of springs and flowing streams. It abounded with all manner of good things, delicacies, fruits, streams of milk and honey, wine with no headache in it, perfumes, and silks, and jewels. In this realm dark-eyed Houris, maidens of rarest beauty, ministered to the wants of the saved.

Mohammed preached that there was but one god, Allah,

who from time to time sent prophets among men to guide and teach them. Such were the prophets of the Hebrews. Jesus too he reverenced as a prophet but not as the son of God. Mohammed was believed by his followers to be the last and the greatest of these prophets. He set up a religious discipline for his followers. Five times a day the Mohammedan was required to turn toward the Kaaba at Mecca for prayer. Almsgiving was required. Fasting, especially during the holy month of Ramadan, was obligatory. And finally the Mohammedan must make at least one pilgrimage in his lifetime to the holy city of Mecca.

The Hegira and After. As Mohammed spread his belief among the Banu Hashim, attacking the traditional worship at many of the Meccan shrines, the Kuraish turned against him. Some of his followers fled to Abyssinia. After the death of Khadijah, Mohammed and a number of his faithful friends fled northward to the city of Medina. This flight is the famous *Hegira* which is the date of the beginning of the Mohammedan calendar.

In Medina, a city some two hundred and seventy miles north of Mecca, Mohammed was well received. He gathered around him many converts and built a mosque as a place of worship and assembly. For a while his role was a peaceful one. But as the number of his followers increased he organized raids on the Meccan caravans trading with Syria. His teachings were spread throughout Arabia and the desert tribes accepted him as a prophet and leader. His following in Medina became so great that he ruled the city. At this point he determined to convert those who resisted his preaching by the sword. Enemies were assassinated. The Jews of Medina were given the choice of accepting conversion or forfeiting their lives. Some six hundred heads of families were killed and their families sold into slavery.

In 630 Mohammed led his forces against the city of Mecca which quickly capitulated. The old idols of the Kaaba enclosure were destroyed but the black stone remained an object of worship. Mecca became a political as well as a religious

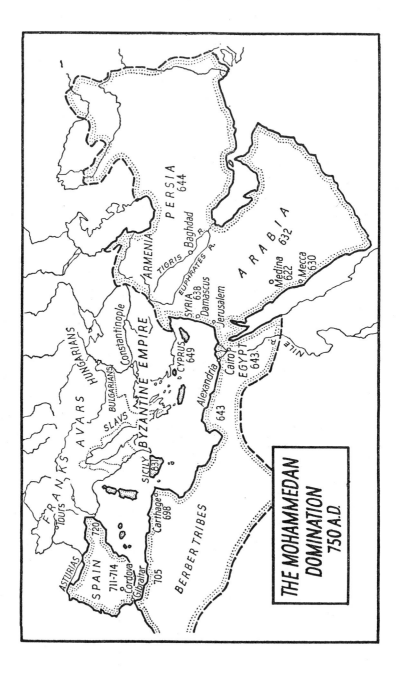

FRANKS
Tours
ASTURIAS
SPAIN
711-714
720
Cordova
Gibraltar
705

AVARS
HUNGARIANS
SLAVS
BULGARIANS
Constantinople

BYZANTINE EMPIRE

SICILY
831
Carthage
698

BERBER TRIBES

ARMENIA
PERSIA
644
TIGRIS R.
Baghdad
EUPHRATES R.
SYRIA
638
Damascus
Jerusalem

CYPRUS
649

Alexandria
643
Cairo
EGYPT
643
NILE

ARABIA

Medina
622
Mecca
630

ARABIA
632

THE MOHAMMEDAN
DOMINATION
750 A.D.

capital for the Arabians and the country exhibited a unity of thought and loyalty that was new in its history.

When Mohammed died in 631, his able kinsman and successor, Abu Bekr, collected his inspired utterances and caused them to be issued in a sacred book, the *Koran*. Those portions of Arabia which had not yet acknowledged Mohammed as prophet and leader were conquered and converted by force. Arabia was unified and Moslem rule was extended to the borders of Persia. Upon the death of Abu Bekr in 634 there began the extraordinary era of Mohammedan conquest which resulted in the creation of the vast empire referred to at the beginning of the chapter.

The Expansion of Islam. The rapid conquest of the Arabs cannot be explained without taking into account the weakened condition of the two great empires which were its chief victims. For the Arabs were not numerous; their land, except in the west, supported only a thin population. True, the Arabs were spurred on by fanatical zeal and the belief that the soul of the soldier who fell fighting for religion was received directly into heaven. But this of itself is not sufficient to explain the capitulation of great and populous regions skilled in the techniques of civilization and experienced in the art of war.

We have already considered how heavy was the burden which the great undertakings of Justinian placed upon the Roman citizenry. The tax-supported bureaucracy continued to grow after Justinian's death. The struggle with Persia was resumed and continued intermittently until both empires were exhausted. Bitter religious schisms divided the Christians of the Eastern Roman Empire, for Arianism was revived and other heresies appeared. Persia too was rent by social and religious discontent.

The Arabs, inured to hardship and warfare, fought with reckless fury. Conquered peoples were offered a triple choice: the Koran, tribute, or the sword. That is, one might accept the Mohammedan religion and be freed from the obligation to pay taxes; one might submit to Mohammedan overlordship, pay tribute, and retain one's religious faith; or one might die in defense of his religious and political allegiance. At this juncture the syncretic character of Mohammedanism became extremely important, for as it embodied the principal beliefs of the people conquered, Christian, Jew, and Zoroastrian often found it easy to accept Mohammed as a prophet without making any important change in beliefs already held.

During the decade of Omar's rule, from 634 to 644, Syria, Egypt, and Persia were subjugated by the Moslems. After the death of Omar dissension within the Arab ranks slowed up their conquests for a time. The Berbers of Africa who, except along the coast, had never been assimilated by Romans or Phoenicians, continued to resist with success for nearly a century. They were finally conquered by the religion of Mohammed rather than by force of arms.

In 711, under the leadership of General Tarik, the Arabs and Berbers crossed the straits into Spain near the great rock which was named in honor of the Arab general Gebr-al-Tarik or Rock of Tarik. Spain was then overrun by the Moslems who crossed the Pyrenees and began a series of raids into Frankish territory. But in 732, at the Battle of Tours, Charles Martel and his Franks checked the further advance of the Arabs into Gaul.

In the eastern Mediterranean the Arabs constructed a fleet and by land and by sea sought to break once and for all the power of the Eastern Roman Empire. Under the able leadership of Leo III, the Isaurian, the city of Constantinople sustained a series of attacks ending with a year's siege in 717–718. With the help of Greek fire, the "liquid fire" of ancient warfare, the Arabs were beaten and their advance into eastern Europe checked.

In the Far East the Arabs reached the mouth of the Indus River in the year 711, the same in which they began their conquest of Spain. They succeeded in subjugating the region of Sind, but further advance was checked by a coalition of the Rajput kingdoms until the end of the tenth century.

In 751 the Arabs defeated the Chinese in battle but they failed to extend their conquest to China. Mohammedanism was spread through China by peaceful means. Active trade developed between the Chinese and the Arabs and this led to an infiltration of Arabs into China. Many of these found employment as mercenaries in the Chinese civil wars. The Chinese were tolerant of Mohammedanism as they were of Christianity and both religions won converts among the Chinese. For a time the Arab empire was ruled by the Omayyad family which established the Moslem capital at Damascus where it remained until 750. But the Arab empire was soon divided by religious and political dissension. In 750 the descendants of Mohammed's uncle, Abbas, overthrew the Omayyads. One member of the deposed dynasty escaped assassination and fled to Cordova in Spain where he set up a new Caliphate. The Abbasids removed the capital to the new city of Baghdad. The splendor of this great city and the Caliphs who ruled there has been made familiar in the tales of the *Arabian Nights*. Many of the stories describe adventures of the famous Caliph Harun-al-Rashid (766–809) who was a wise ruler and a patron of learning.

In the ninth century Egypt, under the leadership of the descendants of Mohammed's daughter Fatima, broke away from the Caliphate of Baghdad. Later Syria came under the control of the Fatimite Caliphate or the Caliphate of Cairo as it was sometimes called.

Moslem Culture. Before closing this discussion of Mohammedan conquest let us take account briefly of the great civilization which continued to flourish under Mohammedan rule for many centuries to come. It is obvious that the Arabs, a fairly primitive tribal people, did not create the civilization which is associated with them and which flourished in Africa, Asia, and Mohammedan Spain, during Europe's Middle Ages. The decline of the Roman West long preceded its political collapse. It was in recognition of this fact that Diocletian and later Constantine centered their administration in Nicomedia and Byzantium respectively, for the eastern Mediterranean had once again become a dominant center of population, wealth, and cultural vitality. The distinctive architectural style which characterized the building of Justinian's era was a product of this eastern civilization which had been developed well before his time. The oriental despotism of the eastern Roman court, its manners, and dress, and ceremony, were all products of the new culture and were something very different from the earlier life which centered about Rome and which derived from ancient Greece.

The Arabs gave a new unity and spiritual impulse to this civilization. They overthrew much of the cumbersome Roman administration and liquidated the burden of debt which weighed so heavily upon the taxpayers. Many cultural elements were brought together and fused; Greek, Babylonian, and even Indian mathematics and science were merged. The fundamental unity of this culture is evident in its architectural monuments. St. Sophia, built by Justinian; the Taj Mahal, constructed by a Moslem ruler of seventeenth-century India; and the mosque at Cordova are all recognizably akin. How profoundly different in concept and feeling they are from the Gothic cathedrals of Medieval Europe or the classical temples of ancient Greece and Rome! The Arabs did not create this civilization; they were assimilated by it.

PART FOUR
Feudal Europe

496	Clovis united Franks and was converted to Roman Catholicism
590–604	Pope Gregory the Great
732	Charles Martel, Frankish Mayor of the Palace, defeated the Mohammedans at Tours
756	Donation of Pepin
771–814	Charlemagne
786–809	Harun-al-Rashid, Caliph of Baghdad
800	Charlemagne crowned emperor at Rome
814–887	Louis the Pious
842	Oaths of Strasbourg
843	Treaty of Verdun
852	Boris, first Christian King of Bulgaria
862	Rurik the Swede founded principality of Novgorod
874	Norsemen settled in Iceland
910	Monastery of Cluny founded
911	Rollo the Norseman settled in Normandy by agreement with Charles the Simple
981	Norsemen reached Greenland
1000	Norsemen reached Vineland, on the mainland of North America

20 THE FRANKS

Although the Moslems extended their conquests through Africa and Asia they were checked at two points when they sought to overrun Europe. The valiant defense of Constantinople under Leo the Isaurian blocked their advance into Europe from the east. And at Tours in 732 the Franks under Charles Martel turned back the plundering armies which had advanced into Europe through Spain. Who were the Franks?

In the middle of the fifth century the Franks were a disunited group of Teutonic tribes settled along the Rhine River. When the Huns attacked the Roman West, the Franks joined the other Germans in turning back Attila at Châlons. They remained disunited until Clovis, king of the Salian group, conquered and united his Frankish neighbors.

Clovis was a barbarian. The Franks had not been converted to Christianity like many of the other German peoples. When the Christianized Germans—Visigoths, Ostrogoths, Vandals, Lombards and others—overran the Roman Empire they imposed their rule upon a civilized population that was Roman in culture and religion. The Germans were Arian Christians and were consequently regarded by their subjects as heretics. The religious difference between the Germans and their subjects was one of many factors that led to trouble between the rulers and ruled. And the Roman clergy, who were in many cases all that remained of the imperial Roman administration, remained leaders and protectors of the subject people.

The Conquests of Clovis. Having conquered the Franks, Clovis turned a covetous eye upon the territories of his near neighbors. He attacked the Alamanni to the south and tried to subdue them. They fought back vigorously and Clovis' situation became desperate. Some time earlier Clovis had married a Burgundian princess, Clotilda, whose family had adopted Roman Christianity and had then been overthrown by their Arian Christian kinsmen. Tradition has it that Clovis prayed to the

Christian god of his wife promising that if Christ would give him victory over his enemies he would adopt the Christian faith for himself and his people. Clovis did win over the Alamanni. Whatever the process by which he was converted to Christianity, the event was of great influence upon his future. For when he began his attacks upon the Arian rulers of former Roman territories, he appeared to their Athanasian Christian subjects as a deliverer. The support of the Roman Church and of the Roman subjects of his enemies aided him greatly in overthrowing his enemies.

Having subdued the Alemanni, Clovis next turned on the Burgundians and reduced them to the position of a tributary kingdom. He then invaded the Kingdom of the Visigoths and in a surprisingly short time overran all the northern part of their kingdom to the Pyrenees. During the latter part of his reign Clovis devoted his energies to consolidating his conquests. By treachery and murder he eliminated all those who stood in his way. Ruthless as were his methods, he is regarded as the creator of the French nation and the first French king.

Historians used to debate with considerable feeling the question whether France was Roman or German in origin. One group insisted that the population of Gaul was predominantly Latin in blood and culture and that the Germanic conquerors did not change their condition materially. Others insisted that the French institutions of a later age were German in origin. It now seems reasonable to acknowledge the role of both German and Latin influences in the shaping of France.

One unfortunate Frankish custom was the cause of much misfortune and hardship. This was the practice of dividing up the kingdom among the sons of a ruler upon his death. This usually resulted in a struggle among the sons for domination which was attended with destructive civil wars. Clovis parted his kingdom among his four sons and the long period of disunity and strife was begun. However, there were frequent periods when the Frankish domain was reunited under a single ruler and the ideal of unity kept alive.

After Dagobert, who died in 638, there ruled a series of violent Merovingians who occupied themselves with personal squabbles and vicious living. Queen Fredigonda assassinated her husband. Brunhilda debauched her own children in order that she might continue to control the Frankish state. Her end was a fitting one; she was tied to the tail of a wild horse and torn to pieces. During the reign of these corrupt "do-nothing" kings, the Frankish nobles ruled like independent little kings on their own lands. But the unity of France was preserved through the efforts of the Mayors of the Palace. Originally the Mayors of the Palace were stewards in the king's household. But they gradually took over greater functions until they came to be the controlling officers of the court. Under Pepin of Heristal the office of Mayor was made hereditary in Pepin's family. The Mayors became the real rulers of France. They put down rebellious nobles and secured the Merovingian dominion.

One of the ablest of the Mayors of the Palace was Charles Martel. He attacked Aquitania, Alamannia, and Bavaria, all of which had overthrown the rule of the Merovingians and restored their own dynasties, and brought them back under the control of the Frankish kings. It was this same Charles Martel who in 732 defeated the Moslems at the battle of Tours and thus saved western Europe from Mohammedan domination.

As we know, the Lombards invaded Italy after the death of Justinian and set up a Germanic kingdom in the northern part of the peninsula. This Lombard conquest cut off Rome from other parts of Byzantine Italy that remained under eastern rule with the result that the pope became the secular as well as the spiritual ruler of central Italy. When the Lombards encroached upon this central Italian domain, the popes appealed to the eastern emperor for aid. When help was not forthcoming, they appealed to the Franks as Catholic Christians to defend them and the people over whom they ruled from Lombard domination.

Charles Martel had been unable to respond to the papal appeal. But so firmly had he restored the unity and power of the Frankish rulers that his son Pepin "The Short," who succeeded him as Mayor of the Palace, was free to give his attention to the Roman problem. First, however, Pepin determined to put an end to the sham of Merovingian rule. With the approval of the pope and the consent of the Frankish nobility, he deposed the last Merovingian king and sent him into a cloister. In 751 he proclaimed himself king and was anointed by the church.

Twice Pepin invaded Italy and defeated the Lombards. He took from them the land along the east coast of Italy which had comprised the Exarchate of Ravenna and instead of restoring it to the eastern emperor he conferred it upon the pope. This is the famous "Donation of Pepin" which, during the Middle Ages, was one of the bases for the papal claim to a temporal domain.

Pepin died in 768 and, according to Frankish custom, divided his kingdom between his two sons, Carloman and Charles. But Carloman died in 771 and the entire domain was left to Charles whom we know as Charles the Great or Charlemagne.

Charlemagne. Charlemagne took up the work of Charles Martel and Pepin. During the forty-six years of his rule he was almost ceaselessly engaged in suppressing those Frankish nobles who were still inclined to resist the monarchy and in extending the borders of the Frankish domain.

Early in Charlemagne's reign the Lombards again seized several papal cities and dispatched an army against Rome. Pope Hadrian I appealed to Charlemagne for help. Failing to bring about a settlement by diplomacy, Charles crossed the Alps with an army and laid siege to Pavia into which the Lombards had retreated. While the siege was in progress in 774, Charles visited Rome where he confirmed the territorial Donation of Pepin. Upon the collapse of Lombard resistance, he deposed Desiderius, the Lombard king, and assumed for himself the title King of the Lombards.

Saxony, a German kingdom lying between the Ems and Elbe rivers, had given the Franks a good deal of trouble by raiding Frankish territories. Charlemagne determined to subdue these warlike neighbors and secure his borders. But the Saxons resisted all efforts to pacify them and Charlemagne determined to subjugate and Christianize Saxony. Despite the many other problems which demanded his attention he persisted in this undertaking. During a period of thirty years he launched some twenty campaigns against the Saxons. After each conquest they revolted, burned the Christian churches and slaughtered the priests, until Charlemagne adopted the most extreme measures against them. On one occasion ten thousand Saxons were deported after a revolt. On another forty-five hundred were slaughtered at Verdun. Saxony was finally "pacified" in 804. It was formed into a Frankish province under the rule of Charlemagne's counts. Monasteries were established as centers of Christianity and of education, and bishoprics were set up. In time towns developed about many of these religious centers.

In order to secure the borders of his empire Charlemagne extended his conquests further to the east. Bavaria was reconquered. The Avars, an Asiatic people who had entered Europe after the withdrawal of the Huns, were attacked and their chief fortress captured in 796. The Avars became a tributary people.

Aquitania had revolted when Charlemagne succeeded to the Frankish throne. This territory was in its turn subdued and placed under the rule of Charlemagne's counts. Later, Charlemagne's son Louis was made King of Aquitania. From Aquitania Charles advanced across the Pyrenees and established border counties known as *Marches* in Spain. The chief function of the March Count was to maintain a sufficient military force to defend the empire against outside attack.

The Carolingian Empire. In the year 800 Charlemagne visited Rome to investigate charges that had been made against Pope Leo III. The affair was settled and on Christmas Day Charles attended mass in St. Peter's church. There he was crowned emperor by the pope. Charlemagne's secretary and biographer, Einhart, declares that Charles was taken by surprise by this act, but there is evidence that the crowning had been planned in advance by both Charlemagne and the pope.

The coronation of Charlemagne proved to be of great importance for the future of Europe and the papacy. The east-

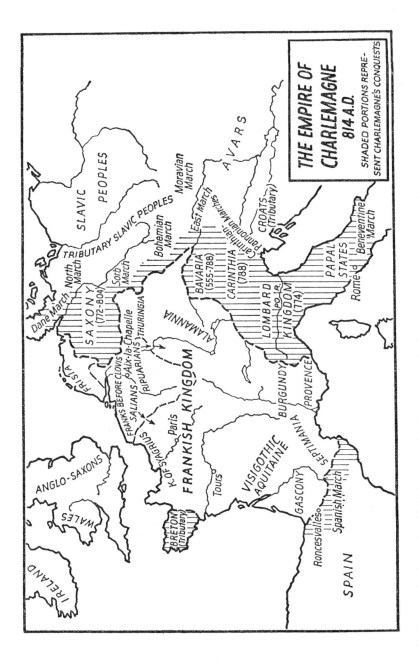

THE EMPIRE OF CHARLEMAGNE 814 A.D.

SHADED PORTIONS REPRESENT CHARLEMAGNE'S CONQUESTS

ern ruler, the notorious Empress Irene, bitterly opposed the restoration of a Western Roman Empire especially as it had been done without her consent. It was not until two years before his death that Charlemagne's title was recognized in the East.

In no sense was the ancient Roman Empire restored by the bestowal of a title upon Charlemagne. Regardless of what name it may have borne the Frankish empire was created by the conquests of her rulers. It was a continental European empire, not a Mediterranean one. The life of its people was primitive and local. Its unity was the energy and activity of Charlemagne and when that force was removed its fundamental disunity was revealed. And yet, such was the genius of this great man that the illusion of unity was not dissipated at his death.

The counts who ruled locally throughout the land had learned that swift punishment would overtake anyone who openly defied the ruler. Perforce they submitted and obeyed Charlemagne's edicts. Interspersed among the territories of the nobles were the estates of the crown, scattered throughout the length and breadth of the empire. The imperial court was wherever Charlemagne happened to be although Rome and Aachen, where the emperor built a palace, were the official capitals. Of necessity Charles was served by a number of officials who looked after the administration of the crown lands and the collection of dues and services owed by the nobles. The church and its administration were also controlled by Charlemagne who appointed bishops and abbots and saw to it that they performed their spiritual and secular duties.

Charlemagne divided his empire into districts into which he sent each year two representatives called *missi dominici,* king's messengers. Their functions were varied. They saw to it that no one took possession of any part of the royal domain, that Charlemagne's edicts or *capitularies* were known and enforced by the counts and their assistant vicars. They heard complaints and made certain that the counts ruled justly and did not abuse their powers. As a rule one of the *missi* was a churchman who visited the monasteries and churches while the other was a noble. In order to improve the condition of his subjects, Charlemagne forced the nobles to endow schools and churches. He improved the education of the clergy in order that they might instruct the youth. He forbade the clergy to marry, to keep concubines, to carry arms, to hunt, or to meddle in worldly affairs. He standardized the church service which in the course of time had been altered and distributed model sermons to the priests as a means of improving the quality of their instruction. He reformed church music and imported singers from Italy to demonstrate the correct performance of the liturgy. Charlemagne founded a palace school at Aachen and brought to it the most distinguished scholars of his day. While the original purpose of this school was the instruction of Charlemagne's children and the children of the nobles who would play a part in the future government of the empire, he admitted on an equal footing children of commoners who displayed an aptitude for learning.

21   BREAKUP OF THE CAROLINGIAN EMPIRE

Louis the Pious and the Grandsons of Charlemagne. When Charlemagne died in 814, he was succeeded by his only surviving son Louis, known in later history as Louis the Pious. Louis was a very different man from Charlemagne. He had been well educated at the palace school founded by his father. He was tolerant, generous, and moral—too civilized a man altogether to command understanding, respect, and obedience from the uncouth and warlike nobility over which he ruled.

Louis applied himself with intelligence to the solution of a number of problems. He proclaimed the unity and indivisibility of the empire and associated with him in the government his oldest son and successor Lothair. His younger sons Pepin and Louis were given the rule of Aquitania and Bavaria respectively but were under the imperial authority.

Charlemagne had not clarified the relationship between the

pope and the empire. Louis now declared the Papal States to be a Frankish protectorate ruled over by the pope for which the pope was obliged to take an oath of allegiance to the emperor. But papal elections were not to be interfered with and the pope was acknowledged the spiritual head of the church.

Charlemagne's nephew Bernard had been placed in charge of the Lombard Kingdom in Italy. Mistrusting Louis' proclamation of the indivisibility of the empire, Bernard revolted. The emperor condemned him to be blinded in punishment for his insubordination. Bernard died from the effects of this barbaric punishment and Louis, holding himself responsible for his cousin's death, then did public penance. Charlemagne would have felt no such scruples. To the rough nobles this Christian act of penance made their emperor seem weak and contemptible.

When Louis sought to create an appanage for Charles the Bald, a fourth son of his second marriage, his other sons, backed by the dissatisfied nobles, revolted. The civil wars thus begun continued after Louis' death in 840 although Pepin had died and Charles the Bald had become ruler of Aquitania. But neither Charles nor Louis of Bavaria were willing to rule as vassals of the emperor Lothair.

At Fontenoy in 841 Lothair was defeated in battle. His brothers then appeared before their assembled supporters at Strasbourg and swore to continue the war until Lothair was defeated. These Strasbourg Oaths are interesting for they reveal the differences between the eastern or German half of the empire and the western Latin half. Louis the German took the oath in the Latin tongue while Charles took his oath in the German speech. This was so that the nobles of the opposite faction might understand to what each brother was committing himself. Thus it becomes clear that whereas the Latin culture and speech of Roman Gaul survived in the region that became France, it had not taken permanent hold in the Rhineland and eastward, for these regions remained predominantly German.

Despite the efforts of Louis, therefore, the old Frankish custom of dividing up the kingdom was re-established. In 843 the brothers drew up a treaty at Verdun which gave Charles most of modern France and Louis most of the German part of the empire including Saxony, Franconia, and Bavaria. Lothair retained the imperial title along with a narrow territory stretching along the Rhine and across the Alps into Italy. Upon the death of Lothair in 855 his brothers seized and divided up the northern part of this domain (Lotharingia, from which came Lorraine) north of the Alps.

Feudalism. The factional struggles which began during the reign of Louis the Pious destroyed the unity that the Carolingian rulers had imposed upon western Europe. The era of feudalism was begun. This period of European history is characterized by ceaseless warfare. The chaos which followed the earlier barbarian invasions once again prevailed. Life became an elementary and violent struggle for bare existence.

The activities of men divided them into three classes or estates. The First Estate comprised the clergy who had the responsibility of caring for the spiritual needs of all Christians. The Second Estate was the nobility, including kings and emperor, the men whose profession was fighting and ruling. The Third Estate was composed of all those whose activities had to do with the economic life of Europe which was mainly agricultural. These were the three conditions of men which made up the society of the Middle Ages, the praying men, the fighting men, the toiling men. And each was dependent upon the other. Obviously the peasant would be unable to till the soil and pasture his cattle in such a time of violence and confusion unless he were protected by the fighting man from the depredations of robber bands and the armies of warring nobles. Nor could the church function in the service of the faithful without similar protection.

The conditions of the time forced men to live in small villages clustered about the walls of the noble's castle. In time of danger the villagers fled into the castle enclosure with their families, livestock, and movable goods, while the noble lord and his men-at-arms sought to drive off the enemy. If the attackers failed to breach the castle walls, they plundered the village and left the fields and dwellings burning as they departed. It was a brutal age. Life was hard for all conditions of men. In winter the peasant slept with his cattle to keep warm; cattle and peasant often shared the same one-room hovel. The noble, living in his grim and damp castle was little better off than the peasant in the matter of physical comfort.

The noble and his followers, when not engaged in warfare, hunted or kept themselves skilled in arms by daily exercise. With his assistant clerks and stewards he furnished the simple government of the feudal community. He heard disputes and administered justice, punished crimes, supervised the periodic distribution of community land among the peasants, and brought in skilled workmen to construct the community oven, the community wine-press, the community mill for grinding grain.

There was no authority to check effectively the brutality or greed of a bad noble. If he treated his peasants cruelly or unfairly, they had to suffer it. If he were wise and kind they thanked God for their good fortune. But whether the lord was cruel or kind the peasant rarely left the manor. He clung to what security he had, knowing full well that in his world freedom would mean no more than freedom to starve by himself or to die a violent death.

Many generations of men were born, lived, and died without ever leaving the manorial village. Travel was extremely hazardous and there was relatively little occasion for it in any case. The manor was practically self-sustaining. Cut off from communication with the rest of the world, men developed local peculiarities of speech and dress and custom which identified them not as Frenchmen or Germans or Italians but as Flemings, Gascons, Saxons, Lombards, and Tuscans. While the manorial serf had heard of the king and pope, many there must have been who knew the name of neither.

Lord and Vassal. And yet in the thinking of the feudal era there remained a concept of the superstate, the empire, which ideally represented the political unity of western Christendom even though the reality was far from such an ideal. Under that ideal no man "owned" land in the modern sense of the word. The earth was God's. Just as God had given the pope charge of the spiritual well-being of men, he had set up a secular ruler, the emperor. From the emperor kings held their kingdoms. From the king the dukes and counts received the lands over which they held sway.

The members of the Second Estate held their lands on the condition of fulfilling certain obligations to the people living under them and to the noble from whom they had received the land or fief. When a feudal noble received a fief he became the vassal of the man who had bestowed it upon him. The bestower of the land became his lord. The vassal owed his lord military service of a specified nature and usually for a specified number of days in the year. This military obligation often involved the services of several knights beside himself. The vassal also agreed to attend court and offer his lord counsel. He undertook to ransom his lord whenever he fell into enemy hands, to contribute to the dowry of the lord's daughter and to make a contribution upon the knighting of the lord's son. In return the lord promised his vassal protection and justice. The lord received into his household the sons of his vassals and there educated the young men for the career of knighthood. The system of allocating land just described is called *infeudation* for it is the process by which fiefs were made.

If a vassal received a large fief, he usually subdivided it. Part he ruled over himself. The rest he assigned to vassals of his own making. When his overlord called upon him for military service, he would then call upon *his* vassals who helped make up the military force with which he was obliged to serve his overlord.

This feudal pattern was further complicated by the fact that bishops and abbots often governed church lands which were held from feudal nobles as fiefs. The demesne revenues from these fiefs would go to support the churches, monasteries, schools, and hospitals which were in charge of churchmen. Often churchmen assigned parts of the land in their charge to noble vassals, fighting men upon whom they could call to protect church property or to fill the military obligations which they owed *their* feudal overlords.

The Serf. We have already taken some account of the toiling man, the serf. The serf was not a vassal. Lords and vassals were members of either the nobility or clergy. The serf dwelt on the land of a feudal noble or the land of the church. He tilled the soil or followed a craft and rendered service to his manorial lord in return for protection, justice, and the security of his life and holdings. His chief obligation was in the form of service, usually some form of labor. He was given a share in the common fields and pastures from which he provided for his own needs. While he was attached to the soil and might not leave it without his lord's consent, it must also be remembered that he could neither be deprived of his share in the land. To that extent he enjoyed an important element of security. To put it in modern language, he could not be fired.

22 THE CHURCH IN FEUDAL EUROPE

When we contemplate the violence and chaos which attended the disruption of Charlemagne's great empire, and when we recall that distracted and disunited Europe was beset upon all sides by enemies—Vikings to the north, Saracens to the south, Magyars and Slavs to the east—we marvel that out of this confusion there arose a great civilization. Throughout these early centuries of turmoil one institution above all others patiently and persistently labored to combat the forces of disintegration and decay. During the era that has long been known as the Dark Ages, it was the Latin Christian Church which succeeded little by little in restraining violence and in restoring order, justice, and decency. A distinguished and critical student of the Latin church has acknowledged that in all the history of mankind no other institution "has exercised so vast an influence on human destinies."

With the collapse of the Roman imperial government in the West, the Christian bishops carried on as administrators and leaders. They continued to administer the Roman law under which the Latin subjects of the new German rulers were governed. Out of the revenues of church lands they dispensed charity and relieved the suffering of those who had been harmed most by warfare and pillage. The monasteries collected and preserved for future ages many of the great achievements of the Roman and Greek past. And it is impossible to estimate the value of the spiritual administrations of the clergy, to know the solace and consolation they brought to sorely tried humankind, how many they saved from utter despair.

Monasticism. When in the fourth century Constantine sought to strengthen the imperial government by seeking the support of the Christians, he made many Christian bishops administrative officials in his government. Numbers joined the church for it became apparent to many whose ambitions were worldly that the church was now the path to office and distinction. But the faithful who had found peace of mind and repose of the spirit by turning away from such worldly ambitions, were disturbed by the new intimate association of church and state.

In their efforts to escape from worldly involvement and to find spiritual repose in prayer and self-discipline, men went out into the deserts and lived as hermits. So great became this eremitical movement that there grew up in north Africa large communities of hermits whose lives of renunciation made a powerful impression upon the Christian world. Men of all types were impelled to take up the hermit's life. Many resorted to extreme and unusual practices in order to subdue their bodies and reduce the demands of the flesh to a minimum. St. Simeon Stylites is one such; he spent many years perched atop a pillar in a space so small there was only room to sit or stand. In many, ascetic discipline became perverted into a form of exhibitionism.

St. Basil, an eastern bishop, tried to check the growth of these extreme and spectacular practices by organizing monasteries in which the ascetic disciplines of fasting, meditation, and prayer would be balanced by useful and healthful activities. But the easterners in general continued to favor the hermit life and ascetic extremes. It was in the West that monasticism flourished. The monk who fixed the pattern of western monastic life was St. Benedict of Nursia (about 480 to 540). At Monte Cassino in Italy he founded his famous monastery and devised a rule which governed the daily living of his followers. St. Benedict's rule was clear and sane. Recognizing that not all men were capable of submitting to monastic discipline, he insisted upon a period of probation or trial before a candidate was allowed to take his final vows of poverty, chastity and obedience. The health of the monks was maintained by an adequate diet. Asceticism was balanced by healthful labor. Understanding the temptations of idleness, Benedict kept his monks constantly occupied with both religious exercises and useful work which usually included some form of manual labor. The monk gave up all property, severed all family connections, and promised unquestioning obedience to his superiors.

In the sixth century the statesman and scholar Cassiodorus became a monk and endowed his monastery with his great library. He established the *scriptorium* where monks copied and preserved the great books of the ancient world, thus preserving through the Dark Ages the learning and literature of Greece and Rome.

In Europe the monasteries played an important role in the life of all men. The monks cultivated their lands and out of their surplus fed the poor. Bridges, essential for communication and trade, were repaired and maintained by them down to modern times—when Henry VIII suppressed the monasteries in England the highways quickly fell into disrepair for it was the monks who had maintained them. By the drainage of swamps and the clearing of forests the monasteries brought new lands under cultivation. Often agricultural experiment on monastic lands taught the peasant how to improve the yield of his flocks and fields.

The monasteries also maintained hospitals and schools and furnished shelter and safety for travelers at a time when travel was very hazardous indeed. Already in Charlemagne's time the church was the only institution in Europe devoted to letters and learning. The educational role of the church was extended when Charlemagne sought by its agency to spread education among his people.

The Papacy. The cloistered clergy, monks and nuns, were known as the *regular* clergy. The bishops and priests, all those whose primary duty it was to serve and instruct the laity, were known as the *secular* clergy. In the West this great body of the clergy, both secular and regular, acknowledged the spiritual and administrative leadership of the bishop of Rome, the pope.

It was but natural for Rome to assume the headship of western Christendom. In the East there were several great centers from which Christianity was spread in the earliest days of its history. Such were Jerusalem, Antioch, Alexandria, and later Constantinople. But in the West there was no rival to Rome which had been the scene of the martyrdom of St. Peter and St. Paul. All roads led to Rome. In the first centuries of the Christian era it was the center of the imperial government, the largest and richest city in the empire to which it had given its name.

The organization and administration of the Christian church naturally followed that of the imperial government. This made it very easy for Constantine later on to associate the Christian bishops in the imperial administration. And when the western empire was officially put an end to in the fifth century, the church continued to carry on many of its functions. In addition, the church had become a great landholder. It is estimated that by the year 600 the land possessed by the papacy in Italy amounted to more than eighteen hundred square miles. This meant that the pope was the greatest prince in Italy on the basis of land alone.

A series of able Roman bishops had greatly enhanced the prestige and authority of the papal office. While the East was rent by schisms, the West remained steadfast in its orthodoxy. Constantine made the pope arbiter in many disputes among eastern bishops and the popes in time came to assert their right to resolve all such questions. They based their claim to primacy upon the doctrine of Apostolic succession from St. Peter, head of the apostles, who had founded the church of Rome and had died there. This claim was vigorously asserted by Pope Leo I (440–461). Pope Gregory I (590–604) assumed the defense of the city of Rome against the Lombards when the emperor was unable to protect Italy. He fed the population which had sought refuge in Rome out of the revenues of church lands. He bought off the Lombards and negotiated a treaty with them. Gregory maintained the papal authority over the churches in Spain and Gaul and spread Christianity further throughout Europe; it was he who sent St. Augustine and his missionaries into England to convert the Anglo-Saxons to the Christian faith. He perfected the ritual and established the style of music that became standard in the service as Gregorian chant.

23 THE NORSEMEN

The Norsemen or Vikings were the Germanic peoples who inhabited the Scandinavian and Danish peninsulas. Neither land was capable of supporting a large population, for Scandinavia is a mountainous region fringed by narrow coasts, and Denmark, a flat land, was covered by dense timber and underbrush. Most of the Norse lived along the coasts and depended upon fishing, trade, and piracy for a livelihood.

Early Norse Attacks upon Europe. Before the death of Charlemagne the Norsemen had begun to venture up the rivers of his empire in their long boats. During the reign of Louis the Pious and after, they appeared in increasing numbers, swooping down suddenly upon the unsuspecting villages and towns which they raided and burned.

The inability of the Carolingian kings to protect the empire against these unpredictable attacks greatly weakened the monarchy. The fortified castles of the nobles became the only security and refuge against this enemy. Thus in feudal Europe the nobles were the real rulers and protectors of their people while the kingly authority was effective only on the personal estates which he ruled like any other feudal lord.

For somewhat more than a century the Norsemen seem to have been satisfied to raid the towns and villages and monasteries of Europe, carrying off what they were able and burning and destroying what they were forced to leave behind. The *Anglo-Saxon Chronicle* first records a Viking attack upon England in the year 787. But the collapse of the Frankish government opened up a new field for rich plunder to the Norsemen and turned many of their number away from England to France. Antwerp was burned in 836. In 845 the raiders sailed up the Seine and plundered Paris. In the same year Seville and the coasts of Spain were attacked. The Norse raiders pushed through the Straits of Gibraltar and entered the Mediterranean. They fought the Moslem raiders and ravaged the coasts of southern Europe. In 860 they reached the shores of Italy and attacked Pisa thinking it was Rome.

While Norsemen from the Danish and the western part of the Scandinavian peninsulas extended their raids westward and southward along the coasts of Europe, those from the region of modern Sweden sailed across the Baltic Sea into the Gulf of Finland and up the great rivers of Russia. Following the course of other rivers which flowed southward, they made their way to the Black Sea and attacked Constantinople. In 862 Rurik founded a Norse dynasty in northern Russia after subduing the Slavic inhabitants of the country. The country took its name from the Swedes who were called Rhos or rowers, hence their land became known as the country of the rowers or Russia.

Still other bands of Norsemen sailed out across the northern Atlantic. Their attacks on the English, Scotch, and Irish coasts were resumed. In 874 these bold adventurers reached Iceland. In 981 they discovered Greenland. And around the year 1000 they reached the coast of North America. They pushed their explorations down the coast and inland along the Great Lakes. It seems possible that they ventured as far west as Minnesota.

Permanent Settlement of the Norsemen. A sharp increase in

population and an ensuing struggle for possession of the land of Scandinavia forced many of the lesser jarls and their followers to seek places of settlement overseas. They settled in such numbers along the northeast coast of England that the Anglo-Saxon king Alfred had to surrender a large part of his domain in order to keep the rest. In 885 by the treaty of Wedmore the Danes, as the English called all the Norsemen, were formally ceded the coastal area north from the Thames River which became known thereafter as the "Danelaw." Another Norse kingdom was founded in Ireland at Dublin.

On the continent of Europe, the Norsemen settled upon the land around the lower Seine and along the coasts. In 912 the French king Charles the Simple decided to come to terms with the Norsemen. As he was unable to drive them out of France, he made a treaty with their chieftain Rollo under the terms of which the Norsemen were assigned a definite territory extending to the borders of Brittany. In accordance with the terms of the treaty the Norsemen adopted the Christian religion and acknowledged the suzerainty of the king of France. This great Norse fief became the Duchy of Normandy and its inhabitants known thenceforth as Normans. Despite their sincere acceptance of Christianity and the suzerainty of the French kings, they remained an adventuresome and violent people. In the next century after their settlement in Normandy, the Normans conquered England and Norman adventurers set themselves up as kings in southern Italy and Sicily.

PART FIVE
Medieval Europe

911	Death of Louis the Child. End of Carolingian line in Germany
962	Otto the Great crowned Holy Roman Emperor in Rome
1000	Hungary became Christian under King Stephen I (997–1038)
1059–1085	Robert Guiscard, Duke of Apulia
1066	Conquest of England by William, Duke of Normandy
1073	The monk Hildebrand became Pope Gregory VII (to 1085)
1077	Henry IV did penance at Canossa
1095	Urban II at Clermont summoned First Crusade
1099	The Crusaders captured Jerusalem
1130	Revival of study of Roman law at Bologna
1147–1149	Second Crusade
1150	Gratian's *Decretum*, digest of canon law
1152–1190	Frederick Barbarossa, Emperor
1158	University of Bologna officially recognized
1180–1223	Philip Augustus, King of France
1182–1226	St. Francis of Assisi
1187	Fall of Jerusalem to Saladin, Sultan of Egypt (1171–1193)
1190–1192	Third Crusade
1194–1260	Building of Chartres Cathedral
1198–1216	Innocent III, Pope
1200	Founding of Universities of Paris and of Oxford
1202–1204	Fourth Crusade
1204	Capture of Constantinople by the Crusaders
1206–1227	Rise of the Mongols under Genghis Khan
1208	First Albigensian Crusade launched
1212	The Children's Crusade
1214	Battle of Bouvines

24 THE HOLY ROMAN EMPIRE

The prestige of Charlemagne and the memory of his great empire was such that his descendants in both France and Germany continued to claim suzerainty over the nobles of the empire. Since they were for the most part men of small accomplishment who offered no serious threat to the independent nobles, there was little disposition on the nobles' part to dispute their shadowy claims.

In 911 the last German descendant of Charlemagne, Louis the Child, died. The chief German nobles assembled and chose as their new king Conrad, Duke of Franconia. When Conrad died in 918 they elected Henry, Duke of Saxony, known in history as Henry the Fowler. There were good reasons for continuing the kingship in Germany. During the century following the death of Charlemagne the Germanies had suffered from the raids of Norsemen, Slavs, and Hungarians. It was the king's task to defend the realm from such attacks.

Henry defeated the Danes and forced them to withdraw beyond the River Eider. He repeatedly attacked the Slavic tribes upon the eastern borders of Germany and erected a series of fortifications along the Slavic frontier. Like Charlemagne, he Christianized the Slavs whom he defeated in battle, hoping by this means to make them more peaceful and friendly toward the Germans. The king of Bohemia was defeated, forced to acknowledge Henry's overlordship and to pay tribute.

Henry wisely refrained from interfering in the affairs of his powerful vassals who jealously guarded their independence against infringement by the monarch. In this way he won their support for his son Otto whom he trained to carry on as his successor. The German dukes of Henry's time were, as we know, extremely independent. They made foreign alliances, coined money, nominated bishops and abbots and invested them in their fiefs, all without interference from king or pope.

During Henry's reign Germany was strengthened by the addition of Lorraine. As a consequence of the civil wars in

France, Gilbert, Duke of Lorraine, renounced his allegiance to the French king and accepted the overlordship of Henry. He cemented this alliance by marrying Henry's daughter Gerberga.

Otto the Great. Upon Henry's death in 936, Otto succeeded to the German throne with the approval of the great German nobles. In foreign affairs Otto continued the policies of his father. He again defeated the Danes who, under Harold Blue Tooth, had broken across the frontier. He sent missionaries among them and re-established the Danish march. When the Magyars, or Hungarians, invaded Suabia Otto gathered together his vassals and defeated the enemy at the battle of Lechfield in the summer of 955. As a protection for his boundaries Otto then set up the Bavarian East Mark later known as Austria and the Magyars settled down in Hungary. Following the custom of Charlemagne, Otto established along his eastern frontier a series of border counties called marks or marches. These were an important factor in spreading German and Christian influence among the neighboring Slavs.

When Otto became king in Germany he determined to unify the German states and to bring the vassals under the control of the crown. Early in his reign his brothers led a rebellion of nobles against him and this gave Otto an opportunity to dispose of the rebellious fiefs. He vigorously suppressed the rebellion and inaugurated the practice of replacing rebellious vassals with members of his own family whose loyalty he believed he could count upon. To keep his vassals in line he established in each duchy a royal officer to protect the interests of the crown. These men were called counts palatine or counts of the palace.

About one third of the land in Otto's Germany was held by the church. In order to bring these territories under the control of the crown Otto created many new bishoprics and appointed his own supporters and members of his family to the vacant offices. This policy was pursued by later German kings also.

Feudalization of the Church and the Plight of Rome. It was inevitable that with the breakup of the Carolingian Empire and the continuing assaults upon Christian Europe of Norsemen, Slavs, Hungarians, and Saracens, the church of Rome would be no more able to maintain control over its far-flung territories and personnel than were the kings and emperors. Vikings, Hungarians, and Saracens attacked Italy. Rome was almost completely cut off from the rest of western Christendom.

When bishops died, the feudal nobles throughout Europe nominated friends or relatives to the vacant offices for in this way they would enjoy control of church lands and revenues. Church discipline was relaxed. Secular-minded churchmen married and raised families. They were often more interested as a consequence in securing positions in the church for their offspring than in the spiritual functions of their office. We have just seen how Otto used the church to strengthen his influence in Germany. It is obvious that under these conditions many men who held church office were not churchmen at all except in name. They were feudal nobles ruling over church lands and their lives and interests were no different from those of any other noble of their day.

Rome, like other feudal towns, was dominated by the Roman nobles. They controlled papal elections and used the offices and property of the church in the interest of themselves and their friends. From 896 to 963 there were twenty popes many of whom were murdered or deposed. For a time Theophylactus and his notorious wife Theodora controlled the papacy. Their daughter Marozia, mistress of one pope, was the mother of another, John XI, whose son in his turn became Pope John XII. At last a discontented faction of the nobles, sent as ambassadors to Otto by Pope John XII, appealed to Otto to intervene in papal affairs. During his lifetime Otto made three trips into Italy.

Otto in Italy. But it was another matter altogether which brought Otto into Italy for the first time in 951. In northern Italy a civil war was in progress between rival claimants to the throne of the Lombard kingdom. Suabia and Bavaria, German duchies which bordered upon Italy, were ruled by Otto's kinsmen. The dukes of Suabia and Bavaria took opposite sides in the Lombard dispute and Otto was obliged to intervene in the interests of peace within the German kingdom. Otto conquered Lombardy, married Queen Adelaide, widow of the former king, and assumed control of the Lombard kingdom. He then returned to Germany.

But in 962 he was again in Italy. This time he made his way to Rome and in order that his authority might not be questioned in Italy, he restored the empire. In 962 Otto and Adelaide were crowned emperor and empress by Pope John XII. The medieval German empire thus established became known in history as the Holy Roman Empire. It lasted for more than eight hundred years until in 1806 it was finally dissolved by Napoleon.

Otto summoned a council of the church to reform the conditions which he found in Rome. John XII was tried and deposed for "murder, sacrilege, and immorality." A dependent of Otto's was placed upon the papal throne as Leo VIII.

The preoccupation of the German emperors with Italian affairs is held by many historians to have had tragic consequences for both Italy and Germany. It is argued that if the German kings had remained at home and devoted themselves to the strengthening of the German kingship, Germany would have become a great and united state much earlier in history than she did instead of remaining a collection of petty principalities down to the nineteenth century. In like manner it is assumed that Italy too would have achieved early nationhood. Maybe so! But we cannot know. The fact is that German emperors did divide their attention between Germany and Italy. And Germany and Italy did remain disunited.

The Successors of Otto. Otto II (973–983) was half Roman in outlook. He tried to unite Germans and Italians in a crusade against the Moslems but died before he could carry out his plan. Otto III (983–1002) who came to the throne as a child of three, grew up to regard himself as the successor of the ancient Roman caesars. He moved the capital of the empire to

Rome and planned that in co-operation with the pope he would make the Eternal City the spiritual and political capital of western Christendom. But Otto died at the early age of twenty-two and was succeeded by his cousin who became Henry II. Henry's reign was unhappy. Germany was threatened on the north by the Scandinavians under Sweyn Forkbeard. The Slavic Poles attacked his empire from the east. And the north Italians refused to accept him as their king until he crossed over into Italy with an army and put down the rebellion.

When Henry II died in 1024 the German barons turned once again to the house of Franconia and elected Duke Conrad their king. Conrad II (1024–1039) brought the Kingdom of Arles or lower Burgundy into the empire by marrying the daughter and heiress of the king of that country. Although he was crowned emperor in Rome, Conrad was primarily interested in Germany. He greatly strengthened the German kingship by cultivating the support of the lesser nobles.

Conrad's son, Henry III (1039–1056), strongly supported by the nobles and the church in Germany, regained Bohemia from Poland, overthrew the Hungarian king and set up another who became his vassal, and established his authority in Italy. Henry III controlled a territory equal to two thirds of Charlemagne's empire. He dominated the church both in Germany and in Italy, nominating five successive popes, all of whom were German.

25 THE RIVALRY OF EMPIRE AND PAPACY

The period during the tenth century when the papal office was in the control of the most disreputable of the gangster politicians of Rome is sometimes called the era of "pornocracy," the rule of the harlots. Otto I rescued the papacy from its desperate plight by deposing John XII and setting up a new pope. But this solution was by no means ideal. For the German emperors insisted upon nominating the popes whenever it suited their interest to do so. The fact that they made wise choices

FRISIA

HOLSTEIN

SLAVS

POLAND

WESTPHALIA SAXONY

Cologne

LOTHARINGIA

THURINGIA

Treves

Mainz

FRANCONIA

Speyer

ALSACE

Strassburg

SUABIA

BAVARIA

BOHEMIA

MORAVIA

AUSTRIA

Salzburg

CARINTHIA HUNGARY

KINGDOM
OF
BURGUNDY
OR
ARLES
(to 1032)

Milan

LOMBARD

Pavia

COMMUNES

Genoa Canossa

March of
Verona CARNIOLA

Venice ISTRIA

CROATIA

ADRIATIC SEA

BYZANTINE

SERVIA

TUSCANY

ROMAGNA SPOLETO

PATRIMONY
OF ST. PETER

Rome

Monte Cassino

Gaeta

Naples

Amalfi

Salerno

BENEVENTO

PETTY LORDS

Bari

Brindisi

Otranto

SARACENS

BYZANTINE

Palermo

THE HOLY ROMAN EMPIRE
ABOUT 1100 A.D.

HOLY ROMAN EMPIRE

BYZANTINE TERRITORY

MOSLEM TERRITORY

does not alter the fact that the papacy, like the other church offices throughout Europe, was politically controlled.

In the tenth century there was begun an important reform movement, the chief object of which was to free the church, and particularly the papacy, from secular control. The movement is associated with the famous French monastery of Cluny and is known as the Cluniac Reformation or the Cluniac Movement.

The Cluniac Movement. In 910 Duke William of Aquitaine founded the monastery of Cluny in Burgundy. The charter of foundation provided that the monastery should be forever free of secular control and that its lands should owe no service to the state. Endowments were showered upon the monastery, for the giver was able to feel that his gift would be protected by Duke William's charter. Its wealth enabled the Cluniac monastery to introduce the practice of founding branch houses in different parts of Europe. In addition, many older monasteries asked to be affiliated with the Cluniac congregation.

As the Cluniac movement spread, its monks developed a program of reforms. They aimed: to free the papal office of secular control, to establish the absolute authority of the pope over all the clergy, to enforce celibacy among the clergy and free them from family preoccupations, and to abolish lay investiture and simony—the investiture of church officials with their lands by secular princes and the sale of church offices. The result of such a program would be the complete freeing of the church from lay control. It was an extraordinarily ambitious program in view of the strong control the powerful princes of Europe exercised over the church. But let us note that such a program in all probability neither would have been conceived nor attempted unless the need for it was recognized by large numbers of men of all classes throughout Europe.

By the middle of the eleventh century the ideals of Cluny were sufficiently understood and approved so that it became possible to translate them into reality. For many years the Cluniac monk Hildebrand, as adviser to the popes, shaped church policy toward the fulfillment of Cluniac ideals. From 1073 to

1085 Hildebrand was himself pope as Gregory VII. In 1059 a church synod issued the Electoral Decree which established that the pope was to be chosen by the college of cardinals. This practice has remained in force down to the present day. The same synod asserted that the marriage of members of the clergy was illegal. Since many of the clergy were already married there was naturally much opposition to this reform and it was a long time before celibacy was enforced among the clergy throughout Europe.

In order to establish the control of the papacy over the clergy, all bishops were required to bind themselves to the pope by a special oath of allegiance. Pope Gregory sent his papal legates throughout Europe and these men, acting for the pope and with his authority, superseded the bishops in authority wherever they happened to be.

Hildebrand became pope in 1073. In 1075, as Gregory VII, he presided over the synod which declared deposed all ecclesiastics who had received investiture from any lay person. This meant that lands which had been at the disposal of the princes for generations were now to be taken out of their hands. It remained to be seen whether the princes would submit passively to this assertion of papal authority and whether the pope would be able to back up and make good his claims. But before we discuss the contest between emperor and pope which grew out of this opposition of interests, we must take account of other factors which were an important part of the situation.

The Normans in Italy. Early in the tenth century the Norsemen, as we saw, were formally established in France as vassals of the French king. They gave their name to the region in which they settled, Normandy. Henceforth we shall refer to them as Normans rather than Norsemen.

The Normans were a prolific people. As the population of their land increased it became difficult for Norman nobles to find fiefs for their many offspring. The case of Tancred is an example of this condition in the eleventh century. Tancred of Hauteville, a small Norman fief, had twelve sons and at least as many daughters. As the sons of Tancred grew to manhood they set out in search of employment for their military skill. By this means they hoped to win lands and fortune. The Normans, now become Christians, often made pilgrimages to the shrine of St. Michael in Apulia in southern Italy. In 1017 some Norman pilgrim-knights took part in a local conflict at Bari and terrified their foes by their ferocity as fighters. The success of the Norman fighting men in southern Italy attracted others to the spot, including several sons of Tancred. One of these, Robert Guiscard, became leader of the Norman adventurers in their attacks upon the lands which still acknowledge the suzerainty of the Byzantine emperor. With the help of his Norman fellows, Robert made himself Duke of Apulia.

But the destruction of life and property in the course of these conquests was such that, responding to the appeal of the people, Pope Leo IX obtained troops from Henry III and led them against the Normans. The papal army was defeated at Civitate in 1053 and the pope taken prisoner. However the Christian Normans treated the pope with much respect and released him.

Hildebrand was at the time adviser to the pope in Rome. He recognized that the Normans were too firmly established to be ousted by force. He therefore decided that more could be done with them as friends than as enemies. The papacy reversed its policy and concluded a treaty with the Normans in 1059. Under the treaty the pope acknowledged the title of the Normans to southern Italy and to Sicily (which was in Moslem hands and remained to be conquered) which they were to hold as a papal fief and for which they were to pay the pope feudal dues. As vassal of the pope the duke promised to protect the pope and the papal states and to assist in forwarding the Cluniac reform program. The warlike energies of the Normans were thus turned against the Moslems in Sicily.

Henry IV and Germany. Henry IV (1056–1106) took over the duties of the German kingship when he reached the age of eighteen in 1069. His most active supporters were the German clergy, for we saw earlier how the German kings had used the church lands to strengthen the royal power. Many of the secular nobles of Germany were suspicious of the growing power of the monarch and rather inclined to resent any extension of kingly authority.

In 1075 Pope Gregory issued the decree which declared illegal the lay investiture of bishops in their lands and offices. It was not to be assumed that Henry would meekly acquiesce and permit his supporters to be dismissed from their offices and fiefs. When the archbishopric of Milan fell vacant, Henry acted promptly and invested his own candidate in the office before the pope had time to act. The issue was now fairly joined.

Gregory summoned Henry to Rome to answer for his act. Henry called together the German clergy at Worms in 1076 and these friends of the king declared the pope deposed. Gregory replied by excommunicating the emperor; this act made him an outlaw from Christian society and dissolved the oaths of fealty taken by his vassals. The pope had acted shrewdly. He knew the temper of the German secular nobles who would be only too glad to break the power of the German king. He also knew that despite their dependence upon Henry many of the clergy would support the pope.

Canossa. Faced with civil war, Henry acted promptly. He crossed the Alps into Italy and appeared before the pope at Canossa as a humble penitent seeking forgiveness for his sins. On three successive days the emperor stood barefooted in the snow before the castle in which the pope was housed. What a contrast this to the relationship that had existed between emperor and pope from the days of Otto I to Henry III! As a priest the pope could scarcely refuse to pardon the penitent ruler.

Henry's act, although humiliating, was good statesmanship. By it he immediately resumed his position as king and emperor and was given time to prepare more skillful measures against the Cluniac reform. So ably did he consolidate his position that when the pope again excommunicated him in 1080, Germany remained loyal to the emperor. He then crossed the Alps with an army and laid siege to Rome.

Gregory withdrew into the fortress of St. Angelo and sent urgent appeals for help to his Norman vassals. As the Normans advanced Henry IV retreated. But when the Normans entered Rome they plundered the city for three days. So indignant were the citizens against the pope, whom they blamed for this outrage, that when the Normans withdrew, Gregory had to leave the city with them. At Salerno, this carpenter's son who had risen through the church to the position of highest authority, who had beheld the emperor a supplicant before him, died an exhausted and saddened man.

After the death of Gregory the investiture question was compromised, not settled. For the interest of Europe was drawn away to matters of more immediate concern to all. These were the Crusades.

26 THE CRUSADES

Less than a quarter century after Mohammed's death the assassination of Othman (644–656) precipitated a civil war among his followers. The division was healed outwardly at least when the Omayyad family established their right to the Caliphate and moved the capital from Medina to Damascus. But the supporters of Ali, cousin and son-in-law of the Prophet, continued to insist that the descendants of Ali and Mohammed's daughter Fatima were the rightful leaders of Islam.

In 750 the Omayyads were overthrown in a palace revolt. All the Omayyad princes were slain except one, Abd-er-Raman (Abdurrahman) who succeeded in escaping to Spain. At Cordova he established a new caliphate which he ruled as an independent state. The new non-Arab rulers in the East were the Abbasid family who transferred the capital from Damascus to Baghdad. This disruption of the religious and political unity of Islam was symptomatic of a tendency which greatly weakened the Mohammedan power. Nevertheless the Moslem world continued to enjoy great prosperity. Although the Emirs or local governors quarreled with one another and ruled as little independent princes, trade and commerce prospered. Although by the beginning of the tenth century the Baghdad caliphs were mere puppets controlled by military chieftains, the Moslem world continued to exhibit great cultural and economic vigor.

The Seljuk Turks. The Turks, dwelling in central Asia north of the Altai Mountains and the Gobi Desert, had become divided into an eastern and western group. The western Turks, weakened by wars with their kinsmen and with China, were conquered by the Arabs during the era of Mohammedan expansion. But as the political unity of the Arab empire was destroyed, the Turkish chieftains led their warlike tribesmen against the Moslem Emirates of western Asia. Seljuk was their leader and as a result they became known as the Seljuk Turks.

The Turkish tribesmen embraced Mohammedanism with the fanaticism which so often characterizes the new convert. This did not prevent them making war on their fellow Mohammedans however. By the end of the first half of the eleventh century, the grandson of Seljuk had overthrown the local chieftain and established his control over the Baghdad caliph. His son in turn subjugated Persia and Armenia and defeated the army of the eastern Roman emperor at Manzikert in 1071.

The coming of the Turks brought about a sudden change in the relationship that had grown up between Christianity and Islam. For while the two civilizations had remained generally hostile to each other—Moslem raiders continued to attack Christian coasts and shipping and the maritime cities of Italy retaliated with increasing vigor—European pilgrims visiting the Christian shrines in Palestine and other Moslem-dominated regions were allowed to come and go in peace and the Christian subjects of Moslem rulers were decently treated. The Turks changed all this. Their successful attacks on the Byzantine empire threatened the destruction of eastern Christendom. Many tales began to reach Europe of atrocities inflicted upon pilgrims and upon the Christian subjects of Turkish rulers. This was the situation when the Byzantine emperors appealed to the West for help.

There was good reason to believe that such help might be

effectively given. An active crusade was in progress against the Moors in Spain. The Italian cities, particularly Genoa and Pisa, had built up their fleets and in 1084 captured the important Moslem stronghold of Tunis in north Africa. In 1072 the Normans took Palermo and in 1091 they completed their conquest of Sicily.

The Council of Clermont. In 1094 the eastern emperor Alexius renewed the appeal to western Christendom addressing his plea to Pope Urban II. The following year there met at Clermont in southern France a great church council which was attended by many nobles and clergy. Toward the close of the session Pope Urban addressed the gathering and proposed a crusade against the Moslems. It was a great speech. Several accounts of it have come down to us. From them we obtain a very clear picture of the situation of Europe at the end of the eleventh century and of the many motives which prompted the military undertakings we know as the Crusades.

The pope pointed out that constant feuds among the European nobles imposed suffering and hardship upon the people of Europe and availed the nobles little. Population had increased to a point where there were not enough fiefs for the noble offspring and destruction of crops had sharpened the threat of famine. He proposed that the nobles call a truce to their private quarrels and direct their warlike energies toward freeing the Holy Land from Mohammedan domination and to rescuing the eastern empire from the Turkish threat. Knowing men, the pope added for the benefit of those who might not be sufficiently stirred by the plight of their fellow Christians the further suggestion that in the wealthy East many might obtain for themselves lands and riches that no longer could be acquired in Europe. He ended his address with a moving portrayal of the sufferings of the eastern Christians. Great numbers immediately took the pledge to go on a crusade and it was arranged that the armies would set out the following year.

The First Crusade. The pope had addressed himself to the nobles, the fighting men of Europe, for this was to be a military enterprise. But the extraordinary enthusiasm aroused by his appeal communicated itself immediately to others. At once self-appointed agitators like Peter the Hermit and Walter the Penniless went about among the peasants stirring up enthusiasm for a crusade. Great numbers of these poor folk packed their families and worldly goods upon carts and, with no notion of the distance to be traveled or of the difficulties to be met with, started off to the East.

As this unorganized rabble passed through Hungary and Bulgaria, living on the country as they traveled, the Christian inhabitants of these lands took up arms to protect themselves and their property. Many of the crusading group died or became lost on the way. Two groups got through to Constantinople arriving in July 1096. We may imagine the feelings of the emperor Alexius when the rabble descended upon his city. He helped them cross over into Asia Minor where they were cut to pieces by the Turks.

In the autumn of 1096 the first of the crusading armies reached Constantinople. The last arrived in the spring of the following year. At once it became apparent that the purpose of the Crusade was one thing to Alexius and quite another to the European nobles. The emperor desired his European allies to restore Asia Minor and Syria to the empire. He was not particularly interested in driving the Moslems out of Palestine for it was a poor country and difficult to defend. The Europeans, on the other hand, were not particularly concerned with Alexius' problems. Their purpose was to free the Holy Land and to carve out fiefs for themselves in the Near East.

As the western armies arrived Alexius required their leaders to take oaths of homage to himself for any of the former territories of the empire which they might conquer. The crusading leaders bitterly resented the emperor's tactics and there were occasional violent outbreaks between the crusaders and the Greeks—Greek was the language of the Eastern Roman Empire and its people were accordingly referred to as Greeks by the Latin Christians. But the crusaders were dependent upon the emperor for guides, siege machinery, and a supporting fleet with supplies. With bad grace they acceded to Alexius' demands.

In April 1097 the crusaders began to cross into Asia Minor. The first Turkish stronghold they encountered was the former Byzantine city of Nicaea. But when the walls were breached the garrison surrendered, by previous arrangement, to the Greeks rather than to the crusaders and the Europeans were thus prevented from plundering the city. Alexius overcame the indignant anger of their leaders with gifts and promises and the armies set out upon their arduous march across Asia Minor. At Dorylaeum the crusaders were ambushed by the Turks who, lightly armored and mounted upon nimble horses, used bow and javelin and avoided coming to close grips with the heavy armored crusaders. The expedition was saved from disaster by a well-timed charge of the Norman knights.

The crusaders, with their woolen and leather garments, heavy armor, and a shortage of pack animals, suffered acutely throughout the whole campaign from heat, shortage of supplies, disease, and the rigors of the march. When the Taurus Mountains were crossed the ambition of many of the crusading princes made itself evident in an immediate scramble for fiefs. Baldwin of Flanders, the landless brother of Godfrey of Bouillon, seized the strategic city of Edessa.

The Siege of Antioch. In October 1097 the crusaders laid siege to the great walled city of Antioch in northern Syria. The crusaders were too few in number to surround the city completely and supplies steadily reached the garrison while the attackers suffered through the winter from lack of food, clothing, and shelter. In the spring reinforcements arrived. Then Bohemund, the Norman leader, bribed a dissatisfied Turkish officer to admit his men and the crusaders poured into the city.

They were just in time, for four days later a Turkish army arrived outside the city and the crusaders, instead of being cut to pieces outside the walls, found themselves besieged in the captured city. They were exhausted from their sack of the city and were still without food and supplies. Their leaders, greedy for fiefs, squabbled over the possession of Antioch. Morale was at low ebb and many crusaders lowered themselves over the walls on ropes during the night and tried to escape through the Turkish lines to the coast. Among these was Peter the Hermit. When the crusaders' plight seemed most desperate a pious monk, Peter Bartholomew, was inspired by a vision to discover the lance which had pierced the side of Jesus as He hung on the cross. The discovery immediately revived the flagging spirits of the crusaders. They issued from the city suddenly and fell upon the Turks, completely defeating them.

In 1099 the rank and file of the army, thoroughly sickened by the quarreling of their leaders, threatened to abandon the crusade unless they were at once led toward Jerusalem. The march was resumed and in June the army arrived before the Holy City. Reinforcements and supplies had reached the crusaders by sea and the siege was brief. In the moment of their triumph the crusaders avenged themselves upon the inhabitants of Jerusalem for all the hardship and despair they had suffered during the two years past. In an enthusiastic letter to the pope, Godfrey of Bouillon wrote that the horses' legs were reddened to the knees from wading among the bodies of the slain.

The Crusading States. European feudalism was at once established in Palestine and Syria. Romanesque churches and feudal castles appeared. The conquered territories were carved up into fiefs and these were subdivided among vassals. Godfrey of Bouillon, who died in 1100, was succeeded by his brother Baldwin, already Count of Edessa, who became King of Jerusalem. Bohemund held the Principality of Antioch. Raymond of Toulouse created for himself the County of Tripoli.

Jerusalem remained in the hands of the crusaders from 1099 to 1187. During all that time there was a constant movement of men and materials back and forth between Europe and the East. No longer was the Mediterranean a Mohammedan lake. The cities of southern Europe built fleets and grew rich upon the traffic in men and goods. Europe found an outlet for her surplus commodities and Europeans developed a taste for the eastern products they had so long been deprived of.

While Europe's fighting men sought careers and lands in the East those who remained at home enjoyed comparative peace and security. Absent nobles often placed their fiefs in the custody of the church and the skillful management of church administrators much improved the condition of these lands and of the people living on them. The Peace of God and the Truce of God were extended throughout Europe and contributed much to the welfare of all. These measures represented the efforts of the church to restrict feudal warfare. The Peace of God, introduced around 990, was a plan whereby the church sought to win from the nobles a promise not to attack women, children, pilgrims, churchmen, and peasants and not to damage churches, and monasteries, crops and cattle and farm implements. The Truce of God, introduced about 1025, suspended fighting on Friday, Saturday, and Sunday. Later it was extended to include "closed seasons" like Lent.

While the nobles were the mounted fighters and leaders of the crusading armies, the "rank and file" was made up of members of the Third Estate. Many peasants undertook pilgrimages to the Holy Land. Some remained in the East. Others returned and settled in the growing towns where they became traders or craftsmen. Travel in Europe became relatively safe and the manor was no longer so completely isolated from the larger world as it had been. The development of a closer, more interdependent, European community was tremendously accelerated by the crusades.

The Crusades Continue. In 1147 an energetic Turkish leader, Zangi, captured Edessa. Europe was at once aroused by the new Turkish threat to the Latin Kingdom of Jerusalem. The Second Crusade was preached by the eloquent monk Bernard of Clairvaux who addressed a council of the French clergy held at Eastertime in the year 1146. King Louis VII of France and many of his nobles took the crusading pledge. In Germany the Emperor Conrad III placed himself at the head of a group of German crusading knights.

The Second Crusade was a miserable failure. Conrad and his Germans were the first to reach the East. They suffered a series of defeats. Upon the arrival of King Louis and the French army the crusade was resumed. The crusaders laid siege to Damascus but failed to take the city. The discouraged monarchs returned home with the remnants of their armies.

Forty years after the fall of Edessa, Western Christendom was electrified by the tidings that Jerusalem had been seized by the great Mohammedan leader Saladin. The tragic news was carried westward in a ship with black sails. In response to the appeal of the pope the three leading rulers of Europe took the Crusaders' Cross. They were Frederick Barbarossa of Germany, Philip Augustus of France, and Richard the Lion Hearted of England.

The formidable German army was the first to arrive on the scene. Its fate was sudden and unexpected. Frederick was drowned while bathing in a stream and his exhausted and discouraged followers turned back and abandoned the crusade. The French and English kings arrived together by sea and joined the siege of Acre which had been going on for two years. Saladin arrived with his army and besieged the besiegers by surrounding their armies.

Philip seems to have regretted his decision to go on a crusade almost from the start. His interests lay at home. He quarreled with Richard and at the first opportunity returned home because of "illness." It might have been a good thing for England had Richard done likewise. Instead Richard left England in the care of his brother John and continued in his role of crusader. He was a man of great personal courage and a doughty warrior. Much inferior to Saladin in intelligence and humaneness, he nevertheless won the respect of his great adversary through his qualities as a warrior. In 1193 a truce was arranged under which the Christians held a strip of the Levant coast with the right of access to the Holy Land for pilgrims. Richard returned home and the following year Saladin died.

The Papacy and the Fourth Crusade. Pope Urban II had launched the First Crusade. Its success brought great prestige to the papacy. During the crusading era the popes were the real heads of Western Christendom. No emperor launched a crusade. When Conrad III and Frederick Barbarossa took the Cross they did so as German rulers and were only equal in authority to the other national monarchs who participated along with them—Louis VII, Philip Augustus, Richard of England. The absence of the more adventuresome nobles from Europe gave the popes the opportunity they had long sought after to re-establish their control over the clergy and over church lands. The reform movement and the extension of the Peace and Truce of God greatly strengthened popular support of the new papal authority. And a series of able popes exercised their authority with good effect.

Pope Innocent III (1198–1216) was the most powerful ruler of his day. He conceived that as the Vicar of Christ the pope was the intermediary between God and men. As ruler over the souls of men his authority was greater than that of king or emperor who ruled merely over their bodies. With Innocent this was no empty theoretical claim. He did not hesitate to make his authority felt.

The church had no armies with which to discipline rulers who might choose to disregard or to defy her authority. But the church possessed powerful spiritual weapons. Chief among them was excommunication and the interdict. By excommunication an individual was declared expelled and outlawed from Christian society and his soul was condemned to Hell for all eternity. If a ruler were excommunicated his subjects no longer owed him obedience; his vassals were immediately relieved of all their feudal obligations to him. An excommunicated man was outside the protection of the law and might be injured or hunted with impunity. The interdict was the suspension of all church offices and of the services of the clergy in the district to which the ban was applied. Administration of the sacraments was suspended. This meant that sinners could not seek forgiveness through the sacrament of penance, that marriages would not be sanctified, that infants would not be baptized, that the dying were deprived of the last rites of the church and final forgiveness for sins. In an age of faith these were terrible weapons indeed. And in addition Innocent did not hesitate to depose kings and to call for crusades against rebellious rulers.

Whereas in former times emperors had chosen popes, Innocent was called upon to decide who should be emperor. Philip Augustus of France, Alfonso IX of Leon, King John of England, all were forced finally to submit to the will of Innocent III; John surrendered England to the pope and received it back as a fief for which English kings paid feudal dues to Rome until 1366. We shall have occasion to refer to these matters again.

In 1202 Innocent issued a call for a crusade. No particular crisis or danger had prompted this call and the response was small. The French nobles who took the Cross decided to go by sea and to attack Egypt which had become the center of Mohammedan power. The Venetians agreed to transport the crusaders for 85,000 marks which was a price of two marks a man and four marks a horse. But when the crusaders arrived in Venice they were fewer in number than had been anticipated and could pay only 51,000 marks.

While the Venetians held the crusaders as "guests" on one of the islands of their city, they negotiated a contract by which the crusaders agreed to attack the Dalmatian city of Zara, a commercial rival of Venice. Of course Zara, a Christian city, belonged to the Catholic king of Hungary who was himself a crusader, but that did not trouble the Venetians. Zara was taken and the pope excommunicated the Venetians. This did not seem to bother them either for they had a still more interesting proposal to put to the crusaders.

Although enjoying a profitable trade with Constantinople and the Byzantine Empire, the Venetians desired a monopoly. They now proposed that the crusaders join them in attacking Constantinople and restoring to the throne the emperor Isaac II and his son Alexius who had been deposed by a palace revolution. Alexius promised money and fiefs to the crusaders and overcame their religious scruples by agreeing to bring about the submission of the Greek church to Rome thereby

uniting eastern and western Christendom under the headship
of the pope.

Constantinople was taken and Isaac and his son were placed
upon the throne. The city rose in revolt and drove them out
but the crusaders retook the city and submitted it to a pillage
that was one of the most disgraceful in history. Some of the
crusaders obtained fiefs which they and their descendants held
for another fifty years. But the Venetians profited greatly.
They took possession of strategic islands and ports and a large
section of the city of Constantinople itself. Their conquest secured them a predominance in eastern commerce which they
held until the age of discoveries opened up new trade routes
around Africa.

The Children's Crusade. The diversion of the Fourth Crusade
and the attacks upon the Christian cities of Zara and Constantinople did much to discredit the movement and to undermine enthusiasm for any future undertakings of the sort.
There were several later crusades against the eastern Mohammedans but they achieved little or nothing. However, mention
should be made of a strange phenomenon of the age of Innocent III, the Children's Crusade, for it will help us to realize
how different was the outlook of the men of that day from
those of our own time.

In 1212 a young shepherd boy, Stephen of Vendôme,
preached a crusade to the children, declaring that God would
open a path through the sea for them as he had for the Is-
raelites of old. Many children left their homes and followed
Stephen to Marseilles where some merchants agreed to transport them to Palestine. A storm overtook the fleet and two
of the ships were sunk with all aboard. The remainder reached
an eastern port where the children were sold in the eastern
slave markets. Another such expedition left Germany headed
by little Nicholas of Cologne. In the course of the march
across the Alps most of the children died of exhaustion and
hunger. The Italian bishops and the pope managed to persuade the survivors to abandon their crusade and return home

although a few still persisted in begging passage on eastbound ships.

27 EFFECTS OF THE CRUSADES UPON EUROPE

The whole life of Europe was affected by two centuries of crusading activity. It is necessary therefore that we make some estimate of the changes which were brought about in Europe as a result of the crusades. And yet it is extremely difficult to know with any degree of certainty just how much of the change observable during the era was caused by the crusades and how much would have occurred in any event. It can be argued that the course of European development would have been pretty much the same had the crusades never taken place. And since the crusades affected men in all walks of life in all parts of Europe it would be possible to attribute nearly every alteration in the life of Europe to the crusading movement. We must bear these possibilities in mind as we seek to arrive at a common-sense judgment of the influence of the crusades upon the life of Europe.

Commercial Expansion. The inhabitants of the Italian maritime cities were among the first to benefit from the crusades. They transported supplies, reinforcements, and pilgrims from Europe to the East. Their returning ships brought back spices, cotton, sugar, silks, and much of the plunder which had been taken from the captured towns of Syria and Palestine. In return for their aid to the crusaders the Italian cities—principally Genoa, Pisa, and Venice—were allotted "quarters" in eastern ports which they ruled in free sovereignty. Here they erected wharves, storehouses, offices, and homes for resident merchants.

Among the eastern products which found a ready market in Europe were rice, garlic, cotton, silk, maize, muslin, damask, purple dye, glass mirrors, spices, perfumes. Most of these were novelties to Europeans and brought high prices. Europe in turn found profitable eastern markets for such commodities as furs, hides, wool cloth, metals. The Italians developed high skill in refining raw products and in converting them into useful and beautiful articles. To this day they are noted for their tooled leather and hand-wrought metal. When commercial relationships became stabilized English raw wool was shipped across the Channel to Flanders and the Low Countries where it was spun into yarn and woven into cloth. A portion of the best cloth was then shipped up the Rhine and across the Alps to Italy where, chiefly in Florence, it was dyed and finished. Much of this finished cloth was then loaded on boats and shipped to the East. The remainder was distributed through European markets. In this instance it may be seen how the opening of an eastern market for woolen cloth stimulated the expansion of the Florentine finishing and dyeing crafts, Flemish spinning and weaving, and English wool growing, as well as extending the activities of all those engaged in transporting the raw, semi-finished, or completed article overland or upon the sea.

The Rise of the Towns. Although town life had not entirely died out during the feudal era the towns were of little importance in the life of Europe during that period. As we saw, the most characteristic form of community was the manorial village dominated and protected by the manor house or the castle of the lord. Manor life was based upon agriculture. A few skilled or semi-skilled craftsmen made shoes and fashioned tools and weapons for the community but even they spent part of their time raising food for their tables.

The peasant was attached to the soil. He held a share of the community land which guaranteed him a living for himself and his family. But he was not free to come and go as he chose. In order to leave the village he had to obtain his lord's permission. Largely self-sufficient and having little contact with even near neighbors, the community tended to produce no more than its needs, for there was little or no profit to be derived from surplus goods.

During the period of the crusades many peasants accompanied their noble overlords as servants, archers, and men-at-arms. Many more joined the eastward movement as pilgrims. Large numbers never returned to their homes but settled in the growing towns where there was bustle and activity and many opportunities for winning a livelihood that had not existed in earlier times.

The organization and provisioning of the crusades was a stimulation to the economic activity of Europe. As goods and men circulated more freely and securely throughout Europe than they had in the past, merchants established themselves at strategic points and sold or traded their wares with all who came their way. Often a trading population grew up around a fortress or burg and thus were born many modern cities, the names of which end in burg. Merchants often settled at the crossing of a river or at its mouth. They settled near monasteries or at the junction of two or more important routes of travel. The names of many European cities indicate their origins: Bruges (bridge), Stamford, Portsmouth, Bordeaux (waters' edge).

Of course the merchants and traders had to come to terms with the feudal noble upon whose land they settled. This usually meant paying taxes to an overlord in return for protection under the law and the right to do business. In general the feudal baron dealt with the merchants as a group or corporate body. This meant that within their own town or borough the merchants controlled their own affairs and established their own local government.

The Guilds. The town dwellers banded themselves together into guilds which were occupational organizations. The earlier guilds were the guilds merchant or trade guilds. Later, handcraft or manufacture was organized in the same way. The guilds enjoyed exclusive privileges and definite responsibilities. For example, a shoemakers' guild might possess the exclusive right to make all the shoes for a given community in return for seeing to it that the community was at all times provided with shoes of good workmanship and material at a reasonable price.

In order to insure the existence of an adequate supply of skilled labor the guild members, "masters" of their craft or trade, took into their shops and homes boys who became apprentices to the trade. While the apprentice learned his craft, the master furnished him room and board. All work done by the apprentice became the property of the master. In other words, the apprentice worked for his education and keep. Apprenticeship was followed by a period during which the craftsman sought employment as a journeyman for a daily wage. He was free to move about from town to town wherever the prospect of employment seemed best. After a number of years during which the journeyman perfected his skill and saved his money, he might become a master craftsman, operate a shop of his own, employ journeymen, and train apprentices. But in order to qualify for full membership as a master in the guild he would have to complete a "masterpiece," a difficult piece of work which would display his mastery of his craft. Once accepted he would pay an initiation fee and dues.

The guild controlled the number of men who might be employed or apprenticed; this was so that there might not be a surplus or shortage of skilled workers. The guild determined the hours and conditions of labor, inspected the merchandise in the shops in order to see that work and materials were up to standard, and held the price down to a fair level. In addition the guild provided many services for its members. There were social gatherings and entertainments. The guilds set up funds to help their members through periods of illness. The guild member contributed to a fund out of which provision was made for the care and support of widows and orphans of guild members.

Money. There was very little use for money on the medieval manor. A peasant might trade some butter for the eggs from his neighbor's hens or he might exchange cheese for beer. He paid his feudal dues to his overlord or to the church in commodities and labor. But with the growth of trade during the crusades the convenience of money was recognized and many different kinds of coin were minted and put into circulation. These varied greatly in size and weight and fineness. As a result, the money changers disregarded the face value of coins and rated them according to the value of the metals they contained.

As the papacy re-established its administrative control over the clergy in charge of the churches and monasteries of Europe it inevitably elaborated departments for the handling of church business and the transfer of revenues. The provisioning and financing of the crusades was an important factor in building up this church bureaucracy. Many types of church institutions concerned themselves with crusades and pilgrimages. There were founded crusading orders of monks, among them the Knights Templars and Hospitalers, who protected the pilgrims and helped them on their way. These orders soon became engaged in banking and commercial activities associated with the crusades. For example, it became customary for a crusading noble to deposit funds with a local branch of such an order in exchange for which he would be given an order or draft. This would enable him to withdraw funds from the treasury of an eastern branch of the order when he arrived at his destination. He was thus saved from the bother and risk of carrying the heavy coin with him during his travels where there was always the danger of loss through shipwreck or piracy. Such withdrawals of funds would naturally be balanced against deposits made by other crusaders or merchants traveling in the opposite direction.

Many a man of wealth wished to go on a crusade but for good reason was unable to do so. There were other able-bodied fighters who could not join the crusades because they lacked equipment and funds with which to pay the cost of their transportation. The church arranged that an individual who was prevented from going on a crusade might share in the spiritual benefits of the enterprise if he would equip and finance a fighting man to go in his stead. Let it be remembered that a crusade was a pilgrimage. The hardship endured by the pilgrim was offered up to God in atonement for the sins he had committed. By the sacrament of penance the repentant sinner, through the agency of the priest, sought God's forgiveness for his sins. But forgiveness did not immediately relieve the sinner of all of the penalties due to sin. A pilgrimage was one of the forms of sacrifice by which the sinner atoned for sin and cleansed his soul of its taint. Under a special dispensation called an indulgence, the sinner was now permitted to substitute a money sacrifice for the actual rigors of a crusade. In an age when money was difficult to come by such a payment represented a very real sacrifice. And let it be understood this was no purchase of forgiveness for sin. Forgiveness was obtained through the sacrament of penance. It is necessary to make this point clear because later on the faithful themselves became confused over the meaning of indulgences.

Reaction to the New Authority of the Church. In all ages there are those who feel that the church's activities should be restricted to purely spiritual matters, who feel that somehow or other the church should be able to maintain its organization, carry on its services to the community, dispense charity, maintain churches and monasteries and schools, and protect its jurisdiction, without becoming involved in business or politics. Such a reaction against the "worldly" involvement of the clergy gave rise to the monastic movement during and after the time of Constantine, as we saw.

During the twelfth and thirteenth centuries, as the church grew powerful and rich, a similar reaction took place. Peter Waldo, a merchant of Lyons, gave away his worldly goods and preached a return to the simple life of the apostolic age. For a while Waldo and his followers, who are known as the Waldensians, had the approval of the pope who was naturally aware that many of the clergy, particularly those in charge of the administration of large benefices, lived more like princes than like churchmen. But the Waldensians soon got into trouble with the local clergy. In denouncing the conduct of worldly and luxury-loving churchmen, the Waldensians began to insist that the faithful were not dependent upon the ministrations of the priest for salvation, that the Bible was the all-sufficient guide to truth and salvation. Thus they denied the necessity of the sacraments and of the priesthood. This was heresy and the Waldensians were condemned by the church. Toward the close of the twelfth century a more extreme heresy arose among a group of reformers in southern France. This became known as the Albigensian heresy because its center was the town of Albi in Toulouse. The Albigensians not only regarded the ministrations of the church as unnecessary to salvation, they insisted that very few men were capable of winning salvation in any case. The souls of sinners, the great majority of men, left their human bodies after death and entered the bodies of animals. Sex, said the Albigensians, was the chief instrument of the devil and should be avoided in all forms. The pure eschewed contact with even those things that had been produced by sex, hence they refused to eat meat, milk, or eggs. The Albigensian heresy spread so widely throughout southern France that a crusade was organized against them and the sect was finally stamped out by force.

Not all reaction against the worldly power of the church was heretical however. Francis, the son of a prosperous merchant of Assisi and a pleasure-loving young man, underwent a spiritual transformation during a period of illness and imprisonment. He devoted himself thereafter to a career of poverty and service, preaching and ministering to the sick and unfortunate. His pure life and inspired preaching won him many followers. So great was his influence that two years after his death in 1226 he was canonized a saint.

St. Dominic was a Spanish priest who visited Toulouse in 1205. He was troubled by the spread of the Albigensian heresy. Adopting a life of poverty, he traveled about among the towns of Toulouse, endeavoring by his preaching and example to win back the heretics to the Catholic faith. In 1216 the Dominican Order of Friars Preachers was formed. They were much like the Franciscans in that they traveled about among the townspeople and lived upon alms instead of retiring from the world into a monastery. But the Dominican friars, unlike the Franciscans, emphasized the training of the intellect. St. Dominic realized that his preachers would have to be very thoroughly educated in order to meet the subtle arguments of the heretics and to avoid falling unconsciously into heresy themselves. The Dominicans became associated with the Inquisition because of their discipline in church doctrine. The Inquisition, set up in 1233, was a court. Its purpose was to determine whether a Christian accused of heresy was in fact guilty of holding heretical beliefs. If he were, the purpose of the court was to persuade him to abandon his false beliefs and repent. If he remained obdurate the court turned him over to the secular authority. Death by burning at the stake was usually the punishment meted out to condemned heretics for a heretic was not much different in popular conception from a witch and witches were customarily burned.

28 THE FLOWERING OF MEDIEVAL CIVILIZATION

In our day the words "Middle Ages" conjure up for many an unpleasant picture in which too often are associated feudal warfare and poor plumbing, serfdom and burnings at the stake, ignorance and superstition.

This is an unfortunate and confusing conception, for in the perspective of history these centuries have a tremendous fascination and character of their own. This is the period when the great Gothic cathedrals were built, when Europe's universities were founded, the period of St. Thomas Aquinas and of Dante.

Medieval Education. The fundamentals of medieval education were the liberal arts. The seven liberal arts were divided into two groups composing the *trivium* of grammar, rhetoric, and logic, and the *quadrivium* of arithmetic, geometry, astronomy, and music. The purpose of medieval education in the liberal arts was to train the intellect. It was not primarily designed to teach a man how to make a living although it was probably assumed that a man who had learned to think clearly was more likely to succeed in making a decent living than one who was mentally confused. The medieval youth did not go to school to learn how to manufacture cloth or to conduct a profitable trade in eastern spices. He acquired those techniques by becoming apprenticed to a master in a craft or trade. Latin was the language of the church and of learning in the Middle Ages. Through a study of the Latin classics the student endeavored to learn how to express himself clearly and accurately. Logic or dialectic further developed his thinking processes. Without statistics on medieval education it is impossible to know how many children received some kind of instruction in letters and simple arithmetic. In the towns many were early apprenticed to the crafts and trades. On the manor a youth with a good head for figures might find employment keeping the accounts in his lord's household or upon one of his manors. Many, of course, entered the church, for in the Middle Ages the church performed many services for the community—like that of education—which in our time are conducted by the government, and many different kinds of careers were open to men through the church.

If a youth chose to follow one of the professions, law or medicine, he would enroll in a university. Were he interested in church law—canon law—he would probably go to the University of Paris which in the thirteenth century was the center of theological studies. If the civil law interested him he would undoubtedly select Bologna where he would study the Code of Justinian and thus become acquainted with the great body of Roman law. For the study of medicine the student might choose Salerno, or Padua, or Montpellier in southern France.

The universities were the creation of the Middle Ages. Many of our famous modern universities were flourishing in the thirteenth century. We have mentioned already some of them. Oxford was founded about 1200 by a group from the University of Paris. Cambridge was founded a little later by a group of Oxford men. The University of Naples was founded in 1224 by Frederick II in order to train state officials. The University of Prague was established in 1347 and that of Heidelberg in 1386.

Medieval Literature. Most of the written literature of the Middle Ages was in Latin and much of it dealt with religion. Collections of anecdotes and fables have come down to us. Many medieval hymns are clearly the work of skilled poets. Among the best known medieval historians are Gregory of Tours, who wrote in the sixth century a *History of the Franks.* In the seventh century Paul the Deacon wrote the *History of the Lombards,* and the Venerable Bede his *Ecclesiastical History of the English Nation* in the eighth century. In the crusading era William, archbishop of Tyre, recorded the *History of the Kingdom of Jerusalem.* The crusades also produced histories in the vernacular or common tongues outstanding among which are the accounts given by Villehardouin and de Joinville. The *Anglo-Saxon Chronicle* in Old English prose is one of the most important historical records of the Middle Ages. It was begun in the reign of Alfred toward the close of the ninth century and was continued for four hundred years.

An early masterpiece of vernacular poetry is the early English poem *Beowulf* which was first written down in the seventh century. In the tenth century the Germans recorded in writing the great epic story of the tragedy of Siegfried and Brunhilde, the *Nibelungenlied.* There were many collections of stories in French known as the *chansons de geste,* accounts of great deeds. Most famous of these is the *Song of Roland* concerning the captain in charge of Charlemagne's rear guard whose force was trapped in the pass of Roncesvalles in the Pyrenees and slaughtered to the last man. The stories of Tristan and Isolde and King Arthur and his knights are products of the medieval imagination.

During the twelfth and thirteenth centuries there traveled about Europe in increasing numbers jongleurs and troubadours, professional entertainers who delighted their hearers by singing and reciting the traditional stories and others of their own devising. Thus there was kept alive and circulated among the people of Europe a literature and music fragments of which were written down and passed on to us.

One of the greatest poets of the Middle Ages was Dante Alighieri (1265–1321). His most famous work is the *Divine*

Comedy in which he is taken through Hell, Purgatory, and Paradise. It is thoroughly medieval in the view of the world which it reveals as it is in its quotation of ancient classical writers and the Bible. This great poem was not written in Latin however but in the popular language of Tuscany. The early development of a vernacular literature in the Tuscan tongue caused it to become the language of all Italy in preference to other dialects.

Gothic Art. One of the crowning glories of the Middle Ages was its art. The great cathedrals which dot the continent of Europe preserve for us overwhelming evidence of the creative imagination and skill of medieval man.

The early Christian churches of southern Europe were quite naturally built upon Roman models; indeed many of the churches of Roman times were originally constructed as pagan temples and later taken over by the Christians. But since the Christian church, unlike the classical temple, was built to house a congregation, the interior space was enlarged by constructing the walls *outside* the pillars which supported the roof. Whenever church buildings were constructed entirely of stone and covered by a vaulted ceiling, it was necessary to build heavy outer walls to take up the side thrust of the masonry roof. The windows which pierced these thick walls were narrow and as a consequence little light was admitted to the interior.

In southern Europe where there is an abundance of bright sunlight during the year, the gloom of the church interior was a pleasant relief from the bright glare of the out-of-doors. And the light filtering in through windows and doors sufficiently illuminated the interior. But in northern Europe the days of bright sunlight were few. Throughout the greater part of the year dark and overcast skies created a problem of lighting in the churches. The medieval architects of northern Europe confronted the problem of so distributing the weight of the heavy masonry vaults which covered their buildings as to permit the opening up of large areas of wall space for windows. In solving this problem they created a structure of surpassing beauty.

In the Gothic church the pointed arch replaced the rounded arch for in this manner the side thrust of the masonry was lessened and the weight was carried more directly to the ground. A series of arched ribs carried the weight of the vaults to points along the walls, and this was concentrated so that slender columns sufficed to support a great weight. The side thrust was carried out over the side aisles of the church by devices known as flying buttresses, curved ribs which carried the weight outward and downward to the ground. The walls between these centers of thrust were thus relieved of the function of supporting the roof. They were accordingly removed and replaced by magnificent curtains of stained glass arranged in intricate and many-colored patterns.

The effect of great weight that we observe in the massive Romanesque churches was largely overcome by this use of ribbed vaults, slender columns, and flying buttresses. An effect of lightness was achieved through the skillful use of decorative detail and the emphasis of vertical lines. Horizontal lines were avoided wherever possible. The surfaces of the building, particularly the façade and towers, were ornamented with intricate carvings and statuary which, at a short distance, produced a lacelike pattern that successfully overcame any remaining effects of heaviness.

The Gothic cathedral represented the whole medieval community as no modern building does. Not only was it erected through the many contributions of the faithful of a locality, its erection was a community enterprise too. The citizens hauled the stone and raised the walls under the direction of architects and builders. Each craft and trade contributed its best to the house of God. Weavers, and painters, and woodcarvers, and metal-workers, and masons—all had a hand in fashioning or equipping the church. And the creative imagination of the individual was not restrained by a detailed plan which must be followed. If a stone-worker were assigned to decorate a spire or a water-spout, he carved such a figure as his mood and fancy suggested. The figure might be rude or humorous or sublime. All this combined effort produced a final result that was at the same time magnificently harmonious and infinitely varied.

Other Aspects. It would be possible to dwell at length upon many other aspects of medieval civilization which compel admiration and respect. Early in our century a distinguished historian was so impressed by the achievements of this era that he published a good-sized volume which acclaimed the thirteenth century the greatest in all the long course of human history.

We could speak of the restrictions placed upon feudal warfare by the extension of the Peace and Truce of God, or of the way in which the rough fighting nobility were restrained and civilized by the code of chivalry. Very much indeed could be written of the great intellectual achievements of the medieval schoolmen like Albertus Magnus, Roger Bacon, and Thomas Aquinas, among whom were some of the greatest minds of all time. It would be interesting to review the efforts through which the church sought to curb human greed by establishing and maintaining a just price for services and commodities.

One of the chief criticisms leveled at medieval society is that it was impossible for a man born of humble parents to rise in the social scale. The medieval records abound with personal histories which contradict this assertion. The popes themselves often were of the humblest origins: Alexander V had been a beggar boy, Sixtus IV was the son of a peasant, Urban IV and John XXII were the sons of cobblers, Benedict XI and Sixtus V were shepherds' sons, and the great Gregory VII was the son of a carpenter. Not that we need exaggerate; the number of men who from humble beginnings reached positions of distinction and influence in society was very limited. But medieval society was by no means as inflexible as we in our time are likely to think.

It is true that men did not enjoy equality before the law. Nor did the great commonalty of men have much to say about their government—the famous thirteenth century *Magna Carta* was not a charter of the people's liberties, it was a feudal agreement imposed by rebellious nobles upon their king. The ideal of human equality is a very new concept among men. It is derived from the Christian teaching reiterated throughout the Middle Ages that the souls of all men are of equal value in the sight of God.

PART SIX
The Formation of European States

1215	Magna Carta signed
1226–1270	Louis IX (Saint Louis)
1260	Kublai Khan, Mongol Emperor in China
1265–1321	Dante
1271	Marco Polo started upon his travels
1273	Rudolf of Hapsburg elected Emperor
1280	Kublai Khan founded the Yuan dynasty in China
1294	Boniface VIII Pope (to 1303)
1302	Calling of French Estates General representing all classes of people
1309–1376	Popes at Avignon, not at Rome
1320–1384	John Wyclif, English Church reform
1327–1377	Edward III, King of England
1337–1453	The Hundred Years' War
1346	Battle of Crécy
1348	The great plague, the Black Death, strikes Europe
1356	Battle of Poitiers
1363	Tamerlane, Mongol conqueror
1369–1415	John Hus, Bohemian church reform
1378	The Great Schism. Urban VI in Rome, Clement VII at Avignon
1405	Death of Tamerlane
1414–1418	Council of Constance, schism healed
1415	Battle of Agincourt
1429	Joan of Arc saves Orléans
1431	Joan of Arc burned at Rouen

29 CAPETIAN FRANCE

The National State. The political history of modern Europe is largely an account of the growth and rivalry of national states. In this it stands in sharp contrast to the history of medieval Europe in which the empire and the papacy played leading roles. The nations of today are obviously very complex phenomena. They did not emerge all of a sudden, but were formed through the centuries by the operation of many forces, cultural, religious, and political. Long before Italy and Germany emerged as unified national states in the nineteenth century Italians and Germans had come to think of themselves as belonging to nations which malignant forces had prevented from achieving political unity. The forging of the sentimental, the cultural, and the ideological bonds which are essential to national being is a subtle process which frequently eludes the historian. Sometimes that process accompanied political unification, sometimes it preceded, sometimes followed.

The French state is largely the creation of its kings. It is reasonable therefore to trace the growth of France through the history of the French monarchy for, to a considerable extent, they are one and the same history.

The Early French Monarchy. The last Carolingian ruler to unite the German and French halves of Charlemagne's empire was the incompetent Charles the Fat who was deposed in 887. The following year the West Frankish bishops and nobles passed over the ten-year-old Carolingian heir and elected as their king Odo, Count of Paris, who had successfully defended Paris against the attacks of the Norsemen. However, there were still many supporters of the Carolingian claims so that upon the death of Odo in 898, the Carolingians were restored to the French throne in the person of Charles the Simple. It was Charles the Simple, we recall, who agreed to the settlement of Rollo and his Norsemen in the district which became known throughout later French history as Normandy.

However, in 987 a descendant of Odo, Hugh Capet, was elected king of "the Franks, Flemish, Bretons, Aquitanians, Burgundians, and Gascons." The Capetian dynasty thus established became one of the principal factors in the rounding out of France. Of course Hugh Capet was only one of a number of influential French nobles of his day. He held the title of king but in fact his powers extended no further than the boundaries of his own fief.

The achievements of the early Capetians may seem small, but they were important. Hugh, before his death in 996, had his son crowned king. By so doing he obviated the calling of a council to bestow the crown upon a successor and established the succession in his own family. The early Capetians were fortunately long-lived; Robert ruled from 996 to 1031, Henry I from 1031 to 1060, Philip I from 1060 to 1108; and the line was unbroken. In addition, the Capetians were favored by the clergy who supported centralized rule because it tended to reduce feudal anarchy and made the administration of the church easier than would have been the case in a France split up into many independent states.

Policies of the French Monarchy. It would not be possible in a brief survey to trace the work of the French monarchs reign by reign. In any case their policy is summed up in the achievements of pivotal figures. Louis VI (1108–1137) strengthened the position of the monarchy by overthrowing the minor nobles who were his vassals within the duchy of France, the limited Capetian realm lying between the Loire and the Somme rivers. This gave his successors full control of the resources of their own fief.

Louis VII (1137–1180) married Eleanor of Aquitaine, the greatest heiress of her day. This marriage might have advanced greatly the fortunes of the French monarchy had it been successful, for the dukes of Aquitaine ruled a territory equal to almost a quarter of modern France. Eleanor's dowry was more than twice the size of the Capetian territories. But the marriage was not a happy one, and during fifteen years of married life Eleanor bore Louis two daughters but no son. During the course of the Second Crusade, the royal pair quarreled. In 1152 the marriage was annulled as a result of the "discovery" that Louis and Eleanor were more closely related than the church law allowed. Complicating matters further, Eleanor then married the young duke of Normandy who was also count of Anjou and Maine. A year after the marriage this young man became king of England as Henry II, thus placing half of France under the rule of the English rather than the French king. Adding insult to injury, Eleanor bore Henry four sons.

Philip Augustus. But by a second marriage Louis had a son who became one of the greatest kings of France. This son was Philip II, better known as Philip Augustus (1180–1223). Philip did much to make Paris the political and cultural center of France. He founded the University of Paris, built a large part of the famous cathedral of Notre Dame, and in other ways beautified and improved the capital city. Philip acquired Artois by marriage, and Amiens and Vermandois as a result of disputes over rights to succession. He withdrew from the Third Crusade, as we saw, and during Richard's absence in the East invaded Normandy. Upon his return from the crusade Richard succeeded in recapturing Normandy from Philip, but in 1199 Richard died and was succeeded by his brother John against whom Philip had better success.

It will be remembered that as king of France Philip was the overlord of the great French nobles. Although John was king of England, he also ruled vast territories in France and as ruler of these French fiefs he was the vassal of Philip. In 1200 John injured one of his French vassals by marrying the vassal's fiancée. John's vassal, Hugh of Lusignan, appealed for justice to this lord's overlord who was Philip of France. Under the feudal code John was entirely in the wrong. Summoned three times to appear before the feudal council in Paris for a hearing, John failed to appear and was accordingly sentenced to the forfeiture of his French fief in 1202 for violation of his feudal obligations to his vassal.

But the judgment of the court was of little significance until enforced. Philip began the conquest of Normandy. With the fall of the great fortress Chateau Gaillard, built by Richard, Normandy went over to Philip. The counties of Maine, Touraine, and Anjou quickly followed suit. And John, in trouble with his English vassals, was unable to launch an expedition against Philip in France.

However, John joined a coalition of princes headed by the emperor Otto IV who invaded France from the east. Philip gathered together his noble and clerical vassals and in addition called upon the towns to aid him with their militia. At Bouvines in 1214 Philip won a great victory over his enemies. The effective support of the townsmen greatly increased the power of the king and by the victory of Bouvines Philip firmly established his hold over the territories he had taken from John. The king of France had become for the first time the strongest feudal noble in France.

France was as divided culturally as it was politically. In the south there flourished a great civilization superior to that of northern France. The area had greatly prospered by the crusades. Its textile industries and sea-borne commerce brought wealth to the region and its cities and court became centers of culture and learning. But the spread of the Albigensian heresy, which has been described elsewhere, was a matter of grave concern to the church and to many Catholic princes of Europe. In 1208 Pope Innocent III proclaimed a crusade against the Albigensians. Philip allowed his son to join in the crusade which was led by the Norman noble Simon de Montfort.

This war between the North and South continued for many years. During its course the civilization of south France was destroyed. The struggle was continued under Louis VIII (1223–1226) and under Louis IX (1226–1270) until 1249 when the brother of Louis IX became count of Toulouse. The migration of northerners of all classes into the conquered territories may be compared with the influx of "carpetbaggers" into the Southern states after the American Civil War. After the death of Alphonse of Poitou during the reign of Philip III (1270–1285) Toulouse was added to the French royal domain. During Philip's reign another large fief was added to the expanded domain of the Capetian rulers. In 1274 the Count of Champagne died leaving as his heir a girl of three. Philip added Champagne to the royal domain and to secure his claim betrothed the Champagne heiress to his son who became Philip IV.

Expansion of Government. The expansion of the territories ruled by the French kings made necessary the creation of an administration to carry on the government of the extended domain. Instead of restoring the feudal custom of investing portions of the kingdom in the hands of the feudal vassals, Philip II divided his realm into administrative districts which he placed in charge of salaried officials, called *baillis,* who were responsible to himself. These men administered justice, collected taxes, and published and enforced the edicts of the king. When this system of government was extended to the south of France the officials were called *seneschals,* but the functions of the office remained substantially the same. Other agents of the government traveled among the bailiwicks and checked the conduct of the local agents.

The character of the Great Council of feudal times gradually became changed. Under Louis IX certain cases were required to be referred to the king's council. The cases became so numerous that a number of the council were formed into a group of justices which became the high court, or *parlement* of France. Under Louis IX a permanent committee was also set up to deal with matters of finance. By such steps the feudal government of the council of nobles was gradually transformed into a royal council representing various departments of government functioning under the authority of the king.

Louis IX. Louis IX is known in French history as St. Louis. He was a wise and capable ruler and his reign was for the most part a happy one for France. The outstanding failures of Louis' career are his two crusades against the Moslems. In 1249 he led a crusade against Damietta in the Nile Delta. The city was captured but was later surrendered when the French army was defeated and Louis himself taken prisoner. In 1270 Louis once again organized a crusade. During the course of the attack against Tunis, Louis died of the plague and the expedition was abandoned. With these failures of St. Louis the crusades came to an end.

30   SAXON AND NORMAN ENGLAND

Earliest Inhabitants. In the Atlantic Ocean off the European coast lie the British Isles, a group of about five hundred islands some of which are visible from the continental mainland. From earliest times successive waves of invaders have crossed over from the European continent and settled upon England's eastern shores. As each new group pressed inland from the coast they drove the earlier inhabitants back into the highlands of Scotland and Wales or into remote corners of the island.

We recall from the early chapters of our history how the Celts, who had begun to make their way westward across Europe as early as the seventh century B.C., had settled in northern Italy and France. Numbers of them crossed over into England and pushed back the earlier dark-skinned and dark-haired inhabitants. The two groups of Celts which settled in the British Isles, the Gaels and the Brythons, maintained contact with their fellows on the European mainland. As a result of this, when the Romans under Julius Caesar conquered Gaul the Brythons sent aid to their cousins the Belgae, and it was this fact which caused Caesar to cross over into Britain in 55 B.C. to punish the allies of the conquered Celts.

But Caesar was recalled from Britain by more important matters, and it was not until the reign of the emperor Claudius that Britain was conquered and subjected to Roman rule (43 A.D.). The Romans subjugated England but never extended their conquests to Scotland or Wales. They built cities and defensive walls, and highways. During four centuries of Roman rule England was Romanized in the same manner as Gaul. But when the barbarians attacked the Roman Empire along its northern and eastern boundaries it became necessary to withdraw the military garrisons from Britain early in the fifth century to defend the threatened frontiers. A large part of the Roman population also withdrew across the Channel leaving Britain to the mercies of the invading Angles, Saxons, and Jutes.

Anglo-Saxon England. After the withdrawal of the Roman armies the Picts and Scots attacked Romanized Britain. Soon Germanic Jutes, Angles, and Saxons raided, then settled upon, the coasts. These Teutonic tribes migrated to Britain in large numbers; the entire Angle nation seems to have moved to Britain for no trace remains of it on the continent. The British population was annihilated or driven back into the mountains. In the course of the Anglo-Saxon conquest Roman civilization in Britain was entirely destroyed. The large numbers of words of Latin origin which have a place in later English speech are not survivals of the Roman occupation of Britain. Many such words became a part of the English language after the Norman Conquest in the eleventh century.

Christians from Roman Britain, Wales and Scotland found their way into Ireland and converted the Irish to Christianity. The most famous among them was Saint Patrick who became the patron saint of Ireland. Toward the end of the sixth century Christian missionaries from Ireland crossed over into England and began to convert the Anglo-Saxons to Christianity. In 597 there arrived in Kent a group of missionaries sent out from Rome to bring Christianity to pagan England. St. Augustine and his missionaries were well received by King Ethelbert who gave them permission to preach freely and hold services. Ethelbert himself was converted. By the end of the seventh century nearly the whole of England was Christian once more.

During the centuries when Christian Ireland had been cut off from contact with Rome, many practices had grown up in the Irish church which were different from those which prevailed on the continent. The Irish calendar placed Easter on a different date from the Roman. These differences gave rise to difficulties among the Anglo-Saxon Christians, some of whom had been converted by Irish and Scottish missionaries while others had been converted by Roman churchmen. In 664 King

Oswy called a synod at Whitby in order to settle the differences between the two groups. The king listened to the arguments on both sides and finally decided that the Roman bishops, as the descendants of St. Peter, should be obeyed in matters of doctrine and church practice. The decision was important for it preserved the unity of western Christendom and brought England into closer contact with the continent.

Schools and churches were established throughout England. Scholars were trained in the liberal arts and many religious centers in England became famous for scholarship and learning. It will be recalled that when Charlemagne established his educational reforms, founded his palace school and many monastic schools throughout his empire, he brought over the great English scholar Alcuin of York and placed him in charge of this great work. One of the famous names associated with this Anglo-Saxon renaissance or rebirth of learning and culture was Bede, whose *Ecclesiastical History of the English Nation* has already been referred to.

The rapid development of Anglo-Saxon civilization was arrested by the coming of the Norsemen. The first recorded attack of the Norsemen upon England occurred in 787. The attacks continued down to the treaty of Wedmore in the year 885. During this time England north of the Thames was repeatedly ravaged by Norse attacks. By 885 the monastic schools in that area had ceased to exist. The kingdom of the West Saxons, Wessex, to the south was still unconquered by the Danes, as the Norse were called by the English, but its plight was serious.

In 870 there came to the throne of Wessex the able king Alfred. For a time the young king was forced to remain hidden in the marshes for the Danes had overrun part of his kingdom. Alfred managed to gather about him a following and to inspire them with fresh courage. His army attacked the Danes and decisively defeated them. This victory was followed by the treaty of Wedmore in 885 by the terms of which Guthrum, the Danish leader, agreed to accept Christianity for himself and his people. Alfred surrendered half his kingdom to the Danes in order to hold the other half. For at least a century the Norsemen continued to migrate to England in large numbers. Alfred built a series of border fortifications to protect his kingdom from the Danes. He organized his subjects so that at all times one third of the able-bodied men were available for immediate military service. Alfred also built a fleet to protect his coasts. Alfred next devoted himself to improving the condition of his people. He studied Latin and translated into his own tongue the books which seemed to him most useful for his purpose. He re-established old laws, imported teachers and founded a school for the instruction of his nobles. His successors carried on his work. Adopting the Danish method of fighting, they succeeded in reconquering bit by bit the lands that had been surrendered to the Danes.

But despite the strong leadership of Alfred and his immediate successors, the growth of feudalism in England weakened the Anglo-Saxon monarchy. The nobles increased their holdings until the great earls of Wessex, Mercia, East Anglia, and Northumberland were more powerful than the king himself.

During the long reign of the weak king Ethelred "the Unready," who came to the throne in 987, England was again repeatedly attacked by the Norsemen. Ethelred resorted to the device of buying off the Danes, and a tax known as the Danegeld was levied upon his subjects for that purpose. In 1016 Sweyn Forkbeard and his son Cnut invaded England and Ethelred fled to the continent. Cnut succeeded his father. Although he had conquered England, he was in turn conquered by Christianity. He became a pious Christian and a good ruler. After his death England broke away from Scandinavia.

Ethelred had married the Norman princess Emma, and upon the conquest of his kingdom by the Danes had fled to Normandy where his son Edward was raised. His widow Emma married the Dane Cnut, who had helped drive her first husband out of England, and thus Edward was in a position to claim the English throne either as the Anglo-Saxon heir of Ethelred or as the stepson of Cnut. He ascended the English throne in 1042, and ruled until the Norman conquest in 1066.

Edward "the Confessor," as we have said, was raised in

Normandy. When he became king of England he surrounded himself with Norman advisers and officials. He appointed Normans to church offices and encouraged the migration into England of Norman traders. The Norman character of Edward's reign provoked an Anglo-Saxon reaction against the Norman influence which was headed by Godwin, earl of Essex. Upon the death of Godwin, his son Harold succeeded him as leader of the Anglo-Saxon group which dominated the feudal council, the Witan.

The Norman Conquest. Edward, who died in 1066, left no direct heirs. As a result there followed a three-cornered contest for the throne of England. Harold Godwinson, who led the Anglo-Saxon faction, was elected king by the Witan although he was not of royal blood. Harold Hardrada, king of Norway, laid claim to the English throne as a descendant of Cnut. The third candidate was Duke William of Normandy, who claimed the English throne had been promised to him by his cousin Edward the Confessor and that Harold Godwinson had promised to support that claim.

Harold Hardrada landed in England with an army of Scandinavians to make good his claim. At Stamford Bridge Harold Godwinson won a brilliant victory over the Norwegian ruler. Meanwhile William of Normandy had landed in the south and was ravaging the countryside. Harold hurried southward with his army which was reduced in numbers and exhausted by the time it encountered William's fresh Norman troops. At the battle of Hastings, Harold lost both the battle and his life.

Norman England. William overcame the English barons and established himself firmly upon the throne of England. He divided up the land, retaining forty percent as his private estate. The lands given to his nobles were so divided up that no feudal baron was powerful enough to offer resistance to the crown. William also assumed control of the English church. No papal bulls or excommunications were to be published in England without the king's consent. William favored the Cluniac reformation then in progress on the continent but insisted that in

England it be conducted under the supervision of the crown. William, the Conqueror, was succeeded by his son, William Rufus, a violent man who seized church lands and their revenues for his own purposes. In 1100 he was found dead in New Forest with an arrow through his heart. Robert, the second son of William I, was away on a crusade. Henry, the youngest, promptly seized the royal treasure, and had himself crowned king. When Robert, Duke of Normandy, returned from his crusade, he gathered his nobles about him and prepared to seize the throne from Henry. He was defeated at the battle of Tinchebrai in 1106, and was kept a prisoner by his brother during the remaining nineteen years of his life.

Henry I strengthened the royal government of England. He created a small council of advisers; he created the office of chancellor to take charge of all records and correspondence of the government; and he placed a treasurer in charge of government finance. He sent out justices who traveled throughout the realm settling cases locally, the modern circuit court.

Upon Henry's death in 1135 his barons elected his nephew, Stephen of Blois, his successor. Matilda, daughter of Henry, landed in England with a group of supporters, and a civil war ensued which lasted for nine years. Stephen lost Normandy to Count Geoffrey who in 1150 turned it over to his young son Henry. Upon Geoffrey's death in 1151, young Henry inherited Anjou, Touraine, and Maine. Then in 1152 he married the great heiress, Eleanor of Aquitaine, whose marriage to King Louis VII of France had just been annulled, as we noted in a previous chapter. Master of half of France, Henry Plantagenet then compelled Stephen to recognize him as heir to the English throne. The following year Stephen died, and Henry Plantagenet became Henry II of England.

Henry II (1154–1189) revived the administrative reforms of Henry I and extended them. All crimes were placed under the jurisdiction of the royal courts and the grand jury was instituted by which criminals were indicted. Henry's justices, traveling from county to county, became thoroughly familiar with local custom and rooted their legal decisions in that custom. They thus established throughout England a justice rooted in the unwritten tradition of England which established what has become known as the common law.

The later years of Henry II's reign were made unhappy by the rebelliousness of his sons, Eleanor having borne him four. Two of those sons predeceased him. The remaining two, Richard and John, contributed little to the well-being of England. Richard was an adventurer. During the eleven years of his reign he spent more than ten of them away from England engaged in wars in France, or in the East, or waiting to be ransomed from his imprisonment. He left no heirs; and upon his death in 1199, the scepter passed to his brother John.

Prince Arthur, the son of an older brother, had a strong claim to the English throne; according to modern notions of succession, a stronger one than John's. But the barons supported John, and to secure the claim Arthur was captured and imprisoned, and shortly afterwards "disappeared." Philip Augustus, as we saw in an earlier chapter, soon seized the French possessions of the English king, and John was left with England. His rule was marked by cruelty, treachery and extortion. He seized churchmen and nobles whose lands he coveted and allowed them to die in prison after hastening their deaths by torture. "His character suffered," explains one historian, "from a lack of good home influence in childhood."

The archbishop of Canterbury was the primate of England; that is, he was head of the English church. The English kings had been in the habit of dictating the choice of the monks of Canterbury who elected the archbishop. Upon the death of Archbishop Hubert Walter in 1205, the monks met secretly and elected one of their number, the sub-prior Reginald, and sent him off to Rome to be invested in his office by the pope before John could interfere. But Reginald indiscreetly let the news out as soon as he had crossed the Channel. When the tidings reached John he was furious. He summoned the monks and commanded that they elect his candidate, John de Gray.

When the situation was reported to Pope Innocent III, he quashed both elections, and made those monks who had gone to Rome with Reginald elect his own candidate, Stephen Langton, a learned and able churchman. John was incensed by the pope's action. He refused to allow Langton to land in England and threatened to cut off the revenues of the English church from the papacy; he confiscated the lands of the archbishop and drove the Canterbury monks out of the country. Pope Innocent responded to this act of defiance by placing all England under an interdict. John then confiscated all church property, and declared that anyone who killed a priest was his friend. Most of the bishops left England. The pope then excommunicated John, declared him deposed from the throne of England, and called a crusade against him. John's plight was desperate. Threatened by a revolt at home and by invasion from abroad, he submitted humbly to the pope, resigned his crown to the papal representative, and received England back as a fief of the papacy for which he pledged an annual tribute to Rome to be paid by himself and his successors.

In January 1215 the barons of England presented to John a demand for the reform of the government of England, and a guarantee of future good conduct. John tried to put them off, but at Runnymede he was compelled to sign the great charter, the famous Magna Carta which defined and guaranteed the rights of his subjects. Not only did this agreement secure the church from kingly intervention in church elections and protect the feudal nobility against the impositions and illegal usages so freely practiced by John; it also secured the free passage of merchants in and out of England and guaranteed that the peasants would not be subjected to arbitrary service and confiscations.

John's promise to respect the charter was worthless. He immediately resumed his war with the barons and met with considerable success, so much so that the barons called upon Louis of France, son of Philip Augustus, to be their king. But in 1216 John died suddenly, and his nine-year-old son came to the throne as Henry III.

During the minority of Henry III, through the Great Council and the regent appointed by it, the barons governed England. But when Henry assumed the direction of affairs, he appointed many Normans to important state and church offices. He married a Frenchwoman, Eleanor of Provence, most of whose relatives and friends came to England and obtained lucrative offices. The pope too flooded the English church with foreign appointees—Gregory IX in 1242 insisted that English livings be provided for 390 Italian churchmen before any Englishmen were appointed. Rome imposed heavy taxes upon the English church for it needed funds to support the struggle with the Emperor Frederick II. Finally, the pope sought to obtain the support of English arms against Frederick by offering the crown of Sicily to the second son of Henry III on condition that the English drive out Frederick. The king accepted and appealed to the Great Council for the necessary funds and military support. The barons refused both.

Interestingly enough, the English barons who were now thoroughly anti-foreign were led by a man of foreign birth, Simon de Montfort, grandson of the leader of the crusade against the Albigensians. In 1258, the year following that in which the Council had refused to support a Sicilian war, the barons met in council at Oxford and presented a series of demands to the king. Magna Carta was to be reissued and observed, the taxation imposed upon the English church by Rome was to be resisted, the foreigners who held favored positions were to be driven from the country, and a permanent committee of the Great Council was to govern England, controlling the acts of the king and his ministers.

The civil war which followed was brief. The king was defeated and taken prisoner. For a year Simon ruled England. During that time he called the first "parliament" which was composed of representatives of all classes of men. The great nobles and clerics were there. From each shire came two knights and from each important town two burgesses.

Young Prince Edward, son of the king, who had been a supporter of Simon de Montfort, now saw that Simon must be overthrown if the monarchy was to be preserved. Simon was defeated and killed at the battle of Evesham in 1265. During the remainder of Henry's life, Prince Edward was the real ruler of England.

As we have said Edward supported the revolution until he saw that under de Montfort's leadership it would destroy the monarchy. He still believed however that the people of England ought to have the opportunity to approve the laws under which they were governed. In 1295 he called into being what has become known as the Model Parliament. It consisted of four houses: one contained the nobles, bishops and abbots of the old Great Council; the representatives of the lower clergy formed a second house; a third was made up of the representatives of the shires; and a fourth of the representatives of the towns. This parliament was not to frame and pass laws; that was still the prerogative of the king. But it did provide an opportunity for the nation's representatives to make known their attitude toward a law before it was put into effect.

31   GERMANY AND ITALY

On the death of Conrad III in 1152, the German barons elected as their ruler Frederick, duke of Suabia, nephew of the deceased emperor. This first Hohenstaufen ruler, known as Frederick Barbarossa, like his predecessors regarded himself as the secular head of western Christendom. Frederick wisely devoted his attention to strengthening his position in Germany before attempting to deal with the larger problem of the empire. He conciliated the rival German factions and bestowed many favors upon the powerful Henry the Lion, duke of Bavaria and Saxony, in order to secure his loyalty.

Frederick crossed into Italy and at Pavia was crowned king of the Lombards. He then moved on to Rome and in 1155 received the imperial crown from the hands of the pope. During his visit in Rome, Frederick was made to realize that the pope, Hadrian IV, considered the emperor inferior in authority to the pope. After he had left Rome, a message reached him from the pope in which reference was made to the many benefits (*beneficia*) bestowed upon the emperor by the papacy. However, the papal messenger, Roland, translated the word *beneficia* as "fiefs." Frederick was highly indignant for he had defended the pope against the king of Naples and Sicily, and had suppressed an anti-papal revolt of the Romans led by Arnold of Brescia.

In 1158 Frederick sought to establish his control of northern Italy which he ruled as king. He insisted upon his right to collect taxes, to levy troops, to establish in each city an imperial governor or *podesta*. He forbade the formation of leagues among the cities, which would have forced the dissolution of the two rival leagues then headed respectively by Milan and Pavia. Milan promptly refused to accept these conditions and Frederick set about the subjugation of the rebellious city. The siege of Milan lasted three years.

Meanwhile Pope Hadrian had died, and the college of cardinals elected as his successor Roland who became Alexander III. Frederick refused to recognize the new pope. He summoned a council at Pavia which deposed Alexander, and elected Victor IV whom Frederick approved. Alexander fled to France and opened negotiations with the Lombard cities. The capture and brutal destruction of Milan had alarmed these cities and forced them to realize that the self-government they had enjoyed for so long was to be ended under the rule of Frederick. Under the leadership of the pope they formed a new league against Frederick.

In 1174 Frederick returned to Lombardy and laid siege to the city of Alexandria, a newly built city that had been named in honor of the pope. The league gathered its forces and met the imperial army at Legnano in 1176. The emperor was completely defeated. The following year the pope and emperor met at Venice where Frederick submitted and signed a truce which was followed in 1183 by the Peace of Constance.

Hohenstaufen Successes. In Germany meanwhile, Henry the Lion had extended his power. He seized the Slav districts of Mecklenburg and Pomerania and sought to Germanize them by building cities and establishing bishoprics and monasteries. He encouraged industry and commerce. He took Lübeck in 1158 and proceeded to break the Danish monopoly of the Baltic trade. Frederick was suspicious of the success of his powerful vassal. Henry's refusal to join his ruler in northern Italy probably contributed to the emperor's defeat at Legnano. As a result, Frederick determined to break the power of his vassal.

Frederick seized Henry's duchies of Saxony and Bavaria and after reducing them in size bestowed them upon other vassals. His success in Germany restored much of the prestige the emperor had lost by his defeat in Italy.

In 1186 Frederick arranged a marriage between his son Henry and Constance, the heiress of the Norman kingdom of Naples and Sicily which was a fief of the papacy. This was a shrewd *coup* which at once strengthened his hold upon Italy, and weakened the papacy by bringing south Italy under Hohenstaufen control.

The following year Frederick took the Crusaders' Cross, and set out upon the Third Crusade. By so doing he hoped to supplant the popes as the leaders of western Christendom in these great enterprises involving all Europe. But as we saw, Frederick's career was abruptly terminated when he was drowned while crossing or bathing in an eastern stream.

Upon his accession Frederick's son, Henry VI, was confronted by rebellion in all quarters. Henry the Lion led the revolt in Germany. He allied himself with his brother-in-law, Richard the Lion Hearted of England, and with Tancred of Sicily who usurped the throne of southern Italy. But the young emperor was a man of energy and ability, and he was aided by fate. Richard the Lion Hearted, returning through Germany from his crusade against Saladin, fell into Henry's hands and was held for a large ransom. Henry the Lion's son fell in love with a Hohenstaufen princess, and when his father died in 1195 the German rebellion came to an end.

Henry VI then crossed into Italy and by shrewdly taking advantage of the jealous rivalry of the north Italian cities he secured their support. He was crowned in Rome, and proceeded into southern Italy where he seized the Norman kingdom and punished its ruler by blinding and mutilation. At the height of his career Henry VI died suddenly in 1197, leaving as his successor his three-year-old son. The following year there came to the papal throne the great Innocent III.

Innocent III and Frederick II. Civil war immediately broke out in Germany. The Hohenstaufens passed over the infant Frederick and acclaimed Henry's brother Philip king. The Guelf faction elected Otto of Brunswick, son of Henry the Lion. Both sides appealed to the pope for support.

Innocent issued a declaration of papal supremacy in which he asserted that the empire was dependent upon the papacy for its origin and authority, and that it was the right and duty of the popes to provide for the empire by bestowing authority upon the emperor. He pronounced in favor of Otto of Brunswick who took the title Otto IV. The Hohenstaufens insisted that it was the right of the German nobles to select the emperor and the struggle continued. The Hohenstaufens allied themselves with Philip Augustus of France, and Otto was supported by Philip's enemy, Richard of England. When it seemed likely Otto would be defeated, Philip of Suabia was murdered by a private enemy, and Otto was then accepted as king in Germany. In 1209 he was crowned emperor in Rome by Innocent III.

Constance, widow of Henry VI and heiress of the Kingdom of Naples and Sicily, became ruler during the minority of her son. Fearing rebellion, she sought the protection of the pope, and shortly before her death in 1198 she placed her son under the pope's guardianship. The pope accepted fully his obligations to the child Frederick. For ten years he fought the Norman barons who sought to disregard Frederick's rights, and in the end he triumphed.

Sicily over which Frederick ruled was at the time perhaps the most prosperous and best organized state in Europe. Palermo was an advanced cultural center and Frederick acquired a fine education. As he grew to manhood the situation in Germany opened up an opportunity for him to regain the German inheritance of which he had been deprived. Otto's policies were such that he lost the support of both the German barons and the pope.

A group of German nobles invited Frederick to assume the German kingship, and with the pope's approval Frederick accepted and was crowned king at Mainz in 1212 at the age of eighteen. He allied himself with Philip Augustus of France. King John of England, defeated by Philip Augustus in France, saw an opportunity to recover his losses by joining Otto. At the Battle of Bouvines in 1214, Philip Augustus and Frederick triumphed.

Innocent III died in 1216. In the same year his successor, Honorius III, crowned Frederick II emperor on condition that the Kingdom of Naples and Sicily be held separate from Germany, and that Frederick go on a crusade. Frederick was not a religious man. He put off the crusade. In other ways his conduct offended the pope, for while he made Palermo a great cultural and intellectual center, he manifested a keen interest in Moslem thought, maintaining a force of Saracen troops, and a harem. For his failure to undertake a crusade, he was excommunicated.

In 1227 he set out on a crusade but returned after three days because of illness. He was again excommunicated, and while still outlawed by the church set out once more and reached the Holy Land. By diplomacy he arranged for the surrender of Jerusalem, Bethlehem, and Nazareth into Christian hands. He had himself crowned king of Jerusalem and returned home.

Frederick next sought to bring northern Italy under his control. In 1237 he defeated the Lombard League, and arranged for the gradual conquest and subjugation of the hostile cities. He then determined to discipline Pope Gregory IX, who had been outspoken in his criticism of Frederick's behavior and morals. He aroused the Roman citizens to revolt against the pope with the result that Gregory's successor, Innocent IV, fled to France from whence he excommunicated Frederick.

In 1250 Frederick II died. Sicilian, partly by blood and wholly by training and interest, he neglected Germany. As a result the history of Germany during and after Frederick's reign is one of disintegration. The Teutonic order of German knights was transferred from Palestine to Prussia in 1230, and Prussia was gradually Christianized. The German nobles and bishops became independent, and German cities fought to free themselves from subjection to their feudal overlords. Many became free cities. This process of disintegration continued until by the close of the Middle Ages the Germanies comprised over three hundred distinct states.

32   RUSSIA AND THE EAST

Eastern Europe in Early Times. The great stretch of continent between the Black Sea and the Gulf of Finland has had a history in large part independent of the developments in Western Europe. Through the ages there had passed across the steppes, forests, and swamps of Eastern Europe many different peoples. Early in our account we traced the advance of the Indo-Europeans from Central Asia across this region into southern and western Europe. Later the Germans traversed the region and settled north of the Black Sea during the second century. Still later the Huns swept in from Asia and set up an extended empire in the region under Attila.

During Justinian's reign in the sixth century, Slavic peoples, whose place of origin is unknown, pressed southward and into the Balkan provinces of the Byzantine empire. In the late seventh century a Ural-Altaic people akin to the Huns crossed from northeast to southwest and eventually settled in the Balkans. These were the Bulgars who, through intermarriage with their Slav neighbors, lost their racial identity and became predominantly Slavic. The Finns, also a Uralic people, settled in the northwest.

Expansion of the Slavs and the Coming of the Rus. During the seventh century the Slavs, who had been located north of the Carpathians, began to expand. They eventually spread themselves over the whole region from the steppes north of the Black Sea to the Gulf of Finland. They traversed the heavily wooded region along the great rivers, the chief means of communication and trade for many centuries.

About the middle of the ninth century, during the era of Norse expansion, some of the Scandinavian Vikings crossed the Baltic, entered the Gulf of Finland and the rivers of northern Russia, and made their way southward into the Ukraine around 859. These Scandinavians who settled in Russia were known as Varangians; as they were also called Rus (meaning rowers), the land which came under their dominion was known as Russia. The Varangians—like their Norse kinsmen in the British Isles, in Northern France, in Iceland, Greenland, and Vineland—set up principalities: at Novgorod, Turov, Polotsk, and Kiev. Rurik, the Scandinavian chieftain, is supposed to have established himself in Novgorod in 862. By the tenth century these Varangian principalities were loosely organized in a great state. This was the work of Rurik and his successors, Igor and Oleg. The people of the Varangian principalities were of course largely Slavic.

Kiev and Novgorod. Kiev became the capital of the Varangian domain and the law of its Grand Prince was respected in all the provinces which paid annual tribute in furs, skins, grain, honey, wax, and slaves. These commodities were sent down the Don and Dnieper to the Black Sea and thence to Constantinople with which a lively commerce had developed.

Byzantine culture and religion spread throughout Russia and became so firmly established that, after the fall of Constantinople in the fifteenth century, the civilization of the Byzantine East survived in that region. At the end of the tenth century, the Grand Prince Vladimir of Kiev was converted to the Byzantine or Greek orthodox form of Christianity. Vladimir made Christianity the religion of Russia. Byzantine artists erected and decorated churches and thereby established the style of later Russian art.

Yaroslav (1016–1054), son of Vladimir, defeated the Petchenegs, who were settled north of the Black Sea. He issued the first code of Russian law. But, like the feudal Franks, he divided up his great empire among his five sons and thus began the disintegration of the great Varangian state. Disintegration was hastened by the invasion of the steppes by an Asiatic horde called the Polovti who severed the trade routes between Russia and the Black Sea and who systematically raided Russian territory during a period of one hundred and fifty years.

The Russians, pushed northward during the twelfth century, migrated into Poland and Lithuania. Others settled around Moscow. Novgorod became the chief center of the new North Russian state. The monarchy was abandoned and a republic was established in its place. Novgorod developed a prosperous commerce in the Baltic with the cities of the Hanseatic League.

The Mongols. In the thirteenth century, the Mongol nomads of the steppes of central Asia were united in a great empire by Genghis Khan. Under the leadership of the great Genghis, the Mongols set out to conquer the world. They seized Turkestan from the kingdom of North China and then conquered the Turkish empire of Kharezm. They then swept westward and by 1223 had reached the Don.

The sons and grandsons of Genghis—among whom was the famous Kublai Khan in China—continued the conquests. The Mongols invaded Russia and took Kiev in 1240. They pursued the Kipchak Turks into Hungary and in 1241 their horsemen reached Italy and the Adriatic. The Europeans knew them as Tatars or Tartars. The Tartars overran Poland and their armies invaded the Moslem East and seized Baghdad, Aleppo, and Damascus.

However, after 1243, the Mongol horde slowly withdrew into Asia. But there remained in Russia the western Mongol Kingdom of the Golden Horde which survived there until the fifteenth century.

The Mongol advance into Europe naturally stimulated European interest in the great eastern empire. In 1250 the Venetian merchants, Nicolo and Matteo Polo traveled into Asia where they were received at the court of the khan. Again in 1271, accompanied by Nicolo's son, Marco Polo, they journeyed across Asia and were received with honors by Kublai Khan. Marco entered the khan's service and traveled widely in the East. Upon his return he dictated *The Book of Marco*

Polo which was translated into many languages and was widely known in Europe during the Middle Ages.

Tamerlane. In 1369 Tamerlane succeeded the Emir of Khurasan. He immediately set about to reconquer the lands that had earlier fallen into Mongol hands. This fierce and barbarous conqueror subjugated a vast territory stretching from Hindustan in northern India to Hungary. He seized Baghdad and Damascus from the Ottoman Turks.

After receiving the homage of the Byzantine emperor in 1402, Tamerlane returned to his capital, Samarkand, north of the Caspian Sea. He was organizing a great invasion of China when he died in 1405. Immediately his great empire collapsed.

The Rise of Moscow. Many of the Russians who had fled northward from the Mongol-Tartars settled around Moscow. The increased population stimulated trade and brought prosperity to the city. Thick forests separated Moscow from the Mongols and protected it against attack. The Muscovite Grand Prince purchased the favor of the Mongols with gifts and was appointed an administrator and tax collector for the khan.

The Moscow princes fostered the prosperity of their city and extended their authority in very much the same fashion as the French Capetian rulers. Two of these Muscovite princes stand out above all others: Ivan the Great and Ivan the Terrible.

The Two Ivans. Ivan III (1462–1505), known as Ivan the Great, ranks as the founder of the Russian empire. He conquered the Republic of Novgorod and incorporated its extensive territories in his domain in 1478. By conquest, purchase, and marriage alliances, he extended his control over the entire Russian North to the White Sea and the Ural Mountains.

Internal dissensions had split the Golden Horde into three khanates: Krim (Crimea), Kazan, and Astrakhan. Ivan freed

Russia from Tartar control and in a series of attacks on the khanates weakened their power.

In 1472 Ivan married Sophia Paleologus, niece of the last emperor and heiress of the Byzantine empire. The Byzantine marriage strengthened the Byzantine tradition in Russia and was also the means of introducing European culture into Moscow, for Sophia brought with her from Italy, to which she had fled after the seizure of Constantinople by the Ottoman Turks, many skilled Italians including architects and artists. It was Ivan III who first assumed the title, Caesar or Czar.

Ivan IV (1547–1584), "The Terrible," was an able ruler who extended Russian territory, introduced many reforms, and strengthened the monarchy. Yet he deserved his title "The Terrible," for his terrible passion combined with a strange cowardice and an utter disregard for human life led him to commit deeds which shocked even the barbarous age in which he lived. His destruction of Novgorod because of a false rumor which he did not investigate, and the slaying of his own son in a fit of fury, are but two of his many deeds of violence.

But Ivan IV was the greatest Russian reformer before Peter the Great. He issued a new code of laws and improved the administration of justice. He reformed the clergy. He strengthened the monarchy by confiscating the estates of the landed aristocracy and redistributed them among a new class. And he gave more attention than his predecessors to the interests of the small landholders.

Ivan IV invaded the khanates of the Golden Horde, which had been weakened by the attacks of Ivan III, and with the help of the Don Cossacks, conquered the khanates of Kazan and Astrakhan. Krim, or the Crimea, had meanwhile been seized by the Turks in whose hands it remained until it became Russian in the reign of Catherine the Great.

33   RIVALRY OF ENGLAND AND FRANCE

While popes and emperors struggled for predominance in Italy—a struggle which, as we have seen, led to the eventual disintegration of Germany—the kings of England and France steadily enlarged their powers and in so doing prepared the way for the final emergence of two great nation-states of Europe.

For a long time however the end to which developments were leading was not apparent. It will be recalled that the Angevin empire of King Henry II of England included England, half of France, with Wales, Scotland, Ireland, and Brittany as vassal states.

The fact that the English kings claimed overlordship of a large part of France determined the major policy of the French kings. The French monarchy, it was recognized, would never be secure so long as English kings claimed part of France. On the other hand, the English rulers in their turn felt that so long as the French monarchy remained powerful their claims to French fiefs would always be disputed. The fundamental issue of the Hundred Years' War was whether France would survive as an independent national state ruled by French kings, or whether it would become part of an Anglo-French empire under English kings.

There were many lesser issues which furnished occasion for launching the long struggle. One was the fact that the herring had shifted their breeding grounds from the Baltic to the North Sea. French and English fishing fleets met at sea and fought for possession of the fishing grounds. This led to an exchange of raids upon English and French coasts and shipping.

Another cause of war was the situation in Flanders. Flanders was a center of cloth manufacture and depended upon England for its chief raw material, wool. The Flemish cities had long enjoyed a large degree of municipal independence and jealously resisted any attempt on the part of the count of Flanders to restrict them in any way, or to share in the profits of their enterprise through increased taxation. In the course of this quarrel between the Flemings and their lord, the count was driven out of Flanders in the early fourteenth century, but was restored to his county through the help of his overlord, the French king, in 1328. The English had not hesitated to make trouble for the French king by encouraging the Flemish revolt. As a result the Flemish count ordered the arrest of all English merchants in Flanders. Edward III of England retaliated by forbidding the export of English wool to Flanders, and as a result the cloth industry of Flanders was brought to a standstill. Under the leadership of Jacob van Artevelde, a merchant of Ghent, the Flemings drove out their count once more, and sought to come to terms with the English with whom they were closely allied in interest.

It should also be mentioned that Bordeaux, in English hands, was the outlet for the sea-borne trade of southwestern France. The French kings were naturally desirous of controlling this seaport and its trade, and that ambition furnished another motive for the war.

In 1340 Philip VI of France determined to avenge the attacks upon French fishermen and to break the English commercial hold in Flanders. He gathered a fleet of Norman and Breton ships and hired forty galleys from Genoa. These he assembled at Sluys in preparation for his attack. Meanwhile Edward had not been idle. With a fleet of English and Flemish ships he appeared outside the harbor of Sluys, and the French issued forth to meet him. The English destroyed or scattered the French fleet, and established a supremacy upon the sea which they maintained throughout the war.

The Flemings meanwhile found themselves in an awkward predicament. They had driven out their count. The count and his overlord, the king of France, both appealed to the pope to condemn and punish the rebellious Flemings for their violation of their feudal obligations to their overlord. Dreading the papal weapons of excommunication and interdict, Jacob van Artevelde hit upon a scheme which would temporarily tie the hands of the papacy. This involved the question of the French royal succession.

The last four Capetian kings prior to 1328 had many daughters but no sons. Upon the death of Charles IV in 1328, it became necessary to determine who was next in line in the succession. If the succession were permitted to pass to a grandson through his mother, Edward III might claim the crown of

France for his mother was a French princess. But the French Estates General ruled out that possibility and bestowed the crown upon a cousin of Charles IV who became Philip VI (1328–1350). At the time Edward III accepted the decision of the Estates General and acknowledged Philip as king of France by doing homage for his French fiefs. Jacob van Artevelde proposed that Edward of England assume the title, "King of France." This would make it necessary to investigate and establish all claims before the papacy would be in a position to take action against the Flemings for disobedience to their overlord.

Crécy. The English king gathered an army which was made up of all classes of Englishmen. The most formidable weapon of the English, as it proved, was the long bow. This bow could be discharged with great rapidity and force, and its steel-tipped arrows were capable of piercing armor at a distance of one hundred yards. Its maximum range was nearly six hundred yards. Years of practice were necessary in order for a man to develop the muscles necessary to draw this powerful bow, so that it was impossible for an army unaccustomed to its use to adopt the weapon quickly.

In 1346 Edward set out from England with an army intending to land at Bordeaux and invade France from the south. Winds held his fleet in the channel. He suddenly changed his plan, and landing at Cotentin in Normandy he marched inland south of the Seine. Along the way he devastated the countryside, burned fields and buildings, and collected an enormous booty. The French hurried up to check his advance. As the French arrived, Edward forded the Seine, intending to join the reinforcements that had been dispatched from Flanders. However, the French army was at his heels, and he was forced to halt and do battle.

The battle site of Crécy was carefully chosen. The English army was disposed upon a slight rise of ground that was protected from flank attack by wooded and marshy lands. At the top of the rise the English knights dismounted and prepared to meet the French charge on foot. To the right and left were companies of bowmen, and hidden in the bushes at the extreme ends were bodies of Welsh knifemen.

The French advanced in customary formation. They were preceded by the Genoese crossbowmen who fired a volley of bolts toward the English ranks with the purpose of breaking up their formation just before the charge of the French knights. However, their volley fell short for a brief shower had wetted and loosened the strings of the crossbows. In their impatience to get at the unmounted English knights the French cavalry charged before the confused crossbowmen had opened their ranks to permit passage of the horsemen. Some confusion resulted.

The English bowmen had protected the strings of their bows against the rain. As the French cavalry charged, slowed down by the rise in the ground and the masses of crossbowmen, the English archers discharged their arrows at long range into the close ranks of the French cavalry. Horses and men went down in great numbers and soon the field was a confused mass of entangled animals and men. When the arrows had done their work, the knifemen closed in and dispatched the knights as they lay struggling on the ground. It is estimated that the French lost between 15,000 and 20,000 killed. The English lost fewer than fifty.

Free from any danger of French attack, Edward next laid siege to the port of Calais which he took and fortified. This gave him a base for future operations in northern France.

The Black Death. After the capture of Calais both nations were so exhausted by the war that the pope's emissaries were able to negotiate a truce. Then in 1347 Europe suffered another disaster. This was the great plague known as the Black Death. The bubonic plague was carried on the bodies of rats which infested the ships trading with the Orient. It is estimated that this dread disease carried off from one-quarter to one half of the population as it swept back and forth across Europe between 1347 and 1350.

Sometimes the entire crew of a ship would die at sea and the ship would drift until driven up on shore where it would at once become a new focal point of infection. The suffering and repulsive appearance of the victims can scarcely be described, and the demoralization it produced among the people can scarcely be imagined. Carts traveled through the towns at night to collect the corpses which were dumped into pits and hastily covered over. Sometimes they were dumped into streams and rivers, and as they were carried away spread the plague in new areas downstream.

Poitiers. During the truce which followed the Crécy campaign the English reinforced their armies in Aquitaine, for the French persisted in their attempts to arouse dissatisfaction with the English rule in that quarter. Edward, heir to the English throne, who is known in history as the Black Prince, decided to resume the war on France. He marched northward into France, plundering and ravaging the countryside as he went. Suddenly he found himself confronted by a French army ten times the size of his own. It was led by King John, who had come to the throne in 1350, and his three sons. The Black Prince offered to make terms with his formidable enemy, for defeat seemed certain, but confident of victory the French king declined the offer.

The battle of Poitiers in 1356 was a repetition of the victory at Crécy. King John and his three sons were taken prisoner and carried off to England with many French nobles to be held for ransom. Many of the common soldiers who had been taken prisoner were slain for they had no value as hostages and their numbers endangered their captors.

This first phase of the Hundred Years' War was brought to a conclusion by the Peace of Bretigny in 1360, which added Poitou to the English possessions in southern France, and confirmed the English possession of Calais and the surrounding county of Ponthieu. The English king was to hold his possessions henceforth in free sovereignty and no longer as vassal of the French monarch.

Civil Strife in France and England. With the cessation of hostilities, thousands of soldiers of both armies found themselves in France without employment. They formed themselves into bands called "free companies" which ravaged the countryside and looted towns and villages. Meanwhile the French were called upon to raise enormous sums of money to ransom their king and his nobles. This was the condition which met Charles, son of King John, who returned to France to establish order and to arrange for the payment of his father's ransom. However, John died in England in 1364 and his ransom was never paid.

We have many times taken account of the tendency of the townsmen to free themselves from their feudal obligations to their overlords and to establish municipal independence under burgher control. In Paris Stephen Marcel was elected provost of the merchants of Paris in 1355. After the disaster of Poitiers in 1356, Marcel saw an opportunity to impose such terms upon the king as would give the burghers a predominance in the French government. Marcel aroused the Paris mob and invaded the palace in order to intimidate the Dauphin Charles. Charles fled from Paris and appealed to the nobles of the country for support. The desperate peasantry, encouraged by the actions of Marcel and the Estates General, broke into revolt and this convinced the nobles of the necessity of supporting the king and restoring law and order. The revolts were put down, and Marcel was assassinated in Paris.

The Dauphin, who became King Charles V in 1364, was fortunate in having the services of an able military commander, Bertrand du Guesclin, who recruited an army from among the free companies and restored order in France. The rule of the Black Prince in Gascony so irked the Gascon nobles that they appealed to Charles V to secure them justice, and the war was resumed. Du Guesclin wisely avoided a pitched battle with the English. He drew the hostilities away from France by an expedition across the Pyrenees and harried the English by guerrilla tactics. In 1376 the Black Prince died of camp fever. By this time English holdings in southern France had been reduced to the coastal region around Bordeaux and Bayonne.

Edward III, who died in 1377, was succeeded by his grandson, Richard II, who arranged the long truce of 1389. England too had suffered a series of revolts. The Black Death had carried off so many of the peasantry that there was a scarcity of labor. The nobles sought to hold the peasants to their feudal condition while their labor was much in demand in the towns and on other estates. In 1381, led by Wat Tyler, a crowd of peasants marched on London and demanded from the king a charter of rights.

The nobles and parliament resisted Richard's rule until, in 1399, he was deposed and was succeeded by his cousin, Henry of Lancaster, who became Henry IV.

Renewal of the War. In 1380 there came to the throne of France Charles VI (1380–1422), an eleven-year-old boy. In 1392 the young king went mad. He could not be deposed however because his insanity was recurrent, interrupted by periods of sanity. In this situation there developed a contest among the great princes of the realm for control of the government.

The Duke of Burgundy, the king's uncle, led one faction. He was opposed by the Duke of Orléans. A bitter civil war was fought between the two factions. In 1407 the Duke of Orléans was murdered in Paris and the leadership of his faction was taken over by the count of Armagnac. The war raged over possession of the capital city, Paris.

Henry V of England aided both sides in order to keep the war going and weaken France. When in 1414 the Armagnacs gained control of Paris, the queen, and the heir to the throne, Henry decided it was time to assume a more active role in the conflict. He invaded France with about fifteen thousand men and besieged Harfleur. As he marched toward Calais after taking Harfleur he was met by a strong French army. The experience of Crécy and Poitiers was repeated once again at Agincourt, and at least ten thousand of the Armagnacs were slain.

The Duke of Burgundy was then able to expel the Armagnacs from Paris. While the French factions continued their struggles with each other, Henry of England systematically reduced and occupied Normandy. In 1420 the Treaty of Troyes was signed which gave the English king a predominant role in France. Under the treaty Henry was to marry Catherine and become regent of France. The Dauphin was excluded from the succession. As regent, Henry proceeded to bring under his control those regions of France that were in Armagnac hands. He cleared his enemies from the north of France, but before he could advance into the south both Henry V of England and Charles VI of France died in the same year, 1422.

Henry's infant son was proclaimed king of England and France while the new king's uncle, the duke of Bedford, became regent of both countries. The son of Charles VI also claimed the French throne as Charles VII, and the wars continued. So long as the able duke of Bedford lived the Anglo-Burgundian alliance was maintained. But English successes were such that the Burgundians now began to fear the consequences of English control of France. In 1435 Bedford died and Charles VII was able to win the Burgundian duke away from his English alliance.

Joan of Arc. Although the Burgundians no longer supported the English, the plight of Charles VII was desperate. The English held all the west and north of France, including the capital, Paris. The Duke of Burgundy held the east including Flanders. Orléans, the temporary capital of the uncrowned French monarch, was besieged by the English and Charles was forced to move from city to city in disguise to escape assassination. His supporters were poor, broken in spirit, and exhausted by the long struggle. The economic life of France was at a standstill. Towns of ten thousand population were frequently reduced to ruined shells sheltering only a few hundred inhabitants.

At this critical point in French history, there appeared before Charles the peasant girl of Domrémy who miraculously saved France. Charles was able to do no more for Joan than to provide her with a suit of armor and a small escort. But as the Maid advanced to the relief of besieged Orléans numbers of soldiers, stirred by the accounts they had heard of the strange Maid, joined the march. Within a few days of Joan's arrival the siege of Orléans, which had lasted nineteen months, was raised. The French once again took heart. In fulfillment of the instructions of the "voices" which had guided Joan, she conducted the king to Rheims where he was crowned with ceremony in the great Cathedral as had been his ancestors before him. This too was a wise move, for the French were made to feel that their king was indeed king. With the crowning of Charles, Joan felt her mission had been fulfilled. But the French wished her to continue to lead them.

However, Joan's military successes were at an end. She was captured by the Burgundians and sold to the English. The French looked upon Joan as a saint and a deliverer. In order to destroy her influence the English had her tried as a witch and heretic. She was condemned and burned at the stake at Rouen in 1431.

But through her martyrdom Joan became a national heroine. The new national enthusiasm enabled Charles to drive the English first out of the north of France and then from the south. In 1453 the English retained of all their French possessions only Calais.

34 THE AVIGNON PAPACY
AND THE GREAT SCHISM

Louis IX, "Saint Louis," was succeeded in France by Philip III and then by Philip IV, "the Fair." Philip addressed himself energetically to the task of broadening the monarchical power. He reorganized administration, increased the number and powers of his officials, and regularized government functions, demanding periodic reports. A privy council replaced the Great Council and functioned as a kind of king's cabinet.

In order to render himself independent of the military support of the feudal nobility, Philip created a national army recruited from all classes of the population and paid out of the national treasury. In order to finance all these new governmental functions, he instituted a system of national taxation. This was naturally resisted because under the feudal system the king, like his vassals, was maintained by the revenues from his own private domain. These feudal revenues were naturally insufficient to support a modern national government.

Throughout his reign Philip was plagued by money troubles. He resorted to many devices to fill the treasury. He banished the Jews from France, and confiscated their property. He then permitted them to return and take up their banking activities upon the payment of heavy fines. He reduced the value of money by decreasing the amount of precious metal in the coin and was thereby enabled to spend the balance.

The great crusading order of Knights Templars, which had grown wealthy through their activities as international bankers, returned to France in 1291. Philip made this order the victim of his need. He suddenly arrested all the Templars in France, brought charges against them of heresy and immorality, burned many of their leaders at the stake, and confiscated their property.

It had become customary for the kings of both France and England to call upon the clergy for gifts to the royal treasury. These gifts had always been given voluntarily. Both Philip IV of France and Edward I of England, who were at war over Guienne, imposed taxes upon the Catholic clergy. The clergy of both countries appealed to the pope. Pope Boniface VIII in 1296 issued the bull *Clericis Laicos* in which he declared that no layman had the right to tax the clergy or church property. Edward responded by outlawing the English clergy with the result that when the protection of the law was removed the English clergy voted the sum their king had demanded. Philip cut off the export of papal revenues to Rome. He arrested a papal legate and tried him for treason.

Boniface replied to Philip's acts with another bull and excommunicated Philip. Philip called together an Estates General in 1302 in which were represented along with the clergy and nobility, the Third Estate with elected representatives from the towns and countryside. Despite the fact that he was successful in persuading the Estates General to give him its support, Philip sent agents to Italy to bring the pope to France. The elderly Boniface received rough treatment at the hands of Philip's agents and died.

The Babylonian Captivity of the Papacy. The archbishop of Bordeaux was elected to succeed Boniface as Clement V. Instead of going to Rome, Clement summoned the cardinals to Lyons where he was crowned pope in 1305. It is true that the quarreling Roman factions threatened the safety of the pope, and Clement remained in France in an effort to save for the church some of the property of the Knights Templars which was dissolved by Philip as we saw. As he continued to live in France, Clement in 1309 transferred the papal government to Avignon.

Clement had not intended to establish the residence of the papacy permanently at Avignon. But as the years passed, he chose new cardinals from among the French clergy so that upon his death the Italians in the College of Cardinals were a minority. From 1305 to 1378 the papacy remained in France, French popes being elected by French cardinals. This is the famous "Babylonian Captivity" of the papacy.

European Reaction to the Avignon Papacy. It was natural that during the course of the Hundred Years' War the English should object to sending revenues of the English church to the French popes at Avignon to be spent in the enemy's country. Whether rightly or wrongly the feeling grew among the faithful throughout Europe that the popes were subject to the influence of the French crown, with the result that papal revenues declined rapidly. In this situation the popes were forced to rely on the French to pay the costs of the papal government and many devices were elaborated to bring fees into church coffers. In time the French came to resent papal taxation to such an extent that by the end of the Babylonian Captivity the papacy had lost prestige throughout all of Europe.

During the absence of the papacy the city of Rome declined. Embassies were sent to Pope Urban V urging the return of the pope to the Eternal City. Urban did pay a visit to Rome to prepare the way for the transfer of the papal government to that city. While in Rome he died. The Romans were now fearful that the election of another French pope might mean the continuance of the papal residence at Avignon. The threat of the Roman mob and a division among the French cardinals resulted in the election of the Italian archbishop of Bari as Urban VI in 1378.

The Great Schism. Urban VI at once vigorously and without tact condemned the morals and manners of the cardinals. His harshness antagonized the cardinals who met in council and, declaring that the election of Urban was invalid because brought about by the compulsion of the Romans, proceeded to elect as pope Robert of Geneva who took the name of Clement VII.

Urban refused to recognize Clement, who took up his residence at Avignon. Thus Europe was confronted with the perplexity of two popes. France, Scotland, and Naples supported Clement. England, the Empire, northern Italy, Hungary and Poland gave their allegiance to the Roman pope Urban. The faithful throughout Europe were troubled. What if the individual unknowingly depended upon the services of the clergy supporting the wrong pope—did this mean that the sacraments so administered were invalid and that his soul would be eternally damned? Men began to ask themselves whether the authority of the papacy was in fact all that had been claimed. The spectacle of two popes making the same claims to that authority provoked doubts.

In 1409 a council of cardinals met at Pisa to deal with the schism. The council declared both the Roman and Avignon popes deposed and elected in their place Alexander V. But neither of the other popes paid any attention to the action of the council of Pisa, with the result that the situation was only further complicated with three popes instead of two.

The Council of Constance. Since the churchmen had failed to heal the schism, the emperor Sigismund called a council of all

Europe to meet at Constance in the Tyrol in 1414. Representatives attended from nearly every country in Europe. At the council of Constance all classes and interests were represented. It was attended by cardinals, bishops, abbots, priests, monks, kings, princes, burghers, peasants, and representatives of the universities and guilds.

The program of the council of Constance was three-fold. It was to deal first with the papal schism. Next came the problem of heresy for during the Babylonian Captivity and Great Schism there arose many preachers who denied doctrines of the church which had been accepted for centuries, and these issues required to be clarified. And finally the council was to address itself to the question of reform within the church.

The council deposed the three papal claimants and elected unanimously Odo Colonna who then became Pope Martin V. At the council were the two Bohemian heretics, John Hus and Jerome of Prague. They were heard by the council and their views declared heretical. When they refused to alter their position, they were condemned and burned at the stake. The representatives of each nation were then asked to draw up a list of abuses which needed reform and submit them to the council.

During the schism many intellectuals, chief among them John Gerson of the University of Paris, had denied the supremacy of papal authority. They held that superior to the pope in authority was the council representing all the faithful. This question was debated and although no final position was reached, the conciliar idea was sufficiently strong so that arrangements were made for the calling of church councils at regular intervals.

In line with this policy a council was called at Pavia in 1423, and in 1431 another council gathered at Basel. But wars and other preoccupations cut down the attendance at these and later councils so that in the long run papal authority was never seriously threatened and the conciliar movement died out.

PART SEVEN
The Renaissance and the Reformation

1400	Death of Chaucer
1446	First printed books (Coster in Haarlem)
1447	Vatican library founded by Pope Nicholas V
1453	Fall of Constantinople, captured by Ottoman Turks
1455–1485	Wars of the Roses
1461–1483	Louis XI, King of France
1462–1505	Ivan III, Grand Duke of Moscow
1469–1492	Lorenzo de' Medici, ruler of Florence
1469	Ferdinand of Aragon married Isabella of Castile
1492	Columbus crossed the Atlantic to America
1497	Leonardo da Vinci's *Last Supper*
1498	Vasco da Gama rounded the Cape of Good Hope to India
	Savonarola executed in Florence
1499	Switzerland became an independent republic
1508–1512	Michelangelo painted ceiling of Sistine Chapel
1509–1547	Henry VIII, King of England
1511	Erasmus' *In Praise of Folly*
1517	Luther's *95 Theses*
1520–1566	Suleiman the Magnificent
1534	Luther's German translation of the Bible
	Ignatius Loyola founded Society of Jesus, or Jesuit order
1545–1563	Council of Trent

35 EUROPE DISCOVERS THE FAR EAST

Venice and the Eastern Trade. During the fourteenth and fifteenth centuries Venice was a great commercial empire lying between Europe and the East. Spices from the Indies, silk from China, gems and fine cotton goods from India, pearls from the Persian Gulf, ivory and emeralds from the east coast of Africa, fine steel weapons from the forges of Damascus and other Moslem cities, were brought together in the ports of the eastern Mediterranean. In exchange for these commodities Venice bartered hides and furs and woolen cloths and copper and many other products which she drew from all Europe.

Each year Venice sent out three great trading fleets, one of which passed through the Straits of Gibraltar, stopped at ports on the west European coast, and ended up in the lowlands where it exchanged its oriental cargoes for the commodities that had been accumulated from the Baltic and the countries of northern Europe. The Portuguese envied the Venetians the monopoly of this rich trade, but continued to depend on them for the spices and other products to which they had grown accustomed.

Henry the Navigator. In the early part of the fifteenth century, the Ottoman Turks, who had settled in Asia Minor, began an expansion and conquest which ultimately gave them control of the entire eastern Mediterranean and brought them into Europe as far as the very gates of Vienna. Once they had established their control of Syria and Egypt, the Turks levied such tolls upon commerce that it became increasingly difficult for Europeans to pay for eastern products.

The Portuguese and the Spaniards had for centuries carried on crusading wars against the Moslems in the Iberian peninsula, and in north Africa. Portuguese and Spaniards had persisted with unflagging zeal in their attempts to break the Moslem power, and to convert the unbelievers to Christianity.

Two powerful motives combined to advance the Portuguese

search for a sea-passage around Africa to the East. One of those motives, the more comprehensible to modern minds, was to open up commerce with the east by a route which would not involve the payment of heavy tolls to the Moslem Turk. The other motive, frequently the more important to

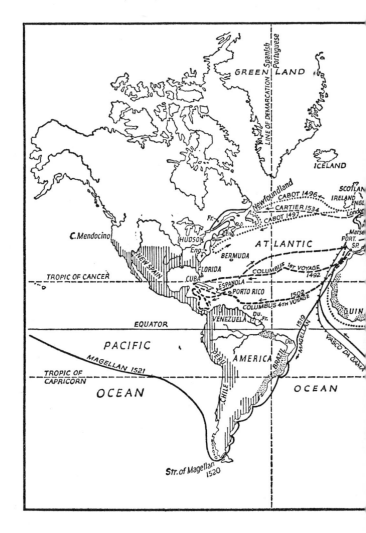

men of the fifteenth century, was to hem in the Turk and to break his hold upon the Holy Land.

The era of exploration was ushered in by Prince Henry of Portugal (1394–1460), known as "the Navigator." After leading crusades against the Moslems in north Africa as a

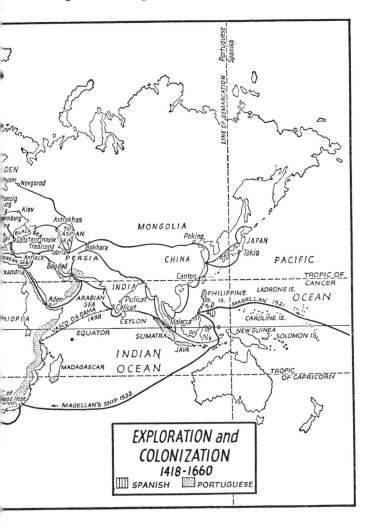

EXPLORATION and
COLONIZATION
1418-1660
SPANISH   PORTUGUESE

young man, he devoted the greater part of his life to organizing and launching explorations along the west coast of Africa. His captains sought a sea-passage to the east and also sought to make contact with the legendary Christian kingdom of Prester John which was believed to exist in the interior of Africa. In alliance with this kingdom the Portuguese hoped to attack the Turk from the Red Sea and free Jerusalem.

By the end of the first decade of Prince Henry's activities, the Madeira Islands and the Azores had been discovered and permanent settlement of them begun. Before Henry's death in 1460 some two thousand miles of the west African coast had been explored.

For a time after Henry's death exploration lagged, but when John II came to the throne in 1481 the work was resumed. In 1486 Bartholomew Diaz reached the Cape of Good Hope.

Columbus. In the meantime a Genoese captain, Christopher Columbus, had advanced the idea that the Indies could be reached by sailing westward from Europe. The conception that the earth was globular was not new in Columbus' day. No matter what most people may have thought about the shape of the earth, scholars all during the Middle Ages had known that the earth was spherical. But Columbus conceived the earth to be much smaller than is actually the case. Failing to obtain the backing of the king of Portugal, Columbus went to the Spanish court and succeeded in winning the sponsorship of Queen Isabella.

On August 3, 1492, Columbus sailed from Palos with three well-equipped and seaworthy ships. The enterprise was intelligently organized as the results proved. On October twelfth the ships came in sight of land. Columbus went ashore and claimed possession in the name of the Spanish crown. He sailed among the islands and explored Cuba and Haiti. Columbus returned to Spain believing the islands he had discovered were in the neighborhood of the Asiatic mainland. Although Columbus made three more trips to the "Indies" before his death it is probable that he never realized he had not reached the East.

The Spanish monarchs appealed to the pope to confirm their

title to the lands discovered by Columbus in order that there might not develop a conflict with Portugal over any rival claims. In 1493 Pope Alexander VI decreed a line of demarcation which granted to Spain all lands not already in the possession of a Christian prince which lay more than a hundred· leagues west and south of the Azores. All lands east of this line were to be claimed by Portugal. The line was readjusted by common agreement the following year.

Further Portuguese Explorations. In 1497 Vasco da Gama set sail from Portugal. He rounded the Cape of Good Hope and reached India in the following year. Despite losses of men and half his ships he returned to Portugal in 1499 with a cargo which paid six thousand percent on the cost of the expedition. Da Gama's expedition was a tremendous incentive to further Portuguese activities.

In 1500 Cabral set sail and circling wide around Africa touched the coast of Brazil. There is now reason to believe that this was not an accident, and that the Portuguese already knew of the existence of land in that vicinity.

Many Portuguese expeditions were sent to the East. The Portuguese established themselves along the coasts of India and Persia and in the Spice Islands of the East Indies.

The Spanish in America. Meanwhile the Spaniards continued their exploration and settlement of the New World. They established themselves firmly in the West Indies. In 1520 and again in 1521 Ponce de Leon landed in Florida. Balboa landed on the Isthmus and, crossing it, learned from the Indians that the Pacific Ocean which he beheld extended a vast distance to north and south. At last it was realized that the lands discovered were not part of Asia.

In 1517 Velasquez, governor of Cuba, sent out an expedition which reached the Yucatan peninsula. Here they found a group of natives living in an advanced state of civilization. The news of the civilization and wealth of these Central American Indians prompted Cortez to set out upon his epic adventures. He reached Mexico with ten small ships and a military

force of slightly more than six hundred. Montezuma, ruler of
the Aztecs, was rightly fearful of what might happen if the
Spaniards reached his capital, Mexico City. He attempted to
buy them off from venturing further inland with presents of
gold. But the sight of the gold whetted the cupidity of the
Spaniards who burned their ships and pressed inland.

Mexico City filled the Spaniards with amazement. Some
could not believe it was real. Its great temples and towers of
solid stone masonry rose directly out of the lake waters and
seemed to float upon its surface. Gaining admittance to the
city, the Spaniards took Montezuma prisoner. The city was
then seized in 1521, and during the course of the next three
years Mexico was made subject to Spain.

Meanwhile, in 1519 Ferdinand Magellan, a Portuguese, set
sail from Seville with five ships, to seek a sea route to Asia.
He traveled along the South American coast to the straits
which bear his name and then struck out across the Pacific.
Magellan of course had no conception of the vast size of the
Pacific. The food supply gave out, and the men were reduced
to eating the leather portions of the ship's gear after soaking
in sea water and cooking. Rats brought high prices. Many of
the men died. After three months and twenty days upon the
Pacific, Magellan's ships reached some islands which he named
the Ladrones (robbers) from the behavior of the natives. Magellan next discovered the Philippines which he named in
honor of the heir to the Spanish throne. Here Magellan was
killed in a quarrel with the natives. The survivors continued
their westward course, reaching Borneo and the Moluccas. At
last in 1522 a single surviving ship of the original five reached
Seville, having completed the first circumnavigation of the
globe.

Meanwhile, in Mexico the Spanish learned of a great civilization which lay south of the Isthmus in South America. In
1524 Pizarro began a search for this fabulous El Dorado, the
land of gold. After three years he reached Peru and the great
Inca empire which flourished there. Although his force contained less than two hundred men and about fifty horses,
nevertheless, Pizarro was successful in subjugating a vast em-

pire which extended more than two thousand miles from north to south. Let us recall in connection with these almost unbelievable exploits of Spanish captains that horses, firearms, armor, and sailing ships were new to the Indians. In addition their civilization was not warlike. Even so, the achievements of the Spanish conquerors stagger the imagination.

When the Spaniards first reached America they quickly realized that these were not the countries which produced the spices and dyes and other products which had been reaching them through the Levant. But they saw that the climate was suitable to the raising of such products. They therefore established permanent settlements, opened up plantations, experimented with a variety of products. Missionaries preached Christianity to the natives, founded universities, and in other ways developed the country, and established European civilization there. But the discovery of the great stores of gold and silver in Mexico and Peru, which attracted many adventurers to those regions, has rather obscured the colonizing work of the Spaniards.

The chief difference between the Portuguese and Spanish colonial empires was that the Portuguese empire was a commercial one; its object was to trade with the populous and civilized lands of Asia and the East. The Spanish empire was a colonial empire. Its success is attested by the fact that with the principal exception of Brazil, which was Portuguese, the vast lands south of the United States are to this day predominantly Spanish in culture and speech.

36 THE AGE OF THE DESPOTS AND THE RENAISSANCE IN ITALY

Throughout the ages Italy has been a land of city-states. The city-state, which was the predominant cultural and political unit of ancient Greek and Roman times remained a fundamental element even during the centuries of the Roman empire. For several centuries a pattern of imperial law and ad-

ministration was superimposed upon the city-state life, but
when the imperial government collapsed in the fifth century
the cities and towns survived, and their municipal life continued through the Middle Ages.

The States of Italy. The long struggle between the emperors
and popes had prevented in both Italy and Germany the sort
of national centralization which took place in France and England and Spain. With the decline of the power of both empire
and papacy during the fourteenth century, the independence
of the Italian city-states became firmly established. The old
Norman kingdom of Naples and Sicily in the south was, of
course, an exception. But Rome, and Florence, and Genoa,
and Milan, and Venice and other towns of lesser prominence,
with the countryside surrounding them, emerged as independent states.

The Papal States of central Italy were ruled by the church.
Slightly to the north of the Papal States was the republic of
Florence which controlled the greater part of Tuscany. In
1434 Cosimo, head of the powerful banking family of Medici,
managed to become ruler of Florence. His family remained in
control of the city for nearly two hundred years. Still further
to the north in the valley of the Po was the duchy of Milan
ruled by the Visconti family. In 1447 the Visconti line died
out. An effort to establish a republic failed, and the military
captain Francesco Sforza made himself duke of Milan. In the
northeast Venice was ruled by a commercial oligarchy which
selected a doge or leader from among the great families. The
powers of the doge were much restricted by the Great Council
which was the real government of Venice.

The mutual jealousies of the Italian cities resulted in almost
constant warfare which was generally waged by hired bands
of mercenary soldiers led by captains, called *condottieri.* This
system of conducting warfare proved fortunate for the Italians. It left the citizens free to go about their business, and as
the object of the *condottieri* was to achieve results with as little
sacrifice in men as possible, the prosperity of Italy was little
impaired by the rivalry of her despotic rulers.

The Renaissance. The word *Renaissance* has many meanings. Literally it means "rebirth." Though many signs of rebirth had made themselves evident during the medieval period from the time of Charlemagne, none had the magnitude and persistence of the change in life and thought which commenced in Italy in the fourteenth century.

A modern historian has described one aspect of the Renaissance as an intensification of the secular spirit. For somehow or other, without denying the Christian teachings of the Middle Ages, men came to be less concerned with religion and their relationship to God and the future life and more interested in the good things of the world. This was partly the result of the tremendous loss in prestige suffered by the church during the Babylonian Captivity and Great Schism. Doubts had been sown in the minds of many men by heretical preaching and the widespread acceptance of the conciliar idea which tended to undermine papal authority even though the conciliar movement failed.

Much of the vigor and enthusiasm of the Renaissance comes from the fresh realization that the world is full of interest and beauty, and many things good in themselves which could be experienced and enjoyed without reference to any larger purpose or foreboding destiny. Let it be remembered that this mood and curiosity were constantly stimulated by increasing contact with the greater world that had begun during the period of the crusades and continued through the era of exploration and discovery.

The Collapse of the Eastern Empire. We have already referred to the conquests of the Ottoman Turks in Syria and Egypt and their effect upon European trade with the East. The Turks extended their conquest to Greece and the Balkan peninsula and finally, in 1453, after long resistance, Constantinople, the capital of the eastern Roman empire, fell to them. Long before this Greeks had been fleeing to Italy in a steady stream. Greek scholars brought with them their libraries which contained many works by ancient Greek and later Saracen authors and scientists which were unknown in Europe.

Humanism. The study of the *humane* or refining and exalting literature of the ancients marks a trend known as Humanism. It stimulated a broad interest in the culture of the ancients which had its influence upon the development of the fine arts as well as upon literature. The sculpture and architecture of the ancient Greeks and Romans, very many examples of which had survived from ancient times, were imitated as carefully by artists as were their literary productions by the Renaissance men of letters.

The wealthy churchmen and princes of Italy assembled libraries of ancient literature, and gave employment to scholars. They employed artists to decorate churches and palaces. The Gothic art of northern Europe, which had never been firmly established in Italy, was abandoned and a new style was employed in the design of churches, public buildings, and monuments. Art and scholarship flourished under generous patronage.

Painting followed a more independent line of development for there were few surviving examples of the work of ancient painters to serve as models. As a result the art of the Renaissance was a completely new achievement, a thoroughly European and modern product. Artists continued to focus their attention upon religious subjects. The Virgin Mary, holding the infant Jesus, was portrayed over and over again. Yet it is apparent that the Renaissance artists were less concerned to convey the spirituality and divinity of the subject than they were to represent naturally and appealingly a young mother and her chubby infant.

Beginning with Giotto (1276–1336) and continuing through Botticelli (1444–1510), Italian painting rapidly increased in beauty and power. The late fifteenth century produced Leonardo da Vinci (1452–1519), Raphael (1483–1520), and Michelangelo (1475–1564), and other artists only slightly less important. And in the following century Titian (1477–1576) led in carrying on the tradition.

In sculpture Ghiberti (1378–1455) and Donatello (1386–1466) prepared the way for Michelangelo, already mentioned as a painter, who in addition designed buildings (including a plan for St. Peter's, Rome), and wrote many superb sonnets still admired. Indeed, the versatility of the Renaissance artists rather overwhelms us today. Cellini (1500–1571), the goldsmith whose exquisite work has delighted his own and later centuries, was also the sculptor of the statue of Perseus (which he cast in bronze himself), the author of an autobiography still read with interest, and an accomplished musician.

Perhaps the greatest and most versatile of these extraordinary men of the Italian Renaissance was Leonardo da Vinci. Most famous of his surviving paintings are the *Mona Lisa* and the *Last Supper*. But he was also a great sculptor, musician, poet, engineer, scientist, inventor, and philosopher. His dissection of human bodies and his anatomical drawings revolutionized the technique of anatomical representation. Among a long list of his inventions are a breech-loading cannon, a submarine, an air-cooling system, canal locks, aerial bombs, a parachute, and a variety of water-driven machines such as pumps and mill saws. His airplane, sound in design, failed because of the lack of adequate motive power.

The art, literature, and outlook of the Renaissance spread throughout Europe.

37   THE REFORMATION

Like other important events of history the Reformation had its roots deep in the past. We have already noted some of the effects of the Babylonian Captivity of the Papacy upon the faithful throughout Europe. The English people, at war with France, were not willing that the revenues of the English church should be sent to a French papacy resident in France, for inevitably that money, spent in France, would contribute to the prosperity of enemy Frenchmen. But it was a serious matter to refuse to the popes the revenues to which their right had so long been established.

The growing discontent with the situation in the church was intensified by the fact that the papal government was unable to maintain its jurisdiction over the church organization outside of France. Worldly-minded prelates neglected their duties and church discipline became lax. The conduct of bishops and priests and monks often caused scandal and dissatisfaction. The conduct of the clergy provided a further basis for dissatisfaction with the church as an institution. This was naturally true in other places than in England.

John Wyclif. Let us remind ourselves that the medieval Christian church was regarded as an indispensable institution founded by Jesus to guide the faithful in matters of belief and —through the administration of the seven sacraments, the means of grace—to save souls from eternal damnation. The sacraments were the indispensable means of salvation, and were exclusively administered by the clergy. When, in the twelfth and thirteenth centuries, the Waldensians and Albigensians attacked the behavior of corrupt members of the clergy, they were forced by logical necessity to deny the church's exclusive control of the means of salvation before they could cast off their dependence upon a corrupt priesthood.

Many later reformers were prompted by the same logic to the same conclusions. During the Hundred Years' War John Wyclif (1320–1384), an Oxford scholar and English patriot, denounced the evils in the church. He insisted that the church should renounce all temporal authority, and claimed that the English were not obliged to pay taxes to the papacy. He declared that the individual was dependent upon no priestly hierarchy for salvation, but directly upon God. This led him to the conclusion that the Bible was the true and only essential guide to faith. In accordance with these beliefs he translated the Bible into English so that it might be read by the people. He organized preachers, known as the Lollards, to preach to the poorer classes. He denied many Catholic doctrines, including that of transubstantiation which is the belief that in the sacrament of the Eucharist, the bread and wine are actually transformed into the substance of the body and blood of Jesus.

John Hus. In Bohemia a similar religious-patriotic reaction occurred. Hus had studied the writings of Wyclif and adopted most of his religious views.

In Hus's day the Czechs developed a strong national self-consciousness. They resented German domination and inevitably that resentment was turned against the German prince-bishops who ruled extensive estates under the empire. Increasingly to the Czechs the great church-state ruled from Avignon and Rome appeared a foreign institution.

Hus favored the formation of a Czech national church independent of Rome. When indulgences were issued in Bohemia in order to raise money for a crusade against Naples, some of the artisans of Prague cried out that the indulgences were a lie. They were condemned and executed. Hus was excommunicated and Prague was placed under an interdict. Hus was forced by the king to withdraw from the university, and he remained in retirement until the calling of the Council of Constance two years later in 1414.

As we have already recalled, Hus and his fellow heretic, Jerome of Prague, traveled to Constance to argue their case before the council. They were condemned and burned at the stake.

The execution of Hus and Jerome provoked a rebellion in Bohemia. Four hundred fifty-two Czech nobles signed a petition protesting the action of the Council, and banded themselves together for mutual defense. The Bohemian ranks were soon divided by disputes over religious doctrine and a period of civil war ensued. The Emperor Sigismund was called upon to intervene. For eleven years the Bohemian war continued, from 1420 to 1431. Ablest of the radical Bohemian leaders was the John Ziska whose iron-clad wagons, in the role of modern tanks, wrought havoc among the German soldiery. Worn out by the long war the more moderate Bohemian factions finally arranged a compromise settlement.

During the remainder of the fifteenth century the Germanies remained politically disunited and weak. But trade prospered, particularly in western Germany along the Rhine. During this century the famous Augsburg banking family of Fugger extended its operations to the lowlands, the Tyrol and into Italy.

The Abuse of Indulgences. In 1513 there came to the papal throne a member of the famous Medici family of Florence who took the name of Leo X. Leo was a humanist, a student of ancient Latin literature, and a patron of Renaissance art and letters. The building of the great Church of St. Peter in Rome, designed by Bramante and Michelangelo, was a project he advanced with enthusiasm. In order to forward this work he issued indulgences by which the faithful who contributed to the building of St. Peter's would be freed from the penalties merited for their sins—on condition, of course, that they obtained pardon in the usual way through the sacrament of penance.

The archbishop of Mainz, Albert, who was a member of the Hohenzollern family, saw in this indulgence campaign, an opportunity to resolve his financial difficulties. Somewhat earlier Albert had come to the Fugger bankers with an interesting proposition. There were only seven electors of the Holy Roman Empire of which the archbishop of Mainz was one. The emperor Maximilian was old and there were several powerful princes who coveted the title of emperor. Albert reasoned that in the circumstances lavish bribes would be offered the electors, and with this in mind he sought to obtain the appointment to the vacant archbishopric.

Albert already held two church benefices. But he argued that the pope was in need of funds for the building of St. Peter's Cathedral and that if he could anticipate with a cash payment the *annates* or first fruits of his new benefice which were customarily paid to Rome, he would have no difficulty obtaining the appointment. He asked Fugger to advance him the necessary monies. The appointment was made according to plan.

But the health of the emperor was better than Albert had judged, and the revenues of his new benefice less. The interest on his debt to Fugger accumulated faster than Albert could pay it off. He accordingly approached Fugger once more and proposed a similar advance to Rome out of the anticipated returns of the indulgence campaign on condition that Albert be put in charge of it. He hoped to pay his debts out of the indulgence campaign. This, too, worked out according to Albert's designs.

Albert then employed an enthusiastic and irresponsible preacher, John Tetzel, to travel about Germany and persuade the faithful to give generously to the indulgence fund. Tetzel seems to have been carried away by the success of his own oratory. He began to claim that to those who bought indulgences pardon was unnecessary, and that it was even possible to buy forgiveness for sins not yet committed. Such claims shocked many of the more intelligent Germans. Luther protested to the elector, Frederick of Saxony, and to his churchly superior in Germany who was, of course, Albert himself. When the faithful came to confession he refused to recognize Tetzel's indulgences and this naturally caused an uproar.

Martin Luther. Martin Luther was the son of a prosperous peasant and had been trained for a career in the law. Much to the disgust of his father, he gave up his legal studies and entered the Augustinian monastery at Erfurt. He was transferred to Wittenberg where he became a teacher in the university. Luther was a loyal Catholic, and when he first attacked Tetzel's conduct of the indulgence campaign he had no thought of separating himself from the church.

In accordance with the custom of the time, Luther posted upon the door of Castle church at Wittenberg a list of ninety-five theses in which he stated his position on indulgences and allied questions. These theses were immediately translated into German and circulated widely with the result that before the questions were formally debated by the academicians they had already become a popular issue.

All Luther sought after at the moment was the correction of obvious abuses. But Albert's financial interests were involved, and he attempted to suppress his lively and popular critic. The grounds of the controversy were quickly shifted from the indulgence question to the question of whether Luther, whose stand had provoked widespread hostility to the clergy, was a rebellious churchman unwilling to submit to the authority of his superiors. Sure of the rightness of his original stand, Luther was led to insist that he would not submit against the dictates of his conscience. If these were denied by ecclesiastical authority—even the authority of the pope or of a council—Luther declared he would make his appeal to Scripture. Before he realized what had happened to him, Luther found himself defending the teachings of the heretic, John Hus.

Spread of the Lutheran Revolt. Had the controversy occurred a century earlier, it is possible it might have been restricted to church and university circles. But about the middle of the fifteenth century the printing press had been invented, and its use had spread widely. Luther, who was an able pamphleteer, flooded Germany with articles attacking every sort of abuse.

In his *Address to the Nobility of the German Nation,* Luther called upon the Germans to unite and destroy the power of the pope over the German states. This led to a war of the lesser German knights against the greater lay and ecclesiastical princes who were allied by interest with foreign powers. The peasants were stirred up to demand the abandonment of many feudal practices which seriously interfered with their well-being. A bloody revolt followed. Luther was horrified by some of the consequences of his agitation.

Many of the German nobles abandoned the church and adopted Lutheranism. As they promptly confiscated the lands and property of the church, it is evident that their motives were not purely religious. The split-up of Germany into hostile camps of Protestant and Catholic princes brought into being a situation which sorely troubled the reign of the emperor Charles V as we shall have occasion to recall later on.

Zwingli. Independent of Luther a reform movement had begun in Switzerland. Its founder was Ulrich Zwingli, a humanist priest, who was appointed vicar at the Cathedral of Zurich in 1518. Zwingli soon established himself among the prosperous citizens of Zurich. He was a keen critic of abuses in the church. In 1519 he forced a seller of indulgences to leave Zurich. He was strongly opposed to the practice of the young Swiss hiring themselves out all over Europe as mercenary soldiers, and strongly criticized the papacy as one of the chief employers of Swiss mercenary troops. Zwingli followed with close attention the progress of the Lutheran movement in Germany.

In 1532 Zwingli drew up a list of sixty-seven theses containing a statement of his essential position. He went beyond Luther in his rejection of customary ideas and practices, for not only did Zwingli condemn the papacy, priesthood, and monasticism; he also abolished the mass, statues, crucifixes, altars, and pictures in the churches. The points of similarity between Luther's and Zwingli's positions resulted in an attempt to bring them into agreement. The two reformers met but were unable to agree on a number of points.

The spread of Zwingli's doctrines to all but the five forest cantons of Switzerland resulted in the formation of two hostile leagues which prepared for war. In 1531 the Protestant forces were defeated, and Zwingli was killed. The forest cantons remained staunchly Catholic.

John Calvin. The work of Zwingli was taken up some time later by John Calvin, a Frenchman. John Calvin, whose father was employed in the service of the Catholic church, was like Luther educated for the law. He became much interested in the religious controversies of his day, and upon his father's death went into retirement in order to clarify his ideas. In 1534 he severed his connection with the Catholic church and traveled to Switzerland.

In 1536 Calvin published *The Institutes of the Christian Religion* which contained the essentials of his belief. The work was later expanded, and a French translation was dedicated to Francis I, king of France, in an effort to win sympathy for the new ideas. The French king remained a loyal Catholic however, and in 1542 Calvin's book was condemned as heretical.

Geneva under Calvinism. The reforming zeal of Calvin, like that of Zwingli whose work he took up, led him to condemn all outward display connected with religion. The stained glass windows of the Swiss churches were smashed, altars and statues and crucifixes were removed, wall frescoes were white-washed over. This attitude soon affected the social life of Geneva where Calvin established himself.

Calvin went beyond Zwingli and developed the idea of pre-destination. In contemplating the sinfulness of man and the omniscience of God, Calvin was forced to recognize that since God was able to foresee all the future he must in some way have known and accepted in advance the fact that most men would lead sinful lives. Calvin concluded that the number of men who were destined to be saved was very limited, and that God knew who these "elect" were in advance. How then might the individual know whether he was numbered among the elect or whether he was destined to be damned? The only sure sign of God's grace or election was the righteousness of the life of the individual.

Under Calvin's leadership, Geneva developed into a theo-cratic or religious state. The conduct of the citizens was regu-lated in the smallest details. Dancing, card-playing, careless language, vain dress, were strictly forbidden, and the severest punishments were meted out for the violation of such rules.

During his lifetime Calvin maintained a large correspon-dence with converts all over Europe. His religion was spread as much by his writings as by his preaching in Geneva, which was listened to by the many who visited the city. Calvinism spread to Scotland and England, to the Netherlands, into Germany, and later into Bohemia and Hungary with impor-tant consequences which we shall have occasion to deal with.

38   TUDOR ENGLAND

During the course of the Hundred Years' War the nobles of England had managed to build up their power. Most of the land was in the hands of the great feudal families like the Percys, Nevilles, Beauforts and Mortimers. They supported armies of hired retainers, and settled their differences with each other by engaging in private wars as in early feudal times.

The ruling house of Lancaster was in general disfavor because of the failure of English arms and the loss of continental possessions to France. In addition Henry VI (1422–1461) was a weak king and subject to fits of insanity. The dukes of York, descended from a son of Edward III, had a strong claim to the throne. Supported by the earl of Warwick, who became known as the "King-maker," the Yorkist Edward overthrew Henry and became king in his place as Edward IV.

Edward IV disregarded the wishes of Warwick in choosing a wife and quarreled with his powerful backer. Warwick changed sides and re-established Henry on the throne for a brief time. However, Edward recovered the throne, Warwick was killed in battle, and Henry was murdered in the Tower of London. The remainder of Edward's reign was quiet, but when he died in 1483 leaving a twelve-year-old son to succeed him, his brother, Richard, duke of Gloucester, became protector of England. The ambitious noble confined his two young nephews in the Tower of London, and had himself proclaimed king as Richard III. The murder of the little princes in the Tower shocked England, and many rallied to the support of the Lancastrian heir, Henry Tudor, who came over from France with an army. At Bosworth field in 1485, Richard was defeated and slain.

These struggles, known as the Wars of the Roses from the insignia of the rival houses of York and Lancaster, were fought by the nobles and their hired armies. Fearing to arouse the country against them, each side was careful to do as little damage to the countryside as possible, with the result that the economic life of England suffered little. Nevertheless, the bulk of the English people were heartily sick of the nobles and their political ambitions.

The attitude of the country toward the nobility strengthened the position of the Tudor monarchs. The fact that many nobles had been killed during the course of the wars enabled

Henry to create new nobles whose loyalty he could depend upon. Henry Tudor, a Lancastrian, married the heiress of the Yorkist house, thus putting an end to the rivalry of the two families.

The Tudors were absolute monarchs but they were popular rulers. They treated parliament with respect but depended upon it as little as possible. Henry VII surrounded himself with bourgeois advisers and devoted his reign to strengthening the monarchy and fostering the prosperity of England. He well knew that in a crisis the monarchy would be dependent upon parliament for grants of money and new taxes, so during the course of his reign he accumulated a treasure which he passed on to his son.

Henry VIII. Henry VIII (1509–1547) began his reign under most favorable auspices. He was a handsome and amiable young man of eighteen and popular with his people. The courtiers were submissive, the treasury was full, and the expanding commerce of England gave promise of an era of prosperity to come. He was unusually talented, well educated, and was surrounded and counseled by able and experienced men.

Henry quickly appreciated the abilities of a young churchman of middle-class origin, Thomas Wolsey, who had been chaplain at the court of Henry VII. Under the king's patronage Wolsey's rise was rapid. He became chancellor and cardinal in the same year, 1515, thus holding the highest offices in both church and state that any subject could hold in England. Henry was happy to be relieved of the cares of government by so able a man. Wolsey adopted a continental policy that has become famous in English history. England was much inferior in population and wealth to the two strongest continental states—Spain and France. By holding aloof from alliances with either of the great rivals, Wolsey placed England in a position whereby she could determine the balance of power between them, and thus her favor was sought by both sides.

Henry VIII and the Church. Henry was a loyal Catholic. Shocked at Luther's conduct, he published a *Defense of the Seven Sacraments against Martin Luther* in which he met Luther's attack point by point. Pope Leo X was so pleased with Henry's treatise that he bestowed upon him the title "Defender of the Faith."

Henry was married to Catherine of Aragon, daughter of Ferdinand and Isabella of Spain. During fifteen years of married life Catherine bore Henry six children, all of whom died in infancy except one, Mary. Since the Norman conquest only one woman, Matilda, had claimed inheritance of the English throne, thus starting a civil war which lasted fifteen years. Henry wanted a son. He came to the conclusion that his marriage was accursed for he had married his brother's widow, a relationship forbidden by the church. Since the queen was past childbearing, Henry insisted that Wolsey get him a divorce in order that he might remarry and beget a son.

Wolsey's assignment was extremely difficult. The Catholic church did not recognize divorces. Occasionally marriages had been annulled or held to be invalid for technical reasons, but before Henry's marriage to Catherine the precaution had been taken of obtaining a special dispensation from the pope sanctioning the marriage. In addition, Catherine was the aunt of the powerful Emperor Charles V who was also king of Spain. Charles was certain to do everything in his power to protect his aunt's name and interests. Wolsey's failure earned him disgrace. He was deprived of office and ordered to retire to his bishopric. Death saved him from further penalties.

The new archbishop of Canterbury, Thomas Cranmer, convoked the ecclesiastical court, which, after long consideration, declared that Henry and Catherine were never properly married. Meanwhile Henry had secretly married Anne Boleyn who shortly gave birth to a daughter, Elizabeth, in September 1533. Parliament, by the Act of Succession, obligingly legalized what had taken place. In answer to the opposition of Rome, Henry next repudiated papal authority entirely. Parliament passed in 1534 the Act of Supremacy which severed the English church from Rome and made the king and his successors heads of the Church of England.

In 1536 Queen Anne was accused of adultery, condemned, and beheaded, and a short time later Henry married Jane Seymour who gave birth to a son, Edward. A few weeks after the birth of the prince, Jane died. Henry now made a political marriage. To counterbalance the Franco-Spanish alliance, he prepared to ally himself with the Protestant princes of Germany by marrying Anne of Cleves. Thomas Cromwell arranged the match, and submitted a flattering portrait of Anne by the great painter Holbein. But Henry was so repelled by his first sight of the bride-to-be, "the great Flanders mare" he called her, that he could scarcely be persuaded to go through with the ceremony. Cromwell was arrested for treason and executed in 1542.

Let us complete the list of Henry's wives by recalling that he next married the beautiful Catherine Howard who, fifteen months after her marriage, was condemned for immoral conduct and beheaded. Henry's sixth and last wife was the discreet widow, Catherine Parr, who outlived the king.

During the despotic reign of Henry VIII England prospered, this despite the fact that the monarchy was costly, for Henry was lavish in his expenditures. He dissipated the treasure he had inherited from his father. When England separated from Rome, Henry suppressed the monasteries and confiscated their property. This wealth too he used up. Toward the close of his reign he obtained money by debasing the coinage. This reduction of the percentage of gold and silver in the coins lowered the value of money and caused prices to fluctuate, and commerce suffered.

Before his death Henry arranged for the succession by making a will. His son Edward, a sickly youth, was first in line of succession. But in the event that Edward should not survive to leave an heir, the succession was to pass to Henry's oldest daughter, Mary, daughter of Catherine of Aragon. In the event of Mary's death, Elizabeth, daughter of Anne Boleyn, was to be next in line.

The Renaissance in England. During the course of Henry's reign the Renaissance was well established in England. Art, letters, and music flourished. Despite the troubled reigns of Edward VI and Mary, they continued to a high flowering under Elizabeth. The lusty vigor of English life under the Tudors is recalled for us by the extravagant richness of costume which we notice in the portraits by Hans Holbein who painted at the English court, in the daring adventures of Elizabethan freebooters, and above all in the magnificent productions of the dramatists of the period whose crowning genius was William Shakespeare.

After Henry's death the course of English history was much affected by developments on the continent of Europe and elsewhere. It will be convenient therefore to view the reigns of the later Tudors from the broader perspective of European and world-wide developments.

PART EIGHT
The Age of Monarchy

1515–1547	Francis I, King of France
1519–1556	Charles V, Emperor
1519	Magellan's circumnavigation of the globe
1534	The Act of Supremacy
1541	Calvin introduced Reformation into Geneva
1556–1598	Philip II, King of Spain
1558–1603	Elizabeth, Queen of England
1561	Francis Bacon born
1564	Shakespeare born
1571	Battle of Lepanto
1588	Defeat of the Spanish Armada
1598	Edict of Nantes
1598–1605	Boris Godunov, Czar of Russia
1609	Holland proclaimed her independence
1618–1648	The Thirty Years' War
1624–1642	Cardinal Richelieu in power in France
1631	Gustavus Adolphus of Sweden campaigned in Germany
1632–1654	Christina, Queen of Sweden
1642–1715	Louis XIV, King of France
1644	The Manchus ended the Ming dynasty
1648	Treaty of Westphalia
1649–1653	The Commonwealth in England
1658	Cromwell died
1660	Restoration of Charles II as King of England
1689–1702	William and Mary ruled England
1690	Battle of the Boyne in Ireland
1696–1725	Peter the Great, Czar of Russia
1701–1714	War of the Spanish Succession
1704	Battle of Blenheim
1713	Treaty of Utrecht

The Empire of Charles V. Albert of Mainz had foreseen that upon the death of the emperor Maximilian there would be a lively contest over the imperial succession. Three powerful and wealthy monarchs competed in bribing the seven electors of the Holy Roman Empire. It is claimed that the only elector who refused all bribes, and who acted in accordance with his best judgment and his conscience, was Frederick, the elector of Saxony. The three candidates were Henry VIII of England, Francis I of France, and Charles I of Spain.

In the end it was Charles I of Spain, grandson of Maximilian, who was raised to the imperial office as the Emperor Charles V. Charles, who was a Hapsburg, became the greatest ruler in Europe. The Hapsburg family, from very humble beginnings had, by shrewd policy and the patient enlargement of their holdings, risen to the position of first place. This rise began with Count Rudolph in the thirteenth century who, elected emperor in 1273, took advantage of his position to obtain as a personal fief the duchy of Austria. By a series of shrewd marriages the family held its position and increased its possessions. For a while the house of Luxembourg replaced the Hapsburgs on the imperial throne, but in 1440 the Hapsburgs were restored. They continued to rule the empire until it was dissolved in 1806 by Napoleon. They retained Austria until the end of World War I.

Maximilian I (1493–1519) married Mary of Burgundy who brought him Franche-Comté, Luxembourg, Flanders, Artois, and the Netherlands. These possessions were passed on to Charles upon the death of his father in 1506. Charles' father, Philip, had married Juana, daughter of Ferdinand and Isabella, the Spanish rulers. In 1516 the Spanish inheritance passed to Charles. This brought under his control not only Spain itself and the Spanish islands of the Mediterranean; also the Spanish possessions in Italy and the vast and growing

THE EMPIRE OF
CHARLES V

American empire. A mere listing of all of Charles' titles and territories would require pages.

The Many Problems of Charles V. Having been elected emperor, Charles desired nothing so much as to be left alone to establish his administration, to become familiar with his new subjects, and to free himself from his heavy debt to the Fugger bankers who had raised the funds with which he had bought his election. We have already noted the growing nationalism of the peoples of Europe. This new spirit made each part of Charles' empire jealous of the other.

Spain had only recently been united by Ferdinand and Isabella. It was not until 1492 that these rulers drove out the last of the Moslems from Granada where they had been in control since 711. All during the Middle Ages that part of Spain which was not under Moslem control had been made up of small principalities which were almost constantly at war. Charles, who was raised in Flanders, offended his Spanish subjects by appointing Flemings to posts in the Spanish government. When he sought the imperial crown, the Spaniards revolted, fearing Spain would become subordinated to the German empire.

The Situation in France. Francis I, who had lost the imperial election, found his nation, France, surrounded by Hapsburg lands. A glance at the map will help us to understand why Francis felt that the security of France was menaced by Hapsburg power. To the north and east were the Netherlands, Flanders, Luxembourg, Franche-Comté. Across the Alps and to the south and southwest lay the duchy of Milan, Naples and Sicily, Sardinia, Corsica, the Balearics, and of course Spain itself. And to the north, across the Channel, lay England whose king was married to Catherine of Aragon, daughter of Ferdinand and Isabella.

King Francis I adopted a policy which was pursued by his successors for some time to come. That policy was to keep the monarchy strong inside France, and to use every opportunity to break the power of the great Hapsburg empire which surrounded France on three sides. He immediately laid claim to the Italian possessions of the Hapsburgs and attacked the duchy of Milan. The harassed Charles, with unsolved problems awaiting him in Spain and Germany while the Ottoman Turks threatened his empire on the continent and in the Mediterranean, was forced to gather troops and defend his possessions. In 1525 the French were overwhelmingly defeated in northern Italy and Francis was taken prisoner.

The Fugger bankers, already heavily invested in Charles' empire, were slow to provide Charles with the money he needed to pay his troops. In 1527 the unpaid soldiery marched southward to Rome and subjected the city to an eight-day sack. The pope took refuge in the impregnable castle of Saint Angelo which was originally the tomb of the Roman emperor Hadrian. Despite his defeat Francis persisted in his effort to break the Hapsburg power. He made alliances with Denmark, Sweden, with the German princes who opposed the emperor, and even with the Moslem Turk. In 1535 Francesco Sforza, duke of Milan, died and Francis claimed the ducal throne for his son. This started another war which lasted until 1544.

The Turks. In 1520 the sultan, Selim the Grim (1512–1520), was succeeded by Suleiman the Magnificent (1520–1566), under whom the Turkish empire reached the zenith of its power. After the fall of Constantinople in 1453 the Turks had consolidated their control of the Balkans and had extended their conquests elsewhere. In 1521 Suleiman captured Belgrade, a fortress which had checked the Turkish advance into Hungary. In the following year the island of Rhodes, stronghold of the knights of St. John, was taken and the Turks controlled the eastern Mediterranean. At the great battle of Mohacs in 1526, the Hungarian army was routed by the Turks and King Louis II was drowned while fleeing from battle. Thus the bulk of Hungary fell into Turkish hands.

Archduke Ferdinand of Austria, who was the brother of the Emperor Charles V, claimed the throne of Hungary. Invading the country, he took Bucharest. Suleiman then invaded Austria and laid siege to Vienna. The Austrians fought so valiantly that Suleiman was forced to raise the siege, but he returned to the task three years later with a great army.

As ruler of the Germans, as a Hapsburg, and as emperor and therefore the secular leader of western Christendom, Charles was obliged to protect Christian Europe from the Turkish menace. It mattered not that the king of France was his bitter enemy, that the German Protestant princes had formed a league against him, that the English king had cast off his wife, Charles' aunt, and severed England from the church of Rome. Charles raised an army and Suleiman was forced to raise the siege and withdraw. Charles next planned to clear the Moslems from the Mediterranean for, not only did Christian shipping suffer at the hands of the Moslem raiders based in north Africa, the coasts of southern Europe were raided and along with plunder the Saracens carried off youths and maidens to be sold in eastern slave markets and confined in eastern harems.

In the summer of 1535 Charles destroyed a Moorish fleet and seized the Moslem stronghold of Tunis in north Africa. Here he found and released from the filthy and overcrowded Moslem prisons some twenty-two thousand Christians. He was forced to abandon his purpose of clearing the Mediterranean when Francis I of France invaded the duchy of Milan.

Germany in Relation to Charles V. When Charles I, Hapsburg king of Spain, was elected emperor as Charles V, the Germans at once became fearful lest German interests be subordinated to Spanish interests by the emperor. They presented a set of conditions to Charles which he accepted, but this by no means allayed German fears. We saw that Luther's attacks upon the Roman church quickly aroused a strong anti-foreign feeling throughout Germany. Many German nobles took advantage of the spread of Lutheranism to seize church lands and incorporate them into their own estates.

It naturally became the concern of the emperor to end the troubles among his German subjects, to bring about a settlement of the Lutheran controversy, to protect the church and princes from being despoiled of their lands, and to maintain order and peace. A series of synods and diets, over some of which the emperor presided, failed to bring about a conciliation between Lutherans and Catholics. In 1531 the German Protestant princes banded together in an association known as the Schmalkaldic League which soon became involved in a war against the emperor.

The year 1547 developed favorably for Charles V, for both Francis I of France and Henry VIII of England died, a five-year truce was signed with the sultan, and the opposition of the Schmalkaldic League was broken at the battle of Mühlberg. Within three years however Charles was faced by as many difficulties as ever. His wise attempt to create a closer unity in Germany was resisted, his effort to end the religious dispute was resisted by Protestant and Catholic, and Maurice of Saxony led a rebellion against him which was kept alive by the French after Maurice's death in 1553.

Worn out by the cares of a long reign, Charles arranged for a division of the far-flung Hapsburg empire between his son Philip and his brother Ferdinand. In 1555 he surrendered the Netherlands to Philip. In 1556 he resigned the empire to his brother Ferdinand who was already ruling in his name. In 1558 he died quietly in retirement in Spain.

Philip II and England. While Charles had been raised in Flanders and appeared a foreigner in the eyes of his Spanish subjects, Philip, who had been raised and educated in Spain, seemed a foreigner to the Netherlanders for he did not even speak their language. During Charles' reign the Netherlands had remained loyal to their Hapsburg ruler, but under Philip there developed in the lowlands a strong nationalist sentiment.

In 1543, at the age of sixteen, Philip was married to his cousin, princess Maria of Portugal, who died giving birth to Don Carlos. Charles then arranged a second marriage for his son to Mary Tudor, daughter of Henry VIII. This marriage was a failure from the start for Philip was unpopular in England.

During the brief reign of the frail Edward VI (1547–1553), his uncle Edward Seymour, earl of Hertford and duke of

Somerset, became virtual dictator of England as Lord Protector. He was head of the Protestant party, and with the aid of Archbishop Cranmer succeeded in introducing Protestant reforms in the English church. Even though he had broken with Rome, Henry VIII continued to regard himself as a Catholic. He insisted upon maintaining the Catholic dogmas and service and persecuted the Protestants. But by the time Mary came to the throne in 1553 Protestantism had been well advanced in England, for the duke of Northumberland, successor to Somerset, also strongly favored Protestantism.

When Mary came to the throne in 1553, Parliament obligingly repealed the reforms of Edward's reign, discarded Cranmer's Book of Common Prayer, condemned marriage of the clergy, and restored the Latin service of the Catholic church. These changes the English might have accepted calmly, but they were averse to recognizing papal supremacy. Mary secured the repeal of the anti-papal legislation of Henry VIII, received Cardinal Pole, the papal legate, and proceeded to persecute those Englishmen who refused to accept Catholicism. Philip was wrongly blamed by the English for many of Mary's unpopular acts. Englishmen called to him in the streets to hurry up and beget an heir and then take himself off to Spain.

Philip left England in the autumn of 1555. However he returned in 1557 to seek England's aid in his war against France. In spite of popular opposition Mary joined the war with disastrous results, for in 1558 the French took Calais, the last remnant of the once extensive English dominion in France. The childless Mary died in November 1558, and the ties between England and Spain were severed.

The Problems of Philip II. During the first two years of his reign Philip was engaged in a war with France. However both Philip and his enemy Henry II of France were concerned over the spread of Protestantism. In 1559, in the treaty of Cateau-Cambrésis the two monarchs arranged a peace which left them free to suppress the spread of heresy in their respective domains.

Many problems demanded Philip's attention. Charles had not found time to devise a centralized administration for Spain, each of whose many provinces owed him separate allegiance and existed under a separate administration. The Turk was still a menace to Europe both upon land and in the Mediterranean. An administrative problem also confronted Philip in the Netherlands for some sort of unification and centralization was necessary if the seventeen provinces were to be administered efficiently. In addition, Philip regarded himself as the champion and protector of Catholicism all over Europe. This involved him in efforts to suppress Protestantism in the Netherlands, to root out heresy among the newly converted Moors and Jews in southern Spain which had been conquered by Ferdinand and Isabella. It was also necessary to foster the development of the great Spanish empire in America and to protect Spanish shipping from the increasing raids of pirates and freebooters in both the Atlantic and the Mediterranean.

Philip and the Turks. In 1570 the pope, Venice, and Spain, formed a league against the Turk. A fleet of 264 vessels was brought together and placed under the command of Philip's half-brother, Don John of Austria. On October 7, 1571 the fleet met the formidable Turkish force of 300 vessels at Lepanto in the Gulf of Corinth. The overwhelming victory of the Christian fleet was hailed with jubilation throughout Europe. Don John now proposed to seize the Turkish strongholds in the East and free the Mediterranean from Moslem control once and for all, but Venice withdrew her support and proceeded to make a separate treaty and a commercial agreement with the Turks.

In Spain the Moriscos, the Moslems who had been converted to Christianity after the conquest of Granada by Ferdinand and Isabella, were accused of practicing in secret the faith which they had outwardly abandoned. The Inquisition, which had been introduced into Spain under Ferdinand and Isabella and flourished under the famous, or infamous, Torquemada, who became its president in 1483, was employed once again to ferret out heresy. Its activities provoked a rebellion which broke out in 1569, and was put down only after much bloodshed.

The Revolt of the Netherlands. When Philip tried to reform and consolidate the administration of the Netherlands, the Dutch provinces, traditionally jealous of their independence, resisted his efforts. As was natural, Philip employed a good many Spaniards in his administration. Unfortunately they showed little regard for the feelings of Philip's Dutch subjects. When the nobles presented a petition to Philip's regent, Margaret of Parma, a Spanish official contemptuously referred to them as beggars. The Dutch promptly adopted the name and medieval insignia of the beggar.

Before Philip could act upon the petition of his Netherlands subjects, an anti-Catholic riot broke out, led principally by the radical Anabaptist sect which favored the overthrow of government as well as church. Great damage was done to Christian churches. Philip decided that it was too late for conciliatory measures. He dispatched the duke of Alva to the Netherlands with an army. Alva ruled with an iron hand. The rebels were condemned to death after summary trial, and their property was confiscated. Alva succeeded in embittering the Dutch beyond any hope of reconciliation. William, prince of Orange, assumed the leadership of the rebels and a prolonged struggle was begun. The ablest of Alva's successors, Alexander Farnese, was successful in bringing about a division between the Catholic south and the Protestant north of the Netherlands, but it was the most he could achieve. The seven Protestant provinces bound themselves together in a league called the Union of Utrecht in 1581 and renounced their allegiance to the king of Spain. This Union of Utrecht is sometimes called the Dutch Declaration of Independence.

Philip and England. One of Philip's problems was the development and the protection of his American empire. These colonies continued to produce many commodities that were in demand in Europe. But around 1535 there began to arrive in Spain shipments of gold and silver from Mexico and Peru. Enormous as this wealth was, it quickly passed out of Spanish hands for Philip was engaged throughout his entire reign in large and costly enterprises: war with France and with the Turk, rebellion in the Netherlands, in Italy, in Germany, and finally war against England. It is interesting to observe that the precious metals, brought from America and quickly distributed over Europe through the hiring of troops, and the purchase of supplies, contributed substantially to European prosperity by providing the material for new money when new money was needed for the convenience of expanding economic activity.

In 1580 Philip seized an opportunity to extend enormously the Spanish empire and to unite the Iberian Peninsula. In 1580 the throne of Portugal became vacant upon the death of King Henry without heirs. Philip, whose mother was the eldest daughter of King Manuel and whose wife was a Portuguese princess, claimed the throne. Portugal with its great eastern, African, and American empire—for the Portuguese had discovered and developed Brazil—remained under Spanish rule from 1580 to 1640.

Although the pope had divided the non-Christian world between Spain and Portugal, awarding to Portugal Africa and Asia, and to Spain all the Americas except Brazil, the other European states refused to pay serious attention to the agreement. The English, like the Spanish and Portuguese before them, sought to discover a route to the East. During Mary's reign Sir Hugh Willoughby and Richard Chancellor sailed in search of a northeast passage around Europe to China and the Indies. Chancellor entered the White Sea and was taken to Moscow where he arranged a trade treaty with Ivan the Terrible. In 1554 Queen Mary chartered the Muscovy Company to handle the trade with Russia. Later John Davis made three attempts to find a northwest passage around North America to the East between 1585 and 1587.

In the meantime English adventurers sought to break the Spanish and Portuguese monopolies over trade with the East and with the New World. John Hawkins in 1562 seized three hundred Negroes along the Guinea coast of Africa, and carried them to America where he sold them at great profit to the Spaniards who needed laborers on their plantations and in the mines. Hawkins repeated this venture twice again, the third time accompanied by Francis Drake. Their five vessels were attacked by a Spanish fleet and Hawkins and Drake barely escaped. In revenge Drake resorted to buccaneering or piracy, and preyed on Spanish shipping. His example was followed by many other English adventurers. Spanish shipping and the Spanish colonies suffered from their raids.

One of Drake's early adventures was the capture of a treasure caravan and thirty tons of silver in the Isthmus of Panama. In 1577 he rounded South America and sailed up the west coast. The Spanish ships carrying Inca treasure to the Isthmus were taken completely by surprise. Drake explored the California coast in search of a northwest passage, and then turned west and headed across the Pacific. Following Magellan's route, he arrived in England in 1580 with such a cargo of gold and silver and spices and silks as had never been seen in England. He was knighted by Queen Elizabeth.

The Invincible Armada. When Philip's ambassadors protested against the English attacks upon Spanish shipping and settlements, Elizabeth pretended she was unable to control buccaneering activity. Yet she secretly supported many of their enterprises and shared in their profits.

Philip determined to put an end to English piracy. He built a great armada, or fleet of ships, for the invasion of England. In May 1588 Philip's fleet of one hundred and thirty ships set sail carrying 19,000 soldiers and 8,000 seamen. It has been calculated that the total tonnage of the fleet was approximately 57,868 tons, which is less than that of the Cunard liner *Queen Mary*. The English prepared to meet the invasion and collected shipping all along the coast. The opposing fleets were about equal in tonnage, but the English ships were smaller, lighter, more maneuverable, and their guns had a greater range than the Spanish and could be fired faster. With these advantages the English succeeded in damaging and sinking a number of the Spanish ships. With ammunition low, the Spaniards realized the venture was lost. As they turned toward home, a violent storm completed the havoc that had been begun by the English.

The destruction of the Armada did not end the war with England, but Philip's main attention was drawn to other fields. He sent a force into France to help the Catholic League in its war against Henry of Navarre in the hope both of combatting Protestantism and of keeping France engaged in internal strife. And for a time it seemed indeed as if France might lose all that she had gained under her long line of kings.

40 THE ABSOLUTE MONARCHY IN FRANCE

Francis I (1515–1547) had not hesitated to ally himself with the Moslem Turk or with the Protestant princes of Germany when by doing so he was able to cause trouble for the Hapsburgs. However he was not tolerant of Protestantism in France. His motto *Un roi, une foi, une loi,*—one king, one faith, one law—expressed his conception of national unity. This was the view that was held throughout Europe until the middle of the seventeenth century. A subject who differed from his prince in religion was held to be treasonable. The persecution of all those subjects who differed with them in religion by Henry VIII, Mary, Philip II, Francis I, was the normal and expected conduct of the time. When, after the Wars of the Schmalkaldic League, Lutherans and Catholics finally came to terms, the Peace of Augsburg recognized both religions. But when Calvinism spread into Germany, it was no more tolerated by Lutherans than by Catholics. And wherever the Calvinists established themselves they matched and surpassed the intolerance of others. It was an age of strong belief, and such an age is never one of toleration.

In 1547 a special tribunal was added to the Parlement of Paris to deal with cases of heresy. It became known as the Chambre Ardente or Burning Court. Henry II (1547–1559) continued the religious policies of Francis and attempted to establish the Inquisition in France. Nevertheless Protestantism spread. It was Calvin's doctrines which appealed to Frenchmen rather than Luther's. As this new faith spread, principally among the burgher population of the towns, its adherents became known as Huguenots.

Henry II died in 1559 leaving three sons, all of whom became kings of France. They were Francis II (1559–1560), Charles IX (1560–1574), and Henry III (1574–1589). During the brief reign of Francis II, who was the husband of Mary Stuart, Mary's uncles, the cardinal of Lorraine and the duke of Guise, dominated France. But when Charles IX came to the throne his mother, Catherine de' Medici, became regent during his minority.

Catherine was an ambitious woman, a Medici, and a loyal Catholic. She seems to have been less interested in the welfare of France than in extending the influence of her family through good marriage connections and in advancing the interests of the Roman Catholic Church.

The Wars of Religion. In 1562 the duke of Guise came upon a congregation of Huguenots who were holding a church service in defiance of the local law. When the Huguenots were ordered to disperse, a quarrel resulted during which the duke's men killed and injured many of the Huguenots. As the news of the incident spread, the Huguenots took up arms and the long series of religious wars was begun. When in 1563 the duke of Guise was killed, Catherine became the recognized head of the Catholic party.

Despite the wars Calvinism spread. In 1570 Catherine adopted a policy of conciliation toward them. Admiral Coligny, the Protestant leader, was made a member of the cabinet and soon came to exercise a considerable influence over the king. This troubled Catherine who began to foresee the loosening of her dominance of the young king.

Coligny escaped an attempt at assassination, and went direct to the king who promised a thorough investigation. Fearing the exposure of her guilty knowledge of the plot and the consequent loss of her position at court, Catherine gained the king's ear, and won his consent to the famous massacre of the Huguenots which took place on St. Bartholomew's Day 1572.

The slaughter of the Huguenot leaders, including Admiral Coligny, did not break the movement. The St. Bartholomew massacre had spread from Paris to other parts of the country, and the struggle was only further embittered as a consequence. Charles IX died in 1574 and was succeeded by his brother Henry III.

In Henry's reign France became divided into three factions: the extreme Catholic party led by Henry, duke of Guise; the Huguenots, who had as their leader, Henry of Navarre; and a moderate Catholic group known as the *politiques* who were inclined to the view that it was not necessary to exterminate the Huguenots in order to preserve the unity of France. The leader of this group was Henry III, king of France. The later phase of the religious struggles in France therefore is known as the Wars of the Three Henrys.

Philip II of Spain supported the Guises and the extreme Catholic party, who became more powerful than the king. In 1588 Henry of France arranged the assassination of Henry, duke of Guise. He then joined Henry of Navarre, and together they laid siege to Paris which was in possession of the Catholic League. But Henry of France was assassinated in 1589 and there was left Henry of Navarre, leader of the Huguenots, who was heir to the throne of France. Henry knew that while he remained a Protestant he would not be accepted by Catholic France. He therefore became a Catholic, and was crowned Henry IV (1589–1610).

The Reign of Henry IV. Henry was an able and popular ruler. When he ascended the throne the nobility were very powerful. Many of them would have been glad to see a France without a king in which all power would lie in the hands of the nobles. But Henry addressed himself vigorously to the task of asserting and maintaining monarchical authority. In this he began the work which was completed under Richelieu and Mazarin.

In restoring prosperity to France, Henry had the assistance of an able minister of finance, the duke of Sully. Sully stimulated the growth of agriculture and industry, reformed the tax accounting in such a way as to lighten the tax burden, and by economy accumulated a treasury surplus. Henry aimed "to put a chicken in the pot" of every peasant family for Sunday dinner, as he himself expressed it.

In 1598 Henry issued the Edict of Nantes which established the position of the Huguenots in France. By its terms they were granted liberty of belief, and they were to continue to enjoy freedom of worship wherever they had exercised that privilege during the two preceding years. The Huguenots were to be eligible for public office, to be admitted to schools, colleges, and hospitals. They might open up schools of their own. They were to be protected in the courts by the presence of Huguenot as well as Catholic justices. They were allowed their own press. And as a guarantee of all these privileges they were permitted to hold La Rochelle and about one hundred other fortified towns and cities. Interestingly enough this edict was condemned equally by Huguenots and Catholics.

In 1610 the last of the "three Henrys" was assassinated by a religious fanatic. He was succeeded upon the throne by his young son, Louis XIII, whose mother Marie de' Medici became regent of France.

The Regency of Marie de' Medici. Instead of placing herself in the hands of the duke of Sully and other of her husband's able advisers, Marie relied upon the counsels of an Italian adventurer, Concino Concini, and his wife. The nobles grew more powerful and the treasury was emptied. However one act of Marie's proved especially fortunate for France. She appointed to the council the young bishop of Luçon, Armand Jean du Plessis de Richelieu.

When he reached the age of sixteen, the young king seized control of the government. Concini was murdered and his wife executed. Temporarily the queen mother and Richelieu were banished from court, but in 1622 a reconciliation was arranged and Richelieu became a member of the royal council. Louis XIII was quick to recognize the genius of his minister. By 1624 Richelieu was head of the state.

Richelieu. The outline of Richelieu's broad policy is simple. It was to make the monarchy supreme in France and France supreme in Europe.

In order to achieve the first of these purposes it was necessary for Richelieu to break the power of the nobles and of the Huguenots, the latter of whom, with their hundred fortified cities, constituted a state within a state. An uprising of the Huguenots gave Richelieu the opportunity he desired to destroy their military power. He personally organized and conducted the siege of La Rochelle and kept the English from relieving the city by constructing a great mole which closed the harbor. In the peace of Alais (1629) Richelieu confirmed the Huguenots in the possession of their civil and religious rights, but deprived them of the military and political privileges which had made them a separate state inside France.

In 1626 Richelieu decreed the destruction of all fortified castles not necessary for defense against a foreign foe. He enforced the edicts against dueling and forbade private warfare. He established an administration of *intendants* in the provinces and transferred the police, judicial and financial administration from the nobles into the hands of these new representatives of the crown. By these measures Richelieu reduced the power of the nobles.

In order to make France supreme in Europe, Richelieu had to reduce the power of the Hapsburgs. In this he followed the line of Francis I and Henrys II and IV, but with much greater success than his predecessors. When the last of the religious wars broke out in 1618—the Thirty Years' War—Richelieu followed its progress with close attention. Whenever the Hapsburgs seemed to have triumphed Richelieu used the influence of France to reopen the conflict. Finally, after Bohemia, Denmark, and Sweden had each fought and lost a phase of the long struggle, Richelieu took France into the conflict.

Neither Richelieu, who died in 1642, nor his king, Louis

XIII, who died the following year, saw the conclusion of the struggle. But Richelieu had found and trained an able successor who carried on his work. This was Cardinal Mazarin.

During Richelieu's long and successful direction of the government of France, he was confronted by conspiracies and plots of all sorts designed to bring him into disfavor with the king, and to topple him from office. Even the queen, Anne of Austria, and the queen mother, Marie de' Medici, his former patron, were jealous of his power. But Louis was a man sufficiently strong-minded to trust his great minister and to sustain him against attack although it must be admitted that during the early years, before the king had come to know and trust Richelieu thoroughly, there were times when the cardinal's position was very insecure.

Mazarin. Cardinal Mazarin was an Italian churchman whose abilities Richelieu early recognized. He was trained by Richelieu to succeed him as first minister and head of the state under the king. Mazarin was the real ruler of France after the death of Richelieu and during the minority of the young Louis XIV.

Although Mazarin was an able ruler he was a foreigner—he always spoke French with a marked Italian accent—and he was blatantly greedy. He accumulated a great fortune and lavished wealth upon the members of his family who came from Italy and settled in France. It was obvious to the French that the wealth flaunted so arrogantly by the Mazarini had come out of their own pockets. In addition, the nobles made a last attempt to regain their lost power during the minority of Louis XIV.

The revolt of the nobles under Mazarin is called the Fronde. There were two such outbreaks in Paris, both of which were successfully put down with the help of troops returning from the Thirty Years' War which had ended in 1648. It was the last attempt of the nobles against the monarchy. When Mazarin died in 1661, Louis XIV took charge of the government as his own first minister. It was the "sun king," Louis XIV, who splendidly wielded the autocratic power that had

been built up for him during long centuries of struggle by
earlier monarchs and their ministers.

41   GERMANY AND THE
THIRTY YEARS' WAR

In 1555 the Schmalkaldic Wars were brought to a conclusion
by the Peace of Augsburg and Lutheranism was formally recognized. Under the terms of the peace each prince was free
to decide whether Catholicism or Lutheranism would be the
prevailing religion in his domain. Many of the German princes
and bishops who had been converted to Lutheranism had
seized the lands and property of the Catholic church. It was
agreed that all church property appropriated before 1552
would remain in Protestant hands, all seized after that time
was to be returned to the Catholic church. Any ecclesiastical
prince who subsequently became a Protestant was to surrender
his see. Lutheran subjects of Catholic princes were not to be
forced to give up their beliefs.

But the terms of the Peace of Augsburg were disregarded.
Church property was not returned and further confiscations
took place. In addition the Peace had recognized only the
Catholic and Lutheran religions. As Calvinism spread through
the Germanies the Calvinists began to insist upon the same
rights as were enjoyed by the Lutherans. A league of Protestant princes was formed in 1608, under the leadership of the
Calvinist prince Frederick, of the Rhenish Palatinate, to secure
a revision of the settlement.

The Lutheran break with the Church of Rome had brought
about a reformation—or counter-reformation—in the Catholic
church. The Council of Trent, in several sessions between 1545
and 1563, had reaffirmed and clarified the basic Catholic doctrines and had instituted a thorough-going reform of the clergy.
The Society of Jesus, the Jesuit order, was organized by Ignatius Loyola, and the Jesuits devoted themselves to winning
back to the church many who had accepted the teachings of
Luther and Calvin.

In order to offset the influence of the Protestant League, the German Catholic princes formed a league under the leadership of Duke Maximilian of Bavaria. Their object was to prevent further secularization of church property, and if possible to regain some of the lands that had been lost to the church.

The Bohemian Revolt. The incident which precipitated the Thirty Years' War occurred in Bohemia. The Czech nobles, many of whom were Calvinist, feared that upon the accession of Ferdinand of Styria, who was a zealous Catholic, many of their privileges would be curtailed and Calvinism would be prohibited. They asserted the right to elect their own king, and in 1618 a delegation of Bohemian nobles broke into the imperial offices in Prague and hurled Ferdinand's representatives out of a castle window some sixty feet above the ground. They were saved from serious injury by landing in a manure pile. The Bohemians then elected as their king, Frederick, the Palatine elector and leader of the Protestant League.

In 1619 the emperor Matthias died and Ferdinand became emperor as Ferdinand II. He called upon the Catholic League and upon his Spanish cousin, Philip III, for help. The Bohemian phase of the Thirty Years' War was brief. The Protestant princes gave Frederick little support, and at the battle of White Hill in Bohemia he was decisively beaten by the forces of the Catholic League led by Count Tilly. The Spaniards invaded the Rhineland from the Netherlands, and with the assistance of the Bavarians seized the Palatinate which was eventually turned over to Maximilian of Bavaria.

The Danish War. Philip then resumed the Dutch War. England and France supported Holland, but the Spanish were successful against all three enemies. A Dutch attack on Brazil failed, as did an English attack on Cadiz. But the Hapsburg and Catholic successes alarmed the Protestants in northern Europe and Christian IV, the Lutheran king of Denmark (1588–1648), decided to champion the Protestant cause. He was aided by generous grants of money from England.

In 1625 Christian invaded Germany. Tilly and the Catholic

League were aided by the extraordinary adventurer Wallenstein who had managed to acquire much of the wealth of the
deposed Calvinist nobles of Bohemia whose estates were confiscated. Wallenstein raised a motley army of adventurers
from all lands, promising them high pay and plunder. In 1626
at Lutter Christian IV was overwhelmingly defeated by the
combined forces of Tilly and Wallenstein. A peace was finally
arranged at Lübeck in 1629. In the same year the emperor
issued the Edict of Restitution by which all lands confiscated
in violation of the Peace of Augsburg of 1555 were to be restored to the Catholic Church.

Sweden Intervenes. Norway, Sweden, and Denmark had been
united in a single state under the king of Denmark in 1397.
But in the sixteenth century Sweden, with Finland, had broken
away from the union and established an independent state
with Gustavus Vasa (1523–1560) as king. The country had
adopted Lutheranism and the church came completely under
the domination of the crown. The grandson of Vasa, Gustavus
Adolphus (1611–1632), now decided that by assuming leadership of the Protestant cause he would be able to make
Sweden the leading power in northern Europe. In his effort to
dominate the Baltic, he had engaged in a series of wars with
Russia which had won him control of Estonia and Ingria and
confirmation of his possession of Finland. He had wrested
Livonia from Poland in a war which lasted from 1621 to 1629.

Gustavus now sought an opportunity for extending Swedish
domination to the Baltic coasts of Germany. At the same time
the Catholic Cardinal Richelieu cast about for a means of
continuing the German struggle and thus of further weakening
the Hapsburgs. The two arranged an alliance whereby Richelieu provided Gustavus with arms and money on condition
that he would protect the freedom of Catholic worship in conquered territories.

In 1630 Gustavus landed in Pomerania where he occupied
fortresses and opened negotiations with the Protestant princes.
Meanwhile the Catholics besieged Magdeburg in 1630. The
massacre which followed the fall of the city brought Gustavus

the prompt support of the German Protestants. Wallenstein's private army had been disbanded and Tilly, who failed to check the Swedish advance, was killed in battle on the Leck in 1632. Wallenstein was recalled and quickly organized an army. At Lutzen in the same year the two armies met. Wallenstein was defeated, but Gustavus was killed.

Although the struggle was continued the advantage was increasingly with the imperial forces. Then in February 1634 Wallenstein was assassinated. Both sides were exhausted and a peace was arranged at Prague in 1635.

The French Phase of the War. Richelieu now decided that it was time for France to intervene openly in order to break the Hapsburg domination of Europe. He counted upon the Swedes and Protestant princes to continue the fight against the emperor while France broke the power of Spain.

The French period of the war lasted from 1635 to 1648. For a while the seasoned Spanish armies were victorious; in 1636 a Spanish army invaded northern France from the Netherlands and nearly captured Paris. In the following year another army invaded France from Spain. But as the French armies gained in experience they gradually turned the tide. The Dutch joined the French, and in 1640 the Portuguese overthrew Spanish rule and re-established their independence. Revolts broke out in Naples and Aragon. And in 1643 the great reputation of the Spanish infantry was blasted by the French victory of Rocroy.

The Peace of Westphalia. The long struggle was finally terminated by the Peace of Westphalia in 1648. This settlement was a very important one in European history. The empire was seriously weakened for each prince was given practical independence in his own realm, each being permitted to make war and peace without interference from the emperor. France received Metz, Toul, Verdun, and part of Alsace. Sweden obtained part of Pomerania and the bishopric of Bremen. The Hohenzollern state of Brandenburg was awarded eastern Pomerania and several bishoprics. Switzerland and Holland were recognized as independent states. Calvinists were to share the privileges accorded to Lutherans. Church property was to remain in the hands of whoever held it in 1624.

The Thirty Years' War had begun as a religious struggle. Its settlement was mainly political and economic, for by its close Europeans had come to recognize that it was possible for people of different religious faiths to live together amicably in the same state. The Hapsburg predominance was broken and the era of national states, all enjoying an equal international status, was inaugurated. It also inaugurated an era of international law. A study of the relationships between nations, *On the Law of War and Peace,* had been published during the course of the war by Hugo Grotius, a Dutch Humanist. Germany, the chief battleground of the war, was left disunited and impoverished.

The war between France and Spain was not ended by the Peace of Westphalia. That struggle dragged on for another eleven years, until 1659. When it was finally concluded by the Treaty of the Pyrenees, exhausted Spain was already in decline. Philip IV was forced to surrender to France Rousillon and a strip of the Netherlands including Artois. Louis XIV married Philip's daughter and renounced any further claim to Spanish territories in return for a large dowry which Spain found itself too poor to pay.

42 DEVELOPMENT OF CONSTITUTIONAL MONARCHY IN ENGLAND

The last of the Tudor monarchs was Elizabeth. Like her predecessors she was an absolute ruler. And like her predecessors Elizabeth wisely sought the co-operation and support of Parliament in her government of England. This gesture of respect toward the wishes of English subjects coupled with a strong national policy and the material prosperity which marked the Tudor era, contributed to make Elizabeth a popular ruler. Another point worth noting is that while Parliament remained subordinate under the Tudors, the fact that the Tudor mon-

EUROPE after the
PEACE OF WESTPHALIA
1648

|||||| INDEPENDENCE RECOGNIZED
AND GUARANTEED BY THE POWERS

SCOTLAND
Edinburgh

NORTH

SEA

Belfast
IRELAND
Dublin
Cork

ENGLAND

Amsterdam

HOLS
Ham
Bremen
UNITED
PROVS.
Antwerp
SPAN. Brussels Co
NETHERLANDS H
PALAT
Metz M
LORRAINE
Strass.

WALES
Oxford London
Bristol

Plymouth

Portsmouth

CHANNEL IS. Havre Rouen Verdun
Brest Paris Reims
Orleans

ATLANTIC

OCEAN

La Rochelle Nantes
FRANCE

FR.
COMTE
Sp. SWITZER

Lyon

DUCHY
OF S
P.
SAVOY
Avignon Ge
Marseille

Bordeaux
Bayonne
Toulouse LANGUEDOC

PORTUGAL
SPAIN
Saragossa

CORSICA
(Genoa)

Lisbon
Madrid

BALEARIC ISLES

SARDINIA
(Spain)

Seville
Cordova
Granada
Cadiz

MEDITERRAN

archs treated that body with respect greatly increased its prestige and strengthened its claim to represent the nation. Elizabeth's reign was marked by intense patriotism and pride in English achievement. The profitable exploits of the buccaneers was climaxed by the defeat of the Great Armada and the humiliation of Spain. The English Renaissance reached a magnificent flowering during the reign of Elizabeth, particularly in the fields of literature and the drama.

When Elizabeth died in 1603 she was succeeded by her cousin, King James VI of Scotland, son of the tragic Mary Queen of Scots, who ascended the English throne as James I. James very soon found himself at odds with Parliament over the question of royal finance. James was lacking in tact. When Parliament refused the subsidies he demanded, he proceeded to raise money on his own account by imposing customs duties, forced loans, the sale of titles of nobility, and the grant of monopolies. When Parliament protested, he arrested some members and sent others home. In 1621 Parliament drew up a "great protestation" against the king's refusal to allow them to exercise traditional privileges and this was followed by the impeachment of the king's treasurer.

Another cause for dissatisfaction with the Stuart was religious. James had been raised a strict Anglican; that is, he adhered to the doctrines and ceremonies of Catholicism and opposed Protestantism while supporting the separation of the English church from Rome. But during Elizabeth's reign Protestantism had spread widely among the middle classes, and its adherents continued to increase in numbers. We have already noted the Calvinist contempt for frivolity and gaiety and their hatred of "popish" ceremony and pomp in the churches. These Puritans, as they came to be called, tried to reform the Church of England from within and to make it Protestant in character. Others, variously called Congregationalists, Independents, and Separatists, endeavored to form independent congregations. Upon the accession of James, these groups presented a petition calling for the modification of church government and ritual. In 1604 James declared that bishops and kings were set over the people by God, and that he would force the Puritans to conform or harry them out of the land.

The wisdom of James' foreign policy was not appreciated by the English. Scotland had long been an enemy country, and the English defeated James' attempt to unite the two countries. They condemned him for his peaceful policy and his refusal to aid the Bohemians in their revolt against the Catholic emperor. And Parliament repeatedly protested against James' conciliatory policy toward Spain, and his attempt to arrange for the marriage of his son Charles to a Spanish princess. When James died in 1625, the ground had already been prepared for a conflict between the Stuart monarchy on one hand and the Parliament and people on the other.

Charles I. When Charles I (1625–1649) succeeded his father upon the throne, the English people hoped for a time that the contest between king and Parliament might be ended. Charles was personally popular. He assured Parliament that he would grant no concessions to the Catholics. Having been jilted by his Spanish fiancée, he shared Parliament's hostility toward Spain. But at the time of his marriage to Henrietta Maria, sister of Louis XIII of France, he secretly assured the French government that he would make general concessions to the English Catholics.

In anticipation of the war with Spain, Parliament granted subsidies. But Charles used up these funds, and demanded additional grants without showing any inclination to begin hostilities. Parliament then limited the collection of customs duties to one year, withheld further subsidies, and attacked the ambitious favorite of the king, the Duke of Buckingham.

Charles dissolved Parliament. Popular dissatisfaction was further increased by the failure of the English attack on Cadiz, and the failure to relieve the Huguenot stronghold of La Rochelle which was taken by Richelieu in 1628. Charles' attempt to raise money by forced loans failed, and in 1628 he was forced to call Parliament into session. The new Parliament forced the king to sign an agreement, the *Petition of Right*, by which he promised he would not levy taxes without the consent of Parliament or establish martial law or quarter soldiers on private citizens or order arbitrary imprisonment. The assassination of the Duke of Buckingham ended the controversy over his dismissal which was demanded by Parliament.

Exasperated by further parliamentary demands, Charles tried to rule without it from 1629 to 1640. In order to obtain much needed funds, Charles revived old feudal customs, employed the courts to collect enormous fines, and sold trade monopolies which resulted in high prices on commodities. In 1634 he demanded the payment of "ship-money" by the seaboard towns in substitution for the ships which they normally provided for the defense of the kingdom in time of trouble. The trial and condemnation of the Puritan, John Hampden, for his refusal to pay ship-money made him a national hero.

With the appointment of William Laud as archbishop of Canterbury, the laws against Catholics were relaxed and this further aroused the Puritans. And when Charles attempted to reorganize the Scotch church, Scotland revolted. Charles was now forced to call Parliament in order to raise money to protect England against the advancing Scotch armies. This disputatious Short Parliament was quickly dissolved, but Charles was soon forced to summon Parliament again.

The Parliament which met in 1640 is known as the Long Parliament for its session lasted until 1660. Under the leadership of such men as John Pym, John Hampden, and Oliver Cromwell, this Parliament insisted that supreme authority rested in the House of Commons which might disregard the acts of the king and the House of Lords. Archbishop Laud and Thomas Wentworth, earl of Strafford, were impeached and sent to the Tower. Charles' special courts, including the Court of Star Chamber, were abolished. And the king was required to summon a Parliament every three years.

Charles entered the House of Commons and attempted to arrest a number of its leaders. Parliament issued a call to arms and civil war was launched. Around the king rallied the Anglicans and Catholics, those who were opposed to the stern morality and manners of the Puritans. Thus began the struggle between the "Cavaliers" and the "Round-heads," so called because of the close-cropped hair of the parliamentary soldiery. A solemn league and covenant was arranged between Parliament and the Scots by which religious uniformity was to be established on the Presbyterian basis.

The war was brief. Charles was defeated at Marston Moor in 1644. The "New Model" army and Cromwell's cavalry force known as the "Ironsides" who charged into battle singing psalms vigorously carried on the war. At Naseby in 1645 Charles was again defeated. He surrendered the following year. Parliament was purged of its irresolute members by Colonel Pride, and the Independent minority or "Rump" Parliament condemned Charles to death. He was beheaded January 30, 1649.

The Commonwealth and Protectorate. The Rump remained in session and Oliver Cromwell was dispatched to Ireland to put down the Catholic rebellion which had broken out there. Parliament had expected to continue to govern England, but Oliver Cromwell, in 1653, dismissed Parliament and made himself religious and military dictator of England, first with the aid of a legislative body of his own choosing and then under a constitution which set up a "Protectorate."

Cromwell, although representing an insignificant majority of Independents, retained his control of England until his death in 1658. He had the support of a well-disciplined army. He maintained order, and during his rule commerce and industry prospered. He arranged profitable trade treaties with Holland and France, and conducted a war against Spain which won England Dunkirk, the island of Jamaica, and many shiploads of Spanish silver. But upon his death no satisfactory government was established, and in 1660 Charles Stuart, son of the beheaded king, was called to England to assume the throne as Charles II (1660–1685).

The Later Stuarts. The English were sick of Puritan rule with its suppression of dances and games and other healthy forms of recreation. Charles was hailed enthusiastically. The royalist nobility in both Scotland and England were also restored along with the king. These king's supporters were moderate and Anglican in their religious outlook. And they were no more ready to submit to absolute monarchy than were the Puritans.

But Charles and his brother James were staunch Catholics and champions of monarchical absolutism. It was not long before the differences between the Stuarts and their subjects provoked parliamentary opposition to the crown. Parliament tried to control the king by withholding grants, and by claiming the right to devote its grants of funds to specific purposes for which it required an accounting.

When in 1672 James, heir to the throne, openly espoused Catholicism and Charles relaxed the restrictions affecting Catholics, England was thrown into a panic lest, with the aid of foreign troops, the monarch attempt to restore Catholicism in England. In 1679 Parliament attempted to exclude James from the succession because of his Catholicism. But above all else the English wished to avoid the outbreak of another civil war. Two factions, the Whigs and the Tories, disagreed as to how far it might be possible to go without risking another civil war.

When Charles died in 1685 there did occur an insurrection in Scotland, and the duke of Monmouth, Charles' illegitimate son and a Protestant, organized a rebellion. Both outbreaks were put down, however, and the Catholic James took the throne as James II (1685–1688).

James at once attempted to create a standing army officered by Catholics. In 1687 he issued a "declaration of indulgence" which exempted Catholics and dissenters from punishment for the infraction of parliamentary laws against them. In 1688 he issued another such declaration which he ordered to be read in all Anglican churches. For a time the English suffered the rule of James in the expectation that upon his death and the accession of his Protestant daughters there would be a change for the better. But when James' Catholic second wife gave birth to a son, other factions joined the Whigs in putting an end to Stuart rule.

The Glorious Revolution. James' elder daughter Mary was married to William of Orange. Upon the invitation of Whig and Tory leaders, William crossed into England with an army in 1688. James, deserted by his followers, fled to France.

In 1689 Parliament issued a Declaration of Rights, which was enacted into law as the Bill of Rights. It clearly established limitations on the king's power and established in England a rule of king *and* Parliament. Money grants were to be made for the period of one year, which made necessary the regular calling of Parliament.

The English revolution had been attended by violence as we have seen. But despite involvement in foreign wars, the English were able to work out a solution of their problems without foreign interference in their internal affairs. Although stirred into rebellion by the abuse of monarchical power, they were nonetheless unwilling to destroy utterly the institution which had provided a satisfactory national government for so many centuries. Instead of destroying their government, therefore, they addressed themselves to the task of eliminating particular abuses of autocratic power, and of setting up safeguards against the re-establishment of those abuses.

43 RUSSIA AND SWEDEN

During three quarters of a century which elapsed between the election of the Romanoff family to the Russian throne and the accession of Peter the Great in 1689, west Europeans visited Russia in increasing numbers. Through such contacts Russians became familiar with west European customs and ideas. However, while this contact was sufficient to make many Russians aware of the civilization of western Europe it was not sufficient to bring about any important change in Russian life. The Europeanization of Russia was begun in the time of Peter the Great and was continued by Catherine and later rulers down to the present day.

Peter the Great. Peter, who was born in 1672, technically succeeded to the Russian throne when he was ten years old, a rule which he shared jointly with his feeble-minded half-brother Ivan under the regency of an older sister Sophia. In other words he became half-czar along with his half-witted half-brother. He received little formal education and was always uncouth in manner and violent in temper.

When Peter reached the age of seventeen, he and a group of conspirators seized control of the government and placed Sophia in a convent. His reign is usually dated from this act which took place in 1689. Peter grew up to be a man of extraordinary vigor and strength in both body and mind. He was six feet eight and one half inches tall, tireless in body and mind.

Ivan died in 1696 leaving Peter sole czar. Peter had seized Azov from the Turks and determined to strengthen his position by seeking alliances with the European states against the Turkish enemy. He organized an embassy which he himself accompanied as Peter Mikhailov, for he was anxious to study the customs of Europe at first hand. As Peter Mikhailov he visited factories, shipyards, schools, arsenals, docks, hospitals. In Holland he worked as a carpenter in order to master the technique of shipbuilding. He induced craftsmen and technicians of all sorts to return with him to Russia in order to train Russians to a mastery of European techniques.

Peter was suddenly called home by a revolt of his standing army, the Streltsi. By the time he reached home the revolt had been suppressed, but Peter insisted upon inflicting severe punishment. Many were tortured and Peter himself took pleasure in carrying out personally the wholesale executions which he decreed.

Peter's Reforms. Having punished revolt, Peter proceeded to introduce west European innovations into Russian life. He organized and equipped an army along European lines. He built a small navy which met with success against the Swedes in the Baltic and the Turks in the Black Sea. Peter had acquired some knowledge of new mercantilist theory during his travels in Europe and accordingly he sought to build up Russian industries and export manufactured goods in order to make Russia prosperous. He also tried to reform the manners of the Russians by insisting that women leave the harems and appear in public without veils. He taught his courtiers to dance and to smoke tobacco. With his own hands he cut off the beards and the long skirted garments of his Muscovite nobles.

Observing that the conservative Orthodox Church was hostile to his reforms, Peter refrained from appointing a successor to the Patriarch Adrian who died in 1700. He finally abolished the office of patriarch and brought the Russian church under the control of the crown.

War with Sweden. We have elsewhere sketched the founding of an independent Sweden under the house of Vasa, and have reviewed the military exploits of Gustavus Vasa and of his grandson, Gustavus Adolphus. We have also seen how Ivan the Terrible was blocked when he attempted to open a Russian port on the Baltic, a "window to the west." When Peter came to the throne, Russia's only port was Archangel on the White Sea which was ice-blocked a large part of the year. Peter seized Azov on the Black Sea at the opening of his reign. He then turned his attention to the Baltic.

When Charles XI of Sweden died in 1697 he left as his successor a fifteen-year-old son who became Charles XII. At once a group of European powers, Denmark, Poland, and Russia, formed a coalition to seize Swedish territories at a time when the monarchy seemed weak. But the young king proved to be a military genius more than equal to the emergency.

Charles did not wait for his enemies to attack. He moved quickly against each of his enemies in turn before they could join forces. In May, 1700, he invaded Denmark and forced its king, Frederick IV, to withdraw from the coalition. Peter of Russia had meanwhile invaded Ingria and laid siege to Narva. With only 8,000 men Charles attacked the Russian army of about 40,000. The badly organized Russians were put to rout.

Had Charles been able to follow up his victory by pursuing the Russian soldiery he might have forced Russia out of the war. But it was necessary to attack Poland quickly. Here again

Charles met with success. He deposed the Polish Augustus the Strong and forced the Poles to accept a king of his own choosing, Stanislaus Leszczynski.

Charles was occupied with the conquest and reorganization of Poland for seven years during which time Peter created a new army, better equipped and disciplined than the last. To meet this new threat Charles collected an army of 30,000 and in 1708 advanced into Russia. Peter adopted the same tactics which at a later date were to defeat Napoleon. He withdrew before the Swedes, destroying supplies as he went. Swedish stragglers were cut off, and the army was given no rest as the retreating Peter drew the enemy deeper and deeper into Russia.

In June 1709, Peter turned upon his weakened foe. Almost the entire Swedish army was destroyed or captured. Charles XII, however, escaped into Turkey where he succeeded in arousing the Turks to make war on the Russians. During the course of the long Turkish war, Peter was forced to surrender Azov to the Turks. Then when Charles felt he could do no more in Turkey, he crossed Russia in disguise and took up the war at home. In 1718 he was killed while fighting in Norway.

44   THE AGE OF LOUIS XIV

The institution of national monarchy, which we have seen developing in all parts of Europe, became most powerful and glorious in France during the reign of Louis XIV. We have seen how the way was prepared for Louis XIV by the work of Richelieu and Mazarin. Louis was a child of five when in 1643 his father, Louis XIII, died. Although he reached his majority under French law in 1651 when he became thirteen, he took no active part in his government while Mazarin lived. However Louis studied the work of his great minister and, when Mazarin died in 1661, announced that from thenceforth the king would be his own chief minister.

The Government of Louis XIV. Louis worked hard at the business of government. He surrounded himself with able advisers, but all decisions were his. His ministers were grouped into councils of State, Finance, Justice, and Interior. Louis presided in person over all but the court. There was no rigidity to this organization for Louis did not hesitate to shift his able organizer Colbert from one ministry to the other wherever his services might prove most valuable.

Colbert was a bourgeois, that is a non-noble townsman. As finance minister, he reformed many abuses and built up a surplus in the treasury as early as 1667. He was a mercantilist in his views, and accordingly fostered the development of French industry. The mercantile theory of the time held that a nation's economic strength grew in international trade through the export of goods to a greater value than imports. It would be necessary, as a result, for foreign purchasers to pay this "balance of trade" in money. The quantity of precious metals or money in the hands of the people and government of a state thus represented its wealth. Since manufactured goods were of greater value than raw materials, it was the aim of mercantilist statesmen to encourage industry and to discourage the import of manufactures from other countries. To this end Louis' government, under Colbert's management, subsidized new French industries and protected them with tariffs on foreign products.

In 1664 an East India Company and a West India Company were founded. Their purpose was to develop trade and colonization. Attempts were made to establish French settlers in the West Indies, in Madagascar, and in India.

The minister of war, Louvois, reformed and enlarged the French army. He introduced for the first time on any scale a standard uniform, marching in step, and regular drill. Promotions in the army were no longer based upon social position merely—merit was taken account of. Vauban, the great engineer, built a series of fortresses along the eastern boundary of France, and constructed base hospitals and supply depots.

Versailles. As we observed during our review of the Renaissance in Italy, writers, dramatists, poets, artists, sculptors, and musicians depended upon noble, royal and ecclesiastical patrons to provide them with employment and a living. Louis, as the greatest monarch of his time, distributed grants and employments to artists, musicians, and writers—many of whose names are famous in our own time. Lully was brought from Florence to become court musician. Corneille, Racine, Molière, La Fontaine, and Bossuet are some of the names which grace the literature of the period.

Architects, artists, and sculptors were employed in the erection and decoration of the magnificent palace Louis built at Versailles, a few miles ouside Paris. The palace of Versailles was not built merely to gratify a vain monarch. It became to France and to all Europe a symptom or symbol of French greatness. Versailles intensified every Frenchman's pride in being a Frenchman.

Versailles was also the last step in the complete subjection of the nobility to the monarchy. While the nobles were occupied with ceremonies, entertainments, and social intrigues, Louis ruled France. Many of the nobles, who were required to attend court by their king, ceased altogether from personally administering their estates. The peasants paid them taxes, but it was the king who represented government, order, justice, and who reflected the glory and power of France.

Louis and the Huguenots. Louis XIV was a devout Catholic. The pope he acknowledged to be supreme in the matter of doctrine, but in other matters the church was subject to the will of the monarch. The religious unity of the state was an ideal of an earlier age which Louis cherished. By a narrow interpretation of the Edict of Nantes, pressure was brought upon the Huguenots to force their conversion to Catholicism. Finally Louis was assured by his enthusiastic advisers that there were very few Huguenots left in France. In 1681 extreme measures were used to bring these stubborn few into line. Companies of soldiers were quartered in the homes of the Huguenots and were encouraged to conduct themselves in such a way as to break the spirit of the Calvinists. At last, in 1685, the Edict of Nantes was revoked. The king's act was hailed with approval throughout France.

The Wars of Louis XIV. Louis was married to Marie Thérèse, daughter of Philip IV of Spain. Louis, it will be recalled, had agreed to renounce all claims to Spanish territory for his wife or his heirs in consideration of the large dowry to be paid out of the Spanish treasury. But that dowry had not been paid; Spain was too poor. When Philip IV died in 1665 and was succeeded by Charles II, his son by a second marriage, Louis XIV claimed the Netherlands for France. He based his claim upon a Dutch custom under which children of a first marriage inherited their father's property to the exclusion of children of subsequent marriages.

When Louis' armies quickly overran the Spanish Netherlands, the Dutch and the English quickly put an end to their war, and joined Sweden in an alliance against France. This was an effort to maintain the balance of power among the European states and to prevent the domination of Europe by France. Louis withdrew from the war, but retained about a dozen Flemish towns.

Louis next proceeded to isolate Holland diplomatically by making treaties of friendship and non-aggression with her allies Sweden and England. When all was prepared, he invaded Holland without a formal declaration of war in 1672. The Dutch opened the dikes and flooded the country around Amsterdam thus saving the city. William III of Orange then arranged alliances with Austria, Spain, Brandenburg, and Denmark. After several more years of war, the treaty of Nimwegen of 1678 awarded Louis Franche-Comté and a number of Flemish towns. Thus Spain was again the loser.

In the very next year Louis set up Chambers of Reunion which searched the records of the past, and set up claims to territories which had once been dependencies of the territories that had been ceded to France. On the basis of their researches, he claimed all of Alsace as well as other territories, and sent his armies to take possession for him. The nations were alarmed afresh at this latest aggression. Spain, Holland, Savoy, Austria, and many small German states formed the League of Augsburg, and when William of Orange accepted the English throne, England too joined the coalition.

The war of the League of Augsburg lasted nearly a decade. While the French navy was defeated by the combined fleets of the English and Dutch, Vauban's line of fortresses protected France from invasion. Nevertheless, after nine years of warfare France was so exhausted that Louis was forced to give up all the territory he had conquered during the war except Strasbourg.

The War of the Spanish Succession. The idiotic Charles II of Spain was childless. Next in line of succession was the Dauphin of France and his three sons. However, as Louis had renounced all claims to Spanish inheritance, the strongest claim was that put forth by the Hapsburg emperor, Leopold, for his second son, the archduke Charles. But the Spanish remembered that they had been abandoned by the German Hapsburgs at the close of the Thirty Years' War, and were thereby forced to carry on the struggle with France alone. They were therefore inclined to favor the French heir if they could be assured that Spain would not become united to France.

Louis' ambassadors persuaded the feeble-minded Spanish king to will his crown to Louis' grandson, Philip of Anjou. Upon the death of Charles II in 1700, King Louis hailed his grandson as Philip V, king of Spain. Had he reassured the other European states that he had no intention of uniting the crowns of Spain and France, Louis might have avoided another war, but he failed to do so.

The War of the Spanish Succession was fought in Europe and in the colonies. We cannot here follow the development of hostilities in America and in India, in the Netherlands, the Germanies, Spain and Italy. The allied forces were led by the great English general, the duke of Marlborough, and by prince Eugene of Savoy. At Ramillies in 1706, at Oudenarde in 1708, and at Malplaquet in 1709, Louis' armies were defeated by Marlborough.

The war was finally brought to a close in 1713 by the treaties of Utrecht and Rastatt (1714). Philip inherited the Spanish throne as Philip V on condition that the crowns of France and Spain should never be united. The emperor received the Spanish Netherlands which now became the Austrian Netherlands, Naples, Milan, and the island of Sardinia which was later exchanged for Sicily. France retained Alsace, but lost a vast colonial empire; for England received Nova Scotia, the Hudson's Bay territory, Newfoundland, as well as Gibraltar and Minorca. The Hohenzollern elector of Brandenburg became king in Prussia, and the duke of Savoy became king of Sardinia, and each received increases of territory. France, exhausted by the long wars, had had a surfeit of glory. When Louis XIV died in 1715 the French people rejoiced.

PART NINE

Industrial Progress and the Beginnings of European World Dominance

1553	Richard Chancellor reached Russia through White Sea
1600	English East India Company chartered (organized 1609)
1604	First French companies chartered for Eastern trade
1606–1607	Dutch defeats of Spanish-Portuguese at Malacca and Gibraltar open seas to Dutch commerce and colonization
1607	First permanent English settlement in America at Jamestown
1608	Quebec founded by French
1611	First English trading stations opened in India
1619	First Negro slaves landed at Jamestown, Virginia
1620	Mayflower expedition founded New Plymouth
1668	First French trading station in India at Surat
1674	Nieuw Amsterdam finally became British by treaty and was renamed New York
1682	La Salle claimed Louisiana territory for France
1712	Newcomen's steam engine invented. James Watt improved it in 1769, 1781, 1782
1731	Jethro Tull's *Horse-Hoeing Husbandry*
1731–1738	"Turnip" Townshend applied Tull's methods to turnip cultivation
1733	Kay's flying shuttle patented
1750?–1794	Robert Bakewell experimented with cattle breeding
1765	Hargreaves' spinning jenny constructed
1767	Arkwright's water frame
1779	Crompton invented spinning mule
1785	Cartwright's power loom
1793	Eli Whitney invented cotton gin
1807	Robert Fulton's steamboat launched steam navigation

45 EUROPEAN COLONIZATION

One of the most striking developments of modern history is the Europeanization of the globe. This European predominance was attained in two ways: firstly, through exploration and settlement carried on aggressively by the principal European states over a period of several centuries; secondly, by the adoption of many of the techniques of European civilization by the peoples of other sections of the globe. This Europeanizing movement began with the opening of the era of exploration in the fifteenth century.

The Portuguese, who first developed an empire in the East, were seeking primarily trade. They established trading posts along the coasts of Asia and in the islands of the East Indies, but were prevented from attempting colonization by two factors. These were: lack of man power—the Portuguese population in the fifteenth century numbered not more than a million —and the fact that the lands which they visited were for the most part already densely populated.

In the western hemisphere the situation was different. In order for these lands to yield the products that were so much in demand in the European market, it was necessary that they be settled and developed. Consequently the Spaniards settled in America, established plantations, developed agricultural experiment, founded towns and cities and adorned them with churches and schools and universities. This aspect of Spanish colonization is often obscured in the accounts by an emphasis upon the more exciting narrative of the search after gold and silver. Every schoolboy is familiar with Ponce de Leon's picturesque quest of the Fountain of Youth, with Cortez's conquest of Mexico, with Pizarro's search for El Dorado. He is likely to pass lightly over the fact that the great Latin civilization to the south of the United States was the product of centuries of settlement and of patient and intelligent development.

The Search for a Sea Passage to the East. Much of the demand for eastern products was created by the increase of industry throughout all Europe. For example, the English cloth industry relied upon dyes and other products which were brought from the East by Portugal and Spain. So great was England's dependence upon Spain in this respect that in Elizabeth's day it was observed that Spain, by suddenly declaring war upon England, might seize half of English shipping in Spanish waters. The English were, as we saw, eager to find a northwest or a northeast passage to Asia and to free themselves thereby from dependence upon Spain. It was not until English explorers failed in their search for a passage to the East that English colonization was seriously undertaken. Even then, although various plans of colonization were worked out, the English government found them too expensive and risky. English colonization was the result of private enterprise.

French fishermen from Brittany and Normandy voyaged to the Newfoundland fishing grounds as early as 1504 and within a decade this became an annual practice. In 1524 Francis I employed the Florentine Verrazano to explore the North American coast in search of a sea passage to the Pacific. A decade later Cartier explored the St. Lawrence as far as the Lachine (China) Rapids. But it was not until the early seventeenth century that the French established settlements in Nova Scotia, and at Quebec in 1604 and 1608.

Dutch Enterprise. The Dutch were the first to challenge seriously the Portuguese and Spanish monopoly of trade with the newly discovered lands in both hemispheres. By the middle of the seventeenth century, the Dutch mercantile fleet was the largest in the world. Toward the end of the sixteenth century the Dutch landed in Java, expelled the Portuguese, and made treaties with the natives. The rapid Dutch development of trade and colonization in the East Indies led to the formation of the Dutch East India Company which established a governor-general in Java, who supervised Dutch governments in Celebes, Amboyna, Macassar, Malacca, Banda, Ternate, Coromandel, and the Cape of Good Hope. The Dutch by degrees drove the Portuguese out of nearly all their eastern possessions.

As a result of the explorations of Henry Hudson, an Englishman in the employ of the Dutch who explored the Hudson River and claimed the region for Holland in 1609, a Dutch West India Company was formed in 1621. A settlement was made on Manhattan Island and was named New Amsterdam. The Dutch also seized part of Brazil, but were driven out when the Portuguese regained their independence from Spain in 1640.

French Settlement. From Quebec, founded by Champlain in 1608, French trading posts were established throughout the northern part of the North American continent, and a profitable commerce in furs was developed with the American Indians. It was not until the reign of Louis XIV that large scale exploration and settlement were undertaken. La Salle explored the region of the Great Lakes while the Jesuits Marquette and Joliet sailed down the Mississippi in Indian canoes. In 1682 La Salle followed up the explorations of the missionaries and reached the Gulf of Mexico. Claiming the great central region of the American continent for France, he named it Louisiana in honor of the king.

French colonial activity was not confined to America, however. In the seventeenth century, French captains explored the Indian Ocean and claimed the islands of Reunion and Mauritius. With the founding of the French East India Company in 1664 by Colbert, their activities increased. Between 1668 and 1674 depots or factories were established at Surat, Masulipatam, and Pondicherry.

English Colonization. Meanwhile the English had turned from exploration to colonization. A careful study was made of Spanish agricultural experiments in the colonies, and lands were sought suitable for the raising of the products customarily imported from the East. After several unsuccessful attempts, the first permanent English settlement in America was established at Jamestown in 1607 by the Virginia Company.

It was not until more than a dozen years later that permanent settlements were established in the north when the Pilgrim Fathers landed at Plymouth on Cape Cod in 1620. In 1629 the Massachusetts Bay Company was granted a charter and many Puritans sought in the American wilderness the religious freedom that was denied to them at home. Massachusetts, Connecticut and Rhode Island were thus settled. In 1634 Leonard Calvert, son of Lord Baltimore, founded a colony on Chesapeake Bay under a charter granted to his father, as a refuge for Roman Catholics. Other settlements were later founded in Carolina.

Separating the northern and southern English colonies in America was the Dutch territory of New Netherlands. Ignoring Dutch claims, Charles II granted this region to his brother, the duke of York, in 1664, who thereupon seized New Amsterdam and renamed it New York. The coastal region to the south of New York was divided up into New Jersey and Delaware, and in 1681 the unoccupied inland region was awarded to William Penn, and became known as Pennsylvania, or Penn's Woods. In 1682 the Friends, or Quakers, founded the city of Philadelphia which, because of the toleration extended to all faiths, soon attracted settlers from different parts of Europe.

The English also settled in Bermuda and in many islands of the West Indies, which became an important source of the sugar that at a later date was carried to Puritan New England and manufactured into rum.

The East India Company established by Elizabeth in 1600 maintained a spice trade with the East Indies until driven out by the Dutch. The English company then turned its attention to the development of trade with India. Here the English were successful in driving out the Portuguese. Trading depots were set up at Surat, Madras, Bombay, and Calcutta between 1609 and 1690.

The French and English in America. When William of Orange ascended the English throne as William III in 1689, England joined the League of Augsburg in its war against Louis XIV.

In America the war between the French and English and their Indian allies became known as King William's War. With the establishment of peace in Europe in 1697, the colonies were forced to restore the land they had taken from each other.

When France and England were again opposed in Louis XIV's last war, the War of the Spanish Succession, the American colonies took up the struggle in what became known as Queen Anne's War. The colonists and their Indian allies again launched a series of bloody massacres. French Acadia was seized and later became the British colony of Nova Scotia. By the treaty of Utrecht in 1713, as we recalled earlier, France gave up Nova Scotia, Newfoundland, and the Hudson's Bay territory. France retained Louisiana and a large region on either side of the St. Lawrence which extended northeast to Labrador.

The French then built a series of fortresses from the St. Lawrence to New Orleans in order to protect their remaining American possessions. A struggle between England and Spain over the mistreatment of English seamen by the Spaniards became known as the War of Jenkins' Ear because an Englishman of that name brought home with him the ear he claimed had been cut from his head by a Spaniard. This war soon became merged in the War of the Austrian Succession. The French then attacked the English colonists and opened the American phase of the struggle which became known as King George's War (1740–1748). But when peace was restored no change was made in the English and French territories in North America.

The next contest between England and France broke out in the colonies before hostilities were begun in Europe. This was the French and Indian War which was one aspect or phase of the Seven Years' War in Europe. In America hostilities were precipitated by the activities of the French in fortifying the borders of Louisiana and in their incitement of the Indians to attacks upon English colonies. The struggle began unofficially in America in 1755, although war was not declared in Europe until 1756.

The English armies sent to America under the command of General Braddock met with disaster when they encountered Indian fighting. It was only after a series of defeats that the British gave sufficient attention to the war in the colonies. The tide was turned, and a series of British victories sealed the fate of French rule in America. The capture of Louisburg, of Fort Duquesne, of Ticonderoga and Crown Point, and the final brilliant taking of Quebec in 1759 by General Wolfe, mark the progress of the war. West Indian islands, including Martinique and Guadeloupe, were taken from the French as well as posts on the West African coast. From France's ally, Spain, the British took Havana and the Philippine Islands.

In India the French governor of Pondicherry, Dupleix, attacked and took Madras from the British during the War of the Austrian Succession. After the conclusion of peace, he sought to weaken the British in India by cultivating friendships with the Indian princes. But the dazzling success of the Englishman Clive in avenging an Indian attack upon the English post at Trichinopoly raised British prestige and many chiefs transferred their support from the French to the British.

During the Seven Years' War, Clive again won a series of brilliant victories over the native princes and the French with a force almost unbelievably inferior in numbers to the enemy. When peace was concluded in Paris in 1763, the French were allowed to retain only their trading stations in India. Canada and all of Louisiana east of the Mississippi, except New Orleans, was ceded to the British. The remainder of Louisiana was turned over to Spain. In exchange for the return of Havana and Manila the Spanish ceded Florida to the British. The French colonial power was broken, and the foundation of the British empire firmly laid.

46 THE AGRICULTURAL AND INDUSTRIAL REVOLUTIONS

The era of political revolution in Europe was preceded and accompanied by a development of techniques that was at least as revolutionary in its effects. Indeed the two developments are so inextricably intermixed that one is not comprehensible without an understanding of the other. Both the agricultural and the industrial revolutions were the result of the application of scientific knowledge to the techniques of production.

The Agricultural Revolution. It would be possible to trace the history of agricultural improvement in Europe back to the Middle Ages. However, the term agricultural revolution generally refers to the acceleration of that development which occurred in the early eighteenth century. In 1733 Jethro Tull published in England his *Horse-Hoeing Husbandry* which was the product of experiments conducted upon his own farm after extensive observation of agricultural methods employed on the continent. Tull had experimented with a horse-drawn implement of his own devising which broke up the soil and facilitated the nourishment of plants. He also created a machine which deposited seeds in parallel rows, making possible the use of machinery in cultivation.

During the Middle Ages the feeding of livestock during the long winter months had been a serious problem. The supply of natural grasses which could be stored for fodder was limited, and it was the general custom to kill off most of the livestock in the autumn, retaining only sufficient cattle to breed new herds in the spring. Under such conditions, the food supply was strictly limited. During the seventeenth century turnips were grown for fodder, and in the eighteenth century the cultivation of turnips, clover, and artificial grasses provided fodder without exhausting the soil. This obviated the necessity for assigning a portion of the cultivated land to lie idle or fallow while its fertility was restored. It also made possible the maintenance of larger herds of livestock.

In the early eighteenth century Lord Townshend, later nicknamed "Turnip" Townshend, applied the technique developed by Tull to the raising of turnips. He and his successors experimented with various methods of fertilizing the soil, and of preserving its fertility by the rotation of crops.

The improvement of industry and the growth of the towns

increased the market for butcher's meat, and this in turn led to experiments in the improvement of livestock by selective breeding. Robert Bakewell was one of the eighteenth century pioneers in this field. Sheep, which were formerly prized for their wool, were bred by Bakewell for food. He developed a breed known as the New Leicesters which were noted for their large bodies, fine flesh, and which reached maturity a year or two earlier than other breeds. Bakewell's example was quickly followed with the result that during the eighteenth century the size of meat-producing animals was roughly trebled. Similar experiments were conducted with dairy cattle, and thus the milk production of animals was often doubled.

The methods of the innovators were popularized by Arthur Young (1741–1820) who wrote books and lectured about the new agricultural experiments. He founded a monthly magazine, *Annals of Agriculture,* which was subscribed to by gentlemen farmers in France, Prussia, and America, as well as by large numbers of upper-class Englishmen.

But it was necessary to segregate animals which were being bred for the development of special characteristics. This led to the abandonment of the medieval common pasture land used freely by the whole community. The large landholders were able to "enclose" portions of the common lands either by buying out the rights of the small farmer or by ignoring them. The "enclosure" movement, the tendency of landholders to infringe upon the common or public land, was not new; it had been a problem in Tudor times. Clearly the small farmer could not afford to set aside fields for experiment. The men who brought about the agricultural revolution were of the landed aristocracy, men who had accumulated capital in the expanding commerce of England. They were the same merchant-adventurers who formed companies and sent out settlers to establish colonies. They were the leaders of the political revolution which had driven out James and set William upon the English throne. They were the men who ruled England from the "Glorious Revolution" of 1688 until the nineteenth century.

The Industrial Revolution. The industrial revolution was fundamentally the replacement of handcraft by power-driven machinery. It was a change unique in human history. In its broader aspects this revolution involved the development of large-scale capitalistic enterprise, changes in the status of the laboring man, population shifts and increase, and new social, economic and political problems. But none of this was new. Capitalism was not new; big cities were not new; nor were labor problems. In an early chapter we referred to the invention of a steam engine by the Hellenistic Greek, Hero of Alexandria. It is important to note however that Hero's invention remained a curiosity in the museum at Alexandria—it was not put to practical use.

Obviously it is impossible to establish a date for the beginning of what we have come to think of as the industrial revolution. But the changes which characterize it have been evident through the eighteenth century, and have continued down to the present day. A method for smelting iron with coal and lime was discovered in 1709, and thus made available the material out of which most power-driven machinery was made. As early as 1718 a silk factory was opened in Derby which was equipped with power-driven machinery.

Factors which contributed to the rapid development of machinery in England were the expanded commerce which opened up new markets for English goods, the availability of large deposits of coal and iron, inventive genius, and the fact that the wealthy, powerful, and educated classes of England fostered the new development.

It would be possible to list a great many inventions which played a part in the revolution of industrial technique. The water-driven silk-spinning machinery installed in his factory in 1718 by Thomas Lombe stimulated the invention of other types of spinning machinery for both silk and cotton. Kay's flying shuttle was patented in 1733. Hargreaves' spinning jenny of 1765 and Arkwright's water frame were combined by Crompton in 1779 in the mule which was capable of producing cotton threads of new strength and fineness. A cylindrical press for printing colored patterns on cotton fabrics and Cartwright's power-driven loom enabled England to produce cheaply great quantities of fine cotton fabric which she supplied to markets all over the world. The growth of the English textile industry created a huge market for American cotton, and when in 1793 the American Eli Whitney invented the cotton gin for separating cotton fibres from the seed, the American South was able to meet the demands of British industry for raw cotton.

For many centuries the fine hand-spun and hand-woven cotton cloths of India had been a luxury in demand all over the world. Now the machine industry of England produced finer yarns and fabrics, varied in design, so cheaply and in such quantity that English cotton cloth competed successfully with Indian in India itself. In this fashion India was conquered by European industrial technique at the same time that she was gradually falling into political subjection to Europe. Of course, the development of the textile industry is but one phase of the industrial revolution. But let us turn to the effects of the new industry upon the lives of men.

PART TEN

Despotism and Revolution

1740–1786	Frederick the Great, King of Prussia
1756–1763	The Seven Years' War
1759	The British General Wolfe took Quebec
1760–1820	George III, King of England
1762–1795	Catherine the Great, Empress of Russia
1769	Napoleon Bonaparte born in Corsica
1772	First Partition of Poland
1789	Storming of the Bastille in Paris
1793	Second Partition of Poland
	Louis XVI beheaded
1795	Russia, Prussia and Austria join in third partition of Poland
1796	Napoleon's First Italian Campaign
1800–1801	Napoleon's Second Italian Campaign
1801–1825	Alexander I, Czar of Russia
1804	Napoleon became Emperor
1805	Battle of Trafalgar
1806	Dissolution of Holy Roman Empire
1808–1814	The Peninsular War
1812	Napoleon's retreat from Moscow
1814–1815	The Congress of Vienna
1815	The Waterloo campaign
1821	Napoleon died at St. Helena
	The Greek revolt
1829	Greece independent
1832	The First Reform Bill
1837–1901	Queen Victoria
1840	Queen Victoria married Prince Albert of Saxe-Coburg-Gotha
1848	German parliament at Frankfurt

47   THE ENLIGHTENED DESPOTS

During the Eighteenth Century there ruled in Europe a group
of monarchs who became known as enlightened and benevolent despots—enlightened, because they were not only patrons
of learning and the arts but because they were themselves
accomplished in those refinements; benevolent, because they
were hard-working rulers who actively labored to improve the
condition of their subjects because they were intelligent
enough to see that their own prestige and power depended
upon the strength and prosperity of the nation; despots, because they jealously guarded and sought to strengthen their
autocratic hold upon the states which they governed. Chief
among them were Catherine the Great of Russia, Frederick
the Great of Prussia, Maria Theresa and Joseph II of Austria.

Russia and Catherine the Great. Between the death of Peter
the Great in 1725 and the accession of the Czarina Elizabeth
in 1741, Russia was ruled by a number of weak Romanoffs,
two of them women. Elizabeth, who was childless, wished to
preserve the Romanoff succession in Russia. She therefore
called to Russia her nephew, Peter, who was the son of her
sister Anna and the German duke of Holstein-Gathorp, for
whom she then proceeded to arrange a marriage with Sophia
of Anhalt.

The prospective empress, Sophia, gave up her Lutheran
faith and adopted that of the Russian Orthodox Church. She
took the name of Catherine, mastered the Russian language,
and sought to identify herself with her people. But Catherine
found herself neglected and mistreated by her boorish husband. For a time she employed her leisure to become acquainted with the ancient classics and the writings of such
leading contemporary thinkers as Voltaire, Montesquieu, and
the Encyclopedists.

Elizabeth died in 1761 and Peter became czar. Regarding
himself a Lutheran and a German, he treated his subjects and

their church with contempt. It was not long before the Russians came to think of Peter as the foreigner and of Catherine as the Russian. Catherine skillfully fostered hatred of the emperor and loyalty to herself. In 1762, while Peter was at his country estate with his Holstein regiment, Catherine was taken to St. Petersburg where she was acclaimed empress by the Russian troops. A few days later Peter's death was reported.

Catherine immediately assumed the direction of the affairs of state. She employed able men in her government, and showed an appreciation of the services of those who served her well. Catherine revealed her German origins by the attention she gave to building up her European reputation. She corresponded with the foremost philosophers and literary figures of her time, with Voltaire, Diderot, d'Alembert, and discussed reform with such interest that she was hailed as a liberal.

But in fact, while Catherine contemplated and proposed many reforms, she made little actual change in the organization of Russian life. For this she is often severely criticized, although it would be well for us to remember that Russia was in no way ready for the kind of reforms being discussed so widely in western Europe. A series of revolts among the peasants, one of them led by Pugashev in 1773 who pretended that he was Peter III, checked any reform of serfdom that Catherine may have attempted. No general educational reform was possible for there were no teachers. Catherine continued therefore to exercise her autocratic sway in Russia while she pleased the taste of the western élite by giving her encouragement and patronage to the most advanced thinkers of the time.

The territories of Russia were greatly enlarged during the reign of Catherine. It was during Catherine's reign that Russia won access to the Black Sea and a port in the south. Peter the Great, we recall, had held Azov for somewhat more than a decade, but was finally forced to restore the region to Turkey. Catherine provoked the Turks into a declaration of war in 1768. At the conclusion of the struggle in 1774, Catherine was ceded Azov and several strongholds north of the Black

Sea. A second Turkish war, which ended in 1792, sanctioned Catherine's annexation of the Crimea.

The Partitions of Poland. However the greatest accession of territory was achieved at the expense of Poland. In the eighteenth century Poland, extending from the Baltic almost to the Black Sea, was the third largest country in Europe. Only Russia and Sweden were larger. In population it was fourth. But despite its size Poland was a weak state. A very poor peasantry was governed by a stupid and greedy nobility. The kingship was elective and its power curtailed by a diet which, through a practice known as the *liberum veto,* was almost incapable of taking any responsible action. By a single vote any one of the nobles was able to block action by the diet. When the security of Poland was threatened, these men continued to make impossible any effective action to protect the country.

Upon the death of August III in 1763, Catherine sent troops to Poland to support her candidate for the throne, Stanislaus Poniatowski. Soon Catherine and Frederick the Great of Prussia opened negotiations with Maria Theresa of Austria leading to the partitioning of Polish territories. In 1772 the powers agreed that Prussia would take West Prussia excepting the cities of Danzig and Thom; Austria received Galicia; and Russia seized "White Russia" which had been lost to her in the Middle Ages.

In spite of the efforts of Poniatowski to organize and defend what remained of his kingdom, the rest of Poland was seized and divided up in 1793 and by a final partition in 1795.

Prussia and Frederick the Great. The German national state was created by the Hohenzollerns. The Hohenzollerns, like the Austrian Hapsburgs and the House of Savoy under which Italy was united, were for long minor vassals of the Holy Roman Empire. In 1417 Frederick of Hohenzollern, who was burgrave of Nuremberg, was presented with the *mark* or *march* of Brandenburg by the emperor Sigismund in reward for services. By shrewd marriage alliances, and by getting into wars on the winning side, the Hohenzollerns gradually increased their dominion.

The military might of Prussia was founded by Frederick William the Great, Elector of Brandenburg (1640–1688), and built up by Frederick William I, King of Prussia (1713–1740), and Frederick II, "The Great" (1740–1786). When the Great Elector came to the throne, he withdrew from the Thirty Years' War long enough to organize a strong army, and re-entered the war before its close in time to have a voice in the peace and a share of the territorial loot. By changing sides in the Swedish-Polish war that broke out in 1655, Frederick William obtained East Prussia from Poland. In return for aiding the emperor Leopold in the War of the Spanish Succession, the Hohenzollerns were raised to the dignity of the kingship.

The eccentric Frederick William I, father of Frederick the Great, continued the work of his predecessors in building up the army, in fostering the growth of trade, industry, and agriculture, and in making Prussia strong. He deplored his son's taste for music, literature, and French culture, which was dominant in Europe in the eighteenth century as well as in the seventeenth, and publicly caned and humiliated the boy until he planned to run away from the Prussian court with a young friend. Discovering the plot, the king had Frederick's friend beheaded outside his son's window, and put Frederick to work as a clerk in the Chamber of War and Domains.

When Frederick succeeded to the throne in 1740, he dismissed the useless regiment of giants, many of them over seven feet tall, that had been his father's pride. He increased the army and built up supplies and munitions. Frederick did not have to wait long for an excuse to make use of his powerful army.

In 1740 the emperor Charles VI died. Charles had no son, but for many years he had exhausted his treasury in making gifts to the various rulers of Europe in return for their agreement that they would recognize and support the right of his daughter Maria Theresa to inherit his domains. These treaties were known collectively as the Pragmatic Sanction. But

Charles' funeral was scarcely over before the European states asserted claims to parts of Maria Theresa's inheritance. The conflict which resulted is known as the War of the Austrian Succession.

Frederick II was the first to take decisive action. Without declaring war, he marched his army into Silesia. Austria was totally unprepared. France, Spain, Sweden, Bavaria, and Saxony entered the war in the hope of making territorial gains. England, prompted by her bitter colonial rivalry with France, sided with Austria. Maria Theresa appealed directly to her subjects who rallied to her cause. Frederick, who had withdrawn from the war, had to re-enter it as Austrian successes endangered his hold on Silesia. When peace was finally arranged in 1748, Frederick held Silesia although all other conquests of territory were restored.

During the eight years following the peace of Aix-la-Chapelle, a realignment of the European powers took place that was so radical it became known as the "Diplomatic Revolution." Alarmed by the power of Prussia, France, Austria, Russia, Sweden, and Saxony formed an alliance against Frederick, while England abandoned Austria and switched her support to Frederick. The colonial consequences of the Seven Years' War (1756–1763) have been discussed. Hostilities had already begun between England and France in India in 1751 and in America in 1754.

On the continent Frederick commenced hostilities by attacking Saxony. Despite a series of brilliant military victories which won for Frederick his title, "The Great," the weight of the coalition made itself felt. Beginning with the defeat of Kunersdorf in 1759, there followed such a series of disasters that Frederick contemplated suicide. Frederick was saved from complete defeat by the death of the Czarina Elizabeth in 1762 which brought to the Russian throne the half-German Peter III. Peter quickly concluded peace with Frederick, and sent him Russian troops to aid against Russia's former allies.

Frederick gained no territory from the Seven Years' War, but the brilliant conduct of the Prussian armies and their leader established Prussian military prestige. And, as we saw,

in 1772, in collaboration with Catherine of Russia and Maria
Theresa of Austria, he added West Prussia to the Hohenzollern domain.

Austria and Joseph II. The reign of Maria Theresa has been
discussed to some degree in connection with those of Catherine
and Frederick. She was a very different type of person from
her collaborators in the Polish partition. Although an autocrat in her government, she lacked the calculating hardness of
Catherine and Frederick. At least the partition of Poland
made her weep. And she was realistic enough to know that if
she had refused to take part, Poland would have been partitioned anyway.

Joseph II succeeded his father as Emperor in 1765. Upon
the death of his mother, Maria Theresa, in 1780, Joseph inaugurated a series of reforms more sweeping than anything
that had thus far been envisaged in Europe. Joseph sought to
centralize the administration and to unify the language of his
polyglot empire. German was made compulsory in schools,
universities, and in government. This offended all the non-German elements in the empire: Magyars, Czechs, Poles and
Croats.

Another desire of Joseph was to establish equality before
the law for all citizens. All offenders whether noble or peasant,
Christian or non-Christian, were to be treated equally under
the law. The death penalty and extreme punishments were
abolished. This offended many nobles and Christians.

In 1781 Joseph abolished serfdom, which permitted peasants to change their homes, marry at will, own land. The freed
peasants were put under the protection of the state against the
attempts of their lords to fine or punish them. An edict of
Toleration granted religious rights to Protestants and the
Greek Orthodox Catholics, and most of the disabilities of the
Jews were abolished.

Joseph also sought to reform and nationalize the Catholic
Church along somewhat the lines that had been in France. The
number of monasteries was reduced and an amount of church
property was confiscated, although it will be well to remember

that Joseph was a Roman Catholic and had no intention of breaking with Rome.

Not only did the nobles resent the abolition of serfdom; so also did the serfs whom Joseph was trying to help. A peasant rebellion broke out. All classes and all groups in Joseph's domains resented his efforts and resisted them. He was forced to rescind most of his decrees in January 1790. He died the next month. The reaction to Joseph's reforms helps us to understand why Catherine was content to do so little to change conditions in Russia.

48 THE ERA OF REVOLUTION

The American Revolution. This is not the place for a narrative of the causes and events of the American Revolution; that will be dealt with in another chapter. What concerns us here is the European aspect of that event. For the American founding fathers were Europeans in culture and background, and were fully in touch with the philosophical and reforming ideas and ideals of eighteenth century Europe.

The French Revolution. The change in thought which laid the foundation for the overthrow of the political and social institutions of feudalism was brought about by the thinkers and writers—the intellectuals—who were supported and encouraged by the members of the privileged classes, the nobility and higher clergy, and the wealthy and cultured bourgeoisie. It is difficult, in a brief space, to give any satisfactory account of the change of outlook effected.

To the Middle Ages, men were by nature imperfect beings, heirs to sin and error, who could only be saved through God's mercy; for even if a man's intentions were of the purest, and he succeeded in resisting or avoiding temptation, his imperfect judgment might still lead him astray. By the eighteenth century, many were asserting that men are fundamentally good by nature, and that they have become corrupted by institutions. Voltaire imagined the Huron Indian as an unspoiled "natural" man, and in this way tried to show what men would be like if they could free themselves of the past. Throughout most of his career Voltaire attacked the church as one of the evil institutions to be gotten rid of. Rousseau proclaimed that men were born free, yet were found everywhere enchained by the past.

This philosophical revolt against the past suited well with the popular mood for many reasons. The extravagances and wars of Louis XIV and Louis XV had put the French nation hopelessly in debt. The privileged classes expensively adorned Versailles, but served no useful purpose while the bourgeoisie, i.e., the prosperous, town-dwelling, merchant and professional men, who had contributed to the material prosperity of France, were denied privileges and social status merely by reason of birth. Taxes fell upon those who were denied privileges.

When in 1789 King Louis XVI summoned an Estates General to meet at Versailles in order to levy such taxes as would extricate the government from its financial predicament, the representatives brought to the meeting *cahiers,* or written memoranda, of the abuses the people of the nation wished to see corrected. Failing to overawe or cajole the members of the Third Estate into passively voting money, Louis tried to dissolve the session, but was defied by Count Mirabeau, a champion of the popular cause. On June 17th the representatives of the Third Estate constituted themselves a National Assembly, and invited representatives of the other estates to join them. Finally accepted by the king as representing the nation, the group reformed itself as the National Constituent Assembly and appointed a committee to frame a new constitution. Alarmed by the presence of bodies of troops that had assembled to maintain order, the people of Paris armed themselves and stormed the old prison of the Bastille on July 14th. The continued uneasiness of the people of Paris led to an outbreak in October when a band marched to Versailles and brought the king to Paris. He was shortly followed by the Assembly.

The representatives were encouraged to reform their government by the success of the revolutionary movement in England which culminated in the Glorious Revolution of 1688 and by the American Revolution. In England, men of enterprise and property were rising to power, and industry and commerce prospered. The constitution of the new American nation, which was adopted in 1789, the year of the French Revolution, stirred profoundly the people of France and Europe with its assertion of principles and its wise provisions for self-government. The new French constitution of 1791 contained a declaration of the rights of man which asserted all men to be free and equal in rights; assured freedom of conscience, speech, and press; decreed the right of men to possess property. The sovereignty of the people and the separation of governmental powers were principles embodied in the constitution. The monarchy was retained, but the king became a limited and constitutional ruler. The financial difficulties were met by seizing and making public the property of the church. On September 14th King Louis accepted the constitution.

In August 1791 the Emperor Leopold and the king of Prussia issued the Declaration of Pillnitz which stated that they were willing to intervene to restore Louis to his old position, but only with the consent of all the European powers, including England. Alarmed by the threat of intervention, the more radical members of the newly elected Legislative Assembly, the Girondins, aided by the still more radical Jacobin clubs, whipped up a patriotic fervor throughout the country.

In April 1792 France declared war against Austria, and put three armies in the field. News of French reverses caused intense excitement in Paris. Ever since the first revolutionary succession in 1789 Marat, through his journal, the *Ami du Peuple*—the *Friend of the People*—had urged the Paris populace to take matters into their own hands for he feared that the wealthy bourgeoisie might get control and set up an aristocratic regime similar to that which held sway in England. The fearful mob, lashed by Marat's frenzied articles and by their own speakers, attacked the Tuileries palace on August 10 and the king was forced to seek refuge with the Assembly.

The king was imprisoned in the old house of the Knights

Templars and a provisional government was set up in which Danton was the dominant figure. In September, the frenzied mob broke into the prisons and slaughtered thousands of political prisoners. Similar slaughters took place at Versailles, Lyons, Orleans, and Rheims. The national government fell under the domination of the Paris mob.

In late September, 1792, a new representative body met, the National Convention. The monarchy was abolished and France was declared a republic. Aroused by Danton's oratory, the people seized weapons and rushed to the defense of the nation. The tide of war turned in favor of the French. In November the Convention offered French assistance to all peoples who wished to overthrow their governments. The government was puzzled as to what to do with the king, since it was agreed it was not safe to set him free. He was brought to trial, condemned, and beheaded by the guillotine on January 21, 1793.

The execution of the king shocked Europe and the war spread. Fresh French reverses brought the radical Jacobins to the fore, and more moderate members were suspected of treason. Unable to tolerate criticism, the radical Jacobins under Robespierre, instituted a reign of terror during which the most appalling wholesale slaughters took place of all those even vaguely suspected of being critical of the Jacobin rule. The Reign of Terror began in September 1793, and lasted to the sudden fall of Robespierre in July 1794.

The success of French armies and the end of the Reign of Terror restored a degree of calm. In August 1795, a new government was established which placed the executive power in a directory of five, and the legislative function in the hands of two chambers, a Council of Elders and a Council of Five Hundred. Shortly after its establishment a royalist insurrection broke out in Paris, and on the motion of Barras, General Bonaparte, then in Paris without a commission, was put in charge of the troops. His famous "whiff of grapeshot" from the Church of St. Roche broke the uprising.

49 NAPOLEON

Napoleon's successful defense of the government won him the command of the Army of the Interior. The Directory arranged for a triple attack upon the Empire. An army under Jourdan was to advance into the region of the lower Rhine, another under Moreau was to penetrate the upper Rhineland, and a third army under Napoleon was to clear northern Italy of the Austrians, and advance through the Tyrol to join the other two. The armies of Jourdan and Moreau were successful in Germany, and a truce was about to be concluded when the archduke Charles suddenly took the offensive, defeated Jourdan, and drove Moreau back to the upper Rhine.

Before leaving Paris for Italy, Napoleon married Josephine Beauharnais, one of the most popular figures in Paris society. He led his army into Italy along the coast and defeated both the Austrians and Piedmontese. Piedmont ceded Savoy and Nice to France, made peace, and permitted the French to garrison Piedmontese fortresses. Napoleon then pursued the Austrians whom he defeated again at the battle of Lodi on May 10. He entered Milan on May 15, subjugated Lombardy, and set up the Lombard Republic. The pope, the king of Naples, and the dukes of Modena and Parma bought peace by surrendering large sums of money and many art treasures; and Napoleon rapidly advanced across northern Italy, and won a series of victories against the enemy. Threatened again, the pope surrendered Romagna, Bologna, and Ferrara.

During March and April 1797, Bonaparte crossed the Alps to advance into Germany, but the uprising of Venice and the Tyrol against the French forced him to conclude the preliminary peace of Leoben on April 18. The territorial settlement gave France the Belgian provinces, and recognized the Cisalpine Republic which was to be formed in northern Italy. Without waiting to fulfill the other provisions of the treaty, France attacked Venice and overthrew the aristocratic government. The Republic of Genoa was transformed into the Ligurian Republic under French control. The treaty of Campo Formio confirmed many of the provisions of Leoben, and ceded further territories to France, including the left bank of the Rhine. In February 1798 the French occupied Rome, took Pope Pius VI prisoner, and set up the Roman Republic.

The Egyptian Campaign. Pretending to be preparing an invasion of England, Napoleon gathered an army of 35,000, and suddenly sailed for Egypt where he landed July 1, and took Alexandria the following day. The Egyptian army was defeated in the battle of the Pyramids on July 21. But the British admiral, Nelson, located and destroyed the French fleet at Aboukir on August 1, and thus cut Napoleon off from France. Although he invaded Syria, and defeated Turkish and British forces there, Napoleon's army was decimated by losses and the outbreak of the plague, and he beat a hasty retreat into Egypt.

Napoleon's reports of brilliant victories and his suppression of the less favorable aspects of his Egyptian campaign made him a popular hero in France, for during his absence French armies in Germany and Italy were suffering defeat. He abandoned his Egyptian army, and unexpectedly returned to France in August 1799. With the help of his brother Lucien, Napoleon overthrew the now unpopular Directory and formed a new government.

The Consulate. The new Constitution of the Year VIII of the Republic made Napoleon first Consul in association with two other consuls whose functions were however merely advisory. Although the new constitution preserved the appearance of a republic through the institution of elected legislative bodies, it actually established the dictatorship of Napoleon. France was divided into prefectures and sub-prefectures, and new and efficient systems of administration and tax collection were set up.

In spite of Napoleon's offers of peace, the war was resumed. The First Consul led an army into Italy while Moreau advanced into Germany. A series of brilliant French victories in both fields of warfare led to the Treaty of Luneville in February 1801 which confirmed former cessions to France, recognized the satellite Batavian (Dutch), Helvetian (Swiss), Cisalpine (north Italian), and Ligurian (Genoese) republics. The grand duchy of Tuscany was transformed into the Kingdom of Etruria, and Spain ceded Louisiana to France, which sold it to the United States in 1803. A treaty was concluded with Naples, a Concordat was arranged with the pope, and finally in March 1802 peace was arranged with England. Europe was at peace.

The Empire. In May 1804 Napoleon was proclaimed Emperor of the French; he was consecrated by the pope in Paris the following December. In imitation of Pepin and Charlemagne, he placed the crown on his own head. The imperial office was made hereditary in the Bonaparte family. A new nobility was created, and a brilliant court surrounded the emperor. In imitation of the German emperors, Napoleon made himself king of Italy. His stepson, Eugene Beauharnais, was appointed viceroy of Naples, and the Ligurian Republic was made part of France.

In 1805 England, Austria, Russia, and Sweden formed a coalition against Napoleon. In October the British fleet under Lord Nelson, who was killed in the battle, won a great victory at Trafalgar over the combined fleets of France and her new ally, Spain. French naval power was broken, and England controlled the seas. But at Austerlitz, on December 2, Napoleon defeated the combined Russian and Austrian armies. Under the treaty of Pressburg, France received Piedmont, Parma, Piacenza, and the Venetian territory that had been given to Austria at Campo Formio. Joseph Bonaparte became king of Naples, and Louis Bonaparte became king of Holland. Large territories were taken from the Holy Roman Empire, and distributed among the powers, and in August 1806 the emperor Francis II surrendered the crown of the old empire, and was known thenceforth as Francis I, Emperor of Austria, a title he had assumed in 1804. This was followed by the defeat and occupation of Prussia; the extension of Napoleonic domina-

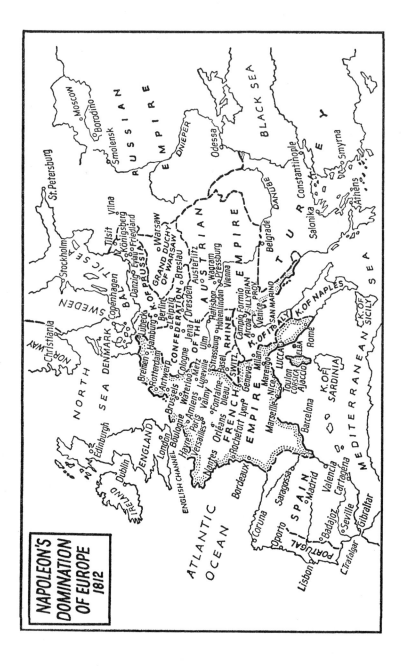

NAPOLEON'S DOMINATION OF EUROPE 1812

tion over other parts of Germany; and a defeat of the Russians which brought about the Treaty of Tilsit, in July, 1807.

Napoleon had been successful against all his enemies except England. Unable to invade the British Isles, he sought to injure England by closing the continent to English trade by the Berlin decree of November 1806. Portugal, which refused to join the blockade, was occupied by the French in 1807 and in 1808 the French invaded friendly Spain, and Napoleon's brother, Joseph, was placed on the Spanish throne. But the Spaniards refused to submit to French rule.

The stubborn resistance of the Spanish people dates the beginning of the decline of Napoleon's power. They were aided by the British under Sir Arthur Wellesley, who became the Duke of Wellington. Although Napoleon succeeded in retaking Spain, a guerrilla warfare continued which was very costly to the French. A new and successful war was waged against Austria in 1809.

From 1810 to 1812 Napoleon was at the height of his power. He divorced Josephine and in 1810 married Marie Louise, daughter of the emperor Francis I of Austria. The birth of a son in 1811 seemed to assure the future of the Bonaparte dynasty. But friction developed between Napoleon and Alexander of Russia over a number of issues, and the French emperor decided upon the invasion of Russia.

Napoleon's Russian campaign has become a familiar story. The Russians adopted a "scorched earth" policy and withdrew before the advancing French. The French entered Moscow on September 14, and the following day the Russians set fire to the city in order to make it untenable. Alexander refused terms, and the frustrated French emperor began, in October, the disastrous retreat which was survived by not more than 100,000 of his original army of about 600,000 men.

The Wars of Liberation. The Russian disaster awakened the hope that Napoleon might at last be overthrown. In 1813 the Prussians reorganized their army. Austria declared war on France, and in September Austria, Russia, and Prussia formed a union against France. At the great Battle of the Nations at

Leipzig in October, Napoleon was defeated by the allies. The English again landed in Spain.

Napoleon fought brilliantly against the greater forces of his enemies, but suffered a series of defeats. On March 31, 1814, the victorious allies entered Paris. Under the influence of Talleyrand, the Senate deposed Napoleon, and the emperor abdicated unconditionally.

The Hundred Days and After. After the first outburst of rejoicing, Napoleon's fall was followed by the relaxation of tension and emotional letdown which usually succeeds a major war. Louis XVIII, brother of the executed Louis XVI (Louis XVII, the young son of Louis XVI had died while a prisoner of the Revolution), seemed a very dull figure after the glamorous Napoleon. The tedious peace negotiations were accompanied, as usual, by the difficulties of internal readjustment, and to the defeated French their great days under Napoleon seemed more and more glorious as time passed.

Napoleon had been imprisoned on the island of Elba off the coast of Italy. On March 1, 1815, he suddenly landed at Cannes in southern France. His old soldiers flocked around him, and even the corps of Marshal Ney, sent to take him prisoner, went over to the old emperor. Napoleon entered Paris in triumph on March 20, and there began the renewal of the war known as the *Hundred Days.*

The Hundred Days was brought to a close by the great battle of Waterloo on June 18. It was a close-fought battle during which Wellington's army of many nationalities withstood a series of terrific attacks by the French. The arrival of Blücher and his Prussians toward the end of the day turned the tide in favor of the allies. Napoleon's defeat was followed by his second abdication on June 22, 1815. This time he was imprisoned on the island of St. Helena in the south Atlantic Ocean where he remained until his death in 1821.

After a quarter-century of war and revolution during which the map of Europe had been remade many times, the representatives of the European states met in the great Congress of

Vienna to deal with the enormously complicated problem of European settlement. The revolutionary governments had collapsed, and it was necessary to set up in their place governments which the people would be able to accept as legitimate and truly representative of their interests. But many of the old ruling houses had died out. In addition there was the delicate problem of territorial settlement to be faced. But despite the many defects of the settlement, the Congress of Vienna did establish a European system bound by treaty obligations, which avoided the demoralization and destruction of a general European war for another century.

50 REACTION AND REVOLUTION

The quarter-century of war through which Europe had just passed had been precipitated by revolution. The restored governments were determined therefore to suppress any revolutionary developments which threatened to precipitate another such disastrous struggle as the one just concluded.

But the governments that had been set up in many parts of Europe during the revolutionary and Napoleonic era had, in truth, destroyed many abuses which had developed out of the feudalism of the past. The Napoleonic administration was highly efficient. Men of all classes, but particularly those of the ancient Third Estate, had enjoyed freedoms, privileges, and opportunities which were once again denied to them as the *émigré* nobles returned with their monarchs and sought to re-establish the privileges they had enjoyed under the old regime. The inevitable economic depression which accompanied the readjustment to peacetime conditions was blamed, and often with reason, upon the measures taken by the restored governments. Actually the old regime was never "restored" in any complete sense, but during twenty-five years the attitude of people had changed, and the restored governments were often unable fully to take account of the fact that they confronted a new and changed Europe.

Liberal and Conservative. The history of the nineteenth century is marked throughout by struggles between "liberals" and "conservatives" or "reactionaries." These words are deceptive for they cover a variety of meanings. It is necessary to take account of the fact that when the Italian or the German spoke of liberalism or liberty he meant something quite different from what the Englishman, the Frenchman, or the American understood the same words to mean. In the latter three countries "liberalism" generally meant the desire for a greater degree of participation on the part of the citizen in determining the policies and important decisions of his government, and a greater degree of freedom for the individual under the law. Those freedoms were variously defined in the bills of rights drawn up during the revolutionary era. But other European peoples conceived a different meaning of the word liberalism.

Long before the French Revolution, as we saw, the people of Europe were developing what we call "national" consciousness. In the Germanies, in the Balkans, in the Austrian Empire, in Italy, and elsewhere, there were Germans, and Hungarians, and Croats, and Bulgarians, and Greeks, and Italians, who found themselves living under governments of foreign princes. By the peace settlement they were held subject to foreign governments and were prevented from uniting with their fellow nationals in other subject territories to form new national states under governments which would be representative of the nation rather than of dynastic interests. To these people liberty meant freedom from foreign rule. They had as yet no experience of national government which would enable them to know what degree of self-government and individual political liberty they would be capable of exercising or even of desiring.

Revolutionary Outbreaks of 1820–1821. In 1820 there occurred in Naples a rebellion against the tyrannical Ferdinand I. The frightened king promptly promised his subjects a constitution modeled upon the Spanish constitution which had been drawn up in 1812. The revolt in Naples was the signal for dissatisfied elements elsewhere to demand changes in government. In Piedmont, the following spring, there occurred a military revolt which brought the abdication of King Victor Emmanuel I in favor of his brother, Charles Felix. The young prince Charles Albert, in the absence of Charles Felix from Turin, proclaimed the Spanish constitution of 1812. A military rebellion which had broken out in Spain quickly spread to the principal cities and early in 1820 the king, Ferdinand VII, promised to support the constitution of 1812. Assassinations and military revolts occurred in Russia, France, Portugal, Germany, and there was an increase of reform agitation and violence in England. In 1821 the Greeks revolted in an effort to free their country from Turkish rule.

The revolts of 1820 and 1821 were ill-organized and poorly carried out. They were conducted by minority groups which, aside from the particular abuse which concerned their own interest, had only a vague notion of what reforms were needed. The Spanish constitution of 1812 was therefore acclaimed as if, by some magic, its mere adoption was sufficient to establish a new and beneficent order on earth. But when the great powers—including France, but not including England —intervened, the revolts were quickly suppressed. The bulk of the population were not behind the revolutionary groups. In Spain the peasants hailed the French soldiers sent to put down the revolution with cries of "Death to the Constitution; long live the absolute king!"

Revolutionary Outbreaks of 1830. In 1825, upon the death of Czar Alexander, a military revolt was staged in an effort to prevent the strong-minded Nicholas I from succeeding to the throne. The effort was a failure, but it is interesting to note that the conspirators adopted the cry of the west European revolutionists. The leaders who wished to place Constantine on the throne had stirred up the troops who started for the palace, shouting, *"Long live Constantine and the Constitution!"* When questioned afterward many of the soldiers revealed that they had thought "Constitution" was the name of Constantine's wife.

During his long exile, while France was in the grip of revolution and dictatorship, Louis XVIII had noted what institutions of the past seemed doomed. He made no attempt to revive them, but issued a *Charter* in 1815 which "granted" to his subjects equality before the law, eligibility to civil and military offices, assured religious liberty, and the taxation of all classes of citizens according to their means. But during the revolutionary excitement which seized Europe in 1820, the duke of Berry, who was in the line of succession to the throne, was assassinated by a fanatical liberal. As a result of this act the French government became more reactionary in its policy and promptly co-operated with the allies in suppressing the rebellion in Spain.

Louis' brother, Charles X, came to the throne in 1824, and immediately adopted measures which aroused consternation among the French. He reduced the interest payments on government bonds, and used the balance to compensate the *émigré* nobles for their losses during the revolution. He dissolved the Chamber of Deputies, placed restrictions on the press, and denied to the French the rights granted in the *Charter*. Paris rose against the king, and barricades were erected in the streets. Charles abdicated and was succeeded by Louis Philippe, a descendant of Henry IV, who had associated with the Jacobins and fought in the republican army.

Encouraged by the success of the new revolution in France, the papal states rose in revolt against the government of Pope Gregory XVI in 1831. Similar outbreaks occurred in Modena and Parma against the Hapsburg rulers who fled to Vienna. But the Austrian minister, Metternich, dispatched troops to Italy which promptly restored the princes and the pope to power.

The Congress of Vienna had united the Belgian and Dutch Netherlands in a single state under the rule of the house of Orange. The Belgians resented the imposition of Dutch laws, Dutch officials, and the Dutch language upon them. In 1830 the Belgian provinces proclaimed their independence, and with the diplomatic support of England succeeded in winning recognition.

Liberal uprisings occurred in the Germanies, and the Poles

in Warsaw revolted against Russia and proclaimed their independence. These attempts were suppressed however.

But the suppression of the uprisings of 1830 and 1831 did not put an end to liberal agitation. It taught the revolutionists, however, that in order to succeed they would need to clarify their aims, perfect their organization, and win the support of a larger part of the population.

51 THE REVOLUTIONS OF 1848

The Industrial Revolution and Liberal Reform. The Industrial Revolution had spread to France, and had brought about altered conditions of living which influenced the demands of the liberals. Before the widespread adoption of machinery in industry, the industrial worker was an individual who, in addition to his skill, usually possessed the tools or implements of his craft and frequently purchased his own supplies of raw material. In other words, the craftsman was in some degree a small businessman whose implements and stock represented his small capital.

There next grew up, especially in England, a system of domestic or home industry under which larger capitalistic enterprisers purchased, at advantageous prices, larger supplies of raw materials which they then "put out" to be manufactured at home by skilled workers who owned their own tools. For example, in textile manufacture, the capitalist devoted his main attention to the purchase of raw materials, and to the marketing of the manufactured fabric. The actual spinning and weaving was done in many cases in the homes of farmers during the winter months. These men owned hand looms, and frequently the whole family was employed for several months during the year in spinning yarns and weaving cloth. The actual "manufacturer" consequently sold to the capitalist enterpriser the services of his hands and his tools.

But when machine manufacture replaced handcraft, this kind of domestic industry found itself unable to compete with the factory. It was impossible for the small craftsman to own and operate the expensive new machinery, and as a result the wealthier capitalist had to set up the plant, install machinery, provide raw materials, and seek a market. Factories were set up at first wherever waterpower was available, and in order to obtain employment the formerly independent farmer-manufacturer had to take up his residence in a factory town, and become a hired worker whose principal asset was now his skilled labor.

With the growth of large-scale scientific farming and the enclosure of the common lands, many small farmers had been able to maintain themselves by the domestic system which combined agricultural and industrial enterprise. Now, unable to maintain himself by agriculture alone, many a small farmer sold his lands, moved to town, and became a hired worker.

Prior to the industrial revolution, large-scale capitalistic enterprise was chiefly commercial, for the assembling of ships and cargoes was obviously a larger undertaking than the manufacture of small quantities of raw materials by hand-operated machinery. But the machine revolution brought about the development of industrial capitalism.

Throughout the nineteenth century liberal reform increasingly concerned itself with the problems of the town-laborer, dependent upon steady employment and wages. His condition was also materially affected by the cost of living which was principally a matter of food and lodging. For the worker was no longer a semi-independent individual who, through the ownership of his own cottage and the production of a large part of his food supply, was rendered relatively independent of the market price of essential commodities.

The complete dependence of the laboring population of the towns upon steady employment and upon a low cost of living, and his serious plight when unsuccessful competition or other causes forced factories to close, gave rise to a number of attempts to envisage a social-political-economic system under which the evils of competitive capitalistic enterprise might be avoided, at least where the interests of the laborer were concerned. Various "socialistic" systems were devised under which, by one means or another, the laborer's "right to work" would be recognized, and he would be secured opportunities for employment either through state enterprise or through the reorganization of the conduct of industrial enterprise.

The French Revolution of 1848. The liberal agitators insisted that the evils of the time could not be corrected until the government was reformed to make it responsive to the wishes of the majority of the citizens. They wished therefore to extend the right of voting to all citizens by repealing the requirements which restricted the voting privilege to those who possessed a certain amount of wealth. They insisted, too, that the monarchy as then constituted was in a position to influence the legislature to make laws contrary to the wishes of the people.

Alarmed by the demands of the socialists, many of whom wished to see the capitalists stripped of their wealth, Louis Philippe resisted liberal changes and tried to prevent the newspapers from agitating reforms. In February 1848 a mob attacked the Tuileries palace. The king abdicated in favor of his grandson, but the crowd invaded the assembly and a provisional government was proclaimed which arranged for the election of a new assembly through universal suffrage. An attempt was made to provide work by the setting up of "national workshops," in which some 117,000 were enrolled at a wage of two francs a day for useless work or mere idleness. When the new Constitutional Assembly abolished the "national workshops," an outbreak occurred in Paris which was put down after much bloody street fighting.

The French elected as president of the new republic, Louis Napoleon, nephew of the great Napoleon. Before his four-year term was up, Louis Napoleon seized control of the government, and had himself elected president for another ten years. One year later, in 1852, he submitted a new constitution to the people which restored the empire. His act was approved by an overwhelming vote, and Louis Napoleon became Napoleon III.

The Revolutions of 1848 in Italy and Germany. The over-throw of Louis Philippe in February 1848 gave rise to a series of revolutionary uprisings throughout Europe. Nationalist and liberal ideas had spread among the many races of the Austrian Empire, which included Slavs, Hungarians, Germans and Italians, so that for a variety of reasons the emperor's subjects wished to put an end to the rule of Metternich who was the archchampion in Europe of the political and social order that had been restored upon the fall of Napoleon. In March Vienna revolted and Metternich fled. At once the Hungarians and Bohemians drew up constitutions for themselves which incorporated the popular reforms—freedom of press, religion, equality of all classes in taxation, and all the rest. However, most of the emperor's subjects wanted a greater degree of freedom under the empire.

In Italy the situation was different. The north Italians wished to free themselves completely from Austrian rule. Milan drove out the Austrians, and Venice followed suit. Charles Albert, king of Sardinia, who had for some years been putting into effect a series of sweeping reforms, now granted his subjects a constitution in response to the demands of the chief liberal journals and spokesmen. On the invitation of Milan, he advanced into Lombardy with an army.

But the Italian effort failed. The Italian states which had sent troops to Lombardy and Venice in the first burst of enthusiasm withdrew their support and Charles Albert was defeated by the Austrian general Radetsky, and compelled to make peace. Florence established a republic. The papal states revolted and upon the flight of the pope, Mazzini proclaimed the Roman Republic.

In Germany, the king of Prussia called an assembly to draft a constitution for Prussia, and an assembly of the German states was convoked at Frankfurt to draw up a constitution for Germany.

But the German revolutions failed of their own accord, or of their own discord. The mixed populations of the empire, with their mutual jealousies, made united action impossible. The Germans of Bohemia opposed the national movement which would make them a minority in a Czech state. The Slavs of Hungary opposed the Hungarians for similar reasons. The nearly six hundred delegates to the Frankfurt assembly talked themselves out, and when Frederick of Prussia refused the German crown, the assembly dispersed.

In Italy the defeat of Charles Albert left the Austrian forces free to suppress the new-born republics. And despite the heroic resistance of Garibaldi, French troops took Rome and restored the papal government.

Reform in England. As a result of the "glorious revolution" of 1688, the wealthier classes of England gained a predominant influence in the government. The powers of the monarch were restricted on the one hand. And the right to vote was withheld from the poorest classes by property qualifications on the other. We have already seen how the increasing seaborne trade of England, the growth of colonies and markets, the agricultural and the industrial revolutions were contributing to increase the wealth of England and the prosperity of the propertied classes.

At the beginning of this chapter we took account of the changes which were being brought about in the status of the small farmer—the tenant farmer, or small property owner— and the town craftsman. With the growth of the towns, many of the well-to-do were shocked at the spectacle of poverty they presented—not that poverty was new, but it became more apparent when the poor were gathered together in one place. This gave rise to a spirit of humanitarianism, a sentimental concern for the improvement of the lot of the least fortunate, which marked the social thinking and behavior of the nineteenth century. It also led, as we saw, to a reform effort which began by insisting that the right to vote should be extended as a first step toward correcting the worst abuses of the factory system.

Throughout the nineteenth century Englishmen struggled to make their government more responsive to the wishes of a larger number of people. At the same time various reforms were instituted which by degrees did succeed in improving somewhat the lot of the industrial worker. The steps by which these changes were brought about are far too complicated to deal with here. In 1832 a reform bill enlarged the influence of the "middle-class," so-called, in the government. A sweeping reform bill was introduced by the Disraeli ministry and passed in 1867. It did give the vote to the town workers, but it was not until 1884 that this privilege was extended to the country dweller.

Another important change which occurred in England in the nineteenth century was a partial abandonment of mercantilist policies for one of free trade. During the eighteenth century, the English government sought to set up a self-sufficient empire in which English ships would carry all the empire trade, in which colonies would provide raw materials and markets for British manufactures. But in the nineteenth century the expansion of the United States and of the South American states provided extensive markets for English goods and capital, while the industrial development of England was so far advanced over that of other countries that she had no need to fear foreign competition. After a long struggle the "Corn Laws," which set protective tariffs on grain imports, were repealed. In 1867 under the Gladstone ministry, the last of the protective duties were lifted.

Meanwhile, beginning in 1828, religious disabilities were removed, first, against Dissenters or Nonconformists, then against Catholics, and finally, in 1858, against the Jews.

Although the struggles over reform in England were often bitter and frequently violent, England escaped a major revolution through the English habit of attacking specific abuses and proposing specific remedies rather than following the continental tendency to overthrow the prevailing system of government.

PART ELEVEN
Nationalism and Imperialism

1820	Revolt in Naples
1821	Revolution in Piedmont
1829	Establishment of independence of Greece
1830	"July Revolution" in Paris. Uprisings in Central Italy
1831	Mazzini founded "Young Italy" Society
1832	English Reform Bill
1846	English abolished "Corn Laws"
1848	"February Revolution" establishing Second French Republic. Italian revolt against Austrian and papal domination. Revolutions in Austria, Germany, Belgium, Poland
1849	Suppressions of revolutionary movements in Italy
1852	Louis Napoleon's *coup d'état,* and beginning of Second French Empire
1854	Commodore Perry landed in Japan
1854–1856	Crimean War
1859–1861	War of Italian liberation. Formation of Kingdom of Italy
1862	Bismarck became chief Prussian minister
1862–1867	Louis Napoleon sought to establish an empire in Mexico
1864	Austro-German-Danish War
1866	Seven Weeks' War—Germany and Italy against Austria
1868	Revolution in Spain
1869	Opening of Suez Canal
1870	Franco-Prussian War
1871	Creation of German Empire
1881	French establish their control of Tunis
1882	British occupation of Egypt
1896	Defeat of Italians at Adowa in Ethiopia
1899–1902	Boer War
1900	Suppression of "Boxer Rebellion" in China
1906	Algeciras Congress and strengthening of French predominance in Morocco
1911	Moroccan Crisis—further strengthening French hold on region
1912	Outbreak of Balkan War

The National Movement in Italy. The nationalist-revolutionary movement in Italy passed through several phases before it became strong enough in popular support, and well enough organized and led to achieve national unity and independence. The secret societies, chiefly the Carbonari and the Freemasons, supplied the agitational ferment which gave rise to the revolutions of 1820–1821.

Although Carbonarist agitation continued in Italy following the failure of these efforts, after 1831 the republicans, stirred up by Mazzini and his "Young Italy" Society, were the most active advocates of revolutionary change. This republican agitation culminated in the outbreaks of 1848. As we saw, the revolutionary governments set up outside of Piedmont—in Milan, in Venice, in Florence, in the Papal States—were republican. But the eventual suppression of all these governments—again excepting Piedmont, which retained the constitution of 1848—discredited the leadership of the republican factions.

All during this time, the old aristocracy of northern Italy, particularly that of Lombardy, had labored patiently to create a solid basis for the ultimate liberation of their country by introducing reforms as rapidly as was possible under the Austrian rule. After the failures of 1848 these men came to look to the rulers of Piedmont and Sardinia, the House of Savoy, to lead the national movement.

The Risorgimento. The *Risorgimento,* literally a resurrection or rebirth, designates the national movement in Italy. It was the name of the newspaper edited by Cavour, who led the demand for a constitution in 1848. Becoming prime minister under King Victor Emmanuel II, Cavour brought the kingdom of Sardinia to the fore in the European concert of nations by joining in the Crimean War of 1853–1856, in which

England and France were aiding Turkey against Russia. He used the platform of the peace conference to condemn the Austrian policy in Italy.

Meanwhile, Napoleon III was seeking an opportunity to win military prestige and territory, for he realized that the reflected glory of his uncle's great name would not maintain his prestige indefinitely. In this need of the French monarch, Cavour saw his chance. Sardinia managed to provoke a war with Austria in 1859. The French promptly joined the Piedmontese and defeated the Austrians at the battle of Magenta. Again the Austrians were defeated at Solferino. Suddenly Louis Napoleon made peace with the Austrians, leaving Venetia still in Austrian hands. The Italians were furious at this desertion, but dared not continue the war by themselves. Lombardy, Modena, Parma, and Romagna were added to Piedmontese territories, and Savoy and Nice were ceded by Victor Emmanuel to France.

But the national movement once begun was not so easily stopped. Garibaldi and his Thousand red-shirts landed in Sicily, conquered the island, and crossed into Naples. He planned to march to Rome, which he had so valiantly defended against the French in 1849, and proclaim the Kingdom of Italy in the city of the Caesars. But Cavour and Victor Emmanuel realized that the seizure of the Papal States would offend Catholic France, and that Louis Napoleon would be forced to take action against the Italians. Victor Emmanuel therefore marched southward to Naples and Garibaldi submitted to the wishes of his king. In February 1861, Victor Emmanuel was hailed as king of Italy by a national parliament representing North and South. But the unification of Italy was not complete. Venice and the Papal States remained to be incorporated in the new national state.

The Prussian Leadership in Germany. In 1858 William became regent in Prussia for his brother, Frederick William IV, who was incapacitated by disease. He immediately strengthened the Prussian armies by increasing the annual levy of troops and extending the term of service to three years. When his military reforms were opposed in the lower house of the German parliament, the Landtag, William summoned to his aid the able Bismarck who carried through the reforms without the money appropriations that had been refused by the Landtag.

The provinces of Schleswig and Holstein, although subject to Denmark, had retained their provincial assemblies and independent status. In 1863 the king of Denmark incorporated Schleswig into his kingdom even though the move was opposed by Prussia because of the predominant German population of the province. Bismarck appealed to Austria to help settle the dispute, and together Austria and Prussia defeated the Danish army and forced the king to surrender Schleswig and Holstein to Austria and Prussia. Bismarck then proposed a settlement which Austria was bound to refuse and, having obtained Louis Napoleon's promise that he would not interfere, Bismarck made war on Austria in 1866.

Bismarck had already arranged with Italy that the Italians would aid Germany in such a war, on the condition that they would be given Venice in return for their assistance. The war began in June. Most of the German states sided with Austria. Prussian troops promptly occupied Hanover, Saxony, and Hesse-Cassel. The Austrians were badly beaten at Sadowa, and within three weeks the war was practically at an end. Although the Italian troops fared badly, Venice was turned over to Victor Emmanuel, in accordance with the Italo-German agreement. Hanover, Hesse-Cassel, Nassau, the free city of Frankfurt, and Schleswig-Holstein were joined with Prussia.

The North German Confederation. Bismarck arranged a federation of the north German states which gave Prussia an unquestioned predominance, but which preserved an appearance of equality among the federated states. He was not ready to proclaim a "German" nation until a closer and practical union had actually been brought into effect. His ultimate plan was the union, under Prussian domination, of all the German states, excluding Austria and her polyglot empire.

53   THE SECOND FRENCH EMPIRE

We have reviewed the steps by which Louis Napoleon made himself emperor of the French. He wished to play a great role in the world, and thus to perpetuate the glory of the name Napoleon. Within France he sought to make himself popular through fostering the material prosperity of the country by negotiating commercial treaties, founding a national bank, establishing agricultural societies. The city of Paris was beautified and modernized, and this work created a demand for labor. He appealed to the financiers and businessmen by lessening the government regulation of industry and by subsidizing a merchant marine. Industry, commerce, and employment were stimulated by the construction of such public works as canals, roads, railroads, and harbors.

The Crimean War. But something more was needed to establish firmly the imperial prestige. In 1853 war broke out between Russia and Turkey over the czar's attempt to establish a protectorate over all Greek orthodox Christians in Turkish territories. Napoleon entered the war on the side of Turkey. The Crimean War, for it was fought in the Crimea from 1853 to 1856, was joined by England and by Piedmont, or the Kingdom of Sardinia, as we recalled earlier. It was perhaps some satisfaction to Napoleon that the peace conference was held in Paris. France obtained commercial privileges in Turkey, and Roman Catholics in the East were saved from Greek domination; but this was small compensation for the cost of the war to France in men and money.

Louis' next opportunity came in the Austro-Italian war of 1859, which we have already reviewed. His victories in northern Italy won him the military prestige he so dearly coveted, and in accordance with the terms of his secret arrangement with Cavour, Savoy and Nice were ceded to France, thus giving him the credit of extending the boundaries of France.

The Mexican Venture. Mexico, engaged in frequent internal squabbles, was heavily in debt to France, England, and Spain. Internal difficulties kept the Mexicans from paying even the interest on that debt, and in 1862, while the United States was engaged in civil war, the creditor nations decided to seize control of the Mexican customs.

Napoleon determined to intervene in Mexico and, by establishing a new imperial government there, to make French influence predominant in that land. To overcome the objections of Austria, Napoleon arranged to have the Mexican crown offered to the Archduke Maximilian of Austria, an attractive young man of thirty who had little understanding of the situation which confronted him. However, promised military support by Napoleon, Maximilian accepted and set out for Mexico in 1864.

Louis Napoleon had thought it safe to ignore the United States. But the American Civil War came to an end, and the United States, then possessed of the most powerful and seasoned army in the world, made clear that she would not permit Mexico to become part of Europe. The Mexican leader, Juarez, kept up a deadly guerrilla warfare, and despite the pleas of the Empress Carlotta, who came to France to seek aid, Napoleon dared not send re-enforcements to Mexico. Maximilian was captured and shot in 1867, and Napoleon's dream, which had developed into a nightmare, was ended.

After the Austro-Prussian war of 1866, Napoleon sought to balance the gains of Prussia by a diplomatic victory. He proposed the annexation of Belgium to France and the purchase of Luxembourg from the king of the Netherlands. But Bismarck got Britain and Russia to back up his refusal, and Napoleon was again thwarted in his design.

The Franco-Prussian War. The incident which precipitated the Franco-Prussian War was the offer of the vacant Spanish throne to Prince Leopold of Hohenzollern. The French were alarmed at the threat of encirclement by Prussian-dominated states. The press and the French government excitedly protested against the acceptance of the offer, and when in June

1870 word was spread that Leopold had accepted, the French newspapers were filled with wild predictions of war. In this situation, the German prince decided to decline the Spanish offer, and the news of his refusal marked an important diplomatic triumph for France.

However, Gramont, the French minister of Foreign Affairs, telegraphed the Prussian king, demanding an assurance that the Hohenzollern candidacy would never be renewed. The impertinent demand was properly refused. This refusal, the famous "Ems Dispatch," was reported by the newspapers as an insult to France. The excited Chamber voted to declare war, and the armies of the two states were mobilized.

Collapse of the Second Empire. Since France was clearly the aggressor, the south German states joined the members of the northern confederation. German mobilization, which had been planned in advance, moved speedily and efficiently. The French mobilized slowly and the troops were scattered along the frontier.

The war was brief. The German general Von Moltke scattered French armies under MacMahon and Bazaine. Mac-Mahon joined Louis Napoleon, the Germans closed in from all sides and at Sedan, the emperor was forced to surrender unconditionally.

When the news reached Paris, the mob filled the streets, shouting, "Down with the empire; long live the republic!" During the two weeks it took the Germans to reach Paris, the city was prepared for a siege. The new government hoped to get off with the payment of an indemnity, but was determined to surrender no land. While the Germans besieged Paris, Gambetta escaped in a balloon and recruited raw troops in the provinces. But the trained German armies prevailed. The besieged city held out for 130 days while the citizens ate rats, cats, and any other food that could be obtained. However, on January 28, 1871, Paris surrendered.

Bismarck imposed a war indemnity of five billion francs. France surrendered Alsace, and part of Lorraine including Metz. The German armies paraded through Paris in triumph.

In the palace of Louis XIV at Versailles, William I of Prussia was proclaimed German Emperor on January 18, 1871. The constitution of the North German Confederation was adjusted to the organization of the empire which now included the south German states. The German state, as Bismarck had planned it, was a reality.

During the war the Italians had attacked the French defenders of the pope in Rome and incorporated the Papal States in the Kingdom of Italy. Italian unity was also finally achieved.

54 IMPERIALISM AND THE EUROPEANIZATION OF THE GLOBE

In our discussion of the earlier Portuguese, Spanish, Dutch, French, and English empires, we noted the fact that mercantilist theories determined the policies that were adopted in the government of the colonies. We shall consider somewhat later how England's efforts to subordinate her American colonies to the interest of the mother country led to the eventual loss of those colonies. We saw that the Portuguese lost a part of their empire to the Dutch. The Dutch lost part of theirs to France and England. In the Seven Years' War (1756–1763) France lost most of what still remained of her colonial empire.

Then in 1776 the American colonies declared their independence of England. In 1822 Brazil won her independence from Portugal. And between 1810 and 1824 Spain lost most of her empire, for the anti-Napoleonic outbreaks, which began in America when Joseph Bonaparte was placed on the throne of Spain in 1808, soon developed into wars of independence. During most of the nineteenth century the nations of Europe were inclined to feel that in the long run colonies were scarcely worth the cost of conquest and development, for it seemed that as soon as they achieved a kind of maturity, they tended to become independent. Free trade thinking is built to some extent upon this presumption.

But during the last quarter of the nineteenth century interest in colonization was revived for a number of reasons, most of them growing out of the changes that had been wrought by the industrial revolution. The rapid accumulation of capital and the expansion of productive capacity which attended industrial development in the nineteenth century made it imperative that outlets be found for both goods and capital. Although the rapid development of the Americas, both North and South, had met those needs during a good part of the century, toward its close capitalist enterprisers were busily seeking markets and opportunities for development and the investment of their capital in other parts of the world.

But in order to secure the control of newly developed markets and to protect investment in the development of new areas, it was almost inevitable that the governments of Europe would become involved in a new imperialistic competition. It was further necessary to secure control of supplies of essential raw material. Thus a new era of mercantilism was introduced which has largely continued on and is an aspect of the conflicts in the world of today.

Interestingly enough, the new imperialism was accompanied and aided by a new missionary zeal among both Protestants and Catholics. Thousands went out to preach Christianity to the natives of Africa, India, China, and the islands of the Pacific. These missionary activities did much to arouse popular interest in the "backward" regions of the globe. And they also helped to demonstrate the unexploited possibilities of these regions while creating among the natives an interest in European goods.

Africa. The Turkish control of north Africa and the discovery of new sea routes to the east and new lands in the western hemisphere distracted the attention of Europe from the African continent for a time except where it was obviously convenient to found depots upon the coasts along the eastern trade routes or where it was found possible to obtain supplies of African slaves for American plantations. But late in the eighteenth century there began a new series of explorations of the interior of the Dark Continent. One of the most famous of these explorers was Mungo Park who in 1795 began his explorations of the upper Niger. During the nineteenth century French, British, German and Portuguese explorers penetrated most of the regions of the unknown continent. The explorations of the Scottish missionary, David Livingstone, and the publicity given African exploration by Stanley in his newspaper articles and books, describing his search for Livingstone and his later travels through Africa, aroused world-wide interest in the region.

In 1875 a relatively small part of Africa was under the control of Great Britain, France, Portugal, and Turkey while Spain held a few scattered bits. Turkish suzerainty was acknowledged by Egypt, the Egyptian Sudan, Tunis, and Tripoli. France held Algeria, a colony in the Senegal River Valley, and a few small posts elsewhere. Britain held the former Dutch settlements in Cape Colony and Natal as well as posts in the Niger Delta, the Gold Coast and at other points. Independent were Morocco, Abyssinia, Zanzibar, Liberia, and the Dutch-settled Boer republics of the Orange Free State and Transvaal. It will be noticed that these settlements lie chiefly along the coasts. The African interior was still in the hands of the natives.

The Struggle for Africa. French expansion in Africa began as a result of the difficulty of safeguarding the desert frontiers of Algeria against raids. The diplomacy of Bismarck was also a factor in focusing the attentions of French and Italian statesmen upon Africa. Following the Franco-Prussian War the French were determined to regain Alsace-Lorraine, and Italy hoped to wrest from Austria the northeastern coasts of the Adriatic which had once belonged to Venice and which were partly Italian in population. In the interests of European peace, Bismarck sought to persuade Italy and France that their aims were futile, and that the future of the two states lay in north African expansion.

The French moved first and occupied Tunis. The Italians were shocked, for they had regarded Tunis as an Italian field for expansion. Realizing the weakness of her isolated position among the European powers, Italy joined Austria and Germany in the famous Triple Alliance in 1882.

Meanwhile the Egyptian ruler, Khedive Ismail, found himself in such serious financial straits that he was forced to sell his Suez Canal stock. This waterway, constructed by the French engineer De Lesseps and completed in 1869, connected the Mediterranean with the Red Sea. France, as a result of the German defeat of 1870–1871, was unable to bid for the stock which was purchased by Great Britain.

But the financial problems of the Khedive remained unsolved. In 1882 an anti-foreign revolt broke out and Britain decided to intervene. When both France and Italy refused to share the venture, the British put down the uprising and established a temporary administration which amounted to the establishment of a protectorate over Egypt.

English and French at once engaged in a competition for control of the Sudan and Somaliland to the south of Egypt. The French obtained possession of the Sahara with the consent of England in 1890. In 1898 a French expedition under Marchand reached Fashoda and threatened to cut off Egypt from the rest of Africa. Lord Kitchener was dispatched with a military force to block the French. For a time the two nations were on the verge of war, but the French gave way, and the English retained the upper Nile valley.

The Italians had established themselves in Eritrea in 1882 and in Somaliland in 1889. But when Crispi attempted to seize Abyssinia, and make it an Italian protectorate, the natives under Menelik, aided by the French, checked the Italians and decisively defeated them at Adowa in 1896.

In central Africa, King Leopold of Belgium succeeded in establishing an independent Congo Free State whose sovereign he became entirely apart from his position as king of Belgium. In exploiting the resources of the region, however, his overseers resorted to such brutal methods that eventually he was forced, in 1908, to cede the Congo Free State to Belgium in return for an indemnity.

The French rapidly extended their dominion through northwest Africa, although both England and Germany obtained territories there, the Germans in Togoland and the Cameroons. The east of Africa was similarly claimed and divided up among the chief European powers.

After the British annexed the Dutch south African colonies in 1815, the Boers, or Dutch colonists, in 1836, migrated northward and set up independent republics in Natal, Orange Free State, and Transvaal. In 1877 Disraeli annexed the Transvaal and thereby provoked the first Boer war which ended in British defeat in 1881.

British control of south Africa was enlarged during the next two decades chiefly through the energy of Cecil Rhodes. The discovery of gold in the independent Dutch states led to an influx of foreigners which was so great that soon they owned two-thirds of the land, and paid 95 percent of the taxes. Nevertheless these Uitlanders were not permitted to participate in the political life of the republics. This situation provoked British intervention in 1899. The Boers waged a guerrilla warfare against the British, and it was three years before the whole of south Africa was finally brought under British control.

Expansion in Asia. Asia was another field for imperialistic expansion. China had sought to resist European penetration, and in the late eighteenth century barred all aliens from China. But the great profits of the tea, silk, and opium trade were such that Europeans persisted in trading with the Chinese. As a result of the Opium War of 1839–1842 which was lost by China, the British were permitted to deal with five treaty ports and were ceded the island of Hong Kong. Other powers —France, Prussia, Belgium, the Netherlands, and the United States—soon obtained similar concessions.

A second Chinese war in 1857–1860 and the Taiping Rebellion (1853–1864), which the Chinese put down with the aid of the British officer, "Chinese" Gordon, led to the partial partitioning of China. The French seized Cambodia, and later added Annam and Tonking. Burma was partly, and later completely, annexed to India by the British. Russia obtained territories in the north. As a result of the Sino-Japanese war of 1894–1895, Japan (which had been opened to western influence earlier by the American Commodore Perry in 1853–1854) obtained as treaty concessions the island of Formosa and the Liaotung peninsula while Korea became an independent state.

In 1899, the American Secretary of State proposed an "Open Door" policy for China which was agreed to in principle by the European powers. The object of this declaration was to secure fair and equal treatment for all in sharing Chinese trade. But foreign aggression in China led to the famous uprising of 1899–1900, known as the Boxer Rebellion. In 1898 the dowager empress Tzu-Hsi had emerged from retirement and seized control of the government. Led by the secret Society of the Harmonious Fists, known as the Boxers, the Chinese attacked the foreigners. The foreign powers intervened, and put an end to the rebellion. They imposed an indemnity of $325,000,000 upon China, and demanded the suppression of all anti-foreign societies. There followed a period of civil strife in China which continued through the early decades of the twentieth century, and which was not interrupted by the establishment of a republic in 1912.

During the nineteenth century, British power was consolidated in India. Indian resistance in the Sepoy Rebellion (1857-1858), like the Boxer Rebellion an anti-foreign revolt, was put down by British troops. The rule of the India Company ended in 1858, and political reforms were introduced. In 1876 Queen Victoria was proclaimed Empress of India.

Late in the eighteenth century the English had begun the settlement of Australia, which early in the seventeenth century had been visited by Portuguese, Spanish, and Dutch explorers. The eastern coast was claimed for England by Captain James Cook in 1770. New Zealand, discovered by the Dutch navigator Tasman in 1642, was also visited by Cook. The native Maori population was given full possession of certain regions when New Zealand became British in 1840.

Changing Attitudes toward Colonies. As reforms in England extended the franchise and liberalized the English government during the course of the nineteenth century, a new attitude toward Britain's colonial subjects developed. Warned by the loss of the Thirteen Colonies, the British government carefully investigated the causes of the Canadian unrest which became acute in the 1830's. The result was a recognition of the fact that the citizen abroad, as well as the citizen at home, had a right to a voice in his own government. Canada was accordingly granted dominion status, which meant in essence that she became a self-governing state associated with Great Britain in allegiance to the crown. Dominion status was eventually granted to other portions of the empire—Australia, New Zealand, and, after the Boer War, South Africa.

It was perhaps inevitable that other colonies would aspire to dominion status, with the result that as the century advanced British administration in the colonies and British colonial education became, without any conscious plan or intent, a kind of tutelage for ultimate self rule. Liberal policy in one quarter inspired liberal aspiration in another.

In 1871, the French, guided by republican principles, united the North African French colony of Algeria with the French state. Algeria was divided into departments under the French administrative system, with representatives in the Senate and Chamber of Deputies.

However, it was not until the close of the First World War that the wide implications of this change in attitude toward colonies was clearly realized. At that time, instead of the enemy's colonies being doled out to the victors as formerly, they were placed, as mandates, under a kind of trusteeship which envisaged ultimate self rule and independence.

PART TWELVE
The United States

1773	Boston Tea Party
1775	Battle of Lexington
1776	Declaration of Independence by United States of America
1781	Adoption of Articles of Confederation
1781	Surrender of Cornwallis at Yorktown
1783	Treaty of Peace between Britain and United States
1789	Adoption of Constitution of the United States of America
1803	Louisiana Purchase
1812–1814	War of 1812
1813	Bolivar led War of Independence in Venezuela
1820	The Missouri Compromise
1823	Monroe Doctrine proclaimed
1836	Republic of Texas established
1845	Annexation of Texas by the United States
1846–1848	War between Mexico and the United States
1848	Discovery of gold in California
1850	Compromise of 1850
1854	Kansas-Nebraska Act repealed Missouri Compromise
1854–1858	War for "Bleeding Kansas"
1860	Election of Abraham Lincoln and secession of South Carolina
1861	American Civil War began with attack on Fort Sumter
1865	Lee's capitulation at Appomattox Court House and end of Civil War
	Assassination of Lincoln
1867	Reconstruction Act
	Purchase of Alaska
1886	American Federation of Labor organized
1889	First Pan-American conference at Washington
1890	Sherman Anti-Trust Law
1896	Klondike gold rush
1898	Spanish-American War
1900	Boxer Uprising in China. U.S. intervened and reaffirmed Open Door policy
1903	Canal Treaty with Panama
1909	Henry Ford begins large-scale manufacture of Model T

1913–1921   Woodrow Wilson, President
1914   Pershing expedition into Mexico
1915   Sinking of *Lusitania* by German submarine
1917   U.S. declared war on Germany

55 THE THIRTEEN COLONIES
AND THE WAR OF INDEPENDENCE

Colonial America. The Colonial Period of American history is inextricably bound up with the history of Europe during that era. In order to avoid repetition in a very crowded volume, we have found it advisable to discuss the settlement of America and the struggles of the colonies against the background of European expansion and national rivalries, for only in that way was it possible to give the reader a perspective which would enable him to understand the forces which brought those colonies into being, and which shaped their development.

The English government was too weak and too poor to undertake to assist and nurture the early English settlements in America. Even those colonies which were supported by companies of adventurers or enterprisers—New Amsterdam and Virginia, for example—or those which enjoyed the backing of rich and influential proprietary patrons—Pennsylvania, Delaware, Maryland—soon discovered that their survival would depend principally upon their own self-reliance rather than upon the assistance that could be dispatched from home. The settlers had carved a domain out of a wilderness. They had made it prosper. They had learned their inter-dependence upon one another, and had developed institutions which served their needs.

But so long as the French and their Indian allies remained a threat to the security and safety of English settlements, the colonists were glad to be able to count upon the support of English soldiers and ships while at the same time they jealously guarded their liberties against parliamentary or royal encroachment. However, when the French surrendered their American empire at the close of the Seven Years' War in 1763, the chief menace to the security of the English colonies was removed. Thereafter, the chief danger to colonial freedom lay in the mercantilist policies of the English government.

In 1651 the English Parliament struck a blow at Dutch shipping in a navigation act which required that colonial products be transported in British ships. An act of 1663 established that European products destined for the colonies must be shipped to England first.

In 1689 King William's War introduced the series of colonial struggles which accompanied the wars between the mother countries in Europe. During the last years of Louis XIV's reign, the colonists were embroiled in the American phase of the War of the Spanish Succession which they knew as Queen Anne's War, 1702–1713. The War of Jenkins' Ear of 1739 became merged in the struggle known in the colonies as King George's War, 1743–1748. And the final struggle which lost France most of her American colonies was known as the French and Indian Wars, 1755–1763.

Background of the Revolution. The French and Indian wars had been a long and costly struggle, and not unnaturally the English government held that the colonists should bear a proportion of the cost to which the mother country had been put in defending their territories. But the colonists were already irritated by the efforts of England to put an end to the illicit trade in sugar and molasses with the French and Dutch West Indies. When in 1765 Parliament passed the Stamp Act taxing legal documents, newspapers, pamphlets, and playing cards, the colonists decided to resist the imposition of taxation which they themselves had not approved. Riots broke out and a Stamp Act Congress, meeting in New York, drew up a Declaration of Rights and Liberties, and addressed memorials to king and Parliament.

Further duties imposed by the Townshend Acts in 1767, a conflict with the British soldiers in 1770 which became known as the Boston Massacre, and the Boston Tea Party of 1773, in which citizens disguised as Indians dumped the taxed tea into the harbor, were a few of many incidents which mark the heightening tension.

The Outbreak of the War. In September 1774 a Continental

Congress assembled in Philadelphia, drew up a Declaration of Rights and Grievances, and discussed methods of co-operation among the colonies. War began when in 1774 British troops, dispatched to destroy stores at Concord, were harassed by "Minute-men" as they withdrew to Lexington and then to Boston. A second Continental Congress met. George Washington was appointed commander-in-chief of the Continental Army. Washington began his career as American commander with the successful siege of Boston, but was defeated in a series of battles around New York and crossed over into Jersey. On July 4, 1776, the Declaration of Independence, drawn up by Thomas Jefferson, was adopted by the Continental Congress.

The British campaign of 1777 was designed to cut the colonies in two along the Hudson Valley by a junction of the armies of General Burgoyne, advancing from Canada, with the army of General Howe, which was to march from New York. But in a series of battles the American General Gates defeated Burgoyne and forced him to surrender. Washington was unable to prevent Howe from taking Philadelphia, and when winter came the American army was forced to winter at Valley Forge where the suffering of the army was extreme.

The Articles of Confederation were agreed upon, and the thirteen colonies became united in a confederacy. France signed a treaty of alliance with the new nation early in 1778. England attempted to come to terms with the colonies, but too late.

The war continued with varying fortunes through 1778, 1779, and 1780. French help increasingly made itself felt. In September 1781, allied armies under Lafayette, Rochambeau and Washington closed in on General Cornwallis in Williamsburg, Virginia, while Admiral de Grasse entered Chesapeake Bay with his French fleet. Cornwallis was bottled up in Yorktown where, after three weeks, he surrendered.

Peace. The American representatives at the peace conference in Paris became impatient of the deliberations and, contrary to their instructions, made a separate peace with England.

Under it England surrendered the land east of the Mississippi to the United States along with full rights in the Newfoundland fisheries.

As usually happens, the war was followed by a severe depression in the United States. Now treated like any other foreign power, many Americans realized for the first time the benefits they had enjoyed as colonies. Their ships were denied participation in the West Indian trade, which had been so important to them before the Revolution. But although there were many reasons for the economic dislocations which followed the war, the Articles of Confederation were thought to be responsible.

In 1787 the Constitutional Convention assembled in Philadelphia. Seldom in history has there been gathered together in the performance of a single task so many men of high political gifts and sincere devotion to the task in hand. The Constitution of the United States of America which they created remains to immortalize the men who made it.

56   GROWTH AND DEFENSE OF THE UNION

The new nation addressed itself to the many knotty problems which confronted it, and which all had to be solved without the aid of precedent. The new President, George Washington, was supported by an able cabinet. Hamilton, in charge of the treasury, established firmly the credit of the United States by taking over state debts and by taking up old securities at par. Treaties with England and Spain clarified boundaries and a reciprocal trade agreement was reached with Britain.

Almost at once political parties developed. Hamilton headed the Federalist, and Jefferson led the Republican, which later became the Democratic party. Opposition between the financial-commercial and the agricultural interests of the nation formed the basis for the two policies. Under John Marshall the supreme court clarified its functions and its jurisdiction.

In 1803 President Jefferson arranged for the purchase of Louisiana from Napoleon for 80,000,000 francs. This extended the nation's boundaries to the Rocky Mountains. The following year the explorations of Lewis and Clark gave the United States a claim to the "Oregon country."

The War of 1812. From 1801 to 1805 the new nation fought a successful war with the Tripolitan pirates of the north African coast. But the rights of American seamen and shipping came into dispute again as a result of the Napoleonic effort to blockade England, and the English attempt to blockade the continent. Although difficulties cropped up in 1806, it was not until 1812 that war was declared against England. The stopping of American ships to remove seamen which the British claimed were deserters was one of many incidents which aroused a war spirit. Another was the conviction that the Canadians had stiffened Indian opposition to the advance of white settlers into the West.

At first American ships met with success in their encounters with the English navy but an attempted invasion of Canada came to nothing. In 1814 the British captured and burned Washington. However, the greatest battle of the war, the defeat of the British at New Orleans by Andrew Jackson, was fought after peace had been declared. Because of the slow communications of the time the news had not reached that quarter. During the war the New England states threatened to secede from the Union, but after the peace they forgot their grievances.

The presidency of James Monroe (1817–1825) is particularly remembered because of the enunciation of a policy that became known as the Monroe Doctrine. It was the result of the threat of the European powers to restore the Spanish colonies which had revolted and declared their independence, and of the aggressive attitude of Russia in the American northwest. It declared that the American continents were not to be considered subjects for future colonization by any European power. Such attempts would be regarded in the light of an unfriendly act by the United States.

The Mexican War. Beginning in 1821, as part of a general

westward movement, American settlers crossed the border into Texas attracted by the generous Mexican land policy. But in 1829 Mexico, like other of the southern republics, abolished slavery. Such a furor was raised in Texas that an exception was made in her case. But when Mexico attempted to restrict further immigration from the United States and to enforce Mexican law, the Texans rebelled.

Texas declared her independence in 1836. The defeat of the Mexicans by Sam Houston and the capture of Santa Anna, who had seized the government of Mexico by a *coup d'état,* won Mexican recognition of Texan independence. Texas then applied for annexation to the United States. However, anti-slavery feeling in the North had reached a point where the admission of Texas, which would increase the number of slave states, was opposed. Texas was not finally admitted to the Union until 1845.

The northeastern boundary between Canada and the United States was settled by treaty in 1842, and in 1846 the Oregon treaty fixed the northwestern boundary of the United States.

President Polk sent a mission to Mexico for the purpose of arranging for the purchase of the territory of New Mexico. The Mexican government refused this, as it had a similar offer for Texas before the Texan revolution. The President then provoked an "incident" which gave him a pretext for declaring war. An army under Zachary Taylor invaded Mexico and won a series of victories over the Mexicans. General Winfield Scott likewise achieved a series of successes culminating in the capture of Mexico City in September 1846. Early in 1848 peace was arranged with Mexico, which surrendered New Mexico and California to the United States and gave up all claims to Texas. Mexico received in return $15,-000,000, and the cancellation of all American claims against her.

Little more than a week before the signing of the treaty with Mexico, gold was discovered in California. This gave rise to the great gold rush which reached its peak in 1849, and brought about the early settlement of California.

Anti-Slavery Agitation. It was inevitable that sooner or later the great principles of human liberty embodied in the Constitution, and in the thinking of men of the revolutionary era, should give rise to a questioning of the institution of slavery. But it would be well for us to remember that slavery had been a respected institution throughout all the centuries of the past in all parts of the world. Its abolition was new and revolutionary.

It will help us to understand the slavery issue, too, if we realize that it was but one aspect, although a very important one, of a larger opposition between two sections of the country representing different economies, different ways of life. The American South was a region in which large-scale agriculture provided cotton, tobacco, and lesser products for a world market. Plantation life produced a society dominated by an aristocratic ideal. It also produced many of the ablest leaders of early American history.

Immediately after the adoption of the Constitution, as we saw, there appeared two political parties, Republican and Federalist, headed respectively by Jefferson and Hamilton, which represented the difference in interest between the agrarian South and the commercial and financial, and increasingly industrial, North. The anti-slavery agitation was, in part, a product of the Northern fear that if new slave territories were admitted into the Union as states, the agricultural group would dominate Congress, and the interests of the North would be neglected. The South was equally unwilling that the commercial and industrial North should dominate the government.

But the abolition of slavery in European countries, and in the Spanish-American republics, brought the question of Negro slavery to the front in American politics. Up to 1819, although the more populous North had 105 members in the House of Representatives against 81 congressmen representing slave states, the balance in the Senate had been kept even by alternately admitting slave and free states to the Union.

In 1820 the Missouri Compromise arranged that slavery would be prohibited in the Louisiana territory north of lati-

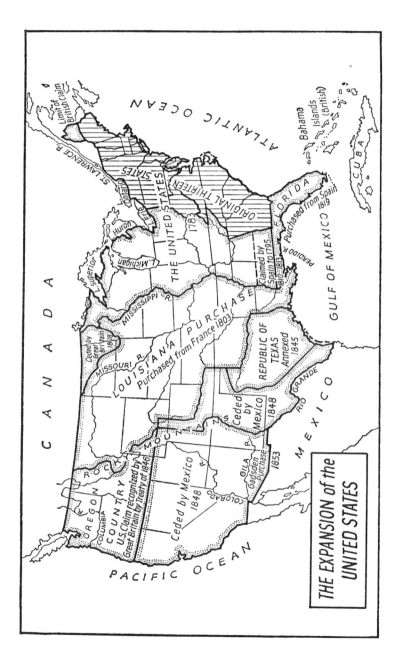

THE EXPANSION of the UNITED STATES

tude 36°30'. Another compromise was reached in 1850 over the admission of California to the Union as a free state and the division of the Mexican territory. But in 1854 the Kansas-Nebraska Act repealed the Missouri Compromise of 1820, and there began a rush of migration to Kansas from both sections of the country in a contest to win the territory for or against slavery. Fraud and violence marked the struggle. The admission of "Bleeding Kansas" was postponed until 1861.

The Civil War. In 1860 Abraham Lincoln, the Republican candidate, was elected on a platform opposing the further extension of slavery to the territories and supporting the tariff. His success was the result of a split in the Democratic party and of the great increase in the laboring population of the North, largely through German immigration. When it became clear that Lincoln had been elected, South Carolina seceded from the Union. The secession movement spread rapidly among the southern states.

Hostilities began with the bombardment of Fort Sumter in Charleston harbor in April 1861. But the first major battle occurred in July at Bull Run where the Union forces were routed. It will be impossible to recount the progress of the war in detail. The Confederate armies had the advantage of a number of excellent generals whose successes inspired the southern armies with confidence and dash.

In 1862 General McClellan advanced on Richmond, but his overcaution and indecision enabled the southern generals to take the initiative and the federal armies withdrew toward Washington. In the following year, General Lee advanced into Pennsylvania in an effort to strike at the northern industrial center, but was checked at Gettysburg.

In 1864 Grant was made commander of the northern armies. While Grant's armies fought those of Lee in western Virginia, Sherman, starting from Chattanooga with about 100,-000 men, marched eastward through Georgia to Atlanta. He destroyed factories and stores, and then proceeded to the sea, ravaging the country as he went.

The Confederate armies were caught between Sherman to

the south and Grant to the north, and were cut off from their food supply. After taking Richmond, Grant pursued and surrounded Lee. On April 9, 1865, Lee surrendered at Appomattox Court House.

57   THE UNITED STATES BECOMES A WORLD POWER

At the close of the Civil War the South was prostrate; the North triumphant, prosperous, and increased in population. The northern industries had been stimulated by war production. Growing American industry and the opportunities afforded by westward expansion attracted immigrants in increasing numbers.

The South after the Civil War. In addition to the destruction of the war, which had been fought mainly in the South, the southern states were exhausted in resources, in man power, in wealth. The dominant class was bankrupt, their wealth confiscated, and they were deprived of the political leadership they had so long exercised. The freeing of four million Negroes, for the most part with little education, presented an enormously difficult problem in itself.

In addition, the South was at once inundated by a wave of political opportunists, the "carpet baggers," anxious to exploit the Negro. This group retained their hold on the South for a decade and seriously impeded its recovery. The assassination of President Lincoln in April 1865 was a tragedy for the South. His wisdom and humanity, coupled with the prestige he had at last come to enjoy, might have enabled him to thwart the greed and the hatred which dictated many of the policies of the reconstruction era.

The Industrial Revolution in the East. Industrialization and invention had already obtained a start in the United States before the Civil War. The industrial prosperity which had been stimulated by the war was fostered by tariffs. Immigration maintained a supply of cheap labor for the new industries. The opening up of the West led to the construction of a great transcontinental railway system, the rapid expansion of which was made possible by government subsidization through the granting of land to the railroad companies. And the West furnished an outlet for eastern manufactures as well as an outlet for occasional surplus labor in periods of readjustment or stress.

An indication of the development of industry is the multiplicity of invention. Although Elias Howe invented the sewing machine in 1846, it was not in general use until Singer popularized it after 1860. It was applied to the making of shoes in 1862. The introduction of the Pullman car in 1864 made travel comfortable. The telegraph was invented in 1844; in 1856 the Western Union Company was organized and communication revolutionized. As important as the discovery of gold in California in the 1840's was the less spectacular discovery of the iron deposits in Michigan in the same decade.

The second half of the nineteenth century was the age of big business in the United States. The mushroom growth of great railroad, and steel, and oil empires was made possible by the existence of the frontier and the fact that American economy was a rapidly expanding economy. Groups of individuals formed combines, and sought to establish "monopolies" through which they could control the market price of commodities or services and thereby assure themselves and their stockholders large profits. In the course of creating a monopoly, it was often necessary to resort to extreme and ugly measures to destroy those competitors who could not be bought out. But along with the ugly side of these struggles for wealth and power is the more palatable fact that the drive and energy and ambition of these men did accelerate American development.

So long as there was a frontier and the country was expanding, there was little inclination to criticize or complain of the conduct of business or political leaders. A man, momentarily thrown out of work, could easily find immediate employment by moving to another locality or by going West. There was little inclination to envy wealth and power when every man had the same opportunities to become rich if he were shrewd and energetic enough.

Toward the close of the century, the young nation, except for the South, was strong and prosperous and proud of its achievement. Culturally, it was crude and a little unsure of itself. The nation was beginning to settle down after its era of hectic growth. For with the settlement of the continental United States and the disappearance of her frontier, expansion was slowed down. A new era of stabilization and adjustment was beginning.

But at the end of the century, American expansion threatened to continue in another form, for this was the era of the new capitalistic imperialism which we have already seen developing in Europe.

The Spanish-American War. In the early part of the century President Polk had tried to purchase Cuba from Spain, but the Spanish had replied that they would rather see the islands sunk to the bottom of the Atlantic. Toward the close of the century maladministration had caused a revolt against the government. The yellow press of the United States had stirred American feelings with tales of atrocities. When, in February 1898, the *U.S.S. Maine* was mysteriously blown up in Havana harbor, there was a popular clamor for war. Although Spain agreed to meet all President McKinley's demands, he asked Congress to intervene. Congress disclaimed any intention of annexing Cuba, but declared war in April 1898.

The outcome of the war, which lasted a little over three months, was foreshadowed by Dewey's victory over the Spanish fleet in Manila Bay. The battles of El Caney and San Juan Hill, and the naval battle of Santiago marked the course of the brief conflict. Peace was signed in Paris late in 1898. Spain withdrew from Cuba and ceded to the United States Puerto Rico, Guam, and the Philippines for which she received $20,000,000. These new territories, particularly the Philippines, along with Alaska, which had been purchased from Russia in 1868 for $7,200,000, and the annexation of the Hawaiian Islands, which was formally accomplished during the progress of the Spanish-American War, gave the United States an empire extending outside the western hemisphere, the defense of which was to involve the country in a world war some decades later.

New Problems and Reforms. The growth and settlement of the United States had been extremely rapid. It had been attended by dislocations of various sorts—economic, social, political, which challenged men of reforming tendencies. During the Civil War there were formed a number of trade union organizations. In 1869 the formation of the Knights of Labor represented an attempt to unite all labor unions in one organization. But in 1886 this organization became involved in a series of railway strikes in which there was much rioting and violence. The Knights of Labor gradually gave way to the American Federation of Labor led by Samuel Gompers. In 1867 the Patrons of Husbandry or the *Grange* was formed by farmers of the middle western states, to protect themselves against the unfair practices of the railway companies and grain elevators on which they depended for the transportation and storage of their product. From 1870 to 1875 a number of states passed laws curbing these abuses and establishing the right and responsibility of state government to regulate the conduct of business in certain situations where the public interest was involved.

Inflation and business panics led to demands for the reform of the currency, financial policy, and banking practices. The discovery of silver, especially the Comstock Lode in Nevada, and its increased production, caused the price to fall. Many believed that the free coinage of silver would raise the price of the metal and provide an abundant supply of money. The silver and money issues were thus linked through the last quarter of the nineteenth century until the discovery of gold in Alaska provided an abundant supply of that metal and forced the silver question into the background.

The growth of monopolistic combinations which were able

to quash competition and maintain high prices led to the enactment of anti-trust legislation. The Sherman Anti-Trust Law of 1890 declared illegal the formation of trusts in restraint of trade and commerce. Treasury surpluses led to attempts to reform the tariff that was no longer needed to protect "infant" industries which had long ceased to be infants.

The period between the Spanish-American War and the World War of 1914–1918 was one during which the chief problems related to the inevitable settlement and stabilization of American life following the era of expansion. The administrations of Theodore Roosevelt, Taft, and Wilson all bear a resemblance in this respect.

Woodrow Wilson came to the White House in 1913 with a program of internal reform which included tariff revision, the reform of the banking system, anti-trust legislation, and tax reform. The program was partly carried out in the Underwood Tariff of 1913, the Federal Reserve Act of the same year, and the Clayton Anti-Trust Act of 1914. In 1914, Wilson was forced to send a military expedition into Mexico as a result of raids into United States territory by the Mexican bandit Villa.

But with the outbreak of war in Europe, the attention of Americans became increasingly focused upon the great struggle in Europe which the country finally entered in 1917.

58 THE UNITED STATES AND LATIN AMERICA

Spanish Rule in America. The Latin civilization of South and Central America is older than the civilization of North America. The Spanish were firmly established in America a century before the first permanent North American settlement was founded at Jamestown in 1607.

The Spanish colonial empire in America was organized from the beginning along mercantilist lines. The subordination and exploitation of the colonies in the interest of Spain remained the unchanged policy of the home government. It was only natural that during the eighteenth century, when new concepts of human rights were being discussed throughout the western world, the colonials would conceive that these rights belonged as fully to men living in colonies as to those in the homeland.

Struggles for Independence. As early as 1721 an insurrectionary movement broke out in Peru in which the sovereignty of the people was asserted. The revolt was not finally suppressed until 1735. Later in the century, in 1780 and 1781, administrative abuses, the forced labor of the natives, and increased taxation caused outbreaks in Peru and Colombia. The last of these early efforts to throw off Spanish rule was led by Miranda, who had been a general in the French revolutionary forces. His effort to liberate Venezuela failed when the English were forced to divert their promised aid to the prosecution of the peninsula campaign against Napoleon.

Spanish exploitation of the colonies and the exclusion of the *creoles* (Spaniards born in America), and the *mestizos* (those of mixed Spanish and Indian blood) from civil and ecclesiastical offices sowed the seeds of discontent. But the general movement for independence began when Napoleon placed his brother, Joseph, upon the throne of Spain in 1808. While some of the colonies declared their allegiance to the deposed Ferdinand VII, others proclaimed their independence. It is likely that the movement for independence would have spread to all the Spanish colonies in any event, but when Ferdinand VII was returned to the throne in 1814 he attempted to restore the old system despite the liberal reforms his agents had granted in the meantime. From then until 1825, when final success was achieved, the revolutionary movement became wholly separatist.

Upon the arrest of Miranda and the collapse of the first Venezuelan Republic, Simon Bolivar assumed the leadership of the revolutionary movement in South America. He set up a second Venezuelan Republic which was crushed in 1814. Undiscouraged, he headed another revolution in Colombia.

Meanwhile, in the South uprisings occurred in Argentina and Chile, led by José de San Martin, Bernardo O'Higgins, and others. The two revolutionary movements, spreading from North and South, became merged when San Martin, in the interests of unified action, withdrew in favor of Bolivar.

Brazilian independence from Portugal occurred during the same period. The break was precipitated by the revolution of 1820 in Portugal which adopted the Spanish constitution of 1812, and summoned the king to return from Brazil, where he had established his government when Napoleon invaded Portugal. The effort of the Cortes to reduce Brazil once again to a position of dependency led to the revolt which ended with the establishment of the independence of the Brazilian Empire under the son of John of Portugal who became Emperor Pedro I in 1823.

Latin America in the Nineteenth Century. Unfortunately, the South American colonies were ill-prepared for independence and even less prepared for self rule. Nevertheless, the liberal aspirations current throughout the western world at that time, and the aggressive enthusiasm of the republicans led to the adoption of republican governments in countries that would have been better served by a strong monarchy.

It will help us to understand the situation of the South American republics if we recall that when their independence was established, the *creole* inhabitants numbered less than one-fifth of the population, the *mestizos* less than one-third. The remainder were mostly Indian, although Negroes comprised about one-twentieth of the total population. The bulk of these people were poor, ignorant, primitive, and the better-educated minority were inexperienced in government for they had been excluded from important political offices under the old regime. It is small wonder that the history of the South American republics has been marked by violence, fraud, and revolution.

Despite this political instability, the introduction of foreign capital and management, and the growth of European migration, contributed to the development of the land. By economic and cultural interest as well as by history, Latin America was more closely linked with Europe than with North America. Its development was primarily agricultural. Europe furnished the market for its produce, and in exchange Latin America provided a market for the European manufactures.

Latin America and the United States. Although the successful rebellion of the North American colonies against England had inspired the Latin American revolutionaries in the nineteenth century, and while the principles embodied in the Declaration of Independence and the United States Constitution were fully accepted by them, the relationship between Latin America and the United States, throughout the nineteenth century, was not marked by any special closeness or friendship. There were a number of reasons for this.

Whatever friendly feelings may have been engendered by the proclamation of the Monroe Doctrine were soon chilled by the realization that, so far as the United States was concerned, this was no self-denying ordinance. The settlement and annexation of Texas, the events of the Mexican War and the annexation of New Mexico, made clear that where United States expansion was involved the territorial rights of Latin American countries were on a par with those of the Indians.

The firm stand taken by the United States against Louis Napoleon's Mexican adventure was scarcely sufficient to offset the effect of earlier aggressions.

The wave of imperialism which stirred the United States around the turn of the century renewed the mistrust which Latin America had felt. American intervention in the affairs of Cuba, and the American declaration of war after Spain had accepted American terms were an indication that formalities would not be allowed to stand in the way of ambition. The impression was confirmed by Theodore Roosevelt's treatment of Colombia when that country delayed in ratifying a treaty which would have ceded a strip of land across the Isthmus of Panama for the canal. A revolution was staged with the aid of ships of the United States fleet, and the new republic, promptly recognized by the United States, as promptly signed a treaty leasing the desired land.

A new era in the relationships between the United States and Latin America opened during the presidency of Woodrow Wilson. In March 1913 he declared that one of the chief objects of his administration would be to cultivate the friendship, and to deserve the confidence of the republics to the south. Although Wilson intervened in Nicaragua and Haiti, the Mexican incident demonstrated the sincerity of his declaration of purpose. The attacks on Americans and upon American property during the troubled regime of Carranza furnished ample warrant for intervention in the affairs of Mexico. Wilson adopted a policy of "watchful waiting" and left Mexico to the solution of its own problems. Some forty thousand United States citizens left Mexico. In 1916 the repeated raids into Texas of the bandit, Villa, forced Wilson to act. A military force under Pershing was sent across the border in pursuit of the bandit who escaped into the mountains. Wilson refused to take advantage of Mexico's weakness to intervene in the affairs of the country, and withdrew the troops.

The policy of collaboration and co-operation with the Latin-American states, inaugurated during Wilson's presidency, was continued by subsequent administrations. It became the "good neighbor" policy of President Franklin D. Roosevelt and the Alliance for Progress of President Kennedy.

In 1915, growing collaboration among the American states was registered in the meeting of a Pan-American financial conference at Washington, and in the conclusion of an arbitration treaty by Argentina, Chile, and Brazil. In 1916, commissions addressed themselves to the problems of improved telegraph and railway communications and the elaboration of uniform commercial law. A Pan-American conference of 1923 provided for fact-finding commissions in cases of disputes and a treaty was signed for their pacific settlement. This work was elaborated at a conference in Washington in 1929. It was continued by conferences in 1933, 1936, and 1938. A declaration of 1938 expressed the determination of the American states to protect themselves against foreign activities that might threaten them. This attitude of hemispheric solidarity was strengthened in important conferences representing all the nations of the Americas, during the difficult years of the early 1940's.

The United States and World History. This section on the United States ends with the period before World War I. In this book, with world history as its subject, later events which concern the United States are presented in international focus in Part Thirteen, "The First World War," Part Fourteen, "The Second World War," and Part Fifteen, "Recent History." In these final sections of the book, dealing with the past half-century, the United States appears at every significant juncture of events. This is so even where specific divisions of chapters may have for their subjects something like "Southeast Asia" or "Developments in Europe." The increasing interaction of political events in recent history, which cuts across any possible geographical division of subject matter, is a major theme in our concluding chapters.

PART THIRTEEN

The First World War

1914   (Aug. 4) Germans crossed Belgian frontier

(Aug. 14–25) French invasion of Lorraine thrown back

(Aug. 26–30) Battle of Tannenberg. Russians defeated by Germans

(Sept. 5–12) Germans checked at first Battle of the Marne

(Dec. 8) Battle of the Falkland Islands

1915   (Jan. 19) First German air raid on England

(Feb. 19) Beginning of naval action against Dardanelles

(Apr. 22–May 25) Allied offensive and second Battle of Ypres. Allies checked by German use of poison gas

Stalemate on Western Front

(May 7) Sinking of *Lusitania*

(May 23) Italy declared war on Austria-Hungary

(Sept. 2) Fourteen Zeppelins raided London

1916   (Feb. 21) Beginning of Battle of Verdun

(May 31–June 1) Naval Battle of Jutland

(June 4) Beginning of Brusilov offensive on Eastern Front

(July 1–Nov. 18) Opening of Somme offensive by British

(Aug. 27) Rumania entered the war on the side of the Allies

(Sept. 15) First use of tanks by the British

(December) Peace negotiations conducted by President Wilson

1917   (Jan. 8) Germany decided to adopt unrestricted submarine warfare

(Mar. 11) Baghdad occupied by the British

(Mar. 12) Russian Revolution. Provisional government set up

(Mar. 15) Czar Nicholas II abdicated

(Apr. 6) United States declared war on Germany

(April) High point of submarine warfare; 875,000 tons of shipping destroyed in one month

(Oct. 24–Dec. 26) Collapse of Italy in the Caporetto campaign

(Nov. 6) Bolshevik *coup d'état* overthrew provisional government in Russia

(Dec. 5) Armistice concluded between Russia and the Central Powers

(Dec. 6) Finland proclaimed its independence

(Dec. 8) General Allenby took Jerusalem

1918   (Jan. 18) President Wilson's Fourteen Points

(Mar. 21–Apr. 5) Great German offensive in an effort to crush Allies before American help could become effective

(Apr. 14) General Foch named commander-in-chief of Allied armies in France

(June 4) American forces broke German advance at Château-Thierry

(Aug. 8) Beginning of Allied offensive

(Sept. 12–13) American forces closed St. Mihiel salient

(Sept. 30) Bulgaria concluded an armistice with Allies

(Sept. 26–Oct. 15) Germans forced back at battles of Argonne and of Ypres

(Oct. 4) German and Austrian governments appealed to President Wilson for an armistice

(Oct. 30) Armistice concluded with Turkey

(Nov. 3) Mutiny of German fleet

(Nov. 7–8) Revolution in Munich

(Nov. 9) Kaiser William II abdicated and fled to Holland the following day

(Nov. 11) Armistice and end of hostilities

1919   Peace conference and peace treaties

1920   Founding of the League of Nations and first meeting

1921   Washington arms conference

1922   Genoa economic conference. Rapallo treaty in which Russia and Germany renounced reparations

1923   French and Belgian occupation of the Ruhr. Germany adopted passive resistance

1924   The Dawes Plan

1925   Locarno conferences and treaties

1926   Admission of Germany to League of Nations

1928   Kellogg-Briand Pact

1929   The Young Plan

1930   London Naval Conference

59 BACKGROUND OF THE FIRST WORLD WAR

The events of the First World War are within the memory of many men and women now living, and numerous others have received some kind of word-of-mouth account of the struggle. Because of its relative nearness in time, historians have not attempted any final judgments. Only in recent years has it been possible to obtain something like a clear perspective in evaluating the causes and summarizing the chief developments of the era.

Economic Background. In another chapter we have already discussed the colonial competition which developed during the last quarter of the nineteenth century and continued into the twentieth; the grab for markets, raw materials, and fields for capitalistic development and settlement. That competition was carried on in other ways as well. Governments subsidized the building of merchant marines which competed for the carrying trade of the world. They subsidized industries and industrial laboratories which tried to improve the quality of manufactures and lessen the cost of their production.

In this competition Germany was well to the fore by 1914. The German chemical industry was the most advanced in the world. And in many other lines she was able to manufacture so well and so cheaply that her products competed successfully in the home markets of the countries which were her industrial rivals. An almost endless variety of cheap manufactured articles bearing the stamp "Made in Germany" flooded the American market in 1914.

In order to protect shipping, and colonies, and concessions in different parts of the world, the great powers constructed navies and built up their armies. But each increase in the English or the German or the French naval or land forces was watched nervously by the others and was soon matched or exceeded by increases in every other country. The naval race in particular stirred up apprehension on all sides and reached the proportions of a panic in England in 1909.

Diplomatic Background. After the Franco-Prussian War, Bismarck was anxious to stabilize Europe and to insure peace for as long as was possible. The Triple Alliance of 1882 between Austria, Italy, and Germany was a defensive treaty. It was renewed at intervals and was in effect at the outbreak of the war in 1914.

In 1887 Bismarck made what he called a "reinsurance treaty" with Russia. There is a tendency to read deep and insidious purposes into these treaties, but on their face they are simply designed to discourage one nation from attacking another. In essence, Bismarck promised Russia that if she were attacked by Austria she could count on Germany's remaining neutral. Russia would have only to deal with Austria. But under the Triple Alliance, Bismarck promised Austria that if she were attacked by Russia, Germany would aid Austria. This was as sensible an arrangement as could very well be devised. It had the added advantage of strengthening Russo-German friendship and making unlikely a Franco-Russian treaty which would encourage France to wage a war of revenge in which Germany would have to fight on two fronts.

But the worst of the alliance system was that the treaties were secret. Even when their terms became known among the governments of Europe, there remained fears that there were special secret clauses whose terms had not been communicated. Like the building up of armies and navies, the system of secret alliances designed to preserve peace actually aroused fears and led to the alignment of the powers in mutually suspicious camps.

The Growing International Tension. When the young Kaiser William II forced the resignation of Bismarck in 1890, he refused to renew the Russian alliance. In the same year, a treaty liquidating grounds for disputes between Germany and England seemed to indicate that England might join the

Triple Alliance. Colonial rivalries had caused friction between England and France, and England and Russia. In 1894 Russia and France made a treaty which obligated both to attack Germany in the event that either was attacked by the Triple Alliance. Competition between Austria and Russia for domination of the Balkans intensified the rivalry of the two alliances.

During the Boer War, the Kaiser offended the English by his outspoken sympathy with the Boers, and excited fears of German intervention. The cooling of Anglo-German friendship was followed by a treaty between England and France in 1904 which dealt chiefly with their North African interests. But it was the beginning of the Entente Cordiale which was strengthened, as time went on, by commitments and agreements of another nature. The commercial and naval competition between Germany and England engendered a mutual mistrust which was strengthened by Germany's project of a Berlin to Baghdad railway which seemed to threaten, not only England's eastern trade, but the security of Suez and her eastern colonies and concessions. A series of minor crises further heightened the European tension and prepared the way for the conflict which began in 1914.

60 THE FIRST WORLD WAR

Outbreak of the War. The incident which precipitated the war was the murder of the Archduke Franz Ferdinand on June 28, 1914, at Sarajevo, capital of Bosnia, by a young student member of the Serbian secret terrorist society, the Black Hand.

It was not until July 23 that Austria presented Serbia with a drastic ultimatum and demanded a reply in forty-eight hours. The Serbian reply was submissive but was not an outright acceptance of all points.

Austria and Russia mobilized their armies. On July 28 Austria declared war on Serbia. Germany declared war on Russia August 1, and on August 3 declared war on France.

EUROPE
BEFORE WORLD WAR I
1914

SWEDEN

Helsingfors
Stockholm
St.Petersburg
BALTIC SEA
Riga
Moscow
Königsberg Vilna
RUSSIA
Danzig
Berlin
ODER R. VISTULA R.
Warsaw
ANY POLAND
Dresden Breslau
Cracow
Kiev
Prague
BOHEMIA
Lemberg
DNIEPER R.
AUSTRIA
DNIESTER R.
Pozsony (Pressburg)
Salzburg Vienna Budapest
Kolozsvar
Odessa
HUNGARY
RUMANIA
Trieste Zagreb Szeged
CROATIA
Venice Fiume
Sevastopol
BOSNIA Belgrade Bucharest Constanta
San Marino Sarajevo
DANUBE R.
BLACK SEA
DALMATIA SERBIA
MONTE- Sofia
ITALY NEGRO
Rome ADRIATIC SEA Cetinje Scutari BULGARIA
Plovdiv Adrianople Chatalja
Naples ALBANIA
Constantinople
Salonika
GREECE OTTOMAN
Palermo Messina
AEGEAN SEA EMPIRE
SICILY
Smyrna
Athens
MEAN SEA

German armies invaded Belgium on August 4 and the same day England declared war on Germany.

Germany was fully prepared for the war. The plan worked out by General von Schlieffen called for an invasion of France through Belgium. Through a concentration of force on the northern wing, the army was to advance in an arc through Belgium and northern France, thus surrounding Paris and the French armies. A quick victory in France would permit the Germans to move their armies rapidly to the east by railway to deliver the knock-out blow to Russia. The armies advanced according to plan. Belgian resistance slowed the advance slightly and the English got 90,000 regulars into France. For ten days these troops fought a rearguard battle but by September 5 the German army was fourteen miles from Paris. The French government moved to Bordeaux.

The Germans were then checked in the first battle of the Marne when the British forced a wedge between the First and the Second German Armies which made it necessary for both to retreat. The Germans entrenched themselves behind the Aisne River. There immediately followed a race to the sea, to break into Belgium beyond the German lines and to protect the Channel ports. With the extension of the lines of both armies to the coast, both sides "dug in" and became deadlocked in trench warfare.

The Eastern Front. In the meantime the Russians advanced quickly into East Prussia, moving much more rapidly than had been anticipated in Berlin and Vienna. The Kaiser then summoned the retired general Hindenburg, who had studied the eastern country. He trapped the Russians in a region of treacherous lakes and marshes and in the battle of Tannenberg destroyed one of the two Russian armies opposed to him. The other was saved by retreat.

The Austrians were repulsed in Serbia. The Russians seized Lemberg and a large part of Austrian Poland. Throughout the remainder of 1914 the armies swept back and forth in attack and counterattack, the general result of which was the defeat of Austria by Russia and the defeat of Russia by Germany.

The War on the Sea. When Turkey attacked Russia, without a declaration of war, England and France promptly declared war on Turkey. The fleet sent to the Dardanelles in February, 1915, failed to smash the Turkish forts, and withdrew. It was important to get munitions through to Russia, however, if she was to continue her resistance to the Germans. Australian, New Zealand, Indian, and French colonial troops were gathered for an attack on Gallipoli at the opening of the Straits. But the Turks, under German command, were well prepared for the attack. After three attempts, the Allied troops were removed to Salonika in Greece.

When war was declared there were some eight German cruisers, as well as other ships, in foreign ports. These immediately put to sea to ravage Allied shipping and coasts. Count von Spee left eastern waters for the South American coast with the cruisers *Scharnhorst, Gneisenau,* and *Nürnburg.* He was joined by the cruisers *Dresden* and *Leipsig* at Easter Island. When he attacked the Falkland Islands off the coast of South America, he was caught by a British fleet. Only the *Dresden* escaped being sunk.

It was not until May, 1916, that the German High Seas Fleet ventured to meet the British in the North Sea. In the battle of Jutland the Germans were forced to withdraw behind the protection of their mine fields. Both sides claimed a victory, but although British losses were double those of the Germans, the Germans never ventured to attack the British fleet again. Thereafter German naval activities were confined to submarine warfare and the sowing of mines.

Italian Entry into the War. In 1915 Italy entered the war on the side of the Allies. However, her chief contribution was that she relieved the French of the necessity of defending her southern border and thus enabled her to concentrate all her troops on the German front. Austria easily defended her mountain approaches. The combined Austro-German forces concentrated against the Russians who were running short of munitions and weapons. The Russians were forced back until winter compelled the Germans to consolidate their lines. In the Balkans, Bulgaria joined the central powers and the Serbians were driven back.

In November, 1914, the British had landed a small force from India and occupied Basra at the head of the Persian Gulf in Mesopotamia in order to protect the oil pipe line from Persia. Activities in the Mesopotamia theater of the war developed on an increasing scale through 1915 and 1916.

The United States and Warring Europe. In the meantime both groups of allies sought to blockade each other. The British drew up a list of goods which would be considered contraband, including foodstuffs, and the Germans resorted to the blockade of England by submarine. Both blockades were relatively successful until the entry of the United States into the war, at which time Britain had only a few weeks' supply of food left.

The United States, which had sought to remain strictly neutral, became a main source of supply of Allied munitions, food, and other essentials. However, Britain, in its determination to prevent the shipment of supplies to Germany by whatever route, halted neutral shipping and lengthened the list of commodities it considered contraband. Feeling was aroused against both England and Germany by their interference with shipping. However it was the German submarine sinkings which finally stirred America to action.

It was the sinking of the liner *Lusitania* in May, 1915, which turned America toward war.

Further Course of the Conflict. At Ypres in April and May, 1915, the Germans won a victory by introducing the use of poison gas against the British, and this upset the British plans for a major offensive. They were unprepared for a gas attack as it had been outlawed by international agreement. It was not until September that the British were able to employ gas against the Germans.

In February, 1916, the Germans began their great offensive against Verdun which was commanded by Crown Prince William. The Germans were held with great losses on both sides. In July the Allied Somme offensive began. Tanks were used for the first time in limited numbers by the British. Again the losses were very great, around 600,000 for the Allies, mostly British, against around 500,000 German.

Late in 1916 the Germans made peace overtures through President Wilson. Wilson submitted a plan of "peace without victory" to both sides, but neither side was prepared to consider terms which would satisfy the other. The opening of unrestricted submarine warfare in 1917 brought about an American declaration of war.

German Successes. In 1917 General von Hindenburg became chief of the German general staff. The German lines were shortened by withdrawal to the strong new position known as the Hindenburg Line. The Allied offensive was a failure. The losses and strain were so great that sixteen French army corps were affected by mutiny, and dissatisfaction was widespread. General Nivelle was replaced by Pétain. In this year the Russian armies collapsed and a revolution overthrew the government. The provisional government of Miliukov and Kerensky, who favored prosecution of the war, was overthrown by the Bolsheviks, who made peace with the Germans.

After two years of military operations the Italians had advanced ten miles toward Trieste. In October the German and Austrian armies attacked in a rigorous offensive. During the Caporetto campaign the Italian armies were broken and driven back to the Piave. British and French troops were rushed to their support and the German-Austrian advance stopped when their armies had overextended their lines of communication and supplies.

The Turn of the Tide. In the spring of 1918 the Germans, aware of the war-weariness of the Allies, decided upon a knock-out offensive in the hope of achieving victory before the Americans could arrive in great force. The Germans drove back the British in the north, and pushed the French to within thirty-seven miles of Paris. At Château-Thierry, the American army played an important part for the first time and in collaboration with the French succeeded in stopping the German offensive.

Then the new head of a unified Allied command, Foch, with French and American troops, drove back the Germans in the second battle of the Marne.

The great final Allied offensive began in August, 1918. During September and October, with the Allied armies advancing, Ludendorff demanded that the German government ask for an armistice while the armies were still able to hold out.

Allied Victory. On October 4 the Germans did ask for an armistice. President Wilson, as spokesman for the Allies, demanded that the occupied territories be evacuated and insisted that the Allies could only treat with a democratic government representing the German people. Meanwhile the British in the north and the Americans advanced rapidly, the Americans reaching Sedan. The sailors of the German fleet at Kiel mutinied and the revolt spread to Hamburg, Bremen, and Lübeck, and then through all Germany. Revolution broke out in Munich. On November 9 the Kaiser abdicated and the following day fled to Holland. On November 11, hostilities ceased on the western front and the slaughter was ended. Its human toll is estimated at 10,000,000 dead and 20,000,000 wounded.

61   THE YEARS AFTER THE FIRST WORLD WAR

The Fourteen Points and the Peace Treaties. President Wilson's Fourteen Points, the statement of American war aims which had been adopted by the Allies, sought to put an end to the system of secret alliances and armament competition by substituting open covenants of peace and disarmament. Territorial readjustments in Europe and in the colonies were to take into account the interests and the national character of the populations. Freedom of the seas and the elimination of economic barriers were to mark the new world order. And a general association of nations was to be set up as an instrument for maintaining international order and for settling international problems and disputes.

In taking into account the deficiencies of the peace settlement, it is necessary to remember that there were delicate and urgent problems of the moment which complicated the application of Wilson's general principles to the specific situation. Just what freedom of the seas might mean in the new world situation was not clear, and the point was dropped. The elimination of economic barriers was another point which could only serve as a guide to future policy but which could not be "enacted" at a peace conference without causing the most serious economic dislocation. Again, it was neither possible nor wise to scrap armaments until some degree of order and stability had been established in the world. Germany was disarmed; and during the decade following Versailles, efforts were made to bring about a general reduction of armaments by progressive stages.

But the territorial readjustment had to be clarified. Belgium was restored, Alsace-Lorraine was ceded to France. In 1920 North Schleswig joined Denmark as the result of a plebiscite taken among its predominantly Danish population. A new Poland with access to the sea was created from certain territories formerly belonging to the German, Austrian, and Russian empires. From the Austro-Hungarian empire, the new nations of Austria, Hungary, Czechoslovakia, and Yugoslavia emerged (the latter also incorporating the old Serbia); and Italy and Rumania also gained territory. Germany's colonial empire, which had been conquered during the war, was not returned to her. It was "mandated" among the different victor nations under a variety of conditions which, in some instances, anticipated eventual independence.

Reparations and the League. The peace settlement failed to take account of the economic needs of post-war Europe. Wilson had not wished to force Germany to assume all costs of the war. He felt that the sooner all nations, including the vanquished, returned to normal life, the better it would be for the whole of Europe and the world. But although the Allied statesmen had accepted Wilson's Fourteen Points, Clemenceau, the French premier, wanted, above everything, security for France and the punishment of Germany. Lloyd George, the British prime minister, promised the British people that Germany would be punished and be required to pay huge reparations.

The peace conference worked under great pressure. The Bolshevik revolution in Russia to a degree communicated itself to Germany, Austria, and, more slowly, to Italy. There was the enormous problem of returning the expanded plants of war-time industry to a schedule of peace-time production. The re-employment and absorption into civilian life of the millions of demobilized soldiers had to be anticipated. Is it any wonder that Wilson was forced to accept compromises in order to hasten the settlement?

The exact amount of reparations to be paid was left undetermined. Germany was to surrender most of her navy, her submarines, and military aircraft, and most of her merchant ships. For five years 200,000 tons of shipping a year was to be built by Germany for the Allies, and for ten years large quantities of coal were to be supplied to France, Belgium, and Italy. Locomotives and railway cars were also surrendered in quantity.

What was overlooked was that Germany, as an industrial nation, could only pay reparations through the revival of her industry. But Allied policy, particularly that of France, tended to demand huge reparations while depriving Germany of the means of paying them.

One point Wilson had insisted upon and that was the formation of a League of Nations. He knew the defects of the Versailles peace, but hoped that after passions had cooled and judgments had become clarified, the League would provide the machinery for the correction of at least the worst mistakes of the peacemakers.

But during Wilson's absence in France, opposition to the League of Nations was fostered in Washington by a group in Congress led by Henry Cabot Lodge of Massachusetts, chairman of the Senate Foreign Relations Committee. It was certainly not difficult to demonstrate that the peace fell far short of what Wilson had promised in his Fourteen Points. His idealism was stressed in such a way as to arouse a popular feeling that an idealist was necessarily impractical. When Wilson returned from his arduous labors at Paris and began a speaking tour to win support for the League, his health gave way. The United States Senate rejected the Versailles Treaty, including the League, on November 19, 1919. The League of Nations was established in 1920 without the participation of the United States.

A Decade of Adjustment. The United States did not conclude treaties of peace with Germany and Austria until August, 1921. But shortly thereafter steps were taken to fulfill one of the promised Fourteen Points. In November, 1921, representatives of nine powers met in Washington to discuss disarmament. Several agreements were reached at the Washington conference. Germany had established itself as a republic under the Weimar Constitution adopted in July, 1919. In the Four-Power Pacific treaty, Britain, the United States, France, and Japan guaranteed each other's rights in insular possessions and agreed to consult whenever those rights were threatened. Two Nine-Power treaties affirmed the principle of the "open door" in China and guaranteed the integrity of Chinese territories and administrative independence. A ten-year naval holiday was declared and the naval strength of the chief naval powers—United States, Great Britain, Japan, France, and Italy—were fixed upon a ratio of 5-5-3-1.67-1.67.

Meanwhile Germany was having difficulty meeting the reparations demands. At the London conference in February, 1921, a schedule of payments was fixed, but the following month Germany was found to be in default. Germany's continued failure to meet the reparations demands despite Allied pressure resulted in a moratorium being declared on reparations payments in March, 1922, over the protest of France.

At another London conference in August, 1922, Britain and France disagreed sharply over what steps should be taken to enforce reparations payments, France favoring confiscation of German properties and the occupation of industrial areas. In January, 1923, after Germany had again been declared in default, French and Belgian troops occupied the industrial Ruhr region in Germany. The German government urged the people of the Ruhr to adopt a policy of "passive resistance" and then developed a policy of currency inflation to provide money to support idle workers. The collapse of the mark affected the French franc which dropped 25 percent and new cooperation was undertaken to avert a world-wide financial collapse. A committee headed by the American, Charles G. Dawes, drew up a plan, known as the Dawes Plan, which provided for a reorganization of the German *Reichsbank,* an Allied loan to Germany, and the Allied supervision of reparations payments.

New Alliances and the Kellogg Pact. In October, 1925, conferences at Locarno resulted in a series of treaties guaranteeing frontiers and the arbitration of disputes. France sought further to secure her own position in Europe by beginning the construction of the defensive Maginot Line along the German frontier. During the decade following the peace, many treaties were arranged among the various European states. A large percentage of these were non-aggression or neutrality pacts designed to remove fears of aggression and to hasten the resumption of normal peaceful intercourse among the states. France, determined to secure her predominance in Europe and to prevent the challenging of that position by a revived and strengthened Germany, concluded a series of military defensive alliances.

As a result of American-French negotiations, the American Secretary of State Kellogg proposed a pact under which the nations would reject aggressive warfare as an instrument of national policy and M. Briand followed with a draft of his own. These proposals resulted in the signing of the Kellogg-Briand Pact or the Pact of Paris of 1928, which was strengthened by a general act of the League of Nations providing for conciliation and arbitration of disputes. The League, established without the adherence of the United States, was functioning actively, with headquarters at Geneva, Switzerland.

In the following year the Young Plan lightened the German reparations burden and provided for its ultimate liquidation. A new naval conference in London further limited armament building.

PART FOURTEEN
The Second World War

1933
(Mar. 4) F. D. Roosevelt became President of the United States

(Oct. 14) Germany withdrew from the Disarmament Conference and from the League of Nations

1935
(Oct. 3) Italian invasion of Ethiopia began

1936
(Mar. 7) German denunciation of Locarno treaties and re-occupation of the Rhineland

(July 18) Outbreak of civil war in Spain

1938
(Mar. 12–13) German invasion and annexation of Austria

(Sept. 12–29) Czechoslovak crisis, Munich Conference, and annexation of part of Czechoslovakia by Germany

1939
(Sept. 1) War between Germany and Poland

(Sept. 3) England and France declared war on Germany

(Nov. 30) Beginning of Russo-Finnish War

1940
(Mar. 8) Russia and Finland concluded peace

(Apr. 9) German armies occupied Denmark and began invasion of Norway

(May 10) Invasion of Netherlands and Belgium

(June 5) Battle of France began

(June 22) German-French armistice

(Aug. 11) Battle of Britain began

(Sept. 3) U.S. and Britain concluded lend-lease agreement involving exchange of fifty destroyers for naval and air bases

(Sept. 27) Rome-Berlin-Tokyo Pact

1941
(June 22) German armies invaded Russia

(Aug. 14) Atlantic Charter drawn up by President Roosevelt and Prime Minister Churchill

(Dec. 7) Japanese attacks on Pearl Harbor, Malaya, and Hong Kong

(Dec. 8) U.S. and Britain declared war on Japan

1942
(Feb. 15) Singapore surrendered to Japanese

(Apr. 9) Japanese captured Bataan

(Apr. 18) American planes bombed Japanese mainland, including Tokyo

(Nov. 7) American forces landed in North Africa

1943	(Feb. 2) Russians defeated Germans at Stalingrad, and began counteroffensive
	(July 13) British troops landed in Sicily
	(Sept. 3) Allies invaded Italian mainland
	(Dec. 3) Roosevelt, Churchill, Stalin met in Teheran, Iran
1944	(June 6) Allies landed in Normandy to begin invasion of Europe
	(Nov. 7) Roosevelt re-elected for fourth term
1945	(Feb. 12) Roosevelt, Churchill, Stalin conferred at Yalta
	(Apr. 12) President Roosevelt died. Harry S. Truman became President
	(Apr. 25) United Nations Security Conference opened in San Francisco to draft charter of United Nations organization
	(May 7) Germany surrendered unconditionally
	(July 17) Truman, Churchill, Stalin conferred at Potsdam
	(July 26) British Labour party won general election and Clement Attlee succeeded Churchill as Prime Minister
	(Aug. 5) American planes dropped first atomic bomb in history on Hiroshima
	(Aug. 14) Japan surrendered, bringing World War II to an end

62 THE ERA OF REPUDIATION

The International Scene in the 1920's. In his Fourteen Points, Woodrow Wilson had laid down the basic principles of a new international order. With these principles as a foundation he believed it possible to erect a structure of international relationships which could inaugurate an era of universal peace, security, and prosperity, under a rule of law. The statesmen who, during the 1920's, sought to create a system of international relationships, followed some of Wilson's principles and ignored others. However, to support a stable structure, the whole foundation was necessary. Is it any wonder then that with its incomplete basis the structure reared during the 1920's collapsed when the first serious strain was placed upon it?

The first four Wilsonian principles provided for open diplomacy, freedom of navigation and of the seas, the removal of economic barriers and the establishment of equality of trade conditions, and the reduction of armaments. These principles were largely ignored in the decade which followed the close of the war, and with fateful consequences.

It was essential for the future stability of Europe that its economic prosperity be restored rapidly. In no other way would it be possible to liquidate the burden of reparations and debts which were the war's legacy, nor could the peoples of the emergent states long remain content with a settlement which lowered their standards of living. The pre-war prosperity of central Europe had rested upon a highly integrated system of production and exchange both within that area and with the rest of the world. The map of Europe had been redrawn to give expression to the principle of political self-determination. But it was nature, not the peace conference, which had distributed Europe's natural resources—coal and iron deposits, fertile lands, natural harbors, rivers which bore much of Europe's commerce, surface contours which determined railway routes. It would seem to have been fairly obvious that the new European states might enjoy in prosperity their newly established political independence only if they recognized their economic dependence upon one another. The problem was, of course, enormously involved. The political and economic crises which immediately confronted the nations were so acute that the peoples and their political leaders inclined to seize the most convenient expedients for protecting monetary reserves by excluding foreign goods and wherever possible monopolizing markets and raw materials. The faultiness of such policies was momentarily obscured by a brief general increase in demand for goods that had not been obtainable during the war, and this gave a temporary stimulation to production and employment, especially in Great Britain and the United States. The economic problem was further obscured and confused by other considerations. The French feared more than anything else a revived and vengeful Germany. Her statesmen opposed the reduction of reparations or any easing of the German situation. This fear also led to the conclusion of a series of alliances with central European states in order to establish "collective security." Hostility and suspicion were thereby emphasized rather than co-operativeness in international policy.

In hampering the economic recovery of Germany, France was, perhaps unwittingly, retarding the material revival of the whole of central Europe and in turn of the rest of the world. The fault was not hers alone for nearly all states erected barriers to international trade. However, the attitude of the French successfully prevented the reform of these conditions, a reform repeatedly urged by the British during the 1920's. The series of economic crises experienced by the states of central Europe during the decade were tided over by international loans and the revisions of reparations already noted in the preceding chapter. But the Wilsonian bases for economic stability—unrestricted trade and freedom of access to markets and raw materials—were not put into effect or even approached.

Some progress was made in relieving the peoples of the world of the burden of armaments. However, from the beginning the French insisted that disarmament was contingent upon security and could be satisfactorily discussed only when adequate provision for international security was made. The British insisted that disarmament, adequately carried out, would provide international security since the re-armament of any nation would give adequate notice of aggressive intent. Throughout the 1920's and early '30's numerous disarmament conferences were held. Partial limitation of armaments was achieved, particularly among the principal naval powers, and to that extent taxpayers were relieved of a burden. But limitation of armaments was only a step toward disarmament, a goal which was not achieved.

The cumulative effect of the economic policies pursued during the first decade of peace were beginning to be felt on a world-wide scale by the end of the period. Emergency lending, both public and private, had repeatedly cushioned the effect of the various crises and postponed the day of reckoning. But restrictions upon the flow of international commerce strangled production, and the strain of emergency financing was beginning to undermine the international credit structure. The effects were already being registered in increasing unemployment throughout the world when the French opposition to the proposed Austro-German economic union and the failure of the Austrian Credit-Anstalt precipitated a world-wide crisis.

The Problem of Reparations and War Debts. For five years Germany had been able to maintain her reparations payments principally because of international loans, most of which had been obtained from American bankers. These reparations payments had enabled the Allied states to make payments in turn on their war debts to the United States—the Young Plan had, in fact, adjusted reparations payments to debt payments. However, partly because of the investment of surplus capital in stock market speculation in the United States, in 1929 Germany found herself unable to obtain sufficient funds from abroad and was forced to depend upon short-term loans and her own resources. She was unable to meet her reparations payments, and the Allied nations were in turn unable to make the payments due on their war debts.

Meanwhile, Austria, deprived of the material resources of her pre-war empire and unable to sustain herself financially, had sought a way out by linking her economy with that of Germany. When she proposed a complete Austro-German customs union, France became fearful that this step might become the means of bringing about through an *Anschluss* or full political union the creation of a single powerful and hostile state. France opposed the economic union and withheld financial support from Austria. Alarmed by this situation, foreign creditors hastily withdrew the short-term credits that had been extended to Austria and Germany. The panic which followed inaugurated an era of world-wide economic depression. President Hoover proposed a moratorium on debt and reparations payments in order to provide an opportunity for a fresh study and adjustment of the whole economic problem. The United States thereby for the first time officially abandoned its position that the two questions of debts and reparations should be treated separately. This acknowledgment led to the suspension of payments to the United States on international debts by all countries except Finland.

The world-wide economic collapse diverted the major attention of statesmen from the international to the local scene where it became necessary to devise expedients to relieve the distress of their own peoples. In the United States, growing unemployment, the stock market collapse, followed by world-wide depression and the repudiation of debt payments, intensified a mood of disillusionment and cynicism, the growth of which had been evident for some time.

A Decade of Growing Disillusionment. The second post-war decade was marked by the gradual abandonment of efforts at international co-operation towards fulfilling the conditions of the peace settlement, and by increasingly bold acts of aggression on the part of the militaristic states in Europe and Asia. The fact that such acts of aggression were permitted with comparatively little protest is an indication of the extent to which apathy and disillusionment had seized the statesmen and peoples of the principal Allied nations. In all likelihood, the prevailing mood of apathy was a major factor in making possible the rise of dictatorship throughout the world.

After four long years of struggle and sacrifice, the war-weary peoples of the victorious Allied countries had anticipated a peace settlement which would punish the guilty and oblige the Central Powers to pay the cost of the war. On the latter score it became clear that neither Austria nor Germany could meet their reparations obligations. As to the responsibility for the war, evidence was unearthed which indicated that war guilt could not be laid at the door of any single nation. Documents were discovered which revealed the complicity of former members of the Serbian government in the plot to assassinate the Archduke Franz Ferdinand, and access of historians to state archives indicated that responsibility for bringing about the war was more complicated than had been assumed and involved other nations as well as the enemy states.

In two respects at least the peace conference had given full support to principles that had been laid down by President Wilson as essential to an enduring peace. The principle of nationality was largely the basis for assignment of territories and determination of boundaries, while new constitutions in both new and old states proclaimed the sovereignty of peoples and set up the forms of representative government. But even before the peace conference met, Poles, Balts, Czechs, and Rumanians seized lands by force so as to establish new national boundaries more favorable than those the peace delegates might be inclined to award. When these arbitrary decisions of violence were set aside by the peace settlement, new difficulties beset the governments set up by peoples without experience of self-government. In time, some form of dictatorship replaced self rule in most of the central European states.

A development in an area of great historic interest, Ireland became an independent republic in 1937. The first step toward freedom for the Irish people was the Irish Free State of

1922. The later step achieving full independence proved the basis for increasingly cordial relations with Great Britain.

Fascism in Italy. It was in one of the victorious Allied states, however, that representative institutions first gave way to dictatorship. Italy had entered the First World War in the hope of winning for herself prestige among the powers. By this means the government hoped also to strengthen its position at home in its dealings with the socialists and other opposition groups. But Italy's military contribution to the war had not been great and her conduct at the peace conference blundering. Her territorial gains were limited to some 9,000 square miles of territory containing a population of 1,600,000.

Dissatisfaction with the peace settlement, the collapse of war industries, debt, the high cost of living, food shortages, a feeling of national humiliation, were some of the factors which oppressed the Italian people in the years immediately following the conclusion of the war. The socialists and other groups employed such tactics as strikes, sabotage, intimidation, and seizure of private property and of municipal governments, seeking to disrupt society to the point where the populace would accept their leadership as the only alternative to continuing chaos. It was this situation which gave Mussolini his opportunity.

In March, 1919, Benito Mussolini, an ex-socialist journalist who had been wounded in the war, called a meeting of ex-servicemen and others who were interested in rescuing Italy from her state of confusion. Under Mussolini's leadership these men were organized into *fasci di combattimento* or "fighting groups" in support of a program of reform which envisaged a change of government.

By 1922 the Fascisti had gained considerable strength. They drove out the Communist government of Bologna and seized the city government of Milan. A Fascist congress was held at Naples in October, 1922, at which Mussolini demanded the resignation of the Facta government which had been unable to re-establish order. Upon Facta's refusal to resign, the Fascists marched on the city of Rome on October 27. The

King refused to declare martial law, Facta resigned, and Mussolini was summoned by Victor Emmanuel to form a cabinet. In November, Mussolini demanded and was granted dictatorial powers by parliament.

The Fascists, soon organized as a militia, by beatings, the administration of castor oil, and by murder, suppressed open opposition and firmly established their control of the country's political administration. However, order was re-established. Industrial arbitration was made compulsory, lockouts and strikes were prohibited. Programs of public works and increases in the armed forces reduced unemployment. Measures were taken to increase the production of food and to reduce the cost of living. A popular achievement was the Lateran Treaties of 1929, under which the Papal and Italian governments adjusted the differences which had existed since the seizure of the Papal States by the Italian troops in 1870. By the agreement, Vatican City was recognized as an independent state under the sovereignty of the Pope.

The Rise of Hitler in Germany. Adolf Hitler, an Austrian subject who had been a corporal in the German army during the First World War, first gained notice in connection with the so-called "Beer Hall Putsch" of November, 1923, in which he associated himself with Ludendorff in leading a group in an attempt to overthrow the Bavarian government. The uprising was put down, and Hitler was imprisoned. While in prison he wrote *Mein Kampf,* outlining his career, his theories, and his program. Released at the end of a year, he devoted his energies to making speeches and organizing the Nazi (National Socialist) party.

Hitler envisaged the formation of a "Third Reich" which would include all Germans in a new and greater German state. This involved the ultimate absorption of German-populated regions in Austria, Czechoslovakia, and Poland—even the Netherlands was looked upon as forming part of the future German state. Hitler sought to restore German pride and self-respect by insisting that the German armies had not been beaten but that revolution at home had occasioned the col-

EUROPE
BEFORE WORLD WAR II

Oslo
NORWAY
NORTH SEA
DENMARK
Copenh
SCOTLAND
Glasgow Edinburgh
Kiel
UNITED
KINGDOM
Ham
Belfast
NORTHERN
IRELAND
Bremen
Amsterdam
GERM
IRELAND
(EIRE)
Dublin
Liverpool
Hull
The Hague
Leipzig
Birmingham
Oxford
NETHERLANDS
Cologne
SAX
Cork
Cobh
London
Dover
BELGIUM
Malmedy
Frankfurt
Bristol
Portsmouth
Calais
Brussels
Namur
LUXEMBOURG
Plymouth
CHANNEL
Lille
SAAR
Stuttgart
ENGLISH
SOMME R.
Reims
Verdun
Strasbourg
Mun
Brest
SEINE
OISE R.
MARNE
BAVAR
BRITTANY
Paris
Basel
Bern Zürich
Innsb
LOIRE R.
SWITZERLAND
JYF
FRANCE
Geneva
Locarno
ATLANTIC
Lyon
Milan
OCEAN
RHONE R.
Turin
Bordeaux
Genoa
Rapa
GARONNE R.
Monaco
Nice
Flo
La Coruña
BASQUE
PROVINCES
ANDORRA
Marseille
Cannes
GALICIA
EBRO R.
CORSICA
DOURO R.
SPAIN
CATALONIA
Barcelona
SARDIN
TAGUS R.
Madrid
PORTUGAL
GUADIANA R.
Valencia
Lisbon
BALEARIC IS.
GUADALQUIVIR R.
Seville
MEDITERRANEA
Algeciras
Gibraltar
Tangier
Ceuta
Algiers
Tunis

lapse of the war effort. He proclaimed that Germany's war guilt had been disproved by Allied historians. Declaring that the Versailles settlement was a betrayal of Germany, he promised his people abrogation of the treaties. He insisted that Jews were an alien race and should not have a place in the Third Reich.

The collapse of German prosperity and the failure of Chancellor Bruening's conciliatory policies to obtain relief for Germany brought the National Socialists to the fore. In January, 1933, Hitler was named chancellor by President Hindenburg, and a new election was held. The National Socialists and their Nationalist allies won control of the Reichstag and Hitler was voted dictatorial powers.

Under the Hitler dictatorship, all opposition parties were liquidated, and in July, 1933, the National Socialist party was declared the only legal party. A boycott of Jewish business and professions in the same year inaugurated a long series of persecutions of the Jews in Germany. A neo-pagan movement was encouraged in opposition to Protestantism and Catholicism. Universal compulsory military service was restored in 1935.

In 1933 Germany withdrew from the disarmament conference and from the League of Nations. In 1934 Hitler concluded a treaty with Poland; and a meeting with Mussolini in Venice paved the way for an alliance between the two dictator states. Immediately on Hitler's return to Germany, there followed the "Blood Purge" of June, 1934, in which 74 members of his own Nazi party were executed, charged with a plot against Hitler. Fresh crises followed rapidly. On July 25, during a Nazi Putsch in Vienna, Chancellor Dollfuss was assassinated, and the Nazis sought to win control of the Vienna government. They probably would have succeeded but for the fact that Mussolini mobilized his troops at the Brenner Pass and by a threat of intervention thwarted the Nazi plot.

The Socialist Experiment in Russia. Between the East and the West lies Russia. During three centuries of Romanoff rule its monarchy had developed into complete autocracy, and Russian dominion had been extended in three continents—Europe, Asia, and North America—until the czars ruled over roughly one-sixth of the earth's surface. During the 19th century continuing Russian expansion brought that nation into conflict with western European nations. The Crimean War of 1853–56, in which Russia was defeated by an alliance of Turkey, France, Britain, and Sardinia, revealed to the Russians that mere size did not constitute strength.

In the years which followed, reforms were undertaken. The abolition of serfdom was begun, laws were codified, the administration of justice was improved, and the creation of the *Zemstvos* (local elective assemblies) provided the opportunity for the Russian people to gain some experience in local self-government.

Russia, at this time, had made relatively little technical progress. She needed industries, railways, organization. The scientific advances of western Europe, which provided the foundation for the agricultural and industrial revolutions of the eighteenth and nineteenth centuries, had been accompanied by changes in social and political outlook which the czars could not contemplate with equanimity. The czars were desirous of strengthening Russia, but progress in the western European sense could only be permitted on condition that it implicated no infringement upon autocratic prerogative.

In 1904–05 the war with Japan once again revealed the weakness of the great Slav empire. Japan, at the time a small nation which had only recently adopted western European techniques and organization, administered to Russia a crushing defeat on land and sea. Soon afterward, in 1905, a revolution broke out, demanding reforms to which the czar was forced to make concessions. Renewed demands for a democratic franchise and civil liberties were accompanied by strikes, violence, and the seizure of land by the peasants, and once again there followed an end of reform and the institution of a policy of repression.

Despite internal weakness, Russia assumed the role of a first class power in her international dealings, and the alliance which she formed with France brought her into the First

World War. The early successes of the Russian armies used up most of her reserve strength in supplies and equipment and Russia's undeveloped industry was unable to supply the lack. The inefficiency and corruptness of the bureaucracy nullified any efforts to organize effectively the patriotic enthusiasm of the people of the vastly extended domain; and with growing belief that the czarina was pro-German, that Rasputin, who exerted a peculiar dominion over the minds of the imperial couple, was in the pay of the enemy, the czarist regime was doomed.

In 1917 the army had been equipped, with Allied help, for a spring offensive. The morale of the troops was high. But bureaucratic ineptness had left the civilian population of Petrograd without supplies of food. During the second week in March, while the czar was with the armies, rioting broke out in Petrograd and spread rapidly throughout the city. The czar sought to deal with the situation by telegraph, but the measures he ordered were inadequate. By March 12 Petrograd was overrun by the revolutionary mob.

The Duma (parliament) seemed the only authority that could control the situation, and crowds of soldiers and civilians rushed to the Tauride palace where the Duma sat, demanding action. That body decided to assume direction of the revolutionary movement. Meanwhile, the Petrograd Soviet (council) of Workers and Soldiers' Deputies was being formed. Although the Petrograd Soviet recognized the leadership of the Duma and dispatched two delegates to represent its interests in that body, it continued to function separately.

The Petrograd revolution was accepted by both the army and the nation. In abdicating, the czar resigned the supreme authority to his brother, Michael Alexandrovitch, who declined the succession and passed the authority on to the Provisional Government. The nobility and the government bureaucracy accordingly accepted the new regime, whose authority was thus legally established. The Provisional Government at once determined to carry on the war while it proceeded with the organization of a new government for Russia. However, as news of the revolution spread throughout Russia, Soviets were organized in all the chief centers and also among the soldiers. The Petrograd Soviet, without regard to the Duma, issued decrees to the nation, and issued orders to the army placing control in the hands of soldiers' committees, a measure which threatened destruction of the whole military organization.

The Provisional Government, the nominal and legal successor to the czars, represented a *political* revolution acknowledging the leadership of the liberal members of the Duma. But the Soviet, which was at the time an unofficial government, aimed at *social* revolution. The members of both groups were largely lacking in practical political experience, a tragic handicap in the complicated crisis which confronted them. The moderate Miliukov, who headed the Provisional Government, was forced out of office and replaced by the Socialist Kerensky.

In April, Lenin, leader of what was to become the Communist Party, had arrived in Petrograd from his place of exile in Switzerland. He called upon the peasants and industrial workers to use the Soviets to organize the overthrow of the Provisional Government. His first revolutionary attempt, in July, 1917, was put down, but his followers succeeded in widening the schism between the Provisional Government and the Soviets, which continued to be an important force. When the army commander-in-chief, General Kornilov, sought the approval of the Provisional Government for his proposal to suppress the Soviet by military force, he was called to Petrograd and arrested on the orders of Kerensky. Reverses in the field won support for the Socialists, who opposed continuation of the war. Disorganization contributed to economic collapse, and as a result of increasing hardships and uncertainty, discontent spread, and propaganda was actively disseminated by both the Socialists and the Bolsheviks (the Socialist minority supporting Lenin).

December 12, 1917, was the date on which the national convention for drafting a Russian constitution was to meet. A national congress of Soviets was called to meet in advance of this date, on November 7. Lenin and the Bolsheviks determined to gain control of the Soviet congress as a necessary step toward Bolshevik dominance of the Russian state. On the night of November 7, Bolshevik troops occupied the government buildings. The printing presses were kept busy, for on the morning of November 8, notices and posters proclaimed the program of the Bolsheviks: 1. seizure of the factories and great country estates by workers and peasants; 2. immediate opening of peace negotiations to end the war; 3. creation of a national government of the Soviets.

The Bolsheviks, who had thus assumed power, were a minority even among the Socialists. They did not represent the nation, only the minority who, with Lenin, sought the immediate establishment of the rule of the proletariat and the division of property. But it was a minority which had organization and purpose and was quite uninhibited with respect to the methods that might be necessary to accomplish its purpose. Kerensky fled from Petrograd and sought to mobilize the armies. But his earlier betrayal of Kornilov handicapped him in his negotiations with the army leaders. In any case, the army was scattered, railway workers refused to transport troops, and soon peasants and workers, led by the Bolsheviks, seized the lands and factories. The complicated civil strife which followed resulted in the triumph of the Bolsheviks.

The newly established government immediately instituted a policy of nationalization of all industry and of land and natural resources in 1921. However, production in all fields, and most seriously in agriculture, immediately declined, resulting in famine in many parts of Russia. To provide incentives to production, the fundamental policy was revised to permit private ownership to a limited extent. This was known as the New Economic Policy (NEP) and was continued until 1928. In 1924 Lenin died and was succeeded by Joseph Stalin, who made the building of a strong Communist state the major concern of the government. The Five-Year-Plan of 1928 and the Second Five-Year-Plan of 1933 increased industrial production while the collectivization of farms raised the agricultural output.

63 A PERIOD OF DEPRESSION AND AGGRESSION

The War of Ideas. We have reviewed the period of protracted efforts to liquidate the First World War and have noted the mood of growing disillusionment.

Accompanying those developments was the war of ideas— the conflict of ideologies or conceptions of the international, political, and social organization of states and of the world. The views of the democracies were opposed by the Nazi-Fascists on one hand and by the Communists on the other.

From 1919 to 1943 the Third or Communist International (Comintern), regarding itself as headquarters for the world army of the proletariat, directed a program designed to carry on international propaganda of Communist ideas, to strengthen the Communist party in all countries, to win leadership of all socialist and labor movements, and to accelerate the development of events toward world revolution.

In Italy the Fascists succeeded in discrediting the parliamentary regime, and thus won popular support for the dictatorship of Mussolini. Fascist propaganda emphasized the weaknesses of parliamentary government. It exalted Italian patriotism, exaggerated the importance of Italy's role in the First World War, blamed parliamentary leadership for Italy's failure to have profited from the war, and asserted Italy's right to a colonial empire which would provide her with natural resources, markets, and a home for her surplus population.

In Germany Hitler exploited the widespread feeling that the peace settlement and the penalties it had imposed upon Germany were unjust. He claimed certain "rights" for the German people, declared his intention of enforcing those rights, and mobilized the human and material resources of Germany in order to be able to back up his demands with force.

One of the chief arguments advanced by the Nazi-Fascists in the economic sphere was that in order for a modern industrial state to exist it must have access to raw materials and markets. To be sure, Wilson in the second and third of his Fourteen Points, recognized that such access was necessary for all nations. But the Nazi-Fascists, representing what were described as "have not" states, made claims far beyond the concept of removal of tariff barriers and other inhibitions to the free flow of goods and transport, asserting that the "have not" states possessed the *right* to seize territories and colonies which would assure them economic self-sufficiency.

One of the consequences of the world-wide economic depression of the 1930's was that the efforts of political leaders were directed away from the international scene to the domestic. Unemployment, the collapse of business, and attendant hardships forced governments to devote their energies to devising means of relieving human suffering and insecurity and to reviving the domestic economy. Taking advantage of this general preoccupation with internal affairs, Japan invaded Manchuria in 1932, and thus launched an "unofficial" war with China.

Among the protests made was that by United States Secretary of State Stimson against Japanese aggrandizement in Manchuria. Although this proved to be little more than a gesture, it was important in its statement of the principle that the United States would not recognize any steps taken in violation of the Kellogg Peace pacts. The League of Nations, appealed to by China, weakly proposed a compromise making Manchuria an autonomous state under Chinese sovereignty but Japanese control. Japan withdrew from the League in March, 1933.

Viewing the declining prestige of the League and disturbed by Hitler's mobilization of German strength and his defiant attitude toward the treaties, France offered to make concessions to Italy in certain French possessions in East Africa. Then the neighboring kingdom of Ethiopia (formerly Abyssinia) became involved along the ill-defined border between Eritrea (at that time an Italian possession) and Ethiopia. Mussolini, eager to enlarge Italy's African empire, invaded Ethiopia. Haile Selassie, Emperor of Ethiopia, appealed to the

League of Nations to arbitrate the dispute, but Italy continued to send troops to East Africa. The League imposed economic sanctions on Italy in October, 1935, but Italy nevertheless carried on full-scale warfare, overrunning all of Ethiopia and annexing it in May, 1936. (In 1941 Ethiopia regained its independence, and in 1952 closely related Eritrea became part of Ethiopia.)

Taking advantage of the Ethiopian crises, Germany, in March, 1936, established a military occupation of the Rhineland, thus violating the treaties of Versailles and Locarno.

In July, 1936, a violent civil war broke out in Spain when a group of monarchist army officers, led by General Francisco Franco, sought to overthrow the Republican government which was in power. Britain and France tried to negotiate an agreement among the large nations not to intervene in the Spanish struggle. Nevertheless, Germany and Italy, recognizing Franco and his Falangists as sympathetic to fascism, sent men and equipment to aid Franco; and simultaneously Russia sent aid to the Loyalists, the forces of the Republican Government. Franco's armies were victorious, and a dictatorship was established in Spain with Franco at its head.

In November, 1936, the already existing alliance between Germany and Italy was enlarged to include Japan, the new alliance becoming known as the Rome-Berlin-Tokyo Axis.

Appeasement. During the years that followed, antipathy to war was so strong among the Western democracies that they hopefully underestimated the extent to which Germany was re-arming herself, accepted at its face value Hitler's announced policy of limiting aggression to correcting injustices of the peace settlement, and similarly refrained from interfering with Mussolini's African conquests on the assumption that his ambitions were limited in scope.

Appeasement of the Nazis by the democracies went even further than this. When Hitler's armies occupied Austria and annexed it to Germany in March, 1938, there was a sense of shock but no opposition whatsoever. When it appeared that Hitler was about to move against Czechoslovakia, with the plan of detaching the Sudeten areas and absorbing them into the growing German state, the peoples of the non-Fascist countries became aroused and alarmed. Chamberlain and Daladier, prime ministers of Britain and France, met with Hitler and Mussolini at Munich in September, 1938, to consider the Czechoslovak crisis. Munich was the high-water mark of appeasement for, to the astonishment of the world, the spokesmen for Britain and France agreed to the dismemberment of Czechoslovakia, and accepted the assurance that Germany would take over only the Sudeten sections and would respect the independence of the rest of the Czechoslovak republic. Nevertheless, Munich also served to awaken the democracies to danger. Realizing how false had been their seeming security and how weak was their military organization, they commenced re-armament on a limited scale.

The uneasy quiet which followed Munich was completely shattered, when, despite all promises, Hitler's forces attacked and overran the independent portions of Czechoslovakia and annihilated the republic in March, 1939. At this point President Roosevelt sent a message to Hitler inquiring as to German intentions, and Hitler in reply denied further aggressive plans.

The shocking truth, however, was revealed in the last days of August, 1939, with the sudden announcement of a Russo-German non-aggression pact, which was followed immediately (Sept. 1, 1939) by a German attack on Poland.

64 THE BEGINNING OF THE SECOND WORLD WAR

When Hitler's armies invaded Poland, France and Great Britain could no longer stand aside. On September 3, 1939, both nations declared war on the Third Reich. The collapse of Poland in a matter of days was incomprehensible to the minds of peacefully inclined peoples, unprepared to envisage the horrors of *blitzkrieg* (lightning warfare). In November, 1939, war broke out between Russia and Finland. Despite heroic resistance, the Finns were forced to conclude an unfavorable peace in March, 1940, involving cession of part of their territory to Russia.

While France and Britain feverishly re-armed, the formidable Maginot Line in eastern France seemed to offer an effective check to a Nazi offensive in the west. But in April, 1940, instead of turning west, Hitler turned north. The occupation of Denmark provided him with a springboard from which to launch his attack upon the Scandinavian peninsula. German ships and planes, aided by a "fifth column" inside Norway, began the invasion of that country. The aid which Britain and France could dispatch to Norway was all too little. While they hampered the enemy's movements and inflicted losses, the small forces landed could not hold their ground against an enemy supported by planes operating from nearby airfields. These forces were withdrawn.

In May, Hitler turned upon the Netherlands and Belgium. The military forces of these small states could only provide a brief check to the Nazi advance. The surrender of the Belgian armies left Hitler free to concentrate his formidable forces against France.

The Collapse of France. When the German armies entered France, their rapidly moving mechanized columns cut behind the French armies, disrupting communications and isolating groups of soldiers. The air force pounded and strafed these groups, prevented their reorganization, and kept the armies informed of the enemy's position and movement. Fifth columnists and forces dropped by parachute behind the enemy lines completed the work of sabotage and disruption. In late May and early June the British troops in France, cut off and almost without hope of survival, were evacuated to England through the port of Dunkirk, together with thousands of French troops caught in the same pocket.

The Battle of France began on June 5, 1940. On June 14, the Germans occupied Paris. On June 10, when it became clear that French power was broken, Mussolini declared war on England and France. On June 17, the aged Marshal Pétain, who had replaced Reynaud as head of the French government the preceding day, asked for peace, and the next day Hitler and Mussolini met to discuss terms for France. The overwhelming success of the Nazi armies was the result of a new technique of warfare which promptly became known as *blitzkrieg*. It involved the close co-ordination of the actions of land, air, and, where possible, sea forces, and the cooperation of a "fifth column" led by saboteurs who had penetrated the country in advance of the attack.

The Battle of Britain. In August, 1940, the Battle of Britain was begun by Hitler with a series of daylight air attacks on an unprecedented scale. Just as *blitzkrieg* had concentrated on the destruction of the enemy's organization and communications, so did the attacks of Hitler's air force seek to destroy the organization of industry, communications, and services in Britain. Concentrated attacks on densely populated industrial cities and towns exacted a fearful toll, but the British people stood firm. In memorable words Prime Minister Churchill expressed the determination of Britain not to yield.

The Battle of The Atlantic. When the failure of the *blitz* against Britain became apparent, Hitler attempted to starve Britain out of the war. Since the attack on British shipping was made from air and naval bases scattered along the extended European coastline from Norway to the Pyrenees, it was impossible for Britain to blockade all of these bases with ships and mines. German bombers pounded London's 1700 wharves, while Nazi submarines inflicted serious losses on British shipping in the Atlantic.

Britain obtained some assistance in the form of fifty over-age American destroyers, which she received in exchange for the lease to the United States of naval and air bases in British possessions in the western hemisphere, including Newfoundland, Bermuda, the Bahamas, various Caribbean islands, and British Guiana.

Britain was unable to use the seaports of Eire, as the Irish state had proclaimed her neutrality in the war. Although she was able to protect shipments of military supplies and reinforcements passing through the Mediterranean to Egypt, Italian naval and air power had largely closed that route to British merchant traffic with the East. The long route around Africa inflicted a serious burden upon British shipping. It became clear that unless Britain received outside help, there was great danger that the Axis would win the battle of the Atlantic.

The Balkans and Libya. Simultaneous with the Battle of the Atlantic was Mussolini's move to cut the British lifeline in the Mediterranean. On October 28, Mussolini ordered his troops to advance into Greece from Albania, which Italy had overrun and occupied in 1939. The massing of Italian troops had prepared the Greeks for this move, and they met the Fascist invasion with a vigor which surprised the Axis powers and heartened their enemies. British naval and air power supported the Greek resistance and launched attacks upon Sicily, southern Italy, and Italian forces in the Balkans. Anglo-Greek successes forced the diversion of German reinforcements for North Africa to the Greek theater of war. This, in turn, permitted General Wavell, who had received heavy reinforcements, to launch an attack against the Italian armies, which had advanced into Egypt. In December, 1940, Wavell succeeded in driving the Italians out of Egypt, and then he and his forces advanced into Libya.

Japanese Activities on the Asiatic Mainland. Meanwhile, faced with the enormous task of defending the British Isles, Britain was in no position to withstand Japanese pressure in the East. Thus in June, 1940, Britain agreed that within the Tientsin Concession Japanese officials might suppress activities prejudicial to the security of Japanese forces. Japanese troops concentrated near Kowloon and Hong Kong, and demanded the stoppage of supplies to Chiang Kai-shek through these points and along the Burma Road. The British agreed to suspend the Burma Road traffic for three months.

Similarly the Japanese wrested concessions from the Vichy

government of France with respect to Indo-China. When, in August, after a demonstration of naval strength, Japan demanded the right to establish naval and air bases and move her troops across Indo-China, both Britain and the United States protested, but in September, France gave in to Japanese demands in return for her promise to guarantee the territorial integrity and French sovereignty of Indo-China. Meanwhile, the Japanese government was reorganized along Fascist lines with Prince Konoye at its head.

The Nazi Attack upon Russia. In August, 1939, as we have already mentioned, the Communist government of Russia concluded a pact with Nazi Germany. While Nazi armies were invading western Poland, Russian troops occupied eastern Poland. Thus Russia had a share in the twentieth-century partitioning of Poland as she had in that of the eighteenth century. While Hitler's armies were overrunning western Europe, Stalin used the moment to strengthen Russia in preparation for a possible clash with the growing Nazi power. The Kremlin was fully aware of the fact that its pact with the Nazis only temporarily disguised the fundamental enmity between the Hitlerites and the Soviet Union. Vital industries were consequently moved from western Russia to locations east of the Urals. Production of the materials of war was mobilized and speeded up. During the summer of 1940, Russia seized the Baltic republics and in the south took Bessarabia and northern Bukovina from Rumania. In April, 1941, the Russians signed a treaty of neutrality and non-aggression with Japan as a precaution against a possible Axis attack upon two fronts. Nevertheless, despite these precautions, Stalin was careful not to antagonize his powerful western neighbor, and Russia delivered to Germany the goods called for by the treaty of 1939. During the winter months of 1940–41, as, under Nazi pressure, the small states of central Europe joined the Axis "new order," Stalin dismissed the representatives of the governments-in-exile of Greece and Yugoslavia, as he had those of Norway and Belgium, and Russia recognized the pro-Axis governments.

On June 22, 1941, without preliminary negotiations or warning, the German armies attacked Russia, thus opening up an eastern front 1800 miles in length. At once it became apparent that the Russians had learned invaluable lessons about defense against *blitzkrieg* from the experience of the western nations. Russian equipment and organization were vastly better than the Germans had anticipated. But the decisive factors were a combination of a "defense in depth" with a "scorched earth" policy.

The Russian lines bent as Hitler's mechanized columns cut forward, but the Russian lines did not break. Her communications and supply lines remained intact, and as the German armies pushed farther into Russia, the Russian air force and Russian guerrillas behind the German lines disrupted German communications.

In the autumn of 1941, the Germans had reached the outskirts of Leningrad in the north, and in central Russia they were close to Moscow. Although the Germans took Odessa and Kharkov in the south during October, and Rostov on the Sea of Azov in November, both Leningrad and Moscow held out. Despite the oncoming of winter, Hitler launched another attack on Moscow, which failed. Then the Russians counterattacked, driving the Germans back from before Moscow, and in the south retaking Rostov and pursuing the Germans forty miles farther westward.

65   THE UNITED STATES AND THE SECOND WORLD WAR

The United States was militarily and psychologically unprepared for the outbreak of a second world war. As we have seen, during the 1930's, events abroad had intensified the mood of cynicism and disillusionment which had begun to manifest itself in the 1920's. A natural reaction to the failure of international cooperation was the growth of "isolationism," the determination to remain aloof from involvement in international problems and disputes. In any case, the attention of the people of the United States was focused upon domestic matters. When Franklin Delano Roosevelt became President of the United States in March, 1933, the main problems he faced were those resulting from the Great Depression. The earliest aggressions of the Axis nations shocked public opinion in America, but that shock was accompanied by a general feeling of thankfulness that these incidents were no concern of ours. During these years, American foreign policy expressed itself through neutrality legislation aiming at the avoidance of incidents which would involve the nation in any conflicts between other countries.

When the Second World War broke out in Europe, the people of the United States soon recognized that their sympathies were emphatically with the Allied cause. The United States had, through the entire course of its history, struggled for the establishment of freedom under law as a basic principle of government within a state and as the basis of a decent international order. It was evident that the aim of the Axis was the establishment of a rule of force, a world domination which would mean the destruction of all that America stood for. Americans watched with growing apprehension the rapid extension of Axis dominance over Austria, Czechoslovakia, Poland, Denmark, Norway, the Netherlands, Belgium, France, Hungary, Albania, Bulgaria, Rumania, Yugoslavia, Greece, and North Africa. Heightening America's reaction was the horror of the German concentration camps, to which the Nazis sent everyone who opposed their doctrines, including many hundreds of thousands of Jews, who were later to be sent to Nazi execution chambers.

Warned by events in Europe and in the East, the United States prepared to make itself the "arsenal of democracy" while building up its own military strength. In the fall of 1940 Congress passed a compulsory military training law and authorized the expenditure of seventeen billion dollars for the construction of a two-ocean navy.

At the same time, the need was felt for a new statement of the basic elements requisite in an international order to which the United States could subscribe. Accordingly, in August, 1941, Prime Minister Churchill and President Roosevelt met in the Atlantic off the coast of Newfoundland and drew up a statement of "certain common principles in the national policies of their respective countries on which they base their hopes for a better future for the world." This statement of principles promptly became known as the Atlantic Charter (see Appendix), and was ultimately accepted as a statement of their aims by all those nations of the world which aligned themselves in a coalition against the Axis.

Prelude to Pearl Harbor. Meanwhile, the American government was growing concerned at the spread of Japanese aggression in Asia. While proceeding with its naval building schedule the United States gave aid and support to China and suspended the shipment of scrap iron to Japan. Later, the United States, along with the Dutch in the Netherlands East Indies, placed embargoes on aviation oil and gasoline intended for Japan.

While attempting by these practical measures to discourage further Japanese aggression, the United States also sought to achieve this end by negotiation with Japan. These went on, were broken off, and were resumed at the suggestion of Japan. In the meantime, the replacement of Prince Konoye by the militaristic Admiral Tojo as prime minister and the concentration of Japanese convoys and naval units brought about a critical situation, and President Roosevelt addressed a personal appeal to the Japanese emperor in the interests of avoiding a precipitation of hostilities.

Pearl Harbor and After. On Sunday morning, December 7, 1941, Japan launched a surprise naval and air attack upon the United States naval base at Pearl Harbor, Hawaii. A large number of vessels of the American Pacific fleet were either sunk or damaged. A few hours later, Japanese planes based on Formosa attacked Clark Field near Manila in the Philippines. On December 8, the United States and Great Britain declared war on Japan. The next day two British battleships, seeking to intercept a Japanese convoy off the Malay coast, were attacked and sunk by Japanese land-based aircraft. Soon the American islands of Guam and Wake fell to the Japanese, as did Hong Kong, the British naval base in southern China.

Having gained control of the air and sea in the East, Japan sent her armies through Indo-China to attack the British in Malaya, forcing them back through the jungles toward Singapore, 400 miles to the south and toward Burma in the west. The great naval base at Singapore, invincible from the sea, but weakly defended on the landward side, fell before a land attack on February 15, 1942.

In Burma the British troops under General Wavell, with air support from the Flying Tigers, an American volunteer group serving with the Chinese, and the assistance of Chinese troops under the command of the American General Stilwell, military adviser to Chiang Kai-shek, at first withstood Japanese attacks; but their numbers and equipment were insufficient, and on April 28, the enemy succeeded in reaching Lashio and the Burma Road, so essential as a supply route to China. When further defense became impossible, the British withdrew from Burma.

Meanwhile there had been important fighting in the Dutch East Indies. A small concentration of Dutch, American, British, and Australian ships, under a Dutch commander, in a six-day battle, January 23 to 29, 1942, destroyed a large number of Japanese ships and transports passing through the Macassar Straits for a Japanese assault on the rich Dutch colonies. However, the Allied force was overwhelmed in a naval battle off Java on February 27, and Java and the other islands of the East Indies, with their rich natural resources, fell to the Japanese.

In the Philippines, the American and Filipino troops under the command of General MacArthur were forced to withdraw from other parts of the islands to Bataan Peninsula, which they continued to hold, along with the fortress of Corregidor, at the entrance to Manila harbor. General MacArthur was called away from Bataan to take charge of American forces in Australia, which was now exposed to the

Japanese attack, and General Wainwright remained in charge in the Philippines. Finally, lack of supplies, food, and medical equipment compelled the heroic group on Bataan to surrender on April 9, and the fortress of Corregidor fell on May 7.

Military Events in Europe and Africa. As the summer of 1942 approached, the Axis powers reached their furthest military advances. The Russians had failed to push back the Germans during the winter of 1941–42. In May, the Germans launched their second Russian offensive, concentrating their efforts in the south. The seizure of Sebastopol in the Crimea deprived the Russians of their chief naval base on the Black Sea; and, pushing eastward and southward into the Caucasus, Hitler's armies captured Maikop and its surrounding oil wells on August 16.

Meanwhile, the German General Rommel, in a new African offensive, forced the British to retreat across North Africa to within sixty miles of Alexandria in Egypt.

At a conference in Washington in December, 1941, representatives of the Allied states met to plan a global strategy and to achieve unity in carrying it out. At this and in subsequent conferences at Moscow and Chungking, it was decided to concentrate first upon the defeat of Germany, and then to turn to Japan. For a year Russia evidenced distrust of her western allies and Stalin remained secretive with respect to the plans and equipment of the Soviet armed forces. However, the conclusion of a twenty-year alliance with Britain, which was signed in May, 1942, paved the way for fuller collaboration. And despite the difficulties of getting aid to Russia over the dangerous northern route to Murmansk or the long southern route around Africa to the Middle East and through the Caucasus, by the end of October, 1943, Russia had received from the United States, large quantities of war equipment, food, and other supplies.

While aiding her allies, the United States rapidly built up all branches of its army and navy. By 1945, the United States had an army equal to Russia's in numbers; and its sea power was greater than that of all the Allied nations combined.

The Turn of the Tide. In the summer of 1942, Rommel's advance into Egypt and the German attack on the Caucasus area threatened to close the Mediterranean and cut off the vital Caucasus supply route to Russia. Allied reinforcements were rushed to Egypt, including quantities of the new American Sherman tanks. In a decisive battle with Rommel's forces (October 23 to November 2), General Montgomery destroyed the enemy's organization. He promptly followed up his advantage and pursued the beaten Nazi forces across North Africa.

Meanwhile, a huge American and British force had gathered secretly in the Atlantic. On November 8, an Allied army carried by 500 ships and accompanied by 350 naval craft, began landings on the Mediterranean coasts of Morocco and Algeria. President Roosevelt, General De Gaulle, leader of the Free French, and General Giraud appealed to the representatives of Vichy France not to resist the landing, and Admiral Darlan gave the necessary order. With the Allies on North African soil, German reinforcements were rushed to North Africa by sea and air. In January, 1943, President Roosevelt and Prime Minister Churchill met for an important conference at Casablanca in Morocco. After a difficult campaign, the Allied armies under General Eisenhower won complete victory in North Africa, with the Nazi surrender on May 12, 1943.

The Russian Front. The Allied landings in North Africa had forced the Germans to shift part of their air force and some of their divisions from the eastern to the Mediterranean front. The Russians then rushed up reserves from Siberia and began their great counter-offensive. The Nazi troops besieging Stalingrad were surrounded and ultimately forced to surrender. Meanwhile, the Russian winter offensive was launched along the entire front. The German defense centers which had held during the preceding winter were all taken and the Russians pushed forward more than 400 miles from Stalingrad.

The Collapse of Italy. From North Africa, the Allied assault upon Sicily began on June 10, 1943. It was preceded by weeks of aerial bombardment of the strongholds and ports of Sicily and southern Italy. An American advance northward cut Sicily in two, while the British pushed the German troops northward and eastward toward Messina. By August 17, the Germans were driven from the island.

Meanwhile, Hitler's refusal to send additional aid to Italy and the Allied successes in Sicily brought about the overthrow of Mussolini, whose resignation was demanded by the Fascist Grand Council on July 24. Marshal Badoglio, upon his appointment as prime minister, decreed the dissolution of the Fascist party. Hitler thereupon rushed some eighteen Nazi divisions into northern and central Italy. Badoglio opened secret negotiations with the Allies and on September 3, 1943, the Italians accepted the armistice terms presented by General Eisenhower, although the occupying Nazis continued opposition.

On September 2, General Montgomery's Eighth Army crossed the straits from Sicily into the toe of the Italian boot and six days later a second force, under the command of General Clark, made an amphibious landing at Salerno. The two armies made contact on September 17, and began the slow northward advance over extremely difficult terrain.

The Assault on Nazi Europe. The Russian summer offensive of 1943 merged into the winter offensive begun in October. As American supplies poured into Russia over shortened routes—for the Allies now dominated the Mediterranean—fresh armies were thrown into the offensive. In August, 1942, the American Air Force had joined operations against Nazi Europe, and the weight of this aerial assault steadily mounted.

The Invasion of France. On June 6, 1944, shortly after the Allied armies in Italy had liberated Rome, American, British, and Canadian troops stormed the beaches of Normandy, and active invasion was under way on a vast scale. Plans had been developed by Roosevelt and Churchill in conferences at Washington and at Quebec in the summer of 1943, and by Roosevelt, Churchill, and Stalin at Teheran in Iran in December, 1943.

The Americans cut across the Cotentin Peninsula and secured the port of Cherbourg, while the British and Canadians held the Germans at Caen. General Bradley's American First Army broke through the German lines and held the gap open while General Patton's armored Third Army rushed through. Spearheads were thrust into Brittany, toward Paris, and toward the mouth of the Seine.

Meanwhile, on August 15, a fresh landing was effectuated in the south of France. The American Seventh Army took Toulon and Marseilles and advanced up the Rhone valley in order to separate the Germans in Italy from those in France. At the same time the French Forces of the Interior—FFI or *Maquis*—arose against the Germans in Paris and throughout France. The Allied armies tore across France and Belgium with such speed that by the middle of September they were at the powerful German West Wall defenses.

Russian Advances in 1944. The Russians opened their summer offensive at several points along the extended eastern front. Finland, which had joined the Nazis in the hope of regaining some of the territory Russia had seized in 1940, was driven out of the war by the middle of September. A second drive, launched against the Baltic states late in July, was pushed on through the fall of 1944. By the end of the year the Nazis had been driven out of Latvia and out of most of Estonia and Lithuania. Farther south a long advance was made from the vicinity of Vitebsk and Orsha into Poland to the outskirts of Warsaw. Still farther south Russian armies penetrated into Galicia. Checked by the German defense at Cracow, the Russian armies then turned southward, late in August, and advanced against Germany's Balkan satellites. Upon the approach of the Russian armies, Rumania and Bulgaria turned upon the Germans and drove them out of the country. The defection of these states forced the Germans to withdraw their forces from Greece, and this withdrawal was hastened by the landing of British troops in the Peloponnesus in October. In Yugoslavia and Albania opposition to the Nazis had never been entirely suppressed. The assistance of Bulgarian troops under Soviet command, plus the advance of the Russian armies, hastened the collapse of Nazi rule in these lands; and Hungary, after a long siege of Budapest, the capital, was liberated in February, 1945.

The Fall of Germany. Early in February, 1945, at the Yalta Conference, attended by Roosevelt, Churchill, and Stalin, the military staffs arranged for the closest co-ordination of effort among the Allies in the assault on Germany. The advance from east and west was accompanied by a terrific aerial attack upon Germany. In February and March the Allied armies in the west achieved one of the greatest victories of the war, the breaching of the West Wall and the crossing of the Rhine. With these barriers overcome, Germany was subjected to the kind of *blitzkrieg* that had overwhelmed France. In the east, the Russians took Vienna on April 13, and advanced on Berlin. General Eisenhower halted the American Ninth and First Armies at the Elbe so as not to interfere with the Russian encirclement of Berlin which took place April 25. Berlin fell on May 2. On May 7 and 8, the formal surrender of the German armies took place.

The Japanese War. The Japanese had invaded northern China in July, 1937, and had pushed southward and westward, so that by the end of 1938, they had occupied the entire coast of China and all the chief eastern cities. The Chinese government, under Chiang Kai-shek, was in Chungking, in western China. The decision of the Allied powers to fight in Europe before turning to Asia resulted in limiting aid to China for several years, to efforts to reopen the Burma Road and to establish a route of supply to China from India, where important American air bases had been established. China's internal situation was complicated by the continuing warfare between Chiang Kai-shek's Nationalist troops and the Chinese Communists.

The first major Allied attack upon Japanese positions in the Pacific was in 1942, when a concentration of Japanese shipping was met off the northeast coast of Australia, in the Coral Sea, by American carrier-based and land-based aircraft, under the command of General MacArthur. In a six-day battle the

Japanese were defeated and turned back. The Japanese then sought to cut off the American naval forces in the southwest Pacific by seizing Midway Island. Here again, in a four-day battle lasting from June 3 to 6, the Japanese fleet was defeated. In April, 1942, American planes bombed the Japanese mainland, including Tokyo.

In August, 1942, an American-Australian naval task force carried a strong force of American marines into the Solomon Islands; and then, in a series of air and naval battles, the Japanese were decisively defeated and the Japanese advance was halted. In November, 1943, American forces under the command of Admiral Nimitz were able to effect landings in the Gilbert and Marshall Islands, at Tarawa and Kwajalein. In June, 1944, American planes raided Japan from Chinese bases, and in November, 1944, began attacks from Saipan in the Marianas. In March, 1945, American forces occupied Iwo Jima in the Bonin Islands, within fighter range of Japan. In June, Okinawa, in the Ryukyus, south of Japan, fell.

By the fall of 1944, the American advance through the Marianas and the Palaus had prepared the way for two objectives: the freeing of the Philippines and the beginning of the aerial assault on Japan. Then on January 9, 1945, General MacArthur and his men landed on Luzon. The liberation of Manila was completed in February, at which time General MacArthur turned over civil control of the city and the island to President Osmena.

The Fall of Japan. On August 6, 1945, Harry S. Truman, who had become President when Roosevelt died during his fourth term of office in April of that year, ordered the dropping of the first atomic bomb—on Hiroshima. On August 8, Soviet Russia declared war on Japan, having renounced her treaty in the spring, and quickly dispatched Russian armies into Manchuria and Sakhalin. On August 9, the second atomic bomb was dropped—on Nagasaki; and on the following day the Japanese government sued for peace. On September 2, 1945, the formal surrender of Japan took place aboard the battleship *Missouri* in Tokyo Bay.

PART FIFTEEN

Recent History

1946   (Jan. 10) United Nations General Assembly met for the first time, in London

(July 4) Philippine Islands gained independence

(Oct. 1) Twelve Nazi leaders sentenced to death by Nuremberg Tribunal

1947   (Mar. 12) President Truman enunciated Truman Doctrine setting limits to Communist expansion

(June 3) India became independent of British rule; Dominions of India and Pakistan set up

(June 5) Secretary of State George C. Marshall announced Marshall Plan for European recovery

1948   (Jan. 30) Mahatma Gandhi assassinated by a Hindu fanatic in New Delhi

(Apr.) 1) Berlin land blockade started by Soviet military government in East Germany; ended Sept. 30, 1949

(May 14) State of Israel proclaimed in Palestine

1949   (Sept. 23) President Truman announced Russia's first atomic bomb test

1950   (Jan. 26) India became a sovereign republic

1952   (Feb. 6) George VI died; Queen Elizabeth II succeeded to British throne

(July 26) King Farouk of Egypt was deposed

(Nov. 1) U.S. exploded first hydrogen bomb in history

1953   (Mar. 5) Death of Joseph Stalin

(Aug. 12) First Soviet hydrogen bomb exploded

1954   (May 7) French defeated at Dienbienphu, Indo-China

(May 17) Racial segregation in U.S. public schools ruled unconstitutional by Supreme Court

(July 21) Geneva truce signed dividing Indo-China

1955   (May 14) U.S.S.R. and 7 East European satellites signed Warsaw Pact for mutual defense

1956   (July 26) Egypt seized Suez Canal

(Oct. 23-Nov. 4) Hungarian revolt put down by Soviet troops and tanks

1957   (Oct. 4) Space age opened with Soviet launch of Sputnik, first artificial earth satellite

1958	(Mar. 27) Khrushchev became Soviet Premier
	(June 1) De Gaulle became French Premier
	(Oct. 28) Pope John XXIII elected
	(Dec. 21) De Gaulle elected President of French Fifth Republic
1959	(Jan. 1) Fidel Castro assumed power in Cuba
1960	(Nov. 8) John F. Kennedy elected U.S. President
1961	(Aug. 12-13) Berlin wall erected by East Germany
1962	(July 3) Independence of Algeria declared
	(Oct. 11) 21st Ecumenical Council opened in Rome
1963	(Oct. 10) Effective date of nuclear test-ban treaty
	(Nov. 22) Assassination of President Kennedy
1964	(May 27) Indian Prime Minister Nehru died
	(Oct. 15) Khrushchev replaced by Leonid I. Brezhnev as First Secretary of Party Central Committee and Aleksei N. Kosygin as Premier of U.S.S.R.
	(Oct. 16) Communist China exploded its first nuclear bomb
	(Nov. 3) Lyndon B. Johnson elected U.S. President
1967	(Apr. 21) Military coup in Greece installed dictatorship
	(June 10) Israel won Six-Day War against Arabs
1968	(Apr. 4) Martin Luther King murdered in Memphis, Tenn.
	(May 10) Vietnam peace talks began in Paris
	(June 5) Robert Kennedy fatally shot in Los Angeles while celebrating presidential primary victories
	(Nov. 5) Richard M. Nixon elected U.S. President
1969	(May 21) Warren E. Burger succeeded Earl Warren as Chief Justice of U.S. Supreme Court
	(July 20) Neil A. Armstrong and Edwin E. Aldrin were first men to land on the moon
	(Nov. 17) Preliminary Strategic Arms Limitation Talks began in Helsinki between U.S. and U.S.S.R.
1970	(Sept. 28) Nasser died and was succeeded Oct. 14 by Anwar Sadat as President of Egypt
1971	(Oct. 28) House of Commons voted approval of British entry into Common Market
	(Nov. 15) Communist China admitted to U.N.
1972	(Jan. 1) Kurt Waldheim of Austria succeeded U Thant as Secretary General of U.N.
	(Feb. 21-28) President Nixon visited Communist China
	(May 22-29) President Nixon visited U.S.S.R.
	(Nov. 7) Richard M. Nixon re-elected U.S. President

66 AFTERMATH OF
THE SECOND WORLD WAR

The speed of transportation by airplane and of communication by radio and television have made events in all parts of the globe the immediate concern of everyone. It is no longer possible to trace the history of nations in isolation. Important events have international significance, and the balance of power as it exists in the world today is nothing less than global. Advances in science, ushering in the "Atomic Age," along with many advantages to life, have nevertheless made global destruction a very real possibility. As opposed to this development, the United Nations makes available an international organization to deal with problems arising between nations or involving the peace and progress of the world as a whole.

At the conclusion of the hostilities in 1945, the United States found itself in a position of world leadership, with responsibilities it had not sought, and which the people accepted with some reluctance yet with recognition that this larger role in international affairs was inescapable. Enabled by natural resources and industrial productivity to assist the nations which had been most scarred by the war, the American government had at the same time to formulate policies of broad international scope for world reconstruction.

Formation and Early Years of the United Nations. The name "United Nations," suggested by President Roosevelt, was first applied during the war to the nations joined together against the Axis. That name was carried over to the new international organization for peace, established during the war to handle postwar problems. In order to meet responsibilities of world-wide scope, several subsidiary agencies of the United Nations were founded in advance of the establishment of the peace organization itself. For example, the United Nations Relief and Rehabilitation Administration (UNRRA) was a three-year program, set up in 1943, to help alleviate the war-caused hardships of millions of people.

The first drafting of proposals to be incorporated in the charter of the United Nations was accomplished in a meeting of representatives of the allied nations at Dumbarton Oaks, near Washington, D.C., in 1944. At Yalta in February, 1945, it was agreed that an international conference was to be held to write the active charter of the organization in the spring of that year. This conference met at San Francisco from April through June, 1945, completing and adopting the charter which provided for an organization with two main bodies: the General Assembly and the Security Council. On October 24, 1945, with ratification of the charter by the twenty-ninth member, the United Nations came into existence.

The General Assembly is composed of representatives of all member nations. The initial meeting was conducted in London in 1946. At first the members were the Allied nations and certain nations which were neutral during the Second World War. In recent years many other nations have been admitted, thus approaching the new goal of universal representation. At the outset, the Security Council had five permanent members—the United States, the United Kingdom, the U.S.S.R., France, and Nationalist China—and six non-permanent members chosen by the General Assembly to serve for two-year periods each. The function of the General Assembly is primarily deliberative, while the Security Council has authority to take definite action, subject, however, to unanimity among the permanent members. The General Assembly has acquired increased power to act in emergencies.

Postwar Demobilization and Disarmament. In the summer of 1947, despite the rapid demobilization of large forces, the United States, Great Britain, and the Soviet Union still had great numbers of soldiers stationed outside their own frontiers. There were more than 2,000,000 Soviet troops in Germany, Finland, Austria, Hungary, Poland, Yugoslavia, Korea, and Manchuria. Nearly 750,000 British troops remained in Germany, Austria, Italy, Greece, Palestine, Iraq, the Suez Canal

Zone, Trans-Jordan, Libya, Eritrea, Italian Somaliland, Egypt, and in the Dutch colonies of Java and Sumatra. Some 650,000 United States troops were located in Germany, Austria, Italy, China, Korea, Japan, the Philippines, Pacific islands, and in scattered air bases, weather stations, and anchorages. Inevitably, the presence of occupation forces gave an international significance to local political issues, with accompanying international friction and rivalry.

To ease this international tension, the United Nations tackled the delicate problem of disarmament, and in December, 1946, the General Assembly called upon all nations to declare their military strength and to permit inspection of weapons of war. In June, 1947, the United States notified the United Nations Atomic Energy Commission that it was willing to destroy its stock of atomic bombs or to surrender them along with the secret of their manufacture to international control, but conditioned this surrender upon the establishment of an effective system of inspection and control of the manufacture and use of atomic weapons throughout the world. This proposal placed the matter in the hands of the Security Council, where Russia opposed the provision relating to inspection and control and insisted that the question of atomic weapons was part of the over-all program of disarmament.

Problems of the Peace Treaties. The series of international conferences, culminating in the one at Potsdam in July and August, 1945, had made plans for the establishment of responsible representative governments in the defeated and also in the liberated countries. However, Germany, Austria, and Korea were occupied by more than one army of the Allies; and the necessary friendly cooperation among the administrative representatives of the various occupying countries proved difficult between the Western powers and Russia. The drawing up of the peace treaties was assigned to the Council of Foreign Ministers, which held nearly two hundred meetings in London, Moscow, Paris, and New York. The actual drafting of treaties began in December, 1946.

Apart from the peace treaties, there was the question of

fixing responsibility for the crimes against humanity committed by the Nazis—the inhuman torture and murder of countless helpless men, women, and children. Agreements reached at the Yalta and Potsdam conferences had introduced a new principle into international law, namely, that of the personal responsibility and accountability of individuals who were guilty of criminal acts in the provocation and conduct of war and in the treatment of civilian populations. In September, 1945, a list of war criminals was published. The chief War Crimes Trials were held in Nuremberg, where an international court tried the principal Nazi leaders (with the exception of Hitler, who, according to the best evidence available, had committed suicide in Berlin during the last days of the war). Sentence was pronounced in October, 1946; ten condemned Nazi leaders were hanged (an eleventh committed suicide). In 1961 the matter of war crimes resulted in the trial by Israel of Adolf Eichmann, one of those in charge of Hitler's program for exterminating Jews; and even more recently, especially in 1964, German courts have been trying other Nazi war criminals.

Throughout these years, the drafting of peace treaties acceptable to both the West and the Soviet Union proved exceedingly difficult; and, in consequence, the actual establishment and recognition of postwar boundaries remained largely in abeyance. Germany and Austria continued to be occupied, and for this purpose zones were established respectively under American, British, French, and Russian administration; Berlin and Vienna were both placed under joint control. Collaboration increased among the three Western powers, and particularly in Germany the Russian zone became markedly separate.

The Iron Curtain. At the time the United States entered the Second World War, all the nations that were fighting against the Axis signed an agreement embodying the principles of the Atlantic Charter as a basis for the establishment of representative governments in the countries whose liberation was one of the goals of Allied victory. Russia found herself at war with Nazi Germany only because Hitler felt himself strong enough to turn on his erstwhile ally. The surrender of Japan on September 2, 1945, ended the fellowship in arms between the Western powers and Russia. As early as the meetings of the Council of Foreign Ministers, the division between Russia and the Western allies became quite apparent. When the war was over, Russia had insisted that for her own protection she must be surrounded by "friendly" neighbors—by which, it soon became clear, she meant Communist-dominated satellite states; and it was not long before an "iron curtain" (Churchill's expression) separated Russia and the neighboring states of Eastern Europe from the Western countries. The cleavage between Eastern and Western Europe in one way or another involved all the European countries.

Most of the Eastern and Central European states were rapidly brought within the Communist orbit. Of the Balkan countries, Rumania, Bulgaria, Albania, and Yugoslavia, and in Central Europe, Poland, Hungary, and later, Czechoslovakia, established governments which looked to the Soviet Union for guidance.

Postwar Europe. In Western Europe the leadership remained with Britain and France, though the extent of their influence was limited by the urgency of their effort toward reorganizing and stabilizing the home economy. Belgium, the Netherlands, and Luxembourg, describing themselves as the Benelux countries, entered into an economic pact and associated themselves in various agreements with Britain and France. Italy, overthrowing the monarchy, established itself as a republic; and its government aligned itself with the United States and the Western powers. Of the Scandinavian countries, Norway, Sweden, and Denmark pursued largely independent courses, but Finland, because of its more easterly location, was forced to make certain geographical concessions to Russia. Portugal looked to the Western powers; but Spain under Franco's fascist rule was largely isolated politically.

Confronted by the steadily widening sphere of Communist influence, American foreign policy began to shape itself toward the support of countries threatened by Communist expansion. This policy, announced by President Truman in 1947, was referred to as the Truman Doctrine, and its first expression was the support of the Greek government by financial aid, the delivery of foodstuffs and other necessities of life, and military advice when needed. This policy was developed further in the Marshall Plan for economic aid to the nations of Western Europe, outlined by Secretary of State George C. Marshall and made a definite program by Congress.

Postwar Asia, Africa, and the Pacific. At their Cairo Conference, Generalissimo Chiang Kai-shek, Prime Minister Churchill, and President Roosevelt had issued a declaration on December 1, 1943, which announced their agreement with respect to the settlement in the Far East to be made at the conclusion of the war with Japan. In accordance with these plans, when peace was made, all territories taken by Japan from China were restored to the Republic. Korea was recognized as independent, but divided into two occupation zones, one American (South Korea) and one Russian (North Korea); as in the case of liberated European areas, this division became the basis of conflict between the Soviet Union and the West.

China was not a unified state at the end of the war, and Chiang Kai-shek could not speak for the entire Chinese people. The kind of aid the West was able to furnish Chiang benefited the commercial and industrial regions along the Chinese coast and did not relieve the distress of the great mass of inland China which was predominantly agrarian. Russia, next-door neighbor to China on the landward side, took full advantage of this situation. With Soviet support and guidance, the Chinese Communists, led by Mao Tse-tung and Chou En-lai, rapidly extended their hold on China.

One of the major developments in Asia after the war was freedom for India. This took the form of a division of the whole Indian subcontinent into two independent countries, one predominantly Hindu, and the other largely Moslem, each state becoming a self-governing member of the British Commonwealth of Nations. The Hindu republic took the name

India; the Moslem state, the name Pakistan. The area of Kashmir has remained a subject of dispute between the two nations.

The continent of Africa was not greatly affected immediately as a result of the Second World War, the only specific question being the disposition of former Italian colonies. French influence in North Africa diminished in the postwar period. By 1956 two of the three former French protectorates, Morocco and Tunisia, had achieved their independence with relative smoothness.

In the Pacific, a significant postwar trend was exemplified early in the achievement of complete independence by the Philippines in 1946, in fulfillment of the promise made in 1934 by the United States. A United Nations trusteeship was given to the United States for large groups of islands captured from the Japanese, most of which had been Japanese mandates rather than possessions. These included the Marshalls, the Marianas, and the Carolines.

A focal point of world attention during the postwar years was Palestine, at the crossroads between East and West. At the end of the First World War, Palestine had been designated a British mandate, with a view to the establishment of a Jewish national home, at the same time providing due consideration for the Arab part of the population. Failing in attempts to reconcile the conflicting claims of these two groups, Britain after World War II turned the question over to the United Nations and announced her surrender of the mandate. In November, 1947 the United Nations proposed the division of Palestine into separate Jewish and Arab states. The neighboring Arab countries—Egypt, Syria, Lebanon, Iraq, Saudi Arabia, Yemen, and Trans-Jordan—opposed this partition. Nevertheless, in May, 1948, basing their action on the partition resolution, the Jews of Palestine established their areas as the independent state of Israel, and the new state was officially recognized by the great powers and the other countries of the world. Israel was immediately attacked by neighboring Arab states. Intervention by the United Nations resulted in a truce, followed by the establishment of armistice lines and the signing of armistices between Israel and individual Arab states. In May, 1949 Israel was admitted to the United Nations.

67   THE FIFTIES AND EARLY SIXTIES

The central political reality continued into the early 1960's to be the split between East and West, with the tensions, aggravations, and dangers consequent upon this pervasive division. The emergence of new nations, whether in Asia or Africa, was not merely the struggle of nationalism against colonialism, but became an event in this total competition of the great power blocs. Even the developments in science and the pursuit of excellence in education could be viewed to a degree as battles in the cold war. The obvious utility of science for the technology of war cannot be gainsaid, but the scientific enterprise, including the adventure of space exploration, is in itself among man's unparalleled achievements, and rich in possibilities for peace. Automation, like science upon which it rests, can be regarded either as a beneficent agent or an instrument of doom. It is certain that automation, in its wholesale displacement of men, will involve the sufferings of many; it is equally certain that future history will be the history of men freed from the burden of much oppressive labor. Beyond the immediate political problems, man must face the problems of the rational distribution of wealth, of work and leisure, and of human populations themselves.

Formation of NATO. Early in April, 1949, a new step in American foreign policy was taken when the North Atlantic Security Treaty, embracing twelve countries of Western Europe and North America, was signed by their foreign ministers in Washington. The scarcely disguised aggressiveness of Russian policy had made it necessary for the European states outside the Iron Curtain to unite their strengths against the possibility of open Russian aggression.

The Atlantic Pact nations (NATO, North Atlantic Treaty Organization) pointed out that the NATO Pact was defensive in purpose and existed within the framework of the United Nations. During 1950, 1951, and 1952, the defensive preparations of NATO were credited with preventing a Russian attack upon Western Europe.

The twelve original NATO countries were the United States, Canada, Great Britain, France, Italy, Denmark, Norway, Belgium, the Netherlands, Luxembourg, Portugal, and Iceland. Subsequently joining NATO were Turkey, Greece, and West Germany.

The Korean War. Korea, as we have seen, was divided into two political entities, South Korea, essentially traditionalist, and North Korea, Communist. In June, 1950, the North Korean army invaded South Korea. The United States promptly brought the crisis to the attention of the United Nations Security Council. The Russians had previously "walked out" of the Council meeting, and the members present voted in favor of military aid to the South Koreans. The United States immediately sent arms and men to Korea, and other members sent smaller forces. Sixteen nations were represented in the United Nations force, which succeeded in repelling the invaders and in moving victoriously far into North Korea, but with tragic loss of American lives and of those of other United Nations troops.

In November, 1950, however, 200,000 Chinese Communist "volunteers" intervened on the side of the North Koreans, and compelled the United Nations armies to retreat into South Korea. During 1951, United Nations counteroffensives drove the invaders north again. Negotiations ensued for a ceasefire which was delayed many months in 1951 and 1952 as representatives of both sides argued about precise terms of an armistice. Finally, in July, 1953, at Panmunjom, near the border between North and South, the Korean armistice was signed between the Communists (North Korean and Chinese) and the United Nations forces. The fighting ceased, but the political separation of North Korea from South Korea continued.

Southeast Asia. For centuries the Netherlands had cultivated the resources and controlled the commerce of what was known then as the Dutch East Indies and is now Indonesia. During the Second World War the islands of this rich empire had fallen to the Japanese, whose propaganda slogan "Asia for the Asians" undoubtedly stirred Indonesian nationalism. The Dutch, who had fought the Japanese vigorously, were unwilling to surrender their claim to their former empire in the period after the war. In the face of Indonesian resistance to the restoration of colonial status, the Netherlands eventually (in 1949) relinquished its hold upon all its territory in the Indies except the western half of New Guinea. In 1963, under UN auspices, this area was also assigned to Indonesia.

As early as 1946 guerrilla fighting had broken out in the region of Southeast Asia known as Indo-China, long under French rule. The principal area of conflict was in Vietnam, the largest Indo-Chinese state. The Vietminh forces, which were Communist, fought local battles for seven and a half years against the French and against the democratic Vietnamese. Finally, France's position was so jeopardized that an international conference of 19 European and Asian nations including France, Britain, and Communist China was held at Geneva, from April 23 to July 21, 1954. Under the agreement reached there, France withdrew from Indo-China; Vietnam was divided (like Korea) into Communist North Vietnam and democratic South Vietnam. Full independence of the other two Indo-Chinese states—Laos and Cambodia—was recognized.

After the partition, North Vietnam, with extensive aid from China and Russia, began a program of rapid reconstruction and expansion of its economy. Soon after this, North Vietnam became involved in aggressive activities against Laos and increasingly against South Vietnam, and gave aid to guerrillas active in those countries.

As Russian aggression became pronounced in Asia, a treaty was signed by eight pro-Western countries in September, 1954. (The signatory nations were the United States, Great Britain, France, Australia, New Zealand, the Philippines, Pakistan, and Thailand.) In addition to mutual protection of member countries, the pact pledged its members' protection to non-member countries of Southeast Asia should their peace or freedom be threatened. The United States specifically interpreted this pledge of help to non-member nations as being relevant only to Communist aggression, an interpretation which was to involve the United States in the affairs of Laos several years later. The group of signing nations became known as SEATO (the Southeast Asia Treaty Organization).

In August, 1960, a military coup forced the resignation of the pro-Western government of Laos, and a revised "neutralist" government was formed. Fighting broke out between the Laotian army and the Pathet Lao, pro-Communist guerrillas. Both the U.S.S.R. and the SEATO countries became involved in the conflict, but the reluctance of both power blocs to allow the Laotian situation to reach the crisis proportions of another Korea led to continuing efforts for a political, rather than a military, settlement.

In 1954 South Vietnam withdrew from the French Union. A republic was proclaimed in October, 1955, headed by President Ngo Dinh Diem, whose government became, in subsequent years, increasingly authoritarian. In 1963, during a period of great internal disorder and unrest, the government of Ngo Dinh Diem was overthrown. In the years following, the political situation became highly unstable; and military problems resulting from Viet Cong (South Vietnamese Communist) guerrilla attacks threatening the security of South Vietnam became so acute that American aid to the country necessarily included air and naval support, aimed at assuring the independence of the country and its participation in a stable development throughout southeast Asia. Later, when North Vietnam invaded South Vietnam, American forces aided South Vietnam in its war against the North Vietnamese and Viet Cong.

Malaya, previously under the British, had been conquered by the Japanese in 1942. After the war, the country experienced over a decade of Communist insurrection as the Chinese, expanding their influence in Southeast Asia, attempted to add Malaya to the Communist empire. In the postwar period Malaya underwent various forms of affiliation with Britain, which was reluctant to grant Malaya its freedom until the guerrillas were subdued. In 1955 the British arranged for free elections and for the formation of a native government. In 1957 the Malay states, plus neighboring Penang and Malacca, gained independence as the Federation of Malaya, which in 1963, with the addition of Singapore, Sabah (formerly British North Borneo), and Sarawak, was renamed Malaysia. Singapore, with strong regional traditions of its own and a large population of ethnic Chinese, left Malaysia in 1965. Malaysian influence on Borneo, most of which is controlled by Indonesia, caused Indonesian guerrilla raids in 1963-1965, but by 1967, after Indonesian President Sukarno's fall from power, normal relations were restored between Indonesia and Malaysia.

Other Far Eastern Matters. The postwar political and economic recovery of Japan commenced slowly. In 1946 a new constitution was adopted and the Emperor renounced his claim of divinity. In 1949 General MacArthur loosened the military bonds on the country, allowing greater local autonomy. In September, 1951, at San Francisco, Japan and forty-eight of those nations with which it had been at war signed a treaty of peace. And in April, 1952, Japan regained sovereignty, affiliating itself to a considerable extent with the Western powers. In 1954 Japan and the United States entered into a bilateral defense agreement. In the fifties, great economic recovery took place, and by the end of the decade Japan had achieved world leadership in cotton textile exports and shipbuilding.

In September, 1949, the Chinese Communists proclaimed the existence of the People's Republic of China under the leadership of Mao Tse-tung, with Chou En-lai as premier and foreign minister. By 1950 Mao was in possession of most of the Chinese mainland, and Chiang and his Nationalists had taken refuge on the island of Taiwan (Formosa). During the early 1950's an almost constant danger of open conflict in the Formosa area threatened to involve the United States, which had given much support to the Nationalists. Gradually, a condition resembling a cease-fire evolved there, with no recognition of Communist China by the United States, and without admitting it to the United Nations. With China's growing power there came in the 1960's a greater independence of the Soviet Union, which was manifested in open ideological conflict between them, with the Chinese at the time frequently more anti-Western than the Russians.

In Tibet, the disputed succession of the tenth Panchen Lama gave the Chinese an excuse to invade that country in October, 1950. While certain old treaties and agreements seemed to support China's claims on Tibet, the invasion was largely another exercise of raw power. In May, 1951, Tibet became an autonomous national territory of China. Extensive land reform and drastic curtailment of the monastic orders gave rise to a rebellion in 1959 which was quickly suppressed by Chinese troops.

During the fifties and later, India played an important role in Asian matters and also became influential in other parts of the world. India manifested a disposition to remain "uncommitted" to either the Western powers or the Soviet Union and Communist China, and therefore could to some extent command the attention of both groups. However, upon the sudden invasion of Indian territory by Communist Chinese armies in 1962, Prime Minister Nehru appealed to the Western powers for military and financial aid, necessitating India's reappraisal of its recent course. Nehru died in 1964, and his successor, Shastri, in 1966. Thereupon, Nehru's daughter, Mrs. Indira Gandhi, became Prime Minister.

Developments in Europe. In the years after the Second World War there was evidence that the Western European nations desired to work toward some form of European unity. Various organizations involving several Western European states evolved in the period between the first idea of the Benelux customs union and the European Economic Community (EEC) or Common Market. The Common Market was an immediate offspring of the European Coal and Steel

Community (ECSC), whose basic intention of building a European economic order it sought to carry out. The EEC treaty was signed in March, 1957, by France, West Germany, Italy, and the Benelux countries. The treaty envisions the gradual removal of tariffs and quantitative restrictions on all commodities from member nations, the development of a single tariff schedule for countries outside the community, coordination of exchange policies, and freedom of movement for workers. Unlike the Common Market, which is primarily economic, the Council of Europe, originating in 1949, was intended to promote political unity. Meeting in Strasbourg, France, it has dealt with social, cultural, and humanitarian issues.

The various efforts to assist and to hasten European economic recovery were quite successful. For example, in ECSC nations, iron and steel production rose by 75 percent and industrial production by 58 percent between 1952 and 1960.

Great Britain, remembering its sovereignty, however abstract, and looking to the Commonwealth in which it still placed great trust, was at first reluctant to join the "Inner Six" of the Common Market. Later the Six were for a time no longer eager to include Britain. In 1960 Britain and six other countries (the "Outer Seven": Britain, Austria, Denmark, Norway, Portugal, Sweden, and Switzerland) formed the European Free Trade Association with more modest aims than those of the Common Market.

The death of Stalin in 1953 did not immediately produce any evident change in the ambitions of the Soviet Union. However, in 1956 the world was startled and reassured by Party Secretary Nikita S. Khrushchev's denunciation of Stalin's autocratic rule. And when Khrushchev became Premier in 1958, the cold war lessened. To ease international tensions, President Eisenhower (inaugurated in January, 1953) met with Prime Minister Eden of Britain, Premier Faure of France, and Marshal Bulganin in July, 1955, at a Summit Conference in Geneva, Switzerland. This important effort stressed the universal recognition of the catastrophic destructiveness which the development of the hydrogen bomb had made possible, and the consequent inescapable need for the prevention of war. The successful launching of the Soviet artificial satellite Sputnik in 1957 continued the East-West competition in another area. Cold war tensions were stirred in the spring of 1960 by revelations of espionage by both the United States and Russia. In 1961 the Soviet Union resumed nuclear tests, but in October, 1963, as a result of the urgent efforts of President Kennedy, an international agreement banning further tests of nuclear weapons in the atmosphere was signed by the United States, the Soviet Union, and Great Britain; and later by over a hundred other nations. The replacement of Khrushchev in October, 1964 by Leonid I. Brezhnev and Aleksei N. Kosygin left to the new leaders the task of healing the breach between the Soviet Union and Communist China, which in the same month exploded its first nuclear device. It appeared that the Soviet Union would continue the policy which Khrushchev had described as peaceful coexistence with the West.

Most of the countries of Central and Eastern Europe (with the important exception of Austria) had become satellites of the Soviet Union, with little or no means of expressing their natural will in a democratic way. The first such nation to separate itself from Russian domination was Yugoslavia under Marshal Tito in the late 1940's. In the fall of 1956, signs of unrest among some of the satellite countries appeared. Poland began to assert its right to greater separation from Moscow's control. And a most powerful drive for freedom appeared in Hungary, where a popular uprising against Soviet domination was put down by the intervention of Russian troops. At about the same time, the resistance to Soviet control was seen to some extent in other satellite countries as well. Thus Rumania has developed considerable local independence in its policies.

In 1955 Germany's sovereignty was established in West Germany, though East Germany continued to be under Soviet control. Relations between West and East Germany became increasingly strained. Experiencing economic deprivation, East

German workers had in 1953 rioted and been subdued by Soviet troops. While East German poverty continued, West Germany, enjoying a remarkable prosperity, strengthened its ties with Western Europe as a member of NATO and the Common Market. In 1961 the Soviets constructed a wall of barbed wire and stone which sealed off the free city of Berlin from the Soviet sector and provided a potent symbol of a people's entrapment. Some relaxation of tension occurred when, beginning in the Christmas of 1963, West Berliners were permitted during holidays to visit relatives in East Berlin.

In June, 1958, following several years of political inactivity and apparent retirement, General Charles de Gaulle returned to prominence as Premier of France, and managed to resolve internal dissension and political unrest. Gaining great popularity, De Gaulle found strong support for his constitution, which extended and strengthened the powers of the executive office, and was elected President of the Fifth Republic of France. During his first few months in office De Gaulle effectively stabilized France's unsettled economy, and brought improved order to domestic governmental affairs. At the same time, he began a vigorous and successful attempt to end the conflict in Algeria, one of the major problems confronting his administration. De Gaulle's foreign policy has sought to increase France's influence in Europe and throughout the world, and although continuing to work within the framework of the NATO alliance in specific situations, his government has preferred considerable independence of action.

Not directly connected with political events in Europe but certain to affect the general temper of the time and of the times to come throughout the world, the Twenty-first Ecumenical Council of the Roman Catholic Church convened at the call of Pope John XXIII in October of 1962. Its hopeful spirit of unity and brotherhood added a stirring new note to the best secular efforts toward world peace and international cooperation. The work of the Council was continued in 1964 under Pope Paul VI.

The Middle East and North Africa. Egypt as early as the end of World War I had sought complete removal of British installations, and in 1954 Britain agreed to withdraw its troops. It was not long after the actual British withdrawal in June, 1956, that it became clear that Egypt, led by Colonel Nasser, was the scene of intense rivalry between the Western allies and the Soviet Union. In other Arab states also, the Russian drive for power in the Mideast was evident. This ambition to push south to the Mediterranean and Indian oceans had been a persistent goal of Russia extending at least as far back as the reign of Peter the Great. Suddenly, Nasser, reacting to the withdrawal of support of the Aswan High Dam project by the United States, Britain, and the International Bank, seized the vital Suez Canal, passing through Egypt, which had long been under international regulation. Further contributing to the unstable situation in the Middle East was the inability of Israel and the Arab states to achieve peace treaties settling their differences. Years of border unrest—economic and strategic blockades, armed raids by Arabs into Israel and by Israelis into Arab territory—reached a crisis when, in the late fall, 1956, Israeli troops crossed the frontier and overran Egypt's Sinai Peninsula. Within two days the British and French attacked the Suez Canal area, seeking to regain the authority there which Nasser had taken from them. The United Nations, strongly supported by the United States, immediately insisted upon the stopping of hostilities and the removal of all troops by the three nations which had attacked Egyptian territory. The use of force as a means of settling disputes was firmly condemned. Both sides submitted to the United Nations' intervention and withdrew their troops as United Nations forces arrived to police the disturbed areas.

In 1958 a new Arab state, the United Arab Republic, was formed, comprising the formerly independent nations of Egypt and Syria. General Nasser became President of the U.A.R., which was joined in a federation agreement by Yemen. This Arab union did not prove to be as stable as Nasser hoped. It dissolved in 1961 when Syria withdrew, and the bond with Yemen was in effect discontinued by civil war there.

Cyprus, which had been a British crown colony since 1925, was long plagued by tension and strife resulting from movements for union of Cyprus with Greece or for partition of the island into Greek and Turkish parts. In 1959, a settlement was finally reached. In 1960 the independence of Cyprus was declared, and it became a member of the United Nations. In 1961 Cyprus joined the British Commonwealth of Nations. However, conflicts between the Greek and Turkish populations of the island broke out again in 1963 and continued in 1964. A United Nations mediator and peace force were able to restrain hostilities, but no definite resolution of the opposing aims was achieved.

Not wholly unrelated to developments in the Middle East was the rise of Arab nationalism in North Africa. Algeria, with a larger European population and a closer identification with France than either Morocco or Tunisia, had since 1954 been the center of the disturbance. De Gaulle, anxious to end the rioting and mob violence that the problem had caused in France as well as Algeria, declared that the policy of self-determination for Algeria was "the only policy worthy of France."

A major stumbling block to achieving a peaceful settlement of the crisis was the division of the rebels into two opposing factions, the Algerian National Liberation Front (FLN) and the Algerian National Movement (MNA), both of which insisted on being consulted exclusively. De Gaulle's position was that the problem could be resolved only after a ceasefire, and that all Algerians, regardless of political affiliation, must have a voice in choosing the form of government that would prevail. In 1961 General de Gaulle made it clear to the Moslem majority, which had sought to solve the issue of Algerian self-determination by force, that they must, within a limited time, come to an arrangement which would also protect the political and economic rights of the European minority, which had lived in Algeria for generations. Early in 1962 an agreement was reached at Evian-les-Bains under which these ends could be achieved. Uncertain of the future, a great many of the Europeans rapidly left for France, where their resettlement was gradually worked out. The agreement, ratified by referenda in both France and Algeria, brought about the independence of Algeria while safeguarding the interests of the Europeans who remained.

Central Africa. In 1914 the West European nations claimed dominion over all of Africa except Liberia and Ethiopia, although the European population throughout most of the African continent constituted only a very small minority. European hegemony largely continued until after the Second World War. However, the probability of national movements for independence in Africa was foreseen by various statesmen, and in many instances colonial governments pursued policies which anticipated and prepared for such an eventuality. When, in the mid-twentieth century, a wave of nationalism swept over Africa, a number of colonies, particularly British ones, found themselves ready to assume the responsibilities of self-government. In 1957 the Gold Coast became independent and, under the name Ghana, was the first purely African self-governing member of the British Commonwealth. In 1950 only four African states were acknowledged to be independent. Ten years later, in the year 1960 alone, sixteen new African countries were admitted to the United Nations.

Following the trend of increasing nationalism among colonial peoples, arrangements were made by Belgian and African leaders for the achievement of independence and self rule by the Belgian Congo. Prior to the establishment of a Congo state, elections were held, after which Patrice Lumumba emerged as the most powerful figure in the Congo. The Republic of the Congo came into being on June 30, 1960, with the radical Lumumba as Premier, the more moderate Joseph Kasavubu as President. Intense civil strife marked the first few days of the republic. There was intertribal fighting, a mutiny of the Congolese army, and attacks by the natives upon "foreign" whites. Katanga province declared its total independence of the other states. With Belgians and Congolese in armed conflict, instability and rivalry among the political factions, and the U.S.S.R. and the NATO countries having sharply divided sympathies, the United Nations sent troops into the Congo to restore order. During this time of chaos, Lumumba was overthrown and, in early 1961, assasinated. Over Russian protests, the delegation of Kasavubu was seated at the United Nations. In September, 1961, while in Africa to seek a cease-fire between U.N. and Katanga forces, Secretary General Dag Hammarskjold was killed in a plane crash. His successor in office was U Thant of Burma.

South Africa. Very special internal problems beset South Africa. For many years the major source of trouble has been *apartheid*—the strict policy of absolute separation of the races militantly championed by the government and detested with equal intensity by the non-white population. This division of the population according to color took rigid form with the passage of laws during the 1920's which limited the opportunities and freedom of non-whites.

In October, 1960, South Africa, which had been a Dominion as the Union of South Africa, voted to become the Republic of South Africa with its own head of state. And at the 1961 Conference of Commonwealth Prime Ministers, Prime Minister Hendrik F. Verwoerd withdrew South Africa from the British Commonwealth. The other prime ministers, while deploring South Africa's racial policies, expressed regret at this move of separation.

Both before and after withdrawal from the Commonwealth, South Africa was the scene of rioting and civil strife arising from *apartheid*. An attempt to discuss the troubles within South Africa by the United Nations brought a denunciation from Prime Minister Verwoerd. The non-white population outnumbers the ruling white population by a ratio of more than three to one, which makes the task of achieving internal peace in South Africa both slow and difficult.

Latin American Developments. Latin America is a source of vast agricultural and mineral riches. The area has provided opportunities for the investment of European and North American capital and skills. The Monroe Doctrine was an early expression of United States interest in Latin American stability and prosperity. Cooperation between the American continents was clearly demonstrated after the Japanese attack on the United States in December, 1941, when a number of Latin American countries immediately declared war on the Axis. Close and neighborly association between the United States and Latin America continued, and found expression in the economic accords providing for beneficial trade in raw materials, in the availability of financial aid and technical skills, and in the interchange of social and cultural activities. The solidarity of the Pan-American nations was confirmed by the Western Hemisphere Defense Treaty, signed in Rio de Janeiro in 1947, and by the Organization of American States, including all the Western Hemisphere nations except Canada, set up in 1948 at Bogota, Colombia.

Accidents of history and geography have conspired to prevent the overwhelming bulk of the population of the Latin American countries from sharing in the riches with which the South American continent is filled. This has resulted in disturbances from time to time coupled with frequent political coups.

Brazil managed to sustain considerable economic progress and industrialization after the Second World War boom in rubber and minerals. There had been a period of relative stability under Getúlio Vargas, President from 1930-1945. His government, essentially a dictatorship, was overthrown and replaced by a democratic government which lasted for six years before Vargas again came to power for a short time. Juscelino Kubitschek was elected President in 1955 and inaugurated the building of Brasília, the new capital of Brazil, along with an extensive program of highway and dam construction. In 1960 the election of a new president and the functioning of the office of president were greatly complicated by a newly constituted parliamentary system. In the national referendum of 1963, the electorate declared in favor of the reinstatement of presidential power. Economic progress through most of the 1960's was hindered by a swift succession of leaders and constitutions.

In Argentina, a "palace revolt" in 1944 brought to power a group of army colonels led by Juan Perón. Perón, in postwar years, was able to establish a popular dictatorship which drew support from the army, from labor unions, from nationalists and reactionaries, and from certain clerical groups. His regime was marked by a totalitarian denial of civil rights and liberties. In 1955, at a time when the economy of Argentina was rapidly deteriorating, Perón, who had already been excommunicated by the Roman Catholic Church, was ousted by a military coup. In 1958 Dr. Arturo Frondizi was elected and attempted to rebuild the shattered economy through an austerity program. He tried also to rid the country of remnants of the Perón regime, but in the 1962 elections the *peronistas* showed great strength. Infuriated at this resurgence, the military arrested Frondizi, and José Maria Guido became President while the real power remained with the military. A general election, the first by proportional representation in the country's history, was held in July, 1963. The victory of Dr. Arturo Illia strengthened the position of the moderates and weakened the forces of former dictator Perón, but it was to be short-lived.

In 1961 President John F. Kennedy announced a program of economic assistance to Latin America known as the Alliance for Progress. This program was designed to aid the individual countries in the solution of economic and social problems. The Inter-American Economic and Social Conference at Punta del Este in August, 1961 formulated a system of capital investment which would bring about a minimum annual increase of 2.5 percent in per capita income.

In Cuba, largest island of the West Indies, a revolutionary movement headed by Fidel Castro overthrew the government of dictator Fulgencio Batista in January, 1959, and assumed power. Promising sweeping economic reforms to help the citizens of his underdeveloped country, Castro was at first hailed as the liberator of the people of Cuba, while the major world powers watched with interest.

It soon became clear, however, that he was closely allied with the policies and ideals of Russia and Red China. By eliminating free elections, silencing the free press, and persecuting political opponents, Fidel Castro revealed his political position. He opposed all United States policies; and in August, 1960, he seized and nationalized numerous United States-owned companies in Cuba.

While committed to a policy of non-intervention in Cuban internal affairs, the United States necessarily felt some sympathy for the anti-Castro factions. The abortive anti-Castro invasion at Cuba's Bay of Pigs in April, 1961, which had in some measure the approval of the United States, caused considerable embarrassment and loss of prestige. Later, however, in the crisis of October, 1962, the forceful stand of President Kennedy, which made the Soviet Union withdraw the offensive nuclear weapons it had supplied to Cuba, constituted a significant victory in the cold war. Still, the presence of a Communist dictatorship so close to the United States remained cause for concern.

Developments in the United States. Outstanding trends of the earlier 1960's in the United States were the increasing role of the federal government in matters relating to the welfare and opportunities of the individual citizen, and the growing concern for civil rights.

During the Eisenhower administration certain projects such as major highway construction received direct federal funds, and sums were made available to the states for use in such fields as housing and schools. In May, 1954, a major blow was struck by the United States Supreme Court against the limiting of civil rights because of prejudice. In a unanimous decision, the Court declared racial segregation in public schools to be unconstitutional. This ruling was aimed at twenty-one states and the District of Columbia, which had separate schools for white and Negro children. The Court's ruling caused much unrest within certain of the states, but firm directives in time gradually brought about increasing compliance.

In January, 1961, John F. Kennedy, a Democrat and senator from Massachusetts, became President. President Kennedy was the youngest man and the first Roman Catholic to be elected to the Presidency. His inaugural address was vigorous, forward-looking, and a notable statement of policy. Calling his program the New Frontier, President Kennedy sought to solve through federal action many of the problems that had also confronted President Eisenhower. The New Frontier called for federal aid to education, health care for older citizens, further conservation of natural resources, help in the field of mental health, a major attack upon poverty, extensive tax relief, the Peace Corps for service abroad, and in foreign affairs strong efforts toward international cooperation. As the new administration progressed, it was clearly recognized that the question of civil rights and integration applied not only to the schools but to the broad moral issue of inequality, and the necessity of new civil rights legislation making explicit many rights such as voting, access to public accommodations, and others which had heretofore been only implied and frequently disregarded, became apparent.

In the field of international relations, two major achievements of the Kennedy administration have been discussed earlier in this chapter: the handling of the Cuban missile crisis and the signing of the nuclear test-ban treaty.

Just when his work was shaping itself, President Kennedy was mortally wounded by an assassin's bullet on November 22, 1963, in Dallas, Texas. Vice President Lyndon B. Johnson of Texas immediately succeeded to the Presidency, making it his purpose to continue the policies of President Kennedy.

In the election of November, 1964, the Republican Barry M. Goldwater, senator from Arizona, who declared himself a conservative in national and international affairs, ran against President Johnson. The election of President Johnson and many Democratic members of Congress by an overwhelming vote indicated the nation's support for a progressive program aimed toward the administration's goal, the Great Society.

The United Nations in the 1960's. The United Nations continued to show capacity for action to preserve and promote peace, and its authority won increasing international recognition, even though certain local problems were dealt with largely by nations immediately affected. Regional associations, which are recognized by the United Nations, sometimes took considerable responsibility, as in the Dominican Republic in 1965, when the Organization of American States, supporting the United States, undertook to settle a threatening internal revolt and the attendant political conflict. The United States continued to give full support to the United Nations as the best present-day agency for international cooperation. The success of the United Nations as an instrument for the establishment of law and order throughout the world may come only through slow steps. But by such slow steps have men advanced from the brutality of primitive existence to the achievements of civilization.

68 THE SIXTIES AND EARLY SEVENTIES

The Changing International Climate. In the 1960's and early 1970's the split between East and West was no longer the focal reality in explaining the rivalries and conflicts of the era. The power balance had undergone important modification. The emergence of Communist China as a major power free entirely of Russian influence showed that world Communism is not a solid bloc.

At the height of the Cold War era, Russia and China each in its own way was engaged in a struggle with the West in bidding for the allegiance of the newly developing nations. Areas such as those in Africa had been colonies of the European powers for a considerable length of time, and had suffered from imperialism's hold on them. Consequently, they were likely to set one major bloc against the other and to weigh the advantages of accepting financial and economic aid, and on occasion, supplies of weapons, from the former imperial and other Western powers, as against offers from the leading Communist nations. It is important to emphasize that the rivalry between the two major ideological groups in relation to the unaligned nations was not merely an attempt to gain political influence over them, but at the same time was a struggle for men's minds and loyalties, which would give permanence and strength to relations with whichever rival power group any previously unaligned nation chose to affiliate itself.

The non-aligned countries included such important nations as India and Indonesia in Asia, the United Arab Republic in the Middle East, the new African states, and some of the countries of Latin America which had needed considerable economic aid over the years. To the extent that these countries do not follow the lead of the great power groups they are sometimes referred to as "the third world." This is not in any sense a formal association, but may express itself in similar stands on specific issues and in their voting in the United Nations.

With the changes which the 1960's brought about, it was no longer desirable or profitable to trade upon the oppositions which still existed between the large power groups. Instead, an accommodation to the group which could offer the most assistance in a given situation seemed the most valuable course. Although many of these nations could conduct themselves in this way, the situation in Vietnam, which had been fraught with danger for several years, became increasingly the scene of relentless warfare. And with North Vietnam seeking arms and aid from both Russia and China, and South Vietnam having the extensive support of the United States, behind the scenes, at least, in this part of the world the confrontation between East and West continued.

The War in Vietnam. The struggle which increased in intensity as the years went by was the warfare between North Vietnam and South Vietnam. The two Vietnams had been declared separate by the treaties at Geneva in 1954, as we have already seen. Coupled with this was the hope that a formula would be found which would make possible a union of the two areas. The United States first became involved when it seemed desirable to offer American guidance and advisors to the military forces of South Vietnam, assuming that this would be sufficient to enable the non-Communist South (with its capital at Saigon) to defend itself from Communist North Vietnam (with Hanoi as its capital). But during President Johnson's administration, the North was making inroads into the territory of the South, and it was decided to have American armed forces participate on the side of South Vietnam. At first only the Air Force and naval craft off the coast were assigned. In August, 1964, a clash between North Vietnamese and United States naval forces in the Gulf of Tonkin led to bombing of the North. Soon thereafter, ground forces joined the action, and these were steadily increased in number until they reached half a million. Australia, South Korea, and Thailand sent regiments to aid the South in the combat. Included in the strategy was the authorization of extensive American and South Vietnamese air attacks on vital military bases and communications centers in North Vietnam.

The North Vietnamese continued, however, to exert strong pressure. And they were able to make use of a trail in neighboring Laos, which permitted their troops to advance from North Vietnam directly into central South Vietnam, bypassing the northern sections of South Vietnam. Laos, which with Vietnam and Cambodia constituted the former French colonial area of Indo-China, was itself divided into non-Communist and Communist regions. The Ho-Chi-Minh trail (named for the president and leader of the people of North Vietnam who died in 1969 at an advanced age) was entirely within the Communist-controlled regions of Laos.

When President Nixon took office in 1969 he expressed his firm intention to find an early and satisfactory conclusion to the war in Vietnam. He began to reduce the number of American troops in the war-torn nation, and he urged the South Vietnamese to take up their own defense.

Hoping thereby to shorten the war, American and South Vietnamese troops made an incursion into neighboring Cambodia, up to that time not involved. The Americans withdrew shortly, and the South Vietnamese remained. Cambodia's government had been headed by Prince Sihanouk, who despite his membership in the royal family of Cambodia had shown sympathetic interest in the political and economic programs of Communism. A conservative local government ousted Sihanouk from power, and he escaped to Peking, hoping to regain his office by working from the capital of mainland China. President Nixon continued his policy of reducing American forces in Vietnam. Meanwhile throughout this period, as also earlier, representatives of the United States and South Vietnam met in Paris with representatives of North Vietnam and the Vietcong (South Vietnamese Communists). These meetings aimed to achieve a political settlement for the seemingly endless conflict. In January, 1973, a cease-fire took place through agreements providing for international observers and setting the guidelines for peace throughout Vietnam.

The Middle East. Another region which for a considerable time has been the scene of unsettled conditions is the Middle East. The uneasy relations between Israel and her Arab neighbors continued, even though the need for replacing the armistice lines by formally negotiated boundaries was generally recognized. During the 1960's a United Nations force had been placed at various points on the temporary boundaries. In 1967 Egypt suddenly asked the U.N. to withdraw all its forces, including those keeping the peace at the vulnerable Straits of Tiran. Immediately following the U.N.'s compliance with Egypt's request, Israel ordered her air force to attack the Egyptian, Syrian, and Jordanian air forces. These were all found on the ground at their military airports and were quickly wiped out. This made it possible for Israel to send ground forces to occupy the whole eastern portion of the Sinai Peninsula right to the Suez Canal; also the western portion of Jordan, leaving the Jordan River as the dividing line; and the Golan Heights of southern Syria which overlook the Sea of Galilee and have made the region subject to Syrian fire. This Israeli military movement completed so swiftly has come to be known as the Six-Day War.

Here, too, some equitable settlement is necessary. The Arabs, especially the Egyptians, ask for the return of all the territory occupied by Israel in 1967. The Israelis point out that the old armistice lines were never intended to constitute national boundaries. They feel that the United Nations resolutions confirm that the old armistice lines must be modified so as to give Israel clearly recognizable and defensible boundaries which will offer to both them and their Arab neighbors the assurance that hostilities will be abandoned, and the hope that they can begin an era of cooperation.

Africa. Many of the newly independent nations in Africa experienced political upheavals. The most bloody and tragic occurred in Nigeria, which from 1967 to 1970 was the scene of civil war. The southeastern area seceded from the country and took the name of Biafra. The other regions refused to recognize this separation, and fought with arms and a food blockade to compel reunion, continuing until they accomplished this in January, 1970. Then they sought to aid their starving opponents by means of a general amnesty.

In the formerly Belgian Congo, also, violence once more erupted when United Nations forces withdrew in 1964. Leftist rebels against the government of Moise Tshombe killed thousands of the foreign mercenaries he had hired to put down the revolt. For a brief period Joseph Kasavubu returned to office, but in 1967 he was succeeded by Joseph D. Mobutu, who took over legislative power from Parliament, quelled another revolt, and in 1970 was elected to a seven-year term. The name of Léopoldville, the capital, was earlier changed to Kinshasa; and later that of the nation was changed from Democratic Republic of Congo to Zaire.

Although by 1970 most of the African countries had some form of self-government, there remained a few outposts of colonialism. Portugal retained Angola, Mozambique, and Portuguese Guinea, countering guerrilla attacks with repressive, white-dominated administrations which were the object of censure by the independent African governments.

The Republic of South Africa came under fire at the United Nations in 1966 for its treatment of the territory of South-West Africa, which had been assigned to it in 1915 as a mandate by the League of Nations. South Africa had never accepted United Nations authority over the mandate. Ethiopia and Liberia accused South Africa of economically exploiting South-West Africa, imposing *apartheid* upon it, and using it for military bases. In 1968 the U.N. General Assembly voted to take over administration of the territory under a new name, Namibia, and lead it to independence. In 1970 the Security Council condemned South Africa for its illegal control of the area; and it appeared that the independence of Namibia would eventually be achieved.

The policy of *apartheid* continued in the Republic of South Africa, even after the assassination of Prime Minister Hendrik F. Verwoerd in 1966 (ironically, by a white fanatic who resented his concessions to the blacks at the expense of the poor whites). He was succeeded by Balthazar J. Vorster.

In 1965 world attention became focused on a comparable situation of "colonialism at home" in Rhodesia. The previous year, when the Federation of Rhodesia and Nyasaland was dissolved and its two northern members were granted independence as Zambia and Malawi, Britain refused to grant independence to the Rhodesia portion until the black majority there were given full representation in the government. Rather than see that this was done, in 1965 Rhodesian Prime Minister Ian Smith unilaterally declared independence from Britain. Britain promptly declared the government illegal and imposed a trade blockade, in which other nations, with the exception of Portugal and South Africa, concurred. Despite this, the Smith government and the Rhodesian economy survived, and in 1970 the rebel nation declared itself the Republic of Rhodesia and severed its last official ties with Britain. Britain continued to seek a compromise, however, and talks in the early 1970's did seem to be developing some sort of acceptable plan for the gradual enfranchisement of black Rhodesians.

Pakistan and India. During the fall of 1971 India and Pakistan found themselves at war with one another with very little warning. The principal cause of conflict was the lack of agreement between West Pakistan and East Pakistan on the claim of East Pakistan to regional autonomy, to lead in time to independence. The two portions of Pakistan—West and East— were widely separated from each other by a broad stretch of India. As we have seen, Pakistan was formed in the late 1940's from the predominantly Moslem sections of India. And because the Moslem population was centered partly in the West and partly in the East, the new state occupied these two regions. The Western part was much the larger, and the Eastern part resented its domination. East Pakistan was populated largely by Bengalis. When the leader of the Bengalis, Sheik Mujibur Rahman, was imprisoned in West Pakistan, the East Pakistanis decided to fight to free their leader and gain independence for their land. India found all her sympathies with the East Pakistanis and sent troops to assist them and to oppose the forces of West Pakistan. The outcome of the conflict was the freeing by West Pakistan of Mujibur Rahman and his return to East Pakistan as the prime minister of that region, which declared itself independent and chose the name of Bangladesh, reflecting the Bengali majority, although there were non-Bengali and even non-Moslem minorities within the relatively small state.

China. When the United Nations was formed, the seat allocated to China was assigned to the Chinese Nationalists, who had been driven off the mainland to the island of Taiwan. Most of China's vast population, however, lived on the mainland. In the fall of 1949 mainland China designated itself the People's Republic of China, and proclaimed its dedication to Communism. During these early years the policies of Communist China seemed to be closely coordinated with those of Russia. This became particularly apparent in North Korea during the Korean War. Cooperation between the two vast countries was less evident in North Vietnam during the war in Vietnam. Although they undoubtedly had many common interests, they had grown increasingly independent of one another.

In the years following 1949, Communist China showed only a limited interest in representation in the United Nations, turning its energies instead to the solution of domestic problems. But in 1971 mainland China indicated a desire to join, on condition that it would be recognized as the sole representative of the Chinese people, and that the Nationalist Chinese on Taiwan would give up whatever U.N. seats and posts they had been holding. The United States, changing its long-held position of opposition to the Communist Chinese, decided that the time had come to welcome mainland China into the U.N.; but the American position was at the same time to arrive at a formula for permitting Nationalist China to retain some representation. However, a majority of the nations of the world favored the claim of mainland China and accordingly were willing to accept the accompanying need to discontinue the membership of Nationalist China. The vote endorsed this position; and Communist China became the official and only representative of China in the United Nations.

Not long after this international action, President Nixon decided to increase contacts between the United States and mainland China. Finding the Chinese cooperative, he visited Peking in February, 1972.

Latin America. The political situation in the countries of South America and Central America has been fairly quiet in the late 1960's and early 1970's. However, a guerrilla movement developed in Bolivia with fighting led by Che Guevara as chief advisor, who evidently sought to introduce into Bolivia concepts of government such as the Communist policies which were being practiced in his native Cuba. Che Guevara was killed in 1967 by Bolivian government troops, and the guerrilla activity subsided.

Wholly different in mood and method was the attainment of power in Chile by a Communist government led by Dr. Salvador Allende, who was elected President in 1970. By the passage of a constitutional amendment he nationalized the copper mines, providing compensation to the owners of the mines. He proceeded further in this manner, thus making possible continued relations with the United States.

Brazil, after a series of governments during the 1960's, found itself at the end of the decade in the hands of military leaders who had virtually stripped congress and local governments of power and instituted imprisonment and torture as a means of dealing with the terrorist movements that flourished from 1968 to 1970. In 1969 a military government under President Emilio G. Medici came to power and finally gained enough stability to make long-needed reforms in the bureaucracy and tax structure. Moreover, though dictatorial in character, it gained considerable popularity from the economic boom which gathered force in the early 1970's, making Brazil's one of the fastest-growing economies in the world.

In Argentina, too, a less repressive government, that of Arturo Illia, was replaced in 1966 by a succession of more dictatorial ones. General Carlos Onganía dissolved congress and political parties and temporarily closed the universities, only to be overthrown in 1970 by another military government which lasted only ten months. A new president, Alejandro A. Lanusse, expressed hope that a non-military, constitutional democracy could soon be restored.

Western Europe. Perhaps the most important development in Europe during the late 1960's and early 1970's was the growth and success of the European Economic Community (Common Market). Between 1958, when it went into effect, and 1970, trade between the "Inner Six"—France, West Germany, Italy, and the Benelux countries—increased over five hundred percent. The abolition of tariff barriers among these countries, plus other steps toward their economic integration, resulted in their unprecedented prosperity. On the other hand, the European Free Trade Association, comprised of the original "Outer Seven" plus Finland and Iceland, who joined later, had more modest goals and enjoyed only a limited success. In 1963, Great Britain, EFTA's principal member, began to seek admission to the Common Market, but for the rest of the decade it met with obstacles both at home and abroad.

At this time, West Germany, still separated from East Germany, was enjoying the most marked prosperity of the EEC countries. In 1963 Konrad Adenauer retired after nearly fifteen years as Chancellor. His immediate successors occupied themselves principally with internal problems while retaining their strong ties with NATO. In 1969, Willy Brandt, widely admired as the Socialist mayor of West Berlin, formed a coalition with the Free Democrats and became Chancellor. Early in his administration he began holding conferences with the East Germans with a view to paving the way to ultimate reunification; and in 1970 he signed a nonaggression treaty with the Soviet Union.

One who opposed the admission of Great Britain to the Common Market was President De Gaulle of France. With the granting of independence to Algeria in 1962 France had given up its last major overseas holding, and it was now ready to focus upon its position as a leader on the European continent. In 1966, in an effort to weaken United States influence in Europe and strengthen that of France, De Gaulle withdrew French forces from NATO, although France retained its membership in the organization. By the strength of his leadership De Gaulle had brought unprecedented stability to postwar France, but in May, 1968, there were student and worker riots which paralyzed the nation. His government weathered this disturbance, but the following year, in April, 1969, when the voters of France did not give him a majority in balloting on constitutional reform, De Gaulle declared that he would not seek reelection for the presidency. He retired to his home in Colombey-les-Deux-Eglises, a small village of eastern France. He died there on November 9, 1970.

He was succeeded by Georges Pompidou, who had been Premier in De Gaulle's cabinet. Pompidou at first adhered closely to De Gaulle's policies, but the tide was turning away from isolation for the Inner Six. With France's attention drawn to internal problems such as the modernizing of industry, Pompidou adopted a more liberal attitude toward the Common Market, and this led to a rapprochement with Great Britain.

Great Britain in the 1960's was no longer an imperial power, and it was failing in its attempts to find a new identity as part of Europe. The result was a stagnant economy. Not only were there difficulties from without in joining the Common Market; Britain had also to cope with its own historically insular position with regard to Europe. Real economic hurdles, moreover, remained to be overcome; for example, EEC membership would raise food prices at home. Nevertheless, the total British economy stood to make great gains. In June, 1970, after almost six years of a Labor government under Harold Wilson, British voters put the Conservative party into power. Edward Heath, who became Prime Minister, had been involved with EEC negotiations since the early 1960's, and his enthusiasm added impetus to Britain's move toward Europe. In May, 1971, Heath and Pompidou ended almost a decade of stalemate by announcing agreement on the terms for Britain's entry into the Common Market, and the following year it became evident that some other EFTA countries would also join.

Northern Ireland. An area of Western Europe that caused world-wide concern commencing in the late 1960's was Northern Ireland, the scene of serious disturbances. The six counties in the north of the province of Ulster had been set apart from the rest of Ireland at the time that the Irish Free State was being formed in 1920-1922, and this division continued when complete independence was achieved by the Irish Republic in 1937. The basis for the separation, and for the establishment of Northern Ireland as a part of the United Kingdom, with representation in Parliament in London, was both political and religious. There has been a Protestant majority in the northern counties since the time when under Elizabeth I large numbers of Scottish Presbyterians were settled there, followed by English Anglicans at the time of Cromwell. Northern Ulster developed as an industrial region, whereas the Republic of Ireland has remained predominantly agrarian.

Today, the inhabitants of Northern Ireland are: about two-thirds Protestants and members of the Unionist party favoring continuing union with Britain; and about one-third Catholics and members of the Nationalist party, which looks to eventual merger with the Republic of Ireland (which has its capital at Dublin). In the early seventies there was much violence between the two factions in Northern Ireland, especially in the cities of Belfast and Londonderry. The provisional Irish Republican Army (affiliated with the I.R.A. of the Republic) has been the principal active opponent of the Protestant forces. The British sent in a limited number of soldiers, hoping thereby to help calm the situation, but actually it created new bitterness. In a later move intended to gain the control needed to make possible an orderly solution, the British government announced the discontinuance for at least a year of the regional Parliament of Northern Ireland (Stormont, just out of Belfast); and put into effect the substitution of direct rule from London, under a representative especially chosen for this post and designated a member of the British cabinet. This is clearly a temporary measure, but it won the approval of the government of the Irish Republic, and it was hoped that it would eventually prove helpful in bringing an end to the hostility and violence, and achieve some form of cooperation between the opposed factions.

The Soviet Union and Eastern Europe. By the 1970's Party General Secretary Leonid I. Brezhnev appeared to be emerging as the principal leader in the Soviet Union; with Kosygin demoted to third place at the Communist Party Congress of 1971. In many ways in the late sixties and early seventies the Soviets seemed to hew to their old line. Some of the intellectuals who pressed for more freedom to dissent were arrested. And world attention noted that the Jews living in Russia were harassed and were prevented from leaving the country. In 1971 matters were eased somewhat when several thousand were permitted to emigrate to Israel.

In the Middle East, Russia continued to court Arab favor, supplying Egypt with arms after the 1967 defeat by Israel. In 1971 Russia signed a fifteen-year friendship treaty with Egypt, pledging both military and economic assistance; but by 1972 relations had cooled somewhat.

One of the major developments of the early 1960's had been Russia's growing quarrel with Communist China. This culminated in 1969 in armed clashes on the Soviet-Chinese border. But by the end of 1970 the two countries had reestablished diplomatic relations and signed an accord for increased trade.

In its relations with the West, Russia showed an increasing openness and desire to negotiate. Progress toward disarmament was furthered by the signing, in 1967, of an outer space arms limitation treaty; in 1968, a treaty limiting the spread of nuclear weapons; and, in 1969, by the beginning of the Strategic Arms Limitation Talks in Helsinki. High-level Soviet officials made increasing visits to the West: in 1965 Foreign Minister Gromyko met with Pope Paul VI; in June, 1967, Kosygin, visiting the United States, had valuable conferences with President Johnson at Glassboro, New Jersey; and in the fall of 1971, all three top Russian leaders made visits abroad, with Kosygin visiting Canada and Brezhnev visiting France (where he signed a trade agreement with President Pompidou).

With regard to Eastern Europe, the decade in general witnessed an easing of the restrictive Communist governments in such countries as Poland, Rumania, and Czechoslovakia. But in 1968, when Alexander Dubcek became First Secretary of the Czech Communist Party, he made dramatically liberal reforms. By June of that year, Soviet tanks, reinforced by troops from the other Warsaw Pact countries, had moved into Prague. Dubcek was replaced by a new Party chief who brought Czechoslovakia quickly back into the old-line fold.

A supporter of the Soviets in putting down the liberal Czech government was Walter Ulbricht, then the leader of East Germany. For nearly twenty-five years he had kept his country strictly within the Communist orbit while it bordered the free and economically booming society of West Germany. The presence of a liberal government on his other border to the East in Czechoslovakia may well have seemed a threat. The long Ulbricht era ended in May, 1971, when he was replaced as Party chief by Erich Honecker. East Germany's years of intransigence on the subject of Berlin also ended, opening the way to a treaty between the four great powers the following September directing East and West Germany to reach an agreement regarding free access to that city.

International Cooperation. The goal of truly peaceful relations between nations, each devoting itself to wholly constructive activities, has not yet been reached. Yet there have been numerous events in recent years which provide encouragement.

The United Nations by 1970 had increased its membership to 126 and hoped in not too long a time to have all nations as members. The seats for non-permanent membership in the Security Council were increased from six to ten, thus giving the smaller nations a stronger voice in that powerful body. By its twenty-fifth anniversary, the U.N. could look back on having controlled impending conflicts in many parts of the world. And it had played a valuable part in bringing about the nuclear limitation treaties of the 1960's. Less spectacular but perhaps ultimately more important was the work of its various agencies behind the scenes in attacking the roots of dissension between nations: backwardness and overpopulation, colonialism, racism, and inequality. Notable also was the work of its agencies such as those governing trade and tariffs, international banking, transportation, postage, and telecommunication—agencies which tend to the mechanics of operating as one world.

One of these agencies, the International Monetary Fund, played a part in easing the world monetary troubles which plagued the 1960's. For years, the United States dollar, backed by gold and one of the world's most stable currencies, had been the standard against which all other currencies were valued; but its value came to be eroded by inflation at home and an adverse balance of payments in its dealings abroad. By the spring of 1971, pressures against the unrealistically high official value of the dollar reached the point where world money trading had to be curtailed for a short period while adjustments were worked out. It has become clear that a better system for international exchange will have to be devised in the near future.

The Cold War had resulted in a number of primarily military alliances such as NATO, SEATO, CENTO, ANZUS, and, on the Communist side, the Warsaw Pact. But gathering momentum in the 1960's was a trend toward international alliances with more constructive aims. We have already noted the remarkable success of the Common Market in achieving benefits for all by giving up a measure of national sovereignty. With the addition of the EFTA countries in the early 1970's the Common Market promised to become an economic force second only to the United States, and there were plans for achieving a unified European currency in the 1980's, as well as for unification in foreign and defense policies and in the development of very costly projects such as supersonic aircraft and nuclear deterrents. Though the Common Market took the limelight, a number of other organizations with similar aims were springing up all over the world: OCAM, formed in 1965 of fifteen French-speaking nations in Africa; ASPAC, formed in 1966 of the non-Communist East Asian nations and Australia; and the Central American Common Market and the Latin American Free Trade Association, both formed in 1960.

Retrospect and a Forward Look. Our backward glance into the recent past focused mainly upon the situations which were a threat to world peace and security. The most serious, it is clear, was the Communist challenge to the non-Communist world. Repeated crises through the years, however, demonstrated that the great powers were determined to avoid a major war. Despite the continuing confrontation in Vietnam, it is possible to detect what seem to be evidences of a lessening of tension, fear, and distrust in the relations of what are currently referred to as the superpowers.

And there has been a definite increase in our feelings of world unity. One of the great events of the period, which was eagerly watched on television by people in all parts of the globe, occurred on July 20, 1969. This was man's first landing on the moon, accomplished by two American astronauts, Neil Armstrong and Edwin Aldrin, aided by their fellow crewman, Michael Collins, who circled the moon while his associates were exploring the surface. Back in 1957, when the Soviets launched the first Sputnik to orbit the earth, the space race was a matter of international competition. But with man's first moon landing in 1969 it seemed immaterial which nation had accomplished it: the inhabitants of the world as a whole were proud that human beings had at last realized their dream of reaching the moon. By the 1970's, when plans were made for joint United States-Soviet space ventures, the space race had gone far toward becoming an area of international cooperation.

Menacing as it was, the threat of nuclear annihilation had the effect of making the superpowers realize that all-out war could no longer be the means of settling their differences. They were thus forced into seeking alternative means, and this undoubtedly had much to do with the increasing pace of international cooperation in the second half of the twentieth century.

In the late 1960's, however, just as the great powers were seeming to minimize the threat of sudden nuclear war, the world became aware of a subtler threat to the human race. Projecting population growth and economic expansion into the future, and comparing these statistics with those of the world's remaining natural resources and the earth's ability to absorb the waste products of its highly industrialized economies, many scientists concluded that unless present trends were reversed, the earth was headed for widespread famine, shortages of the resources necessary for our advanced civilization, and—some even went so far as to predict—perhaps, with sufficient disturbances in the ecological balance, the extinction of life upon the planet. The concept of "ecology"—the idea that in nature each part depends ultimately upon the total system—became widely studied and discussed. Surely man will not be slow to draw the analogy between the balance of nature and his own dependence upon the effective functioning of the world as a whole. Reversing the trend toward wasteful exploitation of the earth's resources at first seemed a formidable task, involving great changes in technology and, more important, in our machinery for cooperation. But a beginning was made. In 1972 the United Nations, continuing its policy over the years of helping guide planning and control of world resources and population, conducted its first Conference on the Human Environment, attended by delegates from most of the nations of the world. It is hoped that conferences with this emphasis will have the success that disarmament conferences began to show in the 1960's, and that this new challenge will call forth man's ever-present ingenuity and stimulate him to new growth toward world-wide responsibility.

Hope for the years ahead seems to lie in three developments: a hard-headed, practical approach to the problems of economic interdependence and cooperation; a new moral leadership, worldwide in scope; and the continuation of restrained and reasonable debate in the areas of international relations where the interests of nations or blocs seem to be in conflict with one another. Whether the desired end can be accomplished in spite of rising and falling international, national, and local passions is the problem of the future.

INDEX

Aachen, 149, 150. *See also* Aix-la-
  Chapelle, peace of
Abbasid caliphs, 139, 175
Abd-er-Raman, caliph, 175
Aboukir, battle of, 334
Abu Bekr, 137
Abyssinia, 359, 360, 422. *See also*
  Ethiopia
Acadia, 315
Achaeans, 43
Achaian Confederacy, 90
Acre, siege of, 182
Actium, battle of, 120-23
Act of Succession, 263
Act of Supremacy, 263, 267
Adenauer, Konrad, 473
Adowa, battle of, 349, 360
Adrianople, battle of, 121
Aedil, 76
Aegean civilization, 23-35
Aeolians, 44
Aeschylus, 56
Aetius, 124, 125
Africa: early exploration, 246; coloni-
  zation, 358-61; postwar, 447; new
  nations, 448, 459-60, 465-66
Agincourt, battle of, 201, 233
Agriculture: in ancient Egypt, 7-8;
  in ancient Mesopotamia, 16-17;
  in ancient Greece, 46; medieval,
  317; agricultural revolution, 317-
  18
Ahmose I, king of Egypt, 12
Ahuramazda, 29
Aitolian League, 88, 90
Aix-la-Chapelle, peace of, 327
Akkad, 1, 15, 18
Alais, peace of, 285
Alamanni, 119, 120, 123, 143, 144
Alamannia, 132, 145
Alans, 119, 120
Alaric, 117, 121, 122, 123
Alaska, 365, 378, 379
Albania, 427, 430, 436, 445
Albert, archbishop of Mainz, 256-57,
  269
Albertus Magnus, 198
Albi, 192
Albigensian heresy, 163, 192, 206, 254
Alcibiades, 60, 61, 70
Alcuin of York, 210
Aldrin, Edwin E., 440, 479
Aleppo, 224
Alexander II, king of Macedonia, 68;
  Alexander III, *see* Alexander the
  Great
Alexander II, Pope, 218; Alexander
  V, 198; Alexander VI, 247
Alexander I, czar of Russia, 321, 337,
  341

Alexander the Great, 34, 35, 41, 63-
  67, 109
Alexandria, Egypt, 66, 68-69, 71-72,
  102, 158, 334
Alexandria, Lombardy, siege of, 218
Alexius I, Roman emperor of the
  East, 177, 178, 179; Alexius V,
  184-85
Alfonso IX, king of Leon, 184
Alfred the Great, 161, 195, 210, 211
Algeciras Congress, 349
Algeria: French possession, 359, 363;
  World War II, 434; independence,
  440, 456, 458-59, 474
Ali, caliph, 175
Allenby, general, 388
Allende, Salvador, 472
Alliance for Progress, 384, 462
Alphabets, early, 7, 17, 27, 31, 35, 120
Alphonse of Poitou, 206
Alsace, 290, 305, 307, 356, 359, 399
Alva, duke of, 278
Amboyna, 312
Ambrose, St., 115
Amenemhet, kings of Egypt, 11
Amenhotep III, king of Egypt, 15;
  Amenhotep IV, *see* Ikhnaton
America: Norsemen in, 141; Spanish
  in, 241, 246-49, 272, 277-80 *pas-
  sim*, 311; English in, 279-80, 307,
  313-16, 327; French in, 312, 313,
  314-16, 327; Dutch in, 313. *See
  also names of American coun-
  tries*
American Federation of Labor, 365,
  379
American Revolution, 329, 331, 368-70
Amiens, 205
Amon, 11, 66
Anabaptists, 278
Angevin rulers, 227
Angles (people), 161, 209
Anglia, East, 211
Anglicanism, 294, 298. *See also* Church
  of England; Protestants: in Eng-
  land
Anglo-Saxon Chronicle, 160, 195
Anglo-Saxons, 161, 209
Angola, 469
Anjou, 206, 213
Annam, 361
Anne of Austria, queen of France,
  286
Anne of Cleves, queen of England,
  264
Anshan, 29
Antigonus, 68, 86
Antioch, 69, 102, 158
Antioch, siege of, 179-80
Antiochus III, king of Syria, 87, 88
Antoninus Pius, Roman emperor, 106

Antwerp, 160
Apartheid, 460, 470
Appomattox Court House, Va., 365, 376
Apulia, 163, 173
Aquitaine, 204, 231. *See also* Aquitania
Aquitania, 123, 132, 145, 147, 150, 151, 204. *See also* Aquitaine
Arabs, 132-40 *passim*, 176, 447. *See also* Moslems
Aragon, 290
Aramaic language, 31
Arbela, battle of, 67
Arcadius, Roman emperor of the East, 117, 121
Archangel, Russia, 301
Argentina, 382, 384, 462
Argonne, battle of, 388
Arian heresy, 113-14, 120, 122, 129, 137, 143, 144
Aristides, 57
Aristogiton, 53
Aristotle, 63
Arius, 113
Arizona, 464
Arkwright, Sir Richard, 309, 319
Arles, Kingdom of, 169
Armada, Spanish, 267, 280-81, 294
Armagnac faction, 233, 234
Armenia, 44, 98, 105, 176
Armstrong, Neil A., 440, 479
Arnold of Brescia, 218
Artevelde, Jacob van, 228, 229
Articles of Confederation, 365, 369, 370
Artois, 205, 269, 291
Aryans, 28-29
Ashur, 110
Asoka the Great, king of Magadha, 2, 36
Assurbanipal, king of Assyria, 1
Assyria: dates, 1; and Egypt, 15; and Hebrews, 25, 27; empire collapses, 29; added to Roman Empire, 105
Astrakhan, 225, 226
Atayatis, 111
Athanasius, St., 113, 114
Athaulf, 123
Athens: ancient, 32, 33, 48-63 *passim*; Sulla seizes, 97; Goths seize, 121
Atlantic, battle of the, 426-27
Atlantic Charter, 405, 431, 444
Atomic bomb, 406, 438, 439, 440, 441, 443. *See also* Disarmament: nuclear; Hydrogen bomb
Aton, 15
Attalus III, king of Pergamum, 90
Attica, 48, 49, 50, 60
Attila the Hun, 117, 124, 125, 126, 143, 222
Attlee, Clement, 406
Augsburg, 255
Augsburg, peace of, 281, 287, 289
August III, king of Poland, 325
Augustine, St., 42
Augustine (Austin), St., 159, 209
Augustinian Order, 257

Augustus, Roman emperor, 41, 103-4, 106, 107, 109, 110. *See also* Octavian
Augustus the Strong, king of Poland, 302
Ausculum, battle of, 78
Austerlitz, battle of, 335
Australia: English settle, 362; dominion status, 363; World War I, 395; World War II, 432, 437, 438; SEATO, 450-51, 467, 479
Austria: early, 166; Turks invade, 273; and Louis XIV, 305, 306; Maria Theresa, 327; Joseph II, 328-29; and French Revolution, 331; and Napoleon, 333, 335, 337; nationalist revolts, 340, 342, 346; 19th cent. wars, 349, 352, 353; Adriatic coast and Italy, 359; Triple Alliance, 360; World War I, 389, 391, 397; between wars, 399, 400, 401, 409, 410, 413, 423; World War II, 405-6, 423, 430; postwar, 442, 443, 444, 454. *See also* Holy Roman Empire
Austro-German-Danish War, 349, 353
Austro-Italian War of 1859, 353, 354
Austro-Prussian War of 1866. *See* Seven Weeks' War
Avars, 129, 132, 147
Avignon papacy, 201, 237-38
Azores Islands, 246
Azov, 300, 301, 324
Aztecs, 248

Babylonia, 1, 2, 18-27 *passim*, 30, 67, 74
Babylonian captivity of the papacy, 237-39, 251, 253. *See also* Avignon papacy; Great Schism
Bacon, Francis, 267
Bacon, Roger, 198
Badoglio, marshal, 435
Baghdad, 141, 224, 225, 387
Baghdad caliphate, 139, 175-76
Bahama Islands, 426
Bakewell, Robert, 309, 318
Balboa, Vasco Nuñez de, 247
Baldwin of Flanders, 179, 180
Balearic Islands, 272
Balkans, 222, 251, 273, 391, 396, 427, 436
Balkan War, 349
Baltimore, lord, 314
Banda, 312
Bangladesh, 471
Barras, vicomte de, 332
Basel, council of, 239
Basil, St., 156-57
Basra, 396
Bastille, storming of, 321, 330
Bataan, 405, 432, 433
Batavian Republic, 335
Batista, Fulgencio, 462
Bavaria, 132, 145, 147, 150, 152, 167-68, 217, 219, 327, 413
Bavarian East Mark, 166
Bayonne, 232
Bazaine, general, 356

Beauharnais, Eugene, 335
Bede, the Venerable, 195, 210
Bedford, John of Lancaster, duke of,
  234
Bedouins, 133
Beer Hall Putsch, 413
Belgae, 208
Belgium: and Napoleon, 333; inde-
  pendence, 342; and Napoleon III,
  355; foreign interests, 360, 361;
  World War I, 394; between wars,
  388, 399, 400, 402; World War II,
  405, 425, 428, 430, 436; postwar,
  445, 449, 454, 459-60
Belgrade, 273
Belisarius, 127, 128
Belshazzar, 30
Benedict XI, Pope, 198
Benedict, St., 117, 157
Benelux customs union, 445, 453
Beneventum, 78
Berbers, 124, 129, 138
Berlin, 391, 437, 439, 440, 444, 456,
  477
Bermuda, 314, 426
Bernard, St., 181
Berry, duke of (1778-1820), 342
Bertrand du Guesclin, 232
Bessarabia, 428
Bethlehem, 221
Biafra, 469
Bible, the, 17, 22, 120, 191, 196, 241,
  254
Bill of Rights (English), 299
Black Death, 201, 230-31, 233. See also
  Plague
Blenheim, battle of, 267
Blitzkrieg, 424, 426, 429, 437
Blücher, general, 338
Boeotia, 50
Boers, 359, 361
Boer Wars, 349, 361, 363, 391
Bohemia, 165, 169, 255, 260, 285, 288,
  328, 346. See also Czechoslovakia
Bohemian Revolt, 288, 295
Bohemian War, 255
Bohemund, 179, 180
Boleyn, Anne, 263, 264
Bolivar, Simon, 365, 381, 382
Bolivia, 472
Bologna, 333, 412
Bologna, university of, 163, 194
Bolsheviks, 388, 397, 400, 419, 420
Bombay, 314
Bonaparte, Joseph, 335, 337, 357, 381
Bonaparte, Louis, 335
Bonaparte, Lucien, 334
Bonaparte, Napoleon. See Napoleon
  I Bonaparte, emperor of France
Boniface VIII, Pope, 201, 236-37
Bonifacius, count, 124
Bordeaux, 188, 228, 229, 232, 394
Boris, king of Bulgaria, 141
Boris Godunov, czar of Russia, 267
Borneo, 248, 452
Bosnia, 391
Bossuet, bishop, 304
Boston, Mass., 368, 369
Boston Massacre, 361
Boston Tea Party, 361, 365

Bosworth Field, battle of, 261
Botticelli, Sandro, 252
Bouvines, battle of, 163, 206, 221
Boxer Rebellion, 346, 362, 365
Boyne, battle of the, 267
Braddock, general, 316
Bradley, general, 436
Bramante (architect), 256
Brandenburg, 290, 305, 307
Brandt, Willy, 474
Brasília, 461
Brazil: Portuguese in, 247, 249; Dutch
  in, 288, 313; independence, 357,
  382; and Pan-Americanism, 384;
  postwar, 461-62, 472-73
Bremen, 290, 398
Bretigny, peace of, 231
Bretons, 204
Brezhnev, Leonid I., 440, 476, 477
Britain. See British Empire; Common-
  wealth of Nations; England
Britain, battle of, 405, 426
British Empire: Gibraltar, Minorca,
  307; economy and colonization,
  312; American colonies, 307, 314-
  16, 357, 367, 368-70; India, 316,
  320, 361, 362; and free trade, 348;
  Africa, 359, 361, 459; Australia,
  362; colonial policy, 362-63. See
  also Commonwealth of Nations,
  British
Brittany, 227, 312, 436
Bruening, chancellor, 416
Bruges, 188
Brunei, 452
Brunhilda, queen of Franks, 145
Brusilov offensive, 387
Brutus, 101, 102
Brythons, 208
Buckingham, George Villiers, 1st duke
  of, 295-96
Budapest, 437
Buddhism, 2, 34, 36
Bukovina, 428
Bulgaria: Christianized, 141; and
  Crusaders, 178; World War I,
  388, 396; World War II, 430, 436;
  postwar, 445
Bulgars, 132, 222
Bull Run, battle of, 375
Burger, Warren E., 440
Burgoyne, general, 369
Burgundians, 119, 123, 126, 144, 204
Burgundy, 132, 169, 171
Burgundy, duke of. See Philip the
  Bold, duke of Burgundy
Burma, 361
Burma Road, 427, 432, 437
Byzantine Empire: dates, 117, 163,
  241; Roman Empire divides, 108-
  9, 112-15, 117, 120-21, 124; Jus-
  tinian, 127-32, 137, 139, 222; Is-
  lamic influence, 137-40; opposes
  Charlemagne, 149; Normans at-
  tack provinces, 173; Seljuk Turks
  attack, 176; Crusaders in, 177-79
  passim, 184-85; culture in Russia,
  223, 226; fall of, 251. See also Constantinople
Byzantium, 114, 139

Cabral, Pedro Alvares, 247
Cadiz, 288, 295
Caen, 436
Caesar, Julius, 41, 98-101, 103, 105, 106
Cairo, caliphate of, 139
Cairo Conference, 446
Calais, 230, 231, 233, 235, 276
Calcutta, 314
Calendar: Egyptian, 7; Sumerian, 17; Caesarean reform, 101; Mohammedan, 135
California, 280, 365, 372, 375, 377
Caligula, 104, 106
Callicrates, 59
Callimachus, 48
Calvert, Leonard, 314
Calvin, John, 259-60
Calvinists, 259-60, 267, 281, 282, 287-91 passim, 304. See also Huguenots; Presbyterians
Cambodia, 361, 450, 467-68. See also Indo-China
Cambridge University, 194
Cambyses, emperor of Persia, 2, 30, 31
Cameroons, 361
Campania, 77, 80, 99
Campo Formio, treaty of, 334, 335
Canaanites, 25, 26
Canada: and Seven Years' War, 316; and War of 1812, 371; U.S. boundary settled, 372; dominion status, 363; World War II, 436; postwar, 449, 461. See also America; England in; America: France in
Cannae, battle of, 84
Cannes, 338
Canossa, 163, 174
Canute, See Cnut
Cape Colony, 359. See also South Africa
Capetian rulers, 204-8, 228
Capitalism, industrial, 344
Capitularies, 149
Caporetto campaign, 387, 397
Cappadocia, 96
Carbonari, 351
Carloman, king of France, 146
Carlotta, empress of Mexico, 355
Caroline Islands, 447
Carolingian rulers, 159-60, 163, 167, 203
Carpet baggers, 376
Carranza, Venustiano, 384
Carthage, 1, 28, 41, 51, 74, 75, 78, 79-86, 95, 117
Cartier, Jacques, 312
Cartwright, Edmund, 309, 319-20
Casablanca Conference, 434
Cassiodorus, 157
Cassius, 101, 102
Castro, Fidel, 440, 462, 463
Cathedrals, medieval, 196-98
Catherine of Aragon, queen of England, 263, 264, 272
Catherine de' Medici, 282
Catherine II the Great, czarina, 226, 299, 321, 323-25, 328, 329

Catholic League, 281, 283, 288-89
Catiline, 98
Cato the elder, 85
Caucasian race, 6, 18
Cavour, Camillo Benso, 351, 352, 354
Celebes, 312
Cellini, Benvenuto, 253
Celts, 29, 68, 208
Chaeronea, battle of, 62
Chaldea, 1, 22, 27, 29, 30
Châlons, battle of, 117, 124, 143
Chamberlain, Neville, 424
Chambre ardente, 281
Champagne, France, 207
Champlain, Samuel de, 313
Chancellor, Richard, 279, 309
Chandragupta I, king of India, 2, 35-36
Charlemagne, 141, 146-50, 157, 158, 159, 165, 166, 195, 210, 251, 335
Charles, archduke of Austria, 333
Charles I, king of England, 295-97; Charles II, 267, 297-98, 314
Charles I, king of France, see Charles II the Bald, Holy Roman emperor; Charles II, king of France, see Charles III the Fat, Holy Roman emperor; Charles III the Simple, 141, 161, 203; Charles IV, 228, 229; Charles V, 232; Charles VI, 233, 234; Charles VII, 234, 235; Charles IX, 282, 283; Charles X, 342
Charles I, Holy Roman emperor, see Charlemagne; Charles II the Bald, 151-52; Charles III the Fat, 203; Charles V, 263, 267, 269-75, 277; Charles VI, 326-27
Charles I, king of Spain, see Charles V, Holy Roman emperor; Charles II, 305, 306
Charles XI, king of Sweden, 301; Charles XII, 301-2
Charles Albert, king of Sardinia, 341, 346, 347
Charles Felix, king of Sardinia, 341
Charles Martel, French mayor of the palace, 138, 141, 143, 145, 146
Charleston, S.C., 375
Chartres cathedral, 163
Château Gaillard, battle of, 206
Château-Thierry, battle of, 388, 398
Chaucer, Geoffrey, 241
Cheops. See Khufu, king of Egypt
Cherbourg, 436
Chiang Kai-shek, 427, 432, 437, 446, 452
Children's Crusade, 163, 185
Chile, 382, 384, 472
Ch'in, China, 37, 38, 39
China: ancient, 2, 33, 36-39; and Islam, 138-39, 176; Mongols, 201, 224, 225; Manchus, 267; Western interests in, 243, 349, 361-62; Sino-Japanese War, 362; republic established, 362, after World War I, 401, 422; World War II, 431, 437; occupied, 443; Communist, 440, 446, 449, 450, 451, 452-

China (cont'd)
53, 455, 463, 465, 466, 467, 471-72,
476
Chinese War of 1857-60, 361
Chosroes I, king of Persia, 127, 128
Chou En-lai, 446, 452
Christian IV, king of Denmark, 288,
289
Christianity: early, 42, 110-15; Ireland converted, 117, 209; Franks
converted, 117; Barbarians converted, 120, 122, 143-44, 146-47;
and Zoroastrianism, 134; and
Islam, 137, 138, 176; Chinese
converted, 139; English converted, 159, 209-11; Norse converted 161; Hungarians converted, 163; Slavs converted, 165;
Normans converted, 173; and
idea of equality, 198-99; Russians
converted, 221, 223; Spanish
Moslems converted, 173; brought
to New World, 249; 19th cent.
missionaries, 358. See also
Church, Roman Catholic; Protestants
Christina, queen of Sweden, 267
Ch'u, China, 37
Chunking, 437
Chunking Conference, 433
Church, Roman Catholic: Council of
Nicaea, 42, 113-14; and Carolingians, 145-53; in feudal Europe, 153, 155-59, 166-67; pope
vs. emperor, 166, 168, 169-71,
174-75; Cluniac reform, 171-72,
173, 174; Crusades, 177, 181, 182-
84; and medieval society, 190,
194, 198-99; indulgences, 190-91,
256-57; heresy and inquisition,
191-93; and William the Conqueror, 212-13; and Plantagenets,
214-16, 236; and Hohenstaufen
emperors, 217-22; and Philip IV
of France, 236-37; Avignon papacy, 237-39; Reformation, 253-
60; and Tudors, 263-64, 276;
and emperor Charles V, 274-75;
Spanish Inquisition, 277-78;
French Inquisition, 282; Counter-
Reformation, 287; Thirty Years'
War, 288-91; and Stuart rulers,
298; and Louis XIV, 304-5; in
Maryland, 314; and emperor
Joseph II, 328-29; and Napoleon,
333, 334; and revolts of 1831 and
1848, 342, 346, 347; English Catholics tolerated, 348; Lateran
treaties of 1929, 413; and Third
Reich, 416; 21st Ecumenical
Council, 440, 456; and Perón,
462; in Northern Ireland, 474-75.
See also Christianity; Papal
States; Protestants
Churchill, Winston, 405, 406, 426, 431,
434, 435, 437, 445, 446
Church of England: founded, 263-
64; and Stuart rulers, 294-98
passim
Cicero, 98

Cimbri, 96
Cimon, 58
Cisalpine Gaul, 83
Cisalpine Republic, 333, 335
Civil War, U.S., 375
Civitate, battle of, 173
Clark, general, 435
Claudius, Roman emperor, 41, 104,
106, 208
Clayton Anti-Trust Act, 380
Clemenceau, Georges, 400
Clement V, Pope, 237; Clement VII,
201, 238
Cleopatra, queen of Egypt, 100, 102-3
Clermont, 163, 177
Clisthenes, 53
Clive, Robert, 316
Clotilda, queen of Franks, 143
Clovis, king of Franks, 117, 132, 141,
143-44
Cluniac reform, 171-72, 173, 174, 212
Cluny, monastery founded, 141
Clusium, 75
Cnut II, king of England and Den-
mark, 211, 212
Code of Hammurabi, 19
Code of Justinian, 130, 194
Colbert, Jean Baptiste, 303, 313
Cold War, 448, 454-55, 465-66, 478
Coligny, admiral, 282, 283
Collins, Michael, 479
Colombia, 381, 383, 461
Columbus, Christopher, 241, 246
Commodus, Roman emperor, 107
Common Market, 440, 453, 454, 456,
473, 474, 475, 478-79
Commonwealth of Nations, British,
439, 446, 452, 458, 459, 460. See
also British Empire; names of in-
dividual members
Communism: in Italy, 412; Third
International, 421; in Southeast
Asia, 449-52, 467-68; in Latin
America, 463, 472; in world, 465,
479. See also China; Russia
Concini, Concino, 284
Concord, Mass., 369
Condottieri, 250
Confucius, 2, 38
Congo, 360, 459-60, 469
Congregationalists, 294
Congress of Vienna, 321, 338-39, 342
Connecticut, 314
Conrad III, king of Germany, 181-82,
183, 217
Conrad II, Holy Roman emperor, 169
Constance, council of, 201, 238-39,
255
Constance, peace of, 218
Constance of Sicily, wife of emperor
Henry IV, 219, 220
Constans, Roman emperor, 114
Constantine I the Great, Roman em-
peror, 42, 108-9, 112, 113, 114,
139, 156, 158; Constantine II, 114
Constantinople: founded, 42, 114; and
Theodoric, 126; and Justinian,
129, 130, 131; attacked, 138,
143, 160; as Christian center,
158; and Crusaders, 163, 178,

Constantinople (cont'd)
   184, 185; trade with Russia, 223;
   fall of, 241, 251, 273. See also
   Byzantine Empire; Byzantium
Constantius, Roman emperor, 108,
   109, 114
Constitution, U.S., 365, 373, 383
Continental Congress: first, 368-69;
   second, 369
Cook, James, captain, 362
Coral Sea, battle of the, 437
Corcyra, 59, 86
Cordova, 140, 175
Cordova, caliphate of, 139
Corinth, 41, 59, 60, 74, 90, 121
Corneille, Pierre, 304
Corn Laws, 348, 349
Cornwallis, general, 365, 369
Coromandel, 312
Corregidor, 432, 433
Corsica, 74, 79, 82, 89, 272
Cortez, Hernando, 247, 311
Coster, Laurens Janszoon, 241
Cotentin, 229
Council of Constance, 201, 238-39,
   255
Council of Europe, 454
Council of Foreign Ministers, 443,
   445
Council of Nicaea, 42, 113-14
Council of Pavia, 239
Council of Pisa, 238
Council of Trent, 241, 287
Cranmer, Thomas, archbishop of Can-
   terbury, 263, 276
Crassus, 41, 99
Crécy, battle of, 201, 229-30, 231
Creoles, 381, 382
Crete, ancient, 1, 11, 14, 23-25, 43, 44
Crimea, 225, 226, 325, 433
Crimean War, 349, 351, 354, 417
Crispi, Francesco, 360
Croats, 328
Croesus, king of Lydia, 30, 47
Cromwell, Oliver, 267, 296, 297, 475
Cromwell, Thomas, 264
Crown Point, battle of, 316
Crusades: dates, 163; background,
   175-77; First, 177-80; Second,
   181-82; Third, 182, 219; Fourth,
   182-85; Children's, 185-86; of
   Louis IX (Sixth), 207-8; of em-
   peror Frederick II (Fifth), 221;
   effects, 180-81, 186-93, 251
Cuba: Spain in, 246, 247; Spanish-
   American War, 378, 383; Castro,
   440, 462-63, 472
Cuneiform, 17, 31
Cyprus: ancient, 11, 14, 23; modern,
   458
Cyrus, king of Persia, 2, 29-30, 47
Czechoslovakia: after World War I,
   399, 411, 413; and Hitler, 405,
   423, 424, 430; and Russia, 445, 477.
   See also Bohemia

Dacia, 105, 129
Dagobert, 144
Daladier, Edouard, 424
d'Alembert, Jean Le Rond, 324

Damascus, 139, 175, 182, 224-25, 243
Damietta, 207
Danegeld, 211
Danelaw, the, 161
Danes, 161, 165, 166, 210. See also
   Norsemen
Danish March, 166
Danish War, 288-89
Dante Alighieri, 195-96, 201
Danton, Georges Jacques, 331
Danzig, 325
Dardanelles, 387, 395
Darius I the Great, king of Persia,
   2, 31-32, 33, 34, 48, 49; Darius III,
   64-67 passim
Dark Ages, 155, 157
Darlan, admiral, 434
David, king of Hebrews, 26
Davis, John, 279
Dawes, Charles G., 402
Dawes Plan, 388, 402
Decius, Roman emperor, 40, 112, 120
Declaration of Independence, U.S.,
   365, 369, 383
Declaration of Pillnitz, 331
Declaration of Rights (1689), 299
De Gaulle, Charles, 434, 439, 440, 456,
   458, 474
Delaware, 314, 367
Delian League, 57, 59-60
Demetrius, king of Corcyra, 86
Democratic party, 370, 375
Demosthenes, 62
Denmark: and Baltic trade, 218;
   and Francis I of France, 273;
   and Thirty Years' War, 285, 288,
   289; and Sweden, 289, 301; and
   Louis XIV, 305; Austro-German-
   Danish War, 353; World War II,
   405, 425, 430; postwar, 445, 449,
   454
Depression, Great, 410, 422, 430
Desiderius, king of Lombards, 146
Dewey, admiral, 378
Diaz, Bartholomew, 246
Diderot, Denis, 324
Diem, Ngo Dinh, 451
Diocletian, Roman emperor, 41, 108,
   109, 112, 114, 139
Disarmament: after World War I,
   388, 399, 401, 403, 405, 408-9;
   nuclear, 440, 443, 454-55, 476-77,
   480
Disraeli, Benjamin, 348, 361
Dollfuss, chancellor, 416
Dominic, St., 192
Dominican Order, 192-93
Domitian, Roman emperor, 42
Donatello, 252
Donation of Pepin, 141, 146
Don Carlos of Austria, 275
Don John of Austria, 277
Dorians, 43
Dorylaeum, 179
Draco, 52
Drake, Francis, 280
Drepana, battle of, 81
Dubcek, Alexander, 477
Dublin, 161
Dumbarton Oaks conference, 442

Dunkirk, 297, 425
Dupleix, 316
Dutch War, 288

East Anglia, 211
Easter Island, 395
East Prussia, 394
Ecbatana, 35
Eden, Anthony, 454
Edessa, 179, 180, 181
Edict of Nantes, 267, 284, 304, 305
Edict of Prices, 42, 108
Edict of Restitution, 289
Edward I, king of England, 216-17;
    Edward III, 201, 228, 229, 232,
    261; Edward IV, 261; Edward VI,
    264, 265, 275
Edward the Black Prince, 231, 232
Edward the Confessor, king of Eng-
    land, 211-12
Egypt: early through New Kingdom,
    1, 6-15; conquered by Assyria, 1,
    22; and east Mediterranean peo-
    ples, 23-28 passim, 44, 46; and
    Persians, 2, 30, 31, 32, 49; Hel-
    lenistic, 66, 68-69, 70; Ptolemies,
    87, 100; and Islam, 138, 139, 163,
    184, 243; 19th cent., 334, 349, 359,
    360; Suez, 349, 360, 439; World
    War II, 427, 434; postwar, 440,
    443, 447, 457-58, 466, 468-69,
    476
Eichmann, Adolf, 444
Einhart, 147
Eire. See Ireland
Eisenhower, Dwight D., 434, 435, 437,
    454, 463, 464
Elamites, 19
Elba, island, 338
El Caney, battle of, 378
Eleanor of Aquitaine, 204-5, 213-14
Eleanor of Provence, queen of Eng-
    land, 215-16
Elizabeth I, queen of England, 263-67
    passim, 280, 291, 294, 312, 314,
    475; Elizabeth II, 439
Elizabeth, czarina, 323, 327
Ems Dispatch, 356
England: early natives, 208; Phoeni-
    cians in, 28; Romans in, 41, 99,
    104, 105, 117, 123, 208-9; Anglo-
    Saxon, 117, 159, 160, 161, 209-12;
    Norman, 163, 212-17; Plantag-
    enet, 182, 187, 205, 236; Hun-
    dred Years' War, 227-35, 237,
    238, 260-61; Wars of the Roses,
    261; early Tudor, 157, 260, 261-
    65, 272, 274, 275-76; Elizabethan,
    279, 280-81, 291-94; early Stuart,
    285, 288, 284-97; Commonwealth,
    267, 297; late Stuart, 297-98;
    William III, 298-99, 305, 307,
    331; and War of the Austrian
    Succession, 327; Industrial Rev-
    olution, 319-20, 343-44; Napole-
    onic era, 335, 337, 338, 342, 371;
    Reform, 340, 341, 347-48; foreign
    involvements, late 19th cent.,
    354, 355; World War I, 389-91
    passim, 394-96 passim; between

wars, 400, 401, 408, 409, 411-12,
    423, 424; World War II, 405-6,
    424-28 passim, 431-37 passim;
    and postwar Europe, 440, 442-45
    passim, 449, 454; and Middle East,
    447, 457; and Asia, 450-51;
    and Common Market, 440, 473,
    474, 475; and Rhodesia, 470; and
    Northern Ireland, 475-76. See also
    British Empire; Commonwealth
    of Nations, British
Entente Cordiale, 391
Epirus, 78
Equestrian class, 91, 97
Erasmus, Desiderius, 241
Eratosthenes, 72
Erfurt, 257
Eritrea, 360, 422-23, 443
Esarhaddon, king of Assyria, 1, 22
Essex, Godwin, earl of, 202
Estonia, 289, 436
Ethelbert, king of England, 209
Ethelred II the Unready, king of Eng-
    land, 211
Ethiopia, 349, 405, 422-23, 459, 469.
    See also Abyssinia
Etruria, Kingdom of, 335
Etruscans, 41, 47, 73-77 passim
Eugene, prince of Savoy, 306
Euripides, 56
European Coal and Steel Community,
    453-54
European Economic Community. See
    Common Market
European Free Trade Association,
    454, 473, 475, 478
Evesham, battle of, 216
Evian-les-Bains, agreement of, 458
Excommunication, 174, 183, 184, 215,
    221, 236, 255, 462
Exploration, era of, 245-49, 251

Fabius, Quintus, Maximus, 84
Facta, Luigi, 412-13
Falangists, 423
Falkland Islands, battle, 387, 395
Farnese, Alexander, 278
Farouk, king of Egypt, 439
Fascism: Italian, 412-13, 421, 435;
    Spanish, 423, 445; Japanese, 428;
    German, see Nazism
Fashoda, 360
Fatima, 139, 175
Fatimite caliphate, 139
Faure, premier, 454
Federalist party, 370, 373
Federal Reserve Act, 368
Ferdinand I, Holy Roman emperor,
    273, 275; Ferdinand II, 288
Ferdinand I, king of Naples, 340
Ferdinand V the Catholic, king of
    Spain, 241, 263, 269, 272, 277;
    Ferdinand VII, 341, 381
Ferdinand of Styria, 288
Ferrara, 333
Feudalism, 152-55, 187-88, 211
Finland: independence, 289, 388;
    Russo-Finnish War, 405, 425;
    World War II, 436; postwar, 410,
    442, 445, 473

Finns, 222
First Estate, 152
Flaminius, general, 87, 89
Flanders, 187, 204, 227-28, 229, 234, 269, 272
Florence, 187, 241, 250, 346, 351
Florida, 247, 316
Flying Tigers, 432
Foch, general, 388, 398
Fontenoy, battle of, 151
Ford, Henry, 365
Formosa. *See* Taiwan
Fort Duquesne, battle of, 316
Fort Sumter, 365, 375
Fourteen Points, 388, 398-99, 400, 401, 406, 422
France: Merovingian, 138, 141, 143-46; Carolingian, 141, 146-52, 157-58; 159-60, 165; Capetian, 181, 182, 203-8, 235-37; Hundred Years' War, 227-35; Avignon papacy, 237-38; struggle with Hapsburgs, 272-73, 274, 276; and Protestants, 259, 281-85; rise of absolute monarchy, 285-87; Thirty Years' War, 288-91; Louis XIV, 302-7; colonies, 312, 314-16, 327, 357, 359, 360-61, 363, 367, 368, 369; War of the Austrian Succession, 327; Revolution, 329-32, 339; Directory, 332-34; Napoleon, 334-39, 371; early 19th cent. revolutions, 340-43, 345, 347, 349; Second Empire, 352, 354-57; World War I, 387-88, 389, 391, 394-95; between wars, 399-402 *passim*, 408-10 *passim*, 422-24 *passim*; World War II, 405, 424-28 *passim*, 434-36 *passim*; and postwar Europe, 439, 444, 445, 449, 454; former colonies, 447, 450-51, 456, 458-59; Fifth Republic, 440, 456, 473, 474. *See also* Gaul
France, battle of, 405, 425-26
Franche-Comté, 269, 272, 305
Francis I, emperor of Austria. *See* Francis II, Holy Roman emperor
Francis I, king of France, 259, 267, 269, 272-73, 274, 275, 281, 312; Francis II, 282
Francis II, Holy Roman emperor, 335, 337
Francis, St., 163, 192
Franco, generalissimo, 423, 445
Franco-Prussian War, 349, 355-57, 359, 390
Franconia, 152
Frankfurt, 321, 346-47, 353
Franks, 117, 119, 120, 123, 126, 132, 138, 141, 143-50, 195, 203, 204
Franz Ferdinand, archduke of Austria, 391, 411
Frederick IV, king of Denmark, 301
Frederick I Barbarossa, Holy Roman emperor, 163, 182, 183, 217-19; Frederick II, 194, 216, 220-21
Frederick, Palatine elector, 287, 288
Frederick II the Great, king of Prussia, 321, 323, 325-28

Frederick, elector of Saxony, 257, 269
Frederick of Hohenzollern, burgrave of Nuremberg, 325
Frederick William the Great, elector of Brandenburg, 326
Frederick William I, king of Prussia, 326; Frederick William IV, 352
Fredigonda, queen of Franks, 145
French and Indian Wars, 315, 368
French Revolution (1789), 329-32, 339
Fronde, the, 286
Frondizi, Arturo, 462
Fugger family, 255, 256, 272, 273
Fulton, Robert, 309

Gaels, 208
Gaiseric, 117, 124, 125
Galba, Roman emperor, 106
Galerius, Roman emperor, 112
Galicia, 325, 436
Gallipoli, 395
Gama, Vasco da, 241, 247
Gambetta, Léon, 356
Gandhi, Indira, 453
Gandhi, Mohandas, 439
Garibaldi, Giuseppe, 347, 352
Gascony, 204, 232
Gates, general, 369
Gaul: ancient 41, 47, 96, 99, 106; barbarian invasions, 117, 122-25 *passim*; Franks settle, 126, 138, 144, 159. *See also* France: Merovingian
Gauls, 68, 76, 77, 82, 86
Geneva, 260, 267, 403
Geneva Conferences: in 1954, 439, 450, 466; in 1955, 454
Genghis Khan, 163, 224
Genoa, 177, 186, 228, 246, 250, 333, 335
Genoa Economic Conference, 388
Genseric. *See* Gaiseric
George III, king of England, 321; George VI, 439
Germany: early, 99; early nationalism, 203, 250, 255; Protestants in, 255-58, 260, 264, 287-88; and Emperor Charles V, 274-75; Thirty Years' War, 288-91; rise of Hohenzollerns, 325; and Napoleon, 334, 335; early 19th cent. revolts, 341-43, 346-47; German Empire, 349, 352-53, 357, 360, 389; and Africa, 359, 361; World War I, 387-89 *passim*, 391, 394-98 *passim*; between wars, 399-403 *passim*, 408-11 *passim*, 413-16, 421-24; World War II, 405-6, 423-30 *passim*, 433-37 *passim*, 444-45; divided into zones, 442-43, 444, 455-56; West Germany, 449, 454, 456, 473-74; East Germany, 477-78. *See also* Holy Roman Empire; Prussia
Gerson, John, 239
Gettysburg, battle of, 375
Ghana, 459. *See also* Gold Coast
Ghent, 228
Ghiberti, Lorenzo, 252
Gibraltar, 307, 309
Gilbert, duke of Lorraine, 166

Gilbert Islands, 438
Giotto, 252
Giraud, general, 434
Girondins, 331
Gladstone, William Ewart, 348
Glorious Revolution, 298-99, 318, 331, 347
Godfrey of Bouillon, 179, 180
Godwin, earl of Essex, 202
Gold Coast, 359, 459
Golden Horde, Kingdom of the, 224, 225, 226
Goldwater, Barry M., 464
Gompers, Samuel, 379
Good Neighbor Policy, 384
Gordon, Charles George (Gordon Pasha), 361
Goths, 119, 120, 121, 122, 129. See also Ostrogoths; Visigoths
Gracchus, Gaius, 94-95
Gracchus, Tiberius, 94, 95
Gramont, Antoine, prince de Bidache, 356
Granada, 272, 277
Granicus, river, battle of, 63
Grant, Ulysses S., 375, 376
Grasse, admiral de, 369
Gratian, Roman emperor, 115, 163
Gray, John de, 214
Great Lakes, 160, 313
Great Schism, 201, 238-39, 251
Greece: early, 1, 25, 29, 32, 43-45; Hellenic, 2, 32-33, 41, 46-61, 70, 71; Alexander the Great, 61-67; Hellenistic, 35, 41, 68-72; in Roman times, 77-78, 79, 81, 87, 88; Byzantine period, 111, 121, 178, 179; achieves independence, 321, 341; World War I, 395; World War II, 427, 428, 430, 436; postwar, 440, 442, 446, 449, 458. See also Byzantine Empire; Macedonia, ancient; Turkey
Greenland, 141, 160
Gregory I, Pope, 159; Gregory VII the Great, 117, 141, 163, 172, 174, 198, see also Hildebrand; Gregory IX, 216, 221; Gregory XVI, 342
Gregory of Tours, 195
Gromyko, Andre, 477
Grotius, Hugo, 291
Guadeloupe, 316
Guam, 378, 432
Gudea, king of Lagash, 18
Guelfs, 220
Guevara, Che, 472
Guíana, British, 426
Guido, José Maria, 462
Guienne, 236
Guilds, medieval, 188-89
Guinea, Portuguese, 469
Guise, François de Lorraine, duke of, 282
Guise, Henry I de Lorraine, duke of, 283
Gustavus I Vasa, king of Sweden, 289; Gustavus II Adolphus, 267, 289-90
Guthrum, king of East Anglia, 210
Gutium, 18

Haarlem, 241
Hadrian I, Pope, 146; Hadrian IV, 217, 218
Hadrian, Roman emperor, 42, 105, 106, 273
Haile Selassie, emperor of Ethiopia, 422
Haiti, 246, 384
Hamburg, 398
Hamilcar Barca, 81, 82, 83
Hamilton, Alexander, 370, 373
Hamites, 6
Hammarskjold, Dag, 460
Hammurabi, king of Babylon, 1, 18, 19, 20
Hampden, John, 296
Hannibal, 83, 84, 85, 87, 88, 122
Hanover, 353
Hapsburg family, 269, 272, 274, 275, 281, 285, 288, 289, 290, 291, 306, 325, 342
Harappa, India, 34
Harfleur, siege of, 233
Hargreaves, James, 309, 319
Harmodius, 53
Harold II Godwinson, king of England, 212
Harold III Hardrada, king of Norway, 212
Harold Blue Tooth, king of Denmark, 166
Harun-al-Rashid, caliph, 139, 141
Hasdrubal (d. 221 B.C.), 82, 83
Hasdrubal (d. 207 B.C.), 84
Hastings, battle of, 212
Hatshepsut, queen of Egypt, 13-14
Havana, 316, 378
Hawaii, 379, 431
Hawkins, John, 279
Heath, Edward, 475
Hebrews, ancient, 1, 2, 17, 22, 25-27
    See also Jews
Hegira, 117, 135
Heidelberg, university of, 194
Hellas, 45
Helsinki, 440, 477
Helvetian Republic, 335
Henrietta Maria, queen of England, 295
Henry I, king of England, 213; Henry II, 205, 213-14, 227; Henry III, 215-16; Henry IV, 233; Henry V, 233, 234; Henry VI, 261; Henry VII, 262, see also Henry Tudor; Henry VIII, 157, 241, 262-64, 269, 275, 276, 281
Henry I, king of France, 204; Henry II, 276, 281; Henry III, 282, 283; Henry IV, 283-84, 342, see also Henry of Navarre
Henry I the Fowler, king of Germany, 165-66
Henry I the Fowler, Holy Roman emperor, see Henry I the Fowler, king of Germany; Henry II, 169; Henry III, 169, 173; Henry IV, 163, 173-75; Henry VI, 219
Henry, king of Portugal, 279
Henry of Navarre, 281, 283. See also Henry IV, king of France

Henry the Lion, duke of Bavaria and Saxony, 217, 218, 219, 220
Henry the Navigator, prince of Portugal, 245-46
Henry Tudor, 261. See also Henry VII, king of England
Heraclea, battle of, 78
Herodotus, 9, 32, 41, 55
Hero of Alexandria, 71, 319
Hesse-Cassel, 353
Hiero, king of Syracuse, 80
Hildebrand, 163, 171-72, 173. See also Gregory VII, Pope
Himera, battle of, 51
Hindenburg, Paul von, 394, 397, 416
Hindenburg Line, 397
Hindus, 446
Hindustan, 225
Hipparchus, 53, 72
Hippias, 53
Hippocrates, 55
Hiroshima, 406, 438
Hitler, Adolf, 413-16, 421-28 passim, 433, 435
Hittites, 1, 15, 20, 21, 24, 25, 44
Hohenstaufen family, 217-21
Hohenzollern family, 290, 307, 325, 326, 328, 355, 356
Holbein, Hans, 264, 265
Holland. See Netherlands
Holstein, 353
Holy Roman Empire: dates, 141, 163, 201, 267, 321; Carolingian empire, 146-52, 165; Otto the Great through Henry III, 166-69; rivals Church, 169-71; Henry IV, 173-75; Hohenstaufen emperors, 181-82, 217-21; Great Schism, 238; Charles V, 269-75; Joseph II, 328-29; dissolution, 331, 333, 335
Homer, 41, 45, 51, 56
Honecker, Erich, 477
Hong Kong, 361, 405, 427, 432
Honorius III, Pope, 221
Honorius, Roman emperor of the West, 117, 121, 122
Hoover, Herbert, 410
Horace, 104
Hospitalers, 190
Houston, Sam, 372
Howard, Catherine, 264
Howe, Elias, 377
Howe, William, general, 369
Hsiang Hsu, 37
Hudson, Henry, 313
Hudson's Bay Territory, 307, 315
Hugh Capet, king of France, 204
Hugh of Lusignan, 205
Huguenots, 282-85, 295, 304-5
Humanism, defined, 252
Hundred Years' War, 201, 227-35, 237, 260-61
Hungarians, 165, 166, 167. See also Magyars
Hungary: Magyars settle, 166; becomes Christian, 163; medieval, 169, 178, 224, 225, 238; Calvinism, 260; national state, 346, 347, 399; World War II, 430, 437; postwar, 439, 442, 445, 455

Huns, 117, 120, 122, 123, 124, 125, 126, 129, 130, 143, 147, 222
Hus, John, 201, 239, 255, 258
Hydrogen bomb, 439, 454. See also Atomic bomb; Disarmament: nuclear
Hyksos, 1, 12, 14, 20, 24

Iberians, 82
Ice Age, 4, 73
Iceland, 141, 160, 449, 473
Ictinus, 59
Igor, Rus chieftain, 223
Ikhnaton, king of Egypt, 1, 15, 24
Illia, Arturo, 462, 473
Illyria, 47, 82, 86, 99, 106, 121
Incas, 248, 280
India: ancient, 1, 2, 28, 34-36, 67; and Islam, 138; and Vasco da Gama, 241, 247; French in, 303, 309, 316, 327; British in, 309, 316, 327; World War I, 396; World War II, 437; independence, 439, 446-47; postwar, 440, 453, 466, 470-71
Indians, American, 7, 33, 313, 315, 316, 329-30, 371, 382. See also Aztecs, Incas
Indies, East, 247, 313, 314. See also Indonesia; Netherlands East Indies
Indies, West, 247, 303, 370. See also Bahama Islands; Cuba; Guadeloupe; Haiti; Jamaica; Puerto Rico
Indo-China, 428, 432, 439, 450. See also Cambodia; Laos; Vietnam
Indo-Europeans, 1, 20, 28-33, 43, 44, 73, 222
Indonesia, 450, 466. See also Borneo; Celebes; Indies, East; Java; Moluccas Islands; Sumatra
Indulgences, sale of, 190-91, 256-57
Industrial Revolution: dates, 309; in England, 319-20; and liberal reform, 343-45; and colonialism, 358; in U.S., 376-78
Ingria, 289, 301
Innocent III, Pope, 163, 183-84, 185, 206, 214-15, 219, 220, 221; Innocent IV, 221
Inquisition, 193, 277-78, 282
International law: beginning of, 291; and war crimes, 444
Ionians, 41
Iran, 29. See also Persia
Iraq, 442, 447. See also Mesopotamia
Ireland: becomes Christian, 117, 209; Norse in, 160, 161; English subject, 227, 267, 297; independence, 411-12, 475; World War II, 426-27
Ireland, Northern, 475-76
Irene, Byzantine empress, 149
Iron Curtain, 444-45, 448
Isaac II, Roman emperor of the East, 184-85
Isabella I of Castile, queen of Spain, 241, 263, 269, 272, 277
Ishtar, 111
Isis, 111
Islam: rise of, 117, 134-40; before

Islam (cont'd)
Crusades, 175-77. See also Arabs;
Moslems; Turkey; Turks
Ismail, Egyptian khedive, 360
Isocrates, 62
Israel, modern, 439, 440, 444, 447-48,
457, 468-69, 476. See also Palestine
Issus, battle of, 64
Italy; after fall of Western Empire,
117, 123, 125-27, 145-46, 151, 158,
159; medieval, 161, 167-69, 172-73,
176, 186-87, 203, 218-19, 224, 238;
Renaissance, 249-53, 255-56, 269;
and Napoleon, 333, 334, 335; nationalism and unification, 340,
346, 349, 351-53, 357, 359; in Africa, 359-60; World War I, 387,
389, 395, 397, 412; between wars,
399, 400, 401, 412-13, 421, 422-23;
World War II, 405, 406, 427, 434-
35; postwar, 445, 447, 449, 454, 473
Ivan III the Great, czar of Russia,
225-26; Ivan IV the Terrible, 226,
301
Iwo Jima, 438

Jackson, Andrew, 371
Jacobins, 331, 332, 342
Jamaica, island, 297
James I, king of England, 294-95;
James II, 298
James, duke of Monmouth, 298
James VI, king of Scotland. See James
I, king of England
Jamestown, Va., 309, 313, 380
Japan: ancient, 33; Perry lands in,
349; Sino-Japanese War, 362;
Russo-Japanese War, 417; after
World War I, 401; World War II,
405-6, 422, 423, 427-28, 431-33,
437-38, 445; postwar, 443, 446,
447, 452
Java, 312, 432, 443
Jefferson, Thomas, 369, 370, 373
Jerome of Prague, 239, 255
Jerusalem: ancient, 2, 26, 41, 110; and
Crusades, 163, 180, 181, 182, 221;
in World War I, 388
Jesuits, 241, 287, 313
Jesus, 41, 109, 113, 135, 180, 252, 254
Jews: derivation of name, 27; and
Rome, 41, 110; and Islam, 135; and
Philip IV of France, 236; in Spain,
277; and Emperor Joseph II, 328-
29; in England, 348; and Third
Reich, 416, 430, 444; in Russia,
476. See also Hebrews; Israel;
Palestine; Semites
Joan of Arc, 201, 234-35
John, king of England, 182, 184, 205,
206, 214, 221
John II the Good, king of France, 231,
232
John XI, Pope, 167; John XII, 167, 168,
169; John XXII, 198; John XXIII,
439, 456
John II, king of Portugal, 246; John
VI, 382
John of Cappadocia, 130

John of Lancaster, duke of Bedford,
234
Johnson, Lyndon B., 440, 464, 467, 477
Joinville, Jean de, 195
Joliet, Louis, 313
Jordan. See Trans-Jordan
Joseph II, Holy Roman emperor, 323,
328-29
Josephine, empress of France, 333,
337
Jourdan, general, 333
Juarez, Benito, 355
Judaism, 110, 134, 135
Jugurtha, 95
Julian, Roman emperor, 114-15
Junonia, 95
Justinian I, Byzantine emperor, 127-
31, 132, 137, 139, 145, 222
Jutes, 209
Jutland, battle of, 387, 395

Kansas-Nebraska Act, 365, 375
Karnak, temple of, 14
Kasavubu, Joseph, 459, 460, 469
Kashmir, 447
Kassites, 1, 20, 24
Kay, John, 309, 319
Kazan, Russia, 225, 226
Kellogg-Briand Pact, 388, 402, 422
Kennedy, John F., 384, 440, 455, 462,
463, 464
Kennedy, Robert F., 440
Kerensky, Alexander, 397, 419, 420
Kharezm, 224
Khrushchev, Nikita S., 439, 440, 454,
455
Khufu, king of Egypt, 9
Khurasan, 225
Kiel, 398
Kiev, 223, 224
King, Martin Luther, 440
King George's War, 315, 368
King William's War, 315, 368
Kipchak Turks, 224
Kitchener, lord, 360
Knights of Labor, 379
Knights Templars, 190, 236, 237, 331
Konoye, prince of Japan, 428, 431
Korea, 362, 442, 443, 446, 449, 467, 471
Korean War, 449, 471
Kornilov, general, 419, 420
Kosygin, Aleksei N., 440, 455, 476, 477
Kowloon, 357
Krim. See Crimea
Kubitschek, Juscelino, 461
Kublai Khan, 201, 224
Kunersdorf, battle of, 327
Kwajalein, 438

Labor unions, 379
Ladrones Islands, 248
Lafayette, general, 369
La Fontaine, Jean de, 304
Lagash, 18
Lake Trasimene, battle of, 84
Lancaster, house of, 261, 262
Langton, Stephen, archbishop of
Canterbury, 214-15
Lanusse, Alejandro A., 473
Laos, 450, 451, 467, 468. See Indo-China

Lao-tze, 37
Lares and Penates, 109
La Rochelle, 284, 285, 295
Lars Porsena, 75
La Salle, Robert Cavelier, 309, 313
Lashio, 432
Lateran Treaties of 1929, 413
Latin League, 76
Latin War, 76-77
Latium, 73, 74, 78
Latvia, 436
Laud, William, archbishop of Canterbury, 296
Lay investiture, 171, 172, 174, 175
League of Augsburg, 306, 315
League of Nations, 388, 399-405 passim, 416, 422, 423, 470
Lebanon, 447
Lechfield, battle of, 166
Leck, battle of the, 290
Lee, Robert E., 365, 375, 376
Legnano, battle of, 218, 219
Leipzig, battle of, 337-38
Lemberg, 394
Lend-lease, 405, 426
Lenin, Nikolai, 419-20
Leningrad, 429. See also Petrograd; St. Petersburg
Leo III the Isaurian, Byzantine emperor, 138, 143
Leo I, Pope, 117, 125, 159; Leo III, 147; Leo IX, 173; Leo X, 263
Leoben, peace of, 333, 334
León (kingdom), 184
Leonardo da Vinci, 241, 252-53
Leonidas, 50
Leopold II, king of Belgium, 360
Leopold I, Holy Roman emperor, 306, 326; Leopold II, 331
Leopold of Hohenzollern, prince, 355-56
Lepanto, battle of, 267, 277
Lepidus, 102
Lesseps, Ferdinand de, 360
Lewis and Clark expedition, 371
Lexington, Mass., 365, 369
Liberia, 459, 470
Libya, 427, 443
Licinius, 109
Ligurian Republic, 333-34
Lincoln, Abraham, 365, 375, 376
Line of demarcation, 247
Lithuania, 224, 436
Liu Pang, 39
Livingstone, David, 359
Livonia, 289
Livy, 104
Lloyd George, David, 400
Locarno conferences, 388, 402, 405, 423
Lodge, Henry Cabot (1850-1924), 401
Lodi, battle of, 333
Lollards, 254
Lombard Kingdom, 151, 167-68
Lombard League, 221
Lombards, 117, 119, 143, 145-46, 151, 195
Lombardy, 74, 218, 333, 346, 351, 352
Lombe, Thomas, 319

London Naval Conference, 388, 403
Long Parliament, 296
Lorraine, 152, 165-66, 356, 359, 387, 399
Lorraine, Gilbert, duke of, 166
Lothair, 150, 151, 152
Lotharingia, 152
Louis I the pious, king of France, see Louis I the Pious, Holy Roman emperor; Louis VI, 204; Louis VII, 181, 182, 183, 204-5; Louis VIII, 206, 215; Louis IX (St. Louis), 201, 206, 207-8, 235; Louis XI, 241; Louis XIII, 284, 285, 286, 295, 302; Louis XIV, 267, 286, 291, 302-7, 313, 314, 315, 330, 368; Louis XV, 330; Louis XVI, 321, 330, 331, 332, 338; Louis XVII, 338; Louis XVIII, 338, 342
Louis II the German, king of Germany, 150, 151, 152; Louis III the Child, 163, 165
Louis I the Pious, Holy Roman emperor, 141, 147, 150-51, 152, 159
Louis II, king of Hungary, 273
Louis I, duke of Orleans, 233
Louis Napoleon. See Napoleon III
Louisberg, battle of, 316
Louisiana Purchase, 335, 365, 370
Louisiana Territory, 309, 313, 315, 316, 335, 373
Louis Philippe, king of France, 342, 345, 346
Louvois, marquis de, 303
Loyola, St. Ignatius of, 241, 287
Lübeck, 218, 398
Lübeck, peace of, 289
Lucanians, 77
Ludendorff, general, 398, 413
Lugalzaggizi, king of Sumer, 17
Lully, Jean Baptiste, 304
Lumumba, Patrice, 459, 460
Luneville, treaty of, 335
Lusitania, S.S., 387, 396
Luther, Martin, 241, 257-58, 259, 263, 274, 281, 282
Lutheranism, 287, 289
Lutter, battle of, 289
Lutzen, battle of, 290
Luxembourg; Hapsburg domain, 269, 272; and Napoleon, 355; postwar, 445, 449, 454
Luxembourg, house of, 269
Luzon, 438
Lydia, Greece, 30, 31, 32, 47
Lyons, France, 191, 237, 332

MacArthur, Douglas, 452
Macassar, 312
McClellan, general, 375
Macedonia, ancient: rise of, 61-63; Alexander the Great, 63-67; Antigonus, 68; Hellenistic world, 70; and Punic wars, 84; Philip V, 87, 88; war with Rome, 90
McKinley, William, 378
MacMahon, Maurice de, general, 356
Madagascar, 303
Madeira Islands, 246
Madras, 314, 316

Magadha, 35
Magdeburg, siege of, 289
Magellan, Ferdinand, 248, 267, 280
Magenta, battle of, 352
Maginot Line, 402, 425
Magna Carta, 198-99, 201, 215, 216
Magnesia, battle of, 88
Magyars, 155, 166, 328. *See also* Hungarians
Maikop, 433
Maine, France, 206, 213
Maine, U.S.S., 378
Mainz, 220, 256
Malacca, 309, 312, 452
Malawi, 470
Malaya: World War II, 405, 432; Communists in, 451; independence, 452. *See also* Malaysia
Malaysia: ancient, 33, 36; modern, 452. *See also* Malacca; Malaya; Singapore
Malplaquet, battle of, 306
Mamertini, 80
Manchu, 267
Manchuria, 422, 438
Manhattan Island, 313
Manila, 316, 431, 432, 438
Manila Bay, battle of, 378
Manuel I, king of Portugal, 279
Manzikert, battle of, 176
Mao Tse-tung, 446, 452
Maquis, 436
Marat, Jean Paul, 331
Marathon, battle of, 41, 48-49, 51
Marozia, 167
Marc Antony, 101, 102, 103
Marcel, Stephen, 232
Marchand, Jean Baptiste, 360
Marcian, Roman emperor of the East, 124
Marcus Aurelius, Roman emperor, 42, 106
Mardonius, 51
Marduk, 19, 22, 110
Margaret of Parma, 278
Marianas, 447
Maria Theresa, archduchess of Austria, 323, 325, 326-27, 328
Marie de' Medici, 284, 286
Marie Louise, empress of France, 337
Marius, Gaius, 95-96, 97, 98, 99
Marlborough, John Churchill, duke of, 306
Marne, first battle of the, 387, 394
Marne, second battle of the, 398
Marquette, Jacques, 313
Marseilles, 74, 185, 436. *See also* Massilia
Marshall, George C., 439, 446
Marshall Islands, 438, 447
Marshall Plan, 439, 446
Marston Moor, battle of, 297
Martin V, Pope, 239
Martinique, 316
Mary I Tudor, queen of England, 263, 264, 265, 275, 276, 279, 281
Maryland, 367
Mary Stuart, queen of Scots, 282, 294
Masinissa, prince of Numidia, 85

Massachusetts, 314
Massilia, 74, 82, 83. *See also* Marseilles
Masulipatam, India, 313
Matilda, queen of England, 213, 263
Matthias, Holy Roman emperor, 288
Maurice of Saxony, 275
Mauritius, 313
Maurya dynasty, 35-36
Maxentius, Roman emperor, 109
Maximian, Roman emperor, 108, 109
Maximilian I, duke of Bavaria, 288
Maximilian I, Holy Roman emperor, 256, 269
Maximilian, emperor of Mexico, 355
Mayflower, 309
Mazarin, cardinal, 283, 286-87, 302
Mazda, 29
Mazzini, Giuseppe, 346, 349, 351
Mecca, 133, 134, 315
Mecklenburg, 218
Medes, 29, 30
Medici, Cosimo de', 250
Medici, Emilio G., 473
Medici, Lorenzo de', 241
Medici family, 256. *See also* Catherine de' Medici; Clement VII, Pope; Leo X, Pope; Marie de' Medici
Medieval culture, 193-99, 329
Medina, 135, 175
Memphis, Egypt, 10
Mencius, 38
Menelik II, emperor of Abyssinia, 360
Menes, king of Egypt, 1, 10
Mercantilism: and Russia, 300; in Louis XIV's France, 303; revived in 19th cent., 358; in American colonies, 367-68, 380-81
Mercia, 211
Merovingian rulers, 144-45, 146
Mesopotamia: ancient, 12, 17-22, 23, 27, 105; fertile crescent, 133; World War II, 396. *See also* Iraq
Messina, 80, 435
Mestizos, 381, 382
Metaurus, battle of the, 84
Metternich, prince von, 342, 346
Metz, 290, 356
Mexican War, 365, 371, 383
Mexico: Spain in, 248, 249, 279; France in, 349; Emperor Maximilian, 355; Pancho Villa and U.S., 365, 380, 384; war with U.S., 372
Mexico City, 248, 372
Michelangelo, 241, 252-53, 256
Michigan, 377
Midway Island, battle of, 438
Milan, 108, 115, 174, 250, 272, 273, 274, 307, 333, 346, 351, 412
Milan, siege of, 218
Miletus, destroyed, 32, 67
Miliukov, Pavel Nikolayevich, 397, 419
Miltiades, 48
Ming dynasty, 267
Minnesota, 160
Minorca, 307
Mirabeau, count, 330

Miranda, Francisco, 381
Missi dominici, 149-50
Mississippi River, 313, 370
Missouri Compromise, 365, 373, 375
Mithridates, 96, 97, 98
Mithraism, 111-12
Mobutu, Joseph D., 469
Model Parliament, 217
Modena, 333, 342, 352
Mohacs, battle of, 273
Mohammed, 117, 133-37
Mohammedanism. *See* Arabs; Islam; Moslems; Turkey; Turks
Mohenjo-daro, India, 34
Molière, 304
Moltke, general von, 356
Moluccas Islands, 248. *See also* Spice Islands
Monasticism, 156-58, 171-72
Money, coined: invented, 31-32; introduced into Greece, 52; in late Middle Ages, 189-90
Mongolians, ancient, 33
Mongols, 163, 201, 224-25
Monmouth, James, duke of, 298
Monroe, James, 371
Monroe Doctrine, 365, 371, 383, 461
Monte Cassino, monastery, 157
Montesquieu, Charles de, 323
Montezuma, 248
Montgomery, general, 434, 435
Montpellier, university of, 194
Moors, 177, 277
Moreau, general, 333, 335
Moriscos, 277
Morocco, 349, 359, 434, 447, 458
Moscow, 224, 225, 226, 279, 321, 337, 429
Moscow conference, 433
Moses, 25
Moslems: threaten Europe, 143, 155, 160, 167, 168, 173; Crusades, 175-85 *passim*, 221; and European trade and exploration, 243-45 *passim*; in Spain, 272, 277; in Pakistan, 446; in Algeria, 458. *See also* Arabs; Islam; Turkey; Turks
Mozambique, 469
Mühlberg, battle of, 275
Munich, 388, 398
Munich conference, 405
Murmansk, 433
Mussolini, Benito, 412, 413, 416, 422-27 *passim*, 435
Mycale, battle of, 51
Mycenae, 23, 25

Nagasaki, 438
Namibia, 470
Nandas rulers, 35
Naples (city), 194, 412
Naples (state): and Hohenstaufen emperors, 217, 219, 220-21; ca. 1400, 238, 250, 255; Spanish dominance, 272, 290; Austrian dominance, 307; and Napoleon, 333, 335; Rebellion of 1820, 340; Garibaldi conquers, 352
Napoleon I Bonaparte, emperor of

France, 168, 269, 321, 332, 333-39, 346, 370, 371, 381; Napoleon III (Louis Napoleon), 345, 349, 352-56 *passim*, 383
Narva, siege of, 301
Naseby, battle of, 297
Nassau, Germany, 353
Nasser, Gamal Abdal, 440, 457
Natal, 359, 361
Nationalism, European: rise of national states, 203-9; German and Italian unity prevented, 250; Reformation and Bohemia, 255; and liberalism, 340; 1848 revolutions, 346-47; Italian unification, 351-52; and Fourteen Points, 399; and Versailles Treaty, 411
National Socialist Party. *See* Nazism
Nations, battle of the, 337-38
NATO, 448-49, 456, 460, 474, 478
Navigation Act, 368
Nazareth, 221
Nazism, 413, 416, 421-22, 430, 436, 437, 439, 444
Nebuchadnezzar II, king of Babylon, 2, 22, 30
Negroes: prehistoric, 33, 73; in ancient Egypt, 7; slavery in U.S., 280, 309, 373-75; in Reconstruction period, 376; in Latin America, 382; schools desegregated in U.S., 439, 463-64; in South Africa, 460, 469-70; in Rhodesia, 470
Nehru, Jawaharlal, 440, 453
Nelson, Horatio, admiral, 334, 335
Nero, Roman emperor, 41, 104, 106, 111
Netherlands: Calvinism in, 260; Hapsburg domination, 269, 272, 275, 277; Union of Utrecht, 278; Thirty Years' War, 288, 290-91; War of the League of Augsburg, 305-6; War of the Spanish Succession, 307; trade and colonization, 312-14, 357, 359, 361, 368; in 19th cent., 335, 342, 355; after World War I, 398, 413; World War II, 405, 425, 430; postwar, 445, 449, 450, 454
Netherlands East Indies, 431, 432, 443, 450. *See also* Indies, East; Indonesia
Nevada, 379
Neville, Richard, earl of Warwick, 261
New Amsterdam, 309, 313, 314, 367
Newcomen, Thomas, 309
New Economic Policy, 420
New England states, 371. *See also names of individual states*
Newfoundland, 307, 315, 370, 426
New Guinea, 450
New Jersey, 314, 369
New Mexico, 372, 383
New Netherlands, 314
New Orleans, 315, 316
New Orleans, battle of, 371
New York, 309, 314, 369
New Zealand, 362, 363, 395, 450-51
Ney, marshal, 338

Nicaea, 179
Nicaea, council of, 42, 113-14
Nicaragua, 384
Nice, France, 333, 352, 354
Nicholas V, Pope, 241
Nicholas I, czar of Russia, 341; Nicholas II, 387
Nicholas of Cologne, 185
Nicias, 60
Nicomedia, 108, 139
Nigeria, 359
Nika riot, 117, 131
Nimitz, admiral, 438
Nimwegen, treaty of, 305
Nineveh, 1, 22, 27
Nivelle, general, 397
Nixon, Richard M., 440, 467, 468, 472
Nomarchs, 11
Noricum, 106
Norman conquest, of England, 209, 212
Normandy, 141, 161, 203, 205, 206, 212, 229, 233, 312
Normandy, Robert II, duke of, 213
Normandy invasion, 406, 435
Normans: settle Normandy, 161; in Italy, 172-73, 175, 177; as Crusaders, 179, 206; in England, 212, 215. See also Norsemen
Norsemen, 141, 155, 159-61, 165, 167, 203, 210, 211, 222. See also Danes; Normans
North Atlantic Treaty Organization. See NATO
North German Confederation, 353, 357
Northumberland, 211
Norway: Danish rule, 289; World War II, 405, 425, 428, 430; postwar, 445, 449, 454
Nova Scotia, 307, 312, 315
Novgorod, 141, 223, 224, 225, 226
Nubia, ancient, 11, 12, 14
Numidians, 79, 85
Nuremberg Tribunal, 439, 444

Octavian, 101-3, 105, 106. See also Augustus, Roman emperor
Odo, count of Paris, king of West Franks, 203, 204
Odoacer, king of Teutons, 117, 126
O'Higgins, Bernardo, 382
Okinawa, 438
Oleg, Rus chieftain, 223
Omar I, caliph, 138
Omayyad caliphs, 139, 175
Onganía, Carlos, 473
Open Door policy, 362, 365, 401
Opium War of 1839-42, 361
Orange, house of, 342
Orange Free State, 359, 361
Oregon, 371
Oregon Treaty, 372
Orestes the Hun, 126
Organization of American States, 461
Orléans, 201, 332
Orléans, Louis I, duke of, 233
Orléans, siege of, 234
Osiris, 8
Osmena, Sergio, 438

Ostrogoths, 117, 119, 120, 126, 143. See also Goths
Oswy, king of Northumbria, 209-10
Othman, caliph, 176
Otto I the Great, Holy Roman emperor, 163, 165, 167-68, 169, 174; Otto II, 168; Otto III, 168-69; Otto IV, 206, 220, 221
Ottoman Empire. See Turkey
Ottoman Turks. See Turkey
Oudenarde, battle of, 306
Oxford University, 163, 194

Padua, university of, 194
Pakistan, 439, 447, 450-51, 470-71
Palatinate, Rhenish, 287, 288
Palermo, 177, 220, 221
Palestine: ancient, 11, 14, 21-22, 25, 26, 27; Crusades, 176, 178, 180, 186, 221; after World War II, 442, 447-48. See also Israel, modern
Palos, Spain, 246
Panama Canal, 365, 383-84
Pan-American conferences, 365, 384-85
Panmunjom, 449
Pannonia, 126, 129
Papacy. See Church, Roman Catholic
Papal States, 151, 250, 342, 346, 351, 352, 357
Paris: medieval, 160, 163, 194, 203, 205, 232, 233, 234; during Reformation, 283, 290; French Revolution, 330, 331, 332; 19th cent., 338, 345, 349, 356; World War I, 394, 398; Vietnam peace talks, 440, 468
Paris, peace of: American Revolution, 369-70; Crimean War, 354; Spanish-American War, 378
Paris, university of, 163, 194, 205
Park, Mungo, 359
Parlement of Paris, 281
Parma, 333, 335, 342, 352
Parr, Catherine, queen of England, 264
Parthenon, 59
Parthia, 105, 132. See also Persia
Pasargadae, 30
Pataliputra, 35
Patesi, 17, 18
Patra, India, 35
Patrician, in early Rome, 75, 76, 91
Patrick, St., 117, 209
Patton, general, 436
Paul VI, Pope, 456, 477
Paul, St., 41, 111, 158
Paul the Deacon, 195
Pavia, 217, 218
Pavia, council of, 239
Pavia, siege of, 146
Pax Romana, 104-5
Peace of God, 181, 183, 198
Pearl Harbor, 405, 431
Pedro I, emperor of Brazil, 382
Peloponnesian War, 41, 59-61
Penang, 452
Peninsular War, 321
Penn, William, 314
Pennsylvania, 314, 367, 375

Pepi I, king of Egypt, 11
Pepin I, king of Aquitaine, 150
Pepin II of Heristal, French mayor of
    the palace, 145; Pepin III the
    Short, 141, 145-46
Pergamum, 87, 88, 90
Pericles, 41, 58-59
Perón, Juan, 462
Perry, commodore, 349, 362
Persepolis, 30, 67
Perseus, king of Macedonia, 88, 90
Pershing, general, 365, 384
Persia: ancient empire, 2, 27, 28, 29-33,
    35, 74; and ancient Greece, 47-51,
    58, 60, 61, 63-67, 68, 70; and
    Roman Empire, 105, 127, 129, 132,
    137; and Islam, 138, 176; Portugal
    in, 247. See also Iran
Peru, 248, 249, 279, 381
Pétain, general, 397, 426
Petchenegs, 223
Peter I the Great, czar of Russia, 226,
    267, 299-302, 324; Peter III, 323-
    24, 327
Peter, St., 41, 112, 158, 159
Peter Bartholemew, 180
Peter the Hermit, 178, 180
Petition of Right, 295
Petrograd, 418, 420. See also Lenin-
    grad; St. Petersburg
Petrograd Soviet, 418, 419
Phalanx, 62
Pharsalus, battle of, 41, 100
Phidias, 59
Philadelphia, Pa., 314, 369
Philip I, king of France, 204; Philip
    II Augustus, 163, 182, 183, 184,
    205-6, 214, 215, 220, 221; Philip
    III, 206; Philip IV the Fair, 207,
    235-37; Philip VI, 228, 229
Philip II, king of Macedonia, 41, 62-
    63, 84; Philip V, 87, 88
Philip I, king of Spain, 269; Philip II,
    267, 278-81, 283; Philip III,
    288; Philip IV, 291, 305; Philip V,
    306, 307
Philip of Anjou. See Philip V, king of
    Spain
Philip of Suabia, 220
Philippi, battle of, 102
Philippines: and Magellan, 248;
    Spain in, 316; U.S. gets, 378;
    World War II, 431, 432, 433,
    438 443; independent, 439, 447;
    SEATO, 450-51
Philip the Bold, duke of Burgundy,
    233, 234
Philistines, 25, 26
Phocaea, 74
Phoenicia, 1, 14, 20, 23-27 passim, 27-
    28, 33, 46-48 passim, 63-64, 74
Phrygians, 44
Piacenza, 335
Picts, 105, 209
Piedmont, 333, 335, 341, 351, 352, 354
Pilgrims (Puritans), 314
Pindar, 63
Piraeus, 57, 59
Pisa, 160, 177, 186
Pisa, council of, 238

Pisistratus, 53
Pius VI, Pope, 334
Pizarro, Francisco, 248, 311
Plague, 129, 201, 208, 230-31, 233, 334
Plataea, 48, 51, 59
Plato, 63
Plebeian, in early Rome, 75, 91, 97
Plymouth, Mass., 309, 314
Podesta, 218
Poeni, 80
Poitiers, battle of, 201
Poitou, 231
Poland: early, 169, 224; and Great
    Schism, 338; and Sweden, 289,
    301-2; partitions of, 321, 325, 326,
    328; 1830 revolts, 342-43; World
    War I, 394; between wars, 399,
    411, 413, 416; World War II, 405,
    424, 428, 430, 436; postwar, 442,
    445, 455, 477
Pole, Reginald, cardinal, 276
Polentia, battle of, 121
Polk, James Knox, 372, 378
Polo, Marco, 201, 224, 225
Polotsk, 223
Polovti, 223
Polybius, 55
Pomerania, 218, 289, 290
Pompey, Gnaeus, the Great, 41, 98, 99,
    100, 101
Pompey, Sextus, the younger, 102
Pompidou, Georges, 474, 475, 477
Ponce de Leon, Juan, 247, 311
Pondicherry, 313, 316
Ponthieu, 231
Pontus, 96
Portugal: foreign exploration, 243-47;
    colonies, 249, 311-14 passim, 357,
    359, 469; Spanish rule, 279;
    independence, 290; and Napoleon,
    337; revolts in, 341; postwar, 445,
    449, 454, 469, 470
Potsdam conferences, 443, 444
Praetorian guard, 103, 106
Pragmatic Sanction, 326
Prague, 194, 225, 288, 477
Prague, peace of, 290
Presbyterians, 297
Pressburg, treaty of, 335
Prester John, 246
Pride, colonel, 297
Printing, invention of, 241, 258
Protestant League, 288
Protestants: in Germany, 274-75, 281,
    287-88; in England, 275, 276, 294-
    98; in France, 276, 281-85 passim,
    304-5; in Spain, 276, 277, 281; in
    Netherlands, 277, 278; in Aus-
    tria, 328; in Northern Ireland, 475.
    See also Reformation; names of
    various sects
Provence, 132
Prussia: becomes Christian, 221;
    Frederick the Great, 325-28;
    fights Napoleon, 325, 337-38; con-
    stitution, 346; leads German Em-
    pire, 352-53; Franco-Prussian
    War, 355-57. See also Germany;
    Holy Roman Empire
Ptolemaic rulers, 68, 71, 87, 100, 102-3

Ptolemy I, king of Egypt, 68; Ptolemy IV, 87
Puerto Rico, 378
Pugashev, Emilyan Ivanovich, 324
Punic Wars, 41, 80-86, 89
Punt, 11
Punta del Este Conference, 462
Puritans, 294, 295, 296, 297, 314
Pym, John, 296
Pyramid of Gizeh, 9-10
Pyramids, battle of the, 334
Pyrenees, treaty of the, 291
Pyrrhus, king of Epirus, 78

Quadrivium, 193
Quakers, 314
Quebec, 309, 312, 313, 316, 321
Quebec Conference, 435
Queen Anne's War, 315, 368
Quinquirems, 80
Quintus Fabius Maximus, 84

Ra, 8, 11, 110
Racine, Jean Baptiste, 304
Radetsky, general, 346
Rahman, Mujibur, 471
Rameses II, king of Egypt, 1, 15, 25
Ramillies, battle of, 306
Rapallo, treaty of, 388
Raphael, 252
Rasputin, 418
Rastatt, treaty of, 307
Ravenna, 122, 125, 131
Ravenna, Exarchate of, 132, 146
Raymond of Toulouse, 180
Reconstruction Act, 365
Reformation: dates, 201; background, 253-54, 256-57; Wyclif, 254; Hus, 255; Luther, 257-58; Zwingli, 258-59; Calvin, 259-60; Henry VIII, 263-64. See also Protestants
Reform Bill of 1832, 321
Reign of Terror, 332
Religion, ancient: Egyptian, 8-9, 15; Mesopotamian, 18, 19-20, 22, 31; Zoroastrianism, 29; Buddhism, 34, 36; Taoism, 37-38; Confucianism, 38; Greek, 56; in Alexandrian Egypt, 66, 110; Roman, 109-10; Hebrew, 110, 134, 135; cults of 3rd cent. A.D., 111
Renaissance: defined, 251; Italian, 250, 252-53; English, 265
Reparations payments, after World War I, 400, 401, 402, 407, 408, 409-10, 411
Republican party, 375
Republican party (Jeffersonian), 370, 373
Reunion Island, 313
Rheims, 235, 332
Rhineland, 288, 405
Rhode Island, 314
Rhodes, 87, 88, 273
Rhodes, Cecil, 361
Rhodesia, 470
Richard I the Lionhearted, king of England, 182, 183, 205, 206, 214, 219, 220; Richard II, 233; Richard

III, 261
Richelieu, cardinal, 267, 283, 284-86, 289, 290, 295, 302
Richmond, Va., 375, 376
Ricimer the Sueve, 125
Risorgimento, 351-52
Robert II, king of France, 204
Robert II, duke of Normandy, 213
Robert Guiscard, duke of Apulia, 163, 173
Robespierre, 332
Rochambeau, general, 369
Rocroy, battle of, 290
Rollo the Norseman, 141, 161, 203
Romagna, 333, 352
Roman Empire. See Byzantine Empire; Rome (nation)
Romanoff rulers, 323
Rome (city): art in, 131, 253, 256; as seat of Holy Roman Empire, 149, 168, 174-75, 217, 219; as seat of papacy, 158, 167, 237-38. See also Papal States; Rome (city), sack of; Rome (nation)
Rome (city), sack of: in 387, 41; in 410, 122; in 455, 125; in 1080, 175; in 1527, 273
Rome (nation): dates, 41, 42, 117; early, 29, 47, 72-74; city-state, 74-76; wars and world dominion, 76-89; rise of dictators, 90-101; empire, 101-8; divided empire, 108-9, 114-15; barbarian infiltration, 119-25; fall of West, 125-27; influence on Dark Ages, 155-57; influence on Renaissance, 252. See also Byzantine Empire; Rome (city), sack of
Rome-Berlin-Tokyo Pact, 405
Rommel, Erwin, general, 433, 434
Romulus Augustulus, Roman emperor of the West, 126
Roncesvalles, battle of, 195
Roosevelt, Franklin D., 384, 405, 406, 424, 430, 431, 434, 435, 437, 438, 441, 446
Roosevelt, Theodore, 380, 383
Rostov, 429
Rouen, 201, 235
Round-heads, 296
Rousillon, 291
Rousseau, Jean Jacques, 330
Rubicon, river, 99
Rudolph I of Hapsburg, Holy Roman emperor, 201, 269
Ruhr, occupation of, 388, 402
Rumania, 399, 411, 428, 430, 436, 445, 455, 477
Rump Parliament, 297
Runnymede, England, 215
Rurik the Swede, 141, 160, 223
Rus, 223
Russia: early, 160, 222-25; Ivan III and Ivan IV, 225-26, 279; Peter the Great, 299-302; Catherine the Great, 321, 323-25, 328, 329; early 19th cent. revolts, 341, 342-43; Crimean War, 354; international influence in 19th cent., 355, 361-62, 371, 379; later Ro-

Russia (cont'd)
  manoffs, 416-18; 1917 revolution,
  388, 397, 400, 418-20; World War
  I, 387-88, 389, 394-96; between
  wars, 399, 400, 420, 424; World
  War II, 405-6, 425, 428-29, 433-
  37 passim; Cold War, 439-50 passim, 453-57 passim, 460, 463, 465,
  466, 471, 474, 476-77, 479
Russo-Finnish War, 405, 425
Russo-German non-aggression pact,
  424
Russo-Japanese War, 417

Sabah, 452
Sadat, Anwar, 440
Sadowa, battle of, 353
Saguntum, 83
St. Bartholomew's Day Massacre, 283
St. Helena, island, 321, 338
St. Mihiel salient, 388
St. Peter's basilica, Rome, 253, 256
St. Petersburg, 324. See also Lenin-
  grad; Petrograd
St. Sophia, church, 130-31, 140
Saipan, 438
Sakhalin, 438
Saladin, sultan of Egypt, 163, 182
Salamis, battle of, 41, 50, 57
Salerno, 175, 435
Salerno, university of, 194
Salian Franks, 143
Salonika, 395
Samarkand, 225
Samnite War, 41, 77
Samnium, 73
San Francisco, peace signed at, 452
San Francisco conference, 442
San Juan Hill, battle of, 378
San Martin, José de, 382
Santa Anna, general, 372
Santiago, battle of, 378
Saracens. See Moslems, Turkey,
  Turks
Sarajevo, 391
Sarawak, 452
Sardinia, 74, 79, 82, 89, 272, 307, 346-
  47, 351-52, 354
Sargon II, king of Assyria, 1, 22
Sargon I, king of Babylon, 1, 18
Satraps, 31, 70
Saudi Arabia, 447
Saul, king of Hebrews, 26
Savonarola, Girolamo, 241
Savoy, 306, 333, 352, 354
Savoy, house of, 307, 325, 351
Saxons, 146, 161, 209
Saxony, 146, 152, 217, 219, 327, 353
Schleswig, 353, 399
Schlieffen, general von, 394
Schmalkaldic League, 275, 281
Schmalkaldic Wars, 287
Scipio the elder, 83, 84
Scipio the younger, 85
Scotland, 208, 209, 227, 238, 260, 294-
  98 passim
Scots, early tribe, 105, 209
Scott, Winfield, general, 372
Scriptorium, 157
SEATO, 450-51, 478

Sebastopol, 433
Second Estate, 152, 154
Secret alliances, 390, 398
Sedan, 356, 398
Seleucus Nicator, 36, 68, 69
Selim the Grim, sultan, 273
Seljuk Turks, 176-77
Semites, 18, 23, 25-27. See also He-
  brews; Jews; Phoenicia
Sempronius, Tiberius, 83
Senegal, 359
Senusret, kings of Egypt, 11
Sepoy Rebellion, 362
Serbia, 391, 394, 396, 399, 411
Serf, 155
Seti I, king of Egypt, 15
Seven Weeks' War, 349, 353, 355
Seven Years' War, 315, 316, 321, 327-
  28, 367
Seville, 160, 248
Seymour, Edward, 275-76
Seymour, Jane, 264
Sforza, Francesco, duke of Milan, 250,
  273
Shakespeare, William, 265, 267
Shastri, Lal Bahadur, 453
Sherman, William Tecumseh, general,
  375
Sherman Anti-Trust Law, 365, 380
Shih Huang Ti, 38, 41
Ship-money, 296
Short Parliament, 296
Sicily: ancient, 41, 46, 47, 60, 74, 77-78,
  79, 96; Norman, 161, 173, 177;
  and Hohenstaufens, 216-21 pas-
  sim; and Hapsburgs, 307; Gari-
  baldi invades, 352; World War II,
  406, 427, 434-35
Sidon, 27
Sigismund, Holy Roman emperor,
  238, 255, 325
Sihanouk, prince of Cambodia, 467-68
Silesia, 327
Silver question, in U.S., 379
Simeon Stylites, St., 156
Simon de Montfort (1160?-1218), 206
Simon de Montfort (1208?-1265), 216
Sinai peninsula, 11
Singapore, 405, 432, 452
Singer, Isaac M., 377
Sino-Japanese War, 362
Sixtus IV, Pope, 198; Sixtus V, 198
Skylax, general, 35
Slavs, 130, 132, 155, 160, 165, 166, 167,
  169, 222, 223
Sluys, battle of, 228
Smith, Ian, 470
Socialism: arises, 344-45; French
  Revolution of 1848, 345; in Italy,
  412; and Bolsheviks, 419, 420
Society of Jesus. See Jesuits
Socrates, 41
Solferino, battle of, 352
Solomon, king of Hebrews, 26
Solomon Islands, battles of the, 438
Solon, 53
Somaliland, 11, 360, 443
Somme offensive, 387, 397
Sophia of Anhalt. See Catherine the
  Great

Sophia Paleologus, czarina of Russia, 226
Sophocles, 56
South Africa, 363, 460, 469-70
South Carolina, 365, 375
Southeast Asia Treaty Organization. *See* SEATO
South-West Africa, 469-70
Soviet Union. *See* Russia
Space exploration, 439, 440, 448, 479
Spain: prehistoric, 4; in classical times, 47, 79, 82, 106; Vandals and Visigoths, 124, 126, 127-28; medieval, 138, 139, 147, 159, 160, 175, 177, 243; exploration of America, 246-49; under Emperor Charles V, 262, 263, 269, 272; Philip II, 275-81, 294; Philip III and Philip IV, 288, 290, 291, 295, 297; and Louis XIV of France, 305, 306; in colonies, 249, 311, 312, 315, 316, 357, 359, 370, 371, 378-83 *passim*; and War of the Austrian Succession, 327; and Napoleon, 335, 337, 338; 19th cent. revolts, 341, 349; and Franco-Prussian War 355-56; civil war, 405, 423; since World War II, 445
Spanish-American War, 365, 378-79
Sparta, 30, 49-55 *passim*, 57-61, 63, 74
Spartan League, 59, 61
Spee, count von, 395
Spice Islands, 247. *See also* Moluccas Islands
Sputnik, 439, 455, 480
Stalin, Joseph, 406, 420, 428, 433, 435, 437, 439, 454
Stalingrad, battle of, 406, 434
Stamford Bridge, battle of, 212
Stamp Act, 368
Stanislaus I Leszczynski, king of Poland, 302; Stanislaus II Poniatowski, 325
Stanley, Henry Morton, 359
Star Chamber, 296
Steam engine, invention of, 71, 309, 319
Stephen of Blois, king of England, 213
Stephen I (St. Stephen), king of Hungary, 163
Stephen of Vendôme, 185
Stilicho, 121-22, 123
Stilwell, general, 432
Stimson, Henry L., 422
Stone Age, 4, 5, 6, 9, 73
Strafford, Thomas Wentworth, earl of, 296
Strasbourg, 306, 454
Strasbourg Oaths, 141, 151
Suabia, 166, 167-68, 217
Sudan, 359, 360
Sudeten, 424
Suevi, 123, 125
Suez Canal, 12, 32, 349, 360, 391, 439, 442-43, 457, 468
Suleiman the Magnificent, sultan, 241, 273, 274

Sulla, L. Cornelius, 95, 96-97, 98, 100
Sully, duke of, 284
Sumatra, 443
Sumerians, 1, 15, 17-18, 19, 23, 25
Surat, 313, 314
Sweden: and Francis I of France, 273; Thirty Years' War, 285, 289-90; Charles XII, 300, 301-2; and Louis XIV of France, 305; size in 18th cent., 325; and War of the Austrian Succession, 327; and Napoleon, 335; postwar, 445, 454
Swedes, 141, 160
Sweyn Forkbeard, 169, 211
Switzerland: prehistoric, 5, 73; independence, 241; and Reformation, 258-60; and Peace of Westphalia, 290-91; Helvetian Republic, 335; joins European Free Trade Assn., 454
Syracuse, Sicily, 41, 60, 74, 84
Syria: ancient, 11, 14, 20, 23, 24, 44, 46, 87, 98; and Islam, 133, 135, 138; Crusades, 178, 179, 180, 186; Ottoman Turks, 243; and Napoleon, 334; postwar, 445, 457-58

Taft, William Howard, 380
Taiping Rebellion, 361
Taiwan, 362, 431, 446, 452, 471-72
Taj Mahal, 140
Talleyrand, 338
Tamerlane, 201, 225
Tancred, king of Sicily, 219
Tancred of Hauteville, 172-73
T'ang dynasty, 117
Tannenberg, battle of, 387, 394
Taoism, 37-38
Tarawa, 438
Tarentum, 41, 74, 77, 78
Tarik, general, 138
Tartars, 38, 120-21, 224, 225, 226
Tasman, Abel Janszoon, 362
Tatars. *See* Tartars
Taylor, Zachary, 372
Teheran Conference, 406, 435
Tell el Amarna, Egypt, 15
Ternate, 312
Terramare, 73
Test ban treaty, 440, 455, 464
Tetzel, John, 257
Teuta, queen of Illyria, 86
Teutonic Order of German Knights, 221
Teutons, 96, 117
Texas, 365, 372, 383
Thailand, 451
Thales of Miletus, 55
Thant, U, 440, 460
Thebes, Egypt, 11-12, 14
Thebes, Greece, 61, 62, 63
Themistocles, 49, 50, 57, 58
Theodora, empress of Byzantium, 131
Theodoric the Ostrogoth, 117, 126
Theodosius I the Great, Roman emperor, 115, 117, 121
Theophylactus, 167
Thermopylae, battle of, 41, 50, 57
Third Estate, 152, 181, 236, 339
Third Reich, 413. *See also* Germany

Thirty Years' War, 267, 285-91, 306, 326
Thom, Poland, 325
Thomas Aquinas, St., 198
Thucydides, 55
Thurii, 77, 78
Thuringia, 132
Thutmose I, king of Egypt, 13; Thutmose II, 13; Thutmose III, 13, 14, 19, 24
Tiberius, Roman emperor, 106
Tibet, 453
Ticonderoga, battle of, 316
Tientsin Concession, 427
Tiglath-pileser I, king of Assyria, 21
Tigranes, king of Armenia, 98
Tilly, count of, 288, 289, 290
Tilsit, treaty of, 337
Tinchebrai, battle of, 213
Tirens, 23
Titian, 252
Tito, marshal, 455
Titus, Roman emporor, 41
Togoland, 361
Tojo, admiral, 431
Tokyo, 405, 438
Tonking, 361
Torquemada, Tomás de, 277-78
Tory party, 298, 299
Toul, 290
Toulon, 436
Toulouse, 192, 206
Touraine, 206, 213
Tours, battle of, 117, 138, 141, 143
Towns, rise of, 187-88
Townshend, Charles "Turnip", lord, 309, 317
Townshend Acts of 1767, 368
Trafalgar, battle of, 321, 335
Trajan, Roman emperor, 42, 104-5, 106
Trans-Jordan, 443, 447, 468
Transvaal, 359, 361
Transylvania, 120
Trent, 241, 287
Tribune, in early Rome, 76
Trichinopoly, battle of, 316
Trieste, 397
Triple Alliance of 1882, 390, 391
Tripoli, 180, 359, 371
Triumvirate: first, 41, 99; second, 102
Trivium, 193
Troubadours, 195
Troy, 25
Troyes, treaty of, 234
Truce of God, 181, 183, 198
Truman, Harry S., 406, 438, 439, 446
Truman Doctrine, 430, 446
Tshombe, Moise, 469
Ts'in, China, 41
Tudor rulers, 261-65, 291
Tuileries palace, 331, 345
Tull, Jethro, 309, 317
Tunis, 177, 208, 274, 349, 359
Tunisia, 447, 458
Turin, 341
Turkestan, 224
Turkey: Ottoman Empire, 225, 226, 241, 243-46 passim, 273-74, 300, 302, 324-25, 341, 354, 359; World

War I, 388; postwar, 449, 458. See also Moslems; Turks
Turks, 176-81 passim, 224. See also Moslems; Turkey
Turov, 223
Tuscany, 74, 250, 335
Tutankhamen, king of Egypt, 1, 15
Tyler, Wat, 233
Tyre, 26, 27, 74
Tyrol, 239, 256, 333
Tzu-Hsi, empress of China, 362

Ukraine, 223
Ulbricht, Walter, 477
Ulfilas, 120
Ulster. See Ireland, Northern
Umbria, 73
Underwood Tariff, 380
Union of Soviet Socialist Republics. See Russia
Union of Utrecht, 278
United Arab Republic, 457-58, 466. See also Egypt; Syria
United Nations, 406, 439, 440, 441-43 passim, 447-49 passim, 452, 453, 457, 458, 460, 465, 466, 468, 469, 470, 471-72, 478, 480
United States: history to 1918, 340, 361-62, 365-80; and Latin America, 355, 371-72, 378-79, 383-85, 461-63, 465, 472; World War I, 387-88, 396, 397-98; between wars, 401-3 passim, 408-10, 422; World War II, 405-6, 429-38; and postwar world, 439-40, 441-55 passim, 457, 461-63 passim, 465, 466-68, 472, 474, 477-79 passim; postwar domestic events, 463-64
Universities, medieval, 194
UNRRA, 441
Ural-Altaic peoples, 222
Urban II, Pope, 163, 177; Urban IV, 198; Urban V, 237-38; Urban VI, 201
Utrecht, treaty of, 267, 307, 315

Valens, Roman emperor of the East, 120-21
Valentinian III, Roman emperor of the West, 124, 125
Valley Forge, Pa., 369
Vandals, 117, 121-27 passim, 143
Varangians, 223
Vargas, Getúlio, 461
Vasa, house of, 301
Vatican City, 413
Vauban, marquis de, 303, 306
Veii, 76
Velazquez, Diego, 247
Venezuela, 365, 381
Venice, 125, 184-86, 218, 243, 250, 277, 333, 335, 346, 351-53 passim, 359, 416
Verdun, 290, 387
Verdun, treaty of, 141, 152
Vermandois, 205
Verrazano, Giovanni da, 312
Versailles, 304, 330, 331, 357
Versailles peace treaty, 399, 400, 401, 416, 423

Verwoerd, Hendrik F., 460, 470
Vespasian, Roman emperor, 41, 106
Vichy government, 426, 427-28, 434
Victor IV, Pope, 218
Victor Emmanuel I, king of Sardinia, 341; Victor Emmanuel II, 351, 352, 353
Victor Emmanuel III, king of Italy, 413
Victoria, queen of England, 321, 362
Vienna, 243, 273-74, 342, 346, 416, 437, 444
Vienna, Congress of, 321, 338-39, 342
Vietnam, 440, 450, 451, 466-68, 471, 479. See also Indo-China
Vikings. See Norsemen
Villa, Pancho, 380, 384
Villehardouin, Geoffroi de, 195
Villiers, George, 1st duke of Buckingham, 296
Virgil, 104
Virginia, 367
Visconti family, 250
Visigoths, 117-26 passim, 143, 144. See also Goths
Vladimir, grand prince of Kiev, 223
Voltaire, 323, 324, 329-30
Vorster, Balthazar J., 470

Wainwright, general, 433
Wake Island, battle of, 432
Waldensian heresy, 191-92, 254
Waldheim, Kurt, 440
Wales, 208, 209, 227
Wallenstein, general, 289, 290
Walter, Hubert, archbishop of Canterbury, 214
Walter the Penniless, 178
War guilt question, 411, 416
War of 1812, 365, 371
War of Jenkins' Ear, 315, 368
War of the Austrian Succession, 315, 316, 327
War of the League of Augsburg, 306
War of the Spanish Succession, 267, 306-7, 315, 326, 368
Warren, Earl, 440
Warsaw, 436
Warsaw Pact, 439, 477, 478
Wars of the Roses, 241, 261
Wars of the Three Henrys, 283
Warwick, Richard Neville, earl of, 261
Washington, D.C., in 1812, 371
Washington, George, 369, 370
Washington Conferences, 433, 435
Waterloo, 321, 338
Watt, James, 71, 309
Wavell, general, 427, 432
Wedmore, treaty of, 161, 210
Weimar Constitution, 401
Wellington, Arthur Wellesley, duke of, 337
Wentworth, Thomas, earl of Strafford, 296
Wessex, 210, 211
Western Hemisphere Defense Treaty, 461
Westphalia, peace of, 267, 290-91
West Saxon Kingdom, 210

Whig party, 298
Whitby, Synod of, 210
White Hill, battle of, 288
Whitney, Eli, 309, 320
Wilhelm II, kaiser of Germany. See William II, emperor of Germany
William I, duke of Aquitaine, 171
William I the Conqueror, king of England, 163, 213, see also William II, duke of Normandy; William II Rufus, 213; William III of Orange, 267, 298-99, 304, 314-15, 318
William, crown prince of Germany, 397
William I, emperor of Germany, 352-53, 357; William II, 388, 390, 398
William II, duke of Normandy, 212. See also William I the Conqueror, king of England
William I the Silent, prince of Orange, 278; William III, see William III of Orange, king of England
William, archbishop of Tyre, 195
Williamsburg, Va., 369
Willoughby, Sir Hugh, 279
Wilson, Harold, 475
Wilson, Woodrow, 365, 380, 384, 387, 388, 397-401 passim, 407, 408, 422
Witan, the 212
Wittenburg, 257
Wolfe, general, 316, 321
Wolsey, Thomas, cardinal, 262, 263
World War I, 387-403
World War II, 405-6, 422-38
Worms, Germany, 174
Wyclif, John, 201, 254, 255

Xantippus, 81
Xenophon, 55
Xerxes I, king of Persia, 49, 50

Yahweh, 110
Yalta Conference, 406, 437, 442, 444
Yaroslav, grand prince of Kiev, 223
Yemen, 133, 447, 457-58
York, house of, 261, 262
Yorktown, 365, 369
Young, Arthur, 318
Young Plan, 388, 403, 409
Ypres, battles of, 387, 388
Yuan dynasty, 201
Yugoslavia: independent, 399; World War II, 428, 430, 436; postwar, 442, 445, 455

Zaire. See Congo
Zama, battle of, 85
Zambia, 470
Zangi, 181
Zanzibar, 359
Zara, 184, 185
Zemstvos, 417
Zeno, Roman emperor of East, 126
Ziggurats, 18, 22
Ziska, John, 255
Zoroaster, 1, 29, 134
Zoser, king of Egypt, 9
Zürich, 258, 259
Zwingli, Ulrich, 258-60